OXFORD MEDICAL PUBLICATIONS

Alcoholism

THE FACTS

Alcoholism

THE FACTS

BY

DONALD W. GOODWIN M.D.

Professor of Psychiatry, The University of Kansas

OXFORD
OXFORD UNIVERSITY PRESS
NEW YORK TORONTO
1981

Oxford University Press, Walton Street, Oxford OX2 6DP

London Glasgow New York Toronto
Delhi Bombay Calcutta Madras Karachi
Kuala Lumpur Singapore Hong Kong Tokyo
Nairobi Dar es Salaam Cape Town
Melbourne Wellington

and associate companies in
Beirut Berlin Ibadan Mexico City

British Library Cataloguing in Publication Data
Goodwin, Donald
    Alcoholism.
    1. Alcoholism
    I. Title
    362.2'92   HV5035   80-42178
    ISBN 0-19-261297-2

Typeset by Hope Services Ltd., Abingdon
Printed in Great Britain by
Richard Clay (The Chaucer Press) Ltd,
Bungay, Suffolk

Preface

This book is written for people who worry about drinking, their own or somebody else's. For the millions of people who have alcoholism in the family, it may have particular appeal.

There is a lot of misinformation about alcoholism. For example, many people, including doctors, take an excessively pessimistic view of the problem. They believe alcoholics never get well. This is untrue.

Many have heard that alcohol causes brain damage. This has not been proved. The newspapers are full of stories about an increase of alcoholism among teenagers and women. This is *impossible* to prove, because nobody knows how many were alcoholic in the past.

I hope to correct some of these misconceptions. At the same time I realize that, as more is learned, today's facts may be tomorrow's fictions.

I have spent most of my professional life doing studies about alcohol and alcoholism. In recent years the studies have dealt more and more with the possible relationship of heredity to alcoholism. This led to an earlier book (*Is alcoholism hereditary?* Oxford University Press, 1976), where some of the information in this book originally appeared. Largely, however, the two volumes differ in content and intended audience. There is no technical language in this book. Nor are sources of information given, although most of the information *has* sources. These are scientific studies, by and large, with a certain amount of personal opinion, which was inevitable.

This is not, I hope, a preachy book. I am convinced that alcoholism is an illness and not a vice. I do not believe victims

Preface

of alcoholism got that way because they exercised free will and chose to get that way.

I don't particularly like the word 'alcoholism'. I use it because it's the word most people use. Those unhappy with the word may substitute 'alcohol dependence'. For brevity, I refer to the alcoholic—the alcohol-dependent individual—in the male gender and the spouse in the female gender, except in the chapter on the woman alcoholic.

As for my own philosophy about drinking, it is captured rather nicely by the quotation introducing Section 1.

Kansas City   DWG
January 1981

Contents

To Sally

Section One

Alcohol

You have asked me how I feel about whisky. All right, here is just how I stand on this question:

If, when you say whisky, you mean the devil's brew, the poison scourge, the bloody monster that defiles innocence, yea, literally takes the bread from the mouths of little children; if you mean the evil drink that topples the Christian man and woman from the pinnacles of righteous, gracious living into the bottomless pit of degradation and despair, shame and helplessness and hopelessness, then certainly I am against it with all of my power.

But, if you when you say whisky, you mean the oil of conversation, the philosophic wine, the stuff that is consumed when good fellows get together, that puts a song in their hearts and laughter on their lips and the warm glow of contentment in their eyes; if you mean Christmas cheer; if you mean the stimulating drink that puts the spring in the old gentleman's step on a frosty morning; if you mean the drink that enables a man to magnify his joy, and his happiness, and to forget, if only for a little while, life's great tragedies and heartbreaks and sorrows, if you mean that drink, the sale of which pours into our treasuries untold millions of dollars, which are used to provide tender care for our little crippled children, our blind, our deaf, our dumb, our pitiful aged and infirm, to build highways, hospitals and schools, then certainly I am in favour of it.

This is my stand. I will not retreat from it; I will not compromise.

—Address to the legislature
by a Mississippi state senator
in 1958

1

Alcoholic beverages

Let us begin at the beginning: with yeast.

When yeast grows in sugar solutions without air, most of the sugar is converted (fermented) into carbon dioxide and alcohol. Carbon dioxide makes the solution bubble ('fermentation' comes from the Latin word for 'boil') and makes champagne corks pop. The alcohol is excreted. Most drinkers do not know they are drinking yeast excrement. Would it matter?

It matters for yeast. When the alcohol concentration reaches about 12 or 13 per cent, the yeast dies of acute alcohol intoxication. This is why unfortified wines, produced by fermentation alone, have alcohol concentrations of no more than 12 or 13 per cent. Sherry, port, and other fortified wines have alcohol added.

As a rule, people do not drink just alcohol. They drink alcoholic beverages. Alcoholic beverages are mostly water and a two-carbon alcohol molecule called ethyl alcohol or ethanol. Tiny amounts of other chemicals, called congeners, also are present. They provide most of the taste and smell and all of the colour, if any.

Because of congeners, beer can be distinguished from brandy, although both consist almost entirely of ethyl alcohol and water. Congeners, depending on the beverage, include varying amounts of amino acids; minerals; vitamins; a one-carbon alcohol called methanol or 'wood alcohol'; plus the 'higher' alcohols with more than two carbons, otherwise known as fusel oil.

Even in small quantities, wood alcohol and fusel oil are poisons. So is ethyl alcohol, but a lot more of it is required to do damage. Is there enough wood alcohol and fusel oil in a cocktail to hurt anyone? Probably not, but no one is sure. To

3

be on the safe side, some people avoid drinks with large amounts of congeners—whiskey and brandies—and drink relatively congener-free vodka. They are not aware that vodka often contains more wood alcohol—the notorious blinder—than other beverages. Although there is almost certainly not enough to blind, wood alcohol certainly does not improve vision.

Congeners vary not only from beverage to beverage but also from brand to brand, and even from bottle to bottle of the same brand. Not all brands (or bottles) of vodka contain relatively high amounts of wood alcohol, but some do. Russian vodka, the favourite of many vodka connoisseurs, sometimes contains considerable wood alcohol, although, again, not enough to be harmful.

There has been a movement in the Unites States to label alcoholic beverages as 'dangerous to your health'. Indeed they are, if taken in excess. Such labels on cigarette packages haven't made much difference, and a more useful label for alcoholic beverages might list the congener content in the same way that ingredients are listed on some food packages.

Apart from man's contribution—the brewer's art, the cosseted grape—beverages differ according to the sugar source. From grapes, wine; from grain and hops, beer; from grain and corn, whiskey; from sugar cane, rum; and originally from the lowly potato, but now mainly from grain, vodka.

Man's great achievement in improving upon yeast's modest productivity was distillation, discovered about 800 AD in Arabia ('alcohol' comes from the Arabic *alkuhl*, meaning essence). Distillation boils away alcohol from its sugar bath and re-collects it as virtually pure alcohol. Then, because pure alcohol is pure torture to drink, water is added back, so that instead of having 100 per cent alcohol, you have 50 per cent or 100 proof alcohol (proof being one-half per cent).

The alcohol content of most distilled alcoholic beverages is expressed in degrees of proof. This term probably developed from the seventeenth-century English custom of estimating content by moistening gunpowder with the beverage and

4

applying a flame to the mixture. The lowest alcohol concentration that would allow ignition—a concentration of about 57 per cent alcohol by volume—was considered to be 'proof spirits'. British and Canadian regulations are still based on this yardstick; a concentration of 57.35 per cent alcohol is considered to be 'proof spirits', while other concentrations are described as 'over' or 'under' proof.

In many ways alcohol resembles water. In the body alcohol behaves like water. It travels everywhere water travels. Because of its water-like properties, ethyl alcohol can be accommodated by the body in vastly greater amounts than any other drug. A person's blood can consist of one half of one per cent of alcohol without producing death or even unconsciousness.

2

Alcohol in the body

What happens to alcohol when you drink it? Essentially the same thing that happens if you don't drink it. It turns to vinegar.*

When alcohol 'sours' in the open air, bacteria are responsible. To become vinegar (acetic acid) in the body alcohol needs two enzymes: alcohol dehydrogenase and aldehyde dehydrogenase. The first is located in the liver in surprisingly large supply. Surprising because, as far as we know, alcohol dehydrogenase does nothing except metabolize alcohol. It is there in all mammalian livers—in the horse's in particular plentitude. Why? Did God anticipate that someday a mammal like man would develop a taste for alcohol and need a way to dispose of it? Or did it happen that millennia ago horses and other vegetarians ate fermenting fruit lying on the ground and their obliging livers evolved a helpful enzyme?†

Nobody knows, but it is a nice enzyme to have in any case. It disposes of 100-proof distilled spirits at the rate of about one ounce per hour, slow enough to soak the brain without, one hopes, pickling it.

Between alcohol and acetic acid is an intermediate step, which is why a second enzyme is required. The intermediate chemical is an aldehyde and very toxic. Again, nature saves the day. The enzyme that destroys the aldehyde is found not just in the liver but throughout the body. It quickly turns the

---

* The reason that fortified wines and distilled spirits do not 'sour' in the open air is that they have concentrations of alcohol above 12 or 13 per cent, which is as lethal for bacteria as it is for yeast.

† A minute amount of ethyl alcohol is produced in the gastrointestinal tract by bacteria, and perhaps this accounts for alcohol dehydrogenase in the liver. Infinitesimal amounts of alcohol may also be produced by normal metabolic processes in the body. If these sources are the reason that the alcohol enzyme is present in such large quantities, it is clearly a case of biological overkill.

6

aldehyde into harmless acetic acid. Fed into the body's normal metabolic machinery, acetic acid becomes carbon dioxide and water, burning or storing seven calories per gram of alcohol in the process.

Vinegar is harmless, but the process that produces it may not be. In being oxidized, alcohol is progressively stripped of hydrogen atoms, which must go somewhere. Where they go results in some interesting biochemical changes which may or may not be harmless (the evidence is not yet clear). Some of the changes are:

1. There is an increase in lactic acid. This is interesting because a connection between increased lactic acid and anxiety attacks has been observed, and heavy drinking is also associated with anxiety attacks.

2. There is an increase in uric acid. This is interesting because increased uric acid is associated with gout, and gout for centuries has been associated with alcohol.

3. There is an increase in fat—not the slow increase that comes from calories (those seven calories per gram) but a rapid increase from the oxidation of alcohol. This fat is seen mainly in the liver or blood. One night of serious drinking—say, six or seven whiskies—discernibly increases the fat content of the liver. The liver will be fattier still if fatty food is also eaten.

Is a fatty liver bad? Admittedly it does not sound good, but on the other hand, the connection between a fatty liver and liver diseases, such as hepatitis and cirrhosis, is unclear. For one thing, the fat goes away soon after the drinker stops drinking. Also, most people drink but most do not develop liver disease. Among those very heavy drinkers we call alcoholics, perhaps only 5 or 10 per cent develop liver disease, although presumably their livers are fatty most of the time. On the other hand, people who develop a particular type of liver disease called Laennec's cirrhosis usually *are* heavy drinkers.

Many disorders associated with heavy drinking are apparently caused by malnutrition, but this may not be true of

7

cirrhosis. Laennec's cirrhosis has been produced in well-nourished baboons after four years of drunkenness. Most of the drunk baboons, however, only had fatty livers, and controversy still thrives about whether alcohol alone causes cirrhosis. Obviously it does not in every case.

Intoxicating amounts of alcohol also increase fat in the bloodstream. In high enough doses, particularly combined with a fatty meal, alcohol may even produce *visible* fat in the blood. The plasma takes on a faint milky tinge, probably a more frightening development for most people than the notion of having fat in their liver. Still, while it does not sound good, nobody knows how bad it is, and possibly it is not harmful at all.

For years people have looked for ways to speed up the elimination of alcohol from the body. The theory was that if alcohol went away faster, some of the ominous things described above might not occur. They probably would occur nevertheless, but speeding up alcohol's elimination would serve one purpose: it would shorten the period of intoxication.

Many things have been tried—insulin, caffeine, exercise—but only one has worked. Fruit sugar (fructose) in large doses definitely speeds the elimination of alcohol. Unfortunately the dose required is so large it is sickening, and most people prefer to remain drunk.

Recent evidence indicates that alcohol intoxication can be reduced *without* lowering blood alcohol. Drugs called narcotic antagonists—antagonists because they block the effects of morphine and other narcotics—also seem to prevent impairment from alcohol. The antagonist has to be given by intravenous injection, which poses a practical problem for bar patrons preparing themselves for a safe drive home. Nevertheless, this finding, if substantiated by further studies, has interesting implications for two effects of alcohol which have never been explained.

These effects are *analgesia* (relief of pain) and *euphoria*. Here, first, is a theory about analgesia.

Recently it was learned that the brain contains substances

resembling morphine. This led to speculation that the body normally responds to painful stimuli by increasing the activity of these natural morphine-like substances. Different people react differently to pain and the reason may be that some of us are 'born' with more 'morphine' in our brain than others. What does this have to do with alcohol? One line of thought holds that alcohol produces analgesia—and possibly euphoria —by stimulating the release of these normally occurring morphine-like substances.

Alcohol also may have morphine-like effects (analgesia and euphoria) in another way. From animal studies it appears that a breakdown product of alcohol combines with a normally occurring chemical in the brain to produce a substance resembling morphine. Thus, alcohol may cause analgesia and intoxication in two ways. It may stimulate the release of morphine-like substances or it may produce new morphine-like substances in the brain. Both may happen, or neither. Alcohol and morphine states are quite different, as are the withdrawal syndromes.

3

Alcohol and behaviour

The effects of any drug depend on the dose. The chance of death occurring from a sip of beer is remote. A quart of whiskey drunk in an hour will kill most men. This dose–effect rule applies to any substance a person consumes. Everything is either a poison or harmless depending on the dose. People die from drinking too little water, and from drinking too much. A little strychnine may even be good for you (it helps rats concentrate). If, when this is read, people are still arguing about whether marihuana is more or less harmful than alcohol, ask the following: Does alcohol refer to a bottle of low-alcohol beer or to a quart of malt whiskey? Does marihuana refer to Kansas hemp (the cannabis equivalent of low-alcohol beer) or to Moroccan hashish (the malt whiskey counterpart)? Drug comparisons are senseless except in terms of amount.

But quantity is not everything. To the amount consumed must be added other factors in determining a drug's effects:

1. *Concentration of alcohol in the blood*

What really counts is not how much alcohol a person drinks but how much gets into the bloodstream. This in turn depends on many things.

Some alcohol is absorbed through the stomach wall but most reaches the bloodstream through the small intestine. Between the stomach and small intestine is a muscular ring called the pyloric valve. (Anatomists point out that the pyloric valve is not a true valve, but merely functions as a valve. This is like saying that the works of Shakespeare were not written by Shakespeare but by another man of the same name.) When the valve clamps shut, as may happen when jolted by a

10

straight shot of whiskey, the alcohol remains in the stomach, where it is absorbed at a very slow pace. For people with sensitive pyloric valves, a strong shot of whiskey or an extra-dry martini may be self-defeating if a quick effect is the goal.

For rapid absorption, it is important that the alcohol reach the small intestine in the highest possible concentration and the shortest possible time. People who have had their pyloric valves removed surgically, as in the treatment of ulcers, find they get drunk faster than previously. Without a pyloric valve to slow down the passage of alcohol, it swooshes into the small intestine and thence into the bloodstream.

Other factors influencing absorption include the presence or absence of food in the stomach and the type of beverage. When alcohol has to compete with other, larger, and often more aggressive molecules in crossing the gastric and small intestinal membranes, it often does not fare well. Figure 3.1 illustrates this. Alcohol in the form of different beverages was given to subjects with and without food. Although the same amount of alcohol was consumed over the same length of time, the blood-alcohol concentration varied greatly. Gin on an empty stomach produced a peak blood-alcohol level above the legal blood-alcohol concentration for drivers in most states in America. Beer combined with a meal resulted in a peak blood level legally compatible with driving in any state in America.

There has been speculation about the difference in alcoholism rates between two wine-drinking countries, France and Italy. Italy, with the lower rate, has a national tradition of drinking wine mainly with meals, while Frenchmen tend to drink wine between meals as well as with them. When wine and spaghetti compete for transport across the intestinal wall, it is not surprising that spaghetti, finishing the race first, will prevent the wine from making much headway.

Mixing food and alcohol produces a slight increase in the oxidation of alcohol and hence its removal from the bloodstream. This may partly explain the lower blood-alcohol level when food and alcohol are combined. It also may partly

11

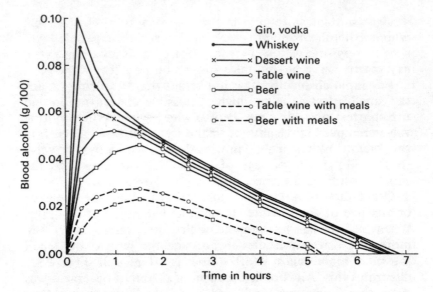

Fig. 3.1. Typical blood-alcohol curves resulting from ingestion of various spirits, wines, and beer, each at amounts equivalent to 0.6 g of alcohol per kilogram of body weight (3 oz. of vodka, three beers, or a large glass of wine). Redrawn from *Alcoholic beverages in clinical medicine* by C. D. Leake and M. Silverman. Copyright © 1966 by Year Book Medical Publishers, Inc., Chicago. Used by permission.

explain the known reluctance of alcoholics to eat while drinking, since presumably the alcoholic has no strong desire to remove alcohol from his bloodstream any faster than necessary.

2. *Rate of absorption*

In addition to how much alcohol is in the blood, it matters how quickly it got there. In general, the faster the rate of absorption, the more striking the effect. This may help explain the popularity of a dry martini before meals.

3. *Duration of drinking*

The body adapts rapidly to chemical insults, including alcohol.

Alcohol and behaviour

The longer there is alcohol in the blood, the more its effects diminish. In practical terms (for a secretary or writer, anyway), if you make five errors per minute while typing sober, you may make 15 errors per minute while typing with a certain blood-alcohol concentration after one hour of drinking, but only seven errors at the same concentration after five hours of drinking. After five hours you may not care how many you make, but that is another consideration.

4. *The slope effect*

Any drinker can tell you he feels better getting drunk than he does sobering up. That is, as the blood-alcohol level climbs from A to B to C, he may feel euphoric at B and C, but as the blood level falls from C to B to A, not only is there no euphoria at B, there is actual discomfort, presaging the hangover to come at A. This 'slope' effect is closely related to and hard to separate from the duration effect.

5. *Tolerance*

As people drink more over days, months, and years, they gradually *need* to drink more to obtain the same effect. This is called tolerance. Its importance is often exaggerated. A seasoned alcoholic at the prime of his drinking capacity may be able to drink, at most, twice as much as a teetotaler of similar age and health. Compared with tolerance for morphine, which can be manyfold, tolerance for alcohol is modest.

More striking than 'acquired' tolerance may be inborn tolerance. Individuals vary widely in the amount of alcohol they can tolerate independent of drinking experience. Some people, however hard they try, cannot drink more than a small amount of alcohol without developing a headache, upset stomach, or dizziness. They rarely become alcoholic but deserve no credit for it. Their 'alcohol problem' is that they *cannot* drink very much.

Others seem able to drink large amounts with hardly any

13

bad effects. It appears they were born with this capacity and did not develop it entirely from practice. They *can* become alcoholic and some do.

Differences in tolerance for alcohol apply not only to individuals but to racial groups. For example, many Orientals develop flushing of the skin, sometimes with nausea, after drinking only a little alcohol. For obvious reasons, alcoholism is rare in these groups. American Indians are also said to be intolerant of alcohol but the nature of the intolerance is more ambiguous and does not appear to discourage heavy drinking.

6. *Set and setting*

Any drug response that involves thinking and mood is bound to be influenced by expectation. Alcohol is no exception. If a person believes alcohol will improve his mood, diminish fatigue, make him feel sexy, or have other salutary effects, the chances that these pleasant changes will occur may be improved. The same goes for expectations of unpleasant changes.

In medicine this is called the placebo effect: drugs tend to do for people what they expect them to do. It presumably has little or no role in the treatment of pneumonia with antibiotics—although one cannot be certain—but it has powerful implications for treating psychiatric disorders. Sometimes sugar pills help almost as much as expensive and potentially toxic tranquillizers or antidepressants.

It is the gap between the sugar pill's performance and that of the 'active' drug that justifies the prescription of the drug, and sometimes the gap is quite small. Placebos can even produce side-effects—headaches, nausea, a rash. Everyone is a little susceptible to suggestion, some more than others.

It is difficult to know how much the effect of alcohol in any given person on any particular occasion is influenced by expectation, or what psychologists call set. Presumably, the stronger the dose, the smaller the placebo effect. But it is a

Alcohol and behaviour

common laboratory and social observation that some people get 'drunk' on very little alcohol. This may be because they want or expect to get drunk quickly.

But set refers to more than expectation. If a person is tired, alcohol may have more of an anti-fatigue effect than usual. If he is hungry, it may make him more hungry (or less). If his mood is good, it may become better. If bad, worse. All of this refers to set—the psychological and physical state of the person at the time he proceeds to drink.

Set, to a considerable extent, is linked to setting. Where is the person drinking? With whom? If he enjoys the people he is with, he may also enjoy the alcohol more. If the occasion is a celebration, a drink may have a livelier effect than would the same amount taken routinely before dinner.

Alcohol is said to make people talk louder, and this often seems true. On the other hand, two men on a deer hunt, taking a nip of scotch to warm up, may talk more softly than usual.

The importance of set and setting in shaping a person's response to alcohol should not be underestimated, although it is difficult to study their relative influence at a given time.

The four stages of intoxication

There is an old saying that alcohol affects a person in four ways. First, he becomes jocose, then bellicose, then lachrymose, and finally comatose.

Comatose he does indeed become if he drinks enough, but the other three stages are not inevitable. Some people hardly feel jocose at all. One reason may be that they do not want to feel jocose. Their reasons for drinking may be purely social: others drink, so do they.

Many people become argumentative when they drink and some combative, but these responses are strongly influenced by social circumstances. The legendary barroom brawl usually occurs in lower-class bars and is a rarity in upper-class saloons. Countless parties are held nightly in middle-class suburbia and, although drinking is common, fighting is not.

15

Alcoholism

This is not to deny that drinking may bring out the beast in man. Alcohol is involved in at least half of all homicides in the USA, with either the attacker, the victim, or both under the influence. This probably explains why more murders occur on Saturday night than on any other evening (the fewest occur on Tuesdays). Again, the connection between alcohol and bellicosity has class overtones, since most murders occur in the lower and lower-middle classes. It has been suggested that one reason fights occur in barrooms is that rarely are so many people thrust together so closely for such long periods, with hardly anything to do but talk, drink, and fight.

One of the paradoxes about alcohol is that people sometimes cry when they drink. Why, then, drink? Isn't the whole point of drinking to feel happier? The fact is, even though some people become anxious and depressed when they drink, they do not give up drinking, which challenges the widely held assumption that people drink mainly to feel less anxious and depressed. The motives for drinking, in truth, are complex and inscrutable, with no single explanation sufficing for all circumstances.

Alcohol is often described as a 'depressant' drug that depresses first the 'higher' centres in the brain and then downwardly anaesthetizes the brain until finally, in lethal dosage, it snuffs out life itself by depressing the respiratory centre at the base of the brain. This, like most things said about alcohol, is an oversimplification.

What is alcohol 'depressing'? Usually not activity. Most people get a 'lift' from alcohol and many become more animated and active. Nerve fibres 'fire' about as readily in an alcohol solution as they do otherwise, unless the concentration is far above what most people can achieve by drinking. It is sometimes said that by depressing the 'higher' centres of the brain, alcohol releases the 'lower' centres and that this is why people are more uninhibited when they drink—the 'animal instincts' are released. The problem is that studies do not support the theory of the top-to-bottom action of alcohol. Co-ordination, a 'lower' function, often is impaired at lower doses of alcohol than is memory, a 'higher' function.

Again, dosage is crucial. Alcohol in rather small dosage may improve certain types of performance. Apparently this is most likely to occur in activities where the person is not very proficient and where the effects of increased confidence might be expected to show up. If he does poorly at hitting the target on a firing range, he may improve somewhat after several drinks of alcohol. On the other hand, if he does well normally, his performance may fall off when he takes in small amounts of alcohol. Nevertheless, in moderate to high amounts, alcohol usually diminishes function across the board.

An interesting exception to this general rule has emerged in several studies. Apparently if a person learns certain things, such as word lists, while intoxicated—even severely intoxicated—he will remember them better when reintoxicated than when sober. Called 'state-dependent learning', this is one of the few exceptions to the overall impairing effect of alcohol at moderate and high dosages.

Alcohol does something else that is almost unique among drugs. It produces a classical amnesia called 'blackout'. While drinking, the drinker does highly memorable things but cannot remember them the next day. Many social drinkers have had this experience, but it occurs most frequently in alcoholics.

Some misconceptions

Some of the physical effects of alcohol should also be mentioned, if only because there are misconceptions about them.

1. It is generally known that alcohol increases urination. It is generally not known that the increase is temporary, and that after a fairly short period of drinking the need to urinate decreases. On the morning after a night of heavy drinking, a person may not urinate at all. No explanation is available.

2. It is commonly believed that alcohol causes dehydration.

It does not. When a person has a dry mouth and thirst after an evening of drinking, it may be because of the astringent effect of alcohol on the mucous membranes of the mouth. If anything, heavy drinkers may be overhydrated because of the large volume of fluid they consume.

3. It is generally known that alcohol produces a feeling of bodily warmth and therefore is just the thing for Saint Bernards to carry around their necks in barrels and for old boys to have at a frosty football game. Alcohol produces a feeling of warmth because it dilates blood vessels in the skin, which is why drinkers have red noses. However, the warmth can be harmfully illusory. A person's resistance to the effects of severe cold, such as frostbite, is in no way increased by alcohol, although the victim may temporarily think it is.

4. It has been reported that alcohol causes cancer. The story seems to be this: if a person is a heavy smoker and also a heavy drinker, he is more likely to develop cancer of the throat, larynx, and oesophagus than if he is simply a heavy smoker. There is no evidence that alcohol *alone* causes cancer. Its role in promoting cancer of the head and neck is a matter of speculation. Alcohol may increase the solubility of carcinogens from tobacco smoke. A second possibility is that alcohol in large amounts depresses the body's immune response (which it does) and thereby lowers the body's resistance to cancer agents as well as infections.

One argument against the latter theory is that alcoholics do not seem especially likely to develop cancer of other organs in the body (except possibly cancer of the liver). Another argument against the lowered-resistance theory comes from the frequent observation by recovered alcoholics that, 'When I was drinking I never had a cold. Now I have them all the time.' This may be so, but the real truth may be that minor ailments are ignored in the haze of intoxication, and it should be said in defence of the lowered-resistance theory that heavy drinking went hand-in-hand with tuberculosis back when tuberculosis was common.

5. It is said that some people are 'allergic' to alcohol.

Alcohol and behaviour

Members of Alcoholics Anonymous sometimes use the word 'allergy' in a metaphorical sense to explain their addiction. Until recently nobody thought alcohol was an allergen in the usual sense. Allergens are usually proteins, while alcohol is, well, alcohol. New evidence, however, suggests that alcohol in some people may indeed cause an allergic response. This refers to the tendency of Orientals, previously mentioned, to develop a blotchy red rash, particularly on the head, neck, and trunk, after drinking a small amount of alcohol. My colleagues and I recently discovered that antihistamines prevent the alcohol-induced flush from occurring. Antihistamines of course are famous for their therapeutic powers in such allergies as hayfever, but this does not prove that the Oriental flushing response is *like* hayfever. Its cause remains —if you will forgive the expression—inscrutable.

4

Alcohol through the ages

The use of alcohol goes back at least to Palaeolithic times. The evidence for this derives from etymology as well as from studies of Stone Age cultures that survived into the twentieth century.

Available to Palaeolithic man, presumably, were fermented fruit juice (wine), fermented grain (beer), and fermented honey (mead). Etymological evidence suggests that mead may have been the earliest beverage of choice. The word *mead* derives—by way of *mede* (Middle English) and *meodu* (Anglo-Saxon)—from ancient words of Indo-European stock, such as *methy* (Greek) and *madhu* (Sanskrit). In Sanskrit and Greek, the term means both 'honey' and 'intoxicating drink'. The association of honey, rather than grain or fruit, with intoxication may indicate its greater antiquity as a source of alcohol.

All but three of the numerous Stone Age cultures that survived into modern times have been familiar with alcohol. 'The three exceptions,' Berton Roueché writes, 'are the environmentally underprivileged polar peoples, the intellectually stunted Australian aborigines, and the comparably lacklustre primitives of Tierra del Fuego.' Early European explorers of Africa and the New World frequently discovered that alcohol was important in the local cultures. The Indians of eastern North America, for instance, were using alcohol in the form of fermented birch and sugar maple sap.

Alcohol has been used medicinally and in religious ceremonies for thousands of years, but it also has a long history of recreational use. Noah, according to the Old Testament, 'drank of the wine and was drunken'. Mesopotamian civilization provided one of the earliest clinical descriptions of intoxication and one of the first hangover cures. Mesopotamian

20

physicians advised as follows: 'If a man has taken strong wine, his head is affected and he forgets his words and his speech becomes confused, his mind wanders and his eyes have a set expression; to cure him, take licorice, beans, oleander . . . to be compounded with oil and wine before the approach of the goddess Gula (or sunset), and in the morning before sunrise and before anyone has kissed him, let him take it, and he will recover.'

One of the few surviving relics of the Seventeenth Egyptian Dynasty, which roughly coincided with the reign of Hammurabi, is a hieroglyphic outburst of a female courtier. 'Give me eighteen bowls of wine!' she exclaims for posterity. 'Behold, I love drunkenness!' So did other Egyptians of that era. Drunkenness was not rare, historians write, and seems to have occurred in all layers of society from the farmers to the gods (or ruling class). Banquets frequently ended with the guests, men and women, being sick, and this did not in any way seem shocking.

Not only descriptions of drunkenness are found in the historical record, but also pleas for moderation. Dynastic Egypt apparently invented the first temperance tract. Moderation was recommended by no less an authority on moderation than Genghis Khan: 'A soldier must not get drunk oftener than once a week. It would, of course, be better if he did not get drunk at all, but one should not expect the impossible.' The Old Testament condemns drunkenness, but not alcohol. 'Give strong drink unto him that is ready to perish,' the Book of Proverbs proclaims, 'and wine unto those that be of heavy hearts. Let him drink, forget his poverty, and remember his misery no more.'

The 'strong drink' of the Bible was probably undiluted wine. 'She hath mingled her wine,' reports Proverbs; a mixture of wine and water was the usual Jewish drink.

Alexander the Great was one of a long line of heavy drinking generals. According to Plutarch, Alexander was under the influence of alcohol at the time of the burning of the royal palace at Persepolis in 330 BC, seven years before his death.

21

Alcoholism

With torch in hand, a drunken Alexander led revellers in a procession in honour of Dionysus and threw the first firebrand, an act he bitterly regretted when sober. The final year of Alexander's life was punctuated with drunken binges and his death may have been hastened by alcohol withdrawal.

Plutarch describes a mass orgy in 325 BC involving Alexander and his Macedonian army: 'Not a single helmet, shield or spear was to be seen, but along the whole line of march the soldiers kept dipping their cups, drinking-horns or earthenware goblets into huge casks and mixing bowls and toasting one another, some drinking as they marched, others sprawled by the wayside.' The history of war is filled with similar scenes.

Alcohol has been the 'intoxicant of choice' in Judaeo-Christian culture. 'To drink is a Christian diversion/Unknown to the Turk and the Persian,' wrote Congreve 300 years ago. It was not *totally* unknown to the Turk and the Persian, but it is true they favoured other intoxicants, notably, the products of the poppy and hemp plant.

One of the myths of our times is that the 'stresses' of modern living have produced a society unusually reliant on alcohol. This is not true. Per capita consumption in the United States was highest, at an estimated six or seven gallons per person, in the early 1800s when whiskey and cider were the favourite beverages. One reason was that whiskey is more portable than grain, and cider more portable than apples. Portability was important before trains came along, especially if you were Westward bound in a covered wagon.

In the United Kingdom, drinking and drunkenness reached a peak during the 'gin epidemic' of the mid-eighteenth century, when gin sold for a few pennies a pint. Probably in no period of history have so many inebriates crowded the streets of a city as occurred in Hogarth's London. Less beer is consumed per capita in the UK now than 100 years ago. Consumption of wine *was* decreasing but started upward again in the late 1960s when the import fees were reduced and the European Common Market influence took hold.

Alcohol through the ages

Fluctuations in consumption also have been influenced by availability of potable water, the introduction of coffee, tea, and cocoa at prices the population could afford, and the waxing and waning of temperance movements.

Today, in the United States, the reported consumption of alcohol (pure alcohol) is about three gallons per person over 14 per annum. This figure is based on tax data. Untaxed sales, such as those on military installations, are not included, so per capita consumption may be underestimated. Also, because consumption estimates are based on the resident population, when residents of one state cross into another state to purchase lower priced alcoholic beverages, the result is a higher per capita consumption figure for the state in which sales occur. Washington, DC and states with high rates of tourism and business travel have higher reported consumption rates because sales to transients are calculated as consumption by the resident population.

There has been a modest increase in taxed alcohol sales in the United States in the past two decades, but the reason may be that people are drinking less untaxed alcohol. There is less available. Moonshine used to be a booming industry in some back country areas, but no longer is today. Making moonshine alcohol mainly was a small family business, and small family businesses in the United States have declined.

Are people drinking different kinds of beverages than formerly? There is not much evidence for this. As noted, the official per capita consumption of alcohol in the United States is about three gallons. Distributed among the three most commonly used beverages—beer, wine, and distilled spirits—the three gallons is equivalent to 320 12 ounce cans of beer, plus 12½ bottles of table wine, plus 10½ bottles of distilled spirits for each US resident aged 14 years or older. The ratios have remained fairly constant since 1945. There is an impression that Americans are drinking more wine than previously, but this does not show up in statistics.

There has been one interesting change in beverage preference. In diet-conscious America people drink more 'light' beer (beer with fewer calories) than regular beer. They also drink more 'white' spirits, such as vodka or gin, than 'brown' spirits (whiskey). The explanation for the latter is not clear, unless people have the notion that white spirits are healthier than brown, which is probably not true.

International comparisons are difficult at best. However, it appears that 'wine countries' such as France and Italy consume more alcohol than do countries where distilled spirits are favoured. Israel has the lowest per capita consumption. Ireland, contrary to its popular image, has a lower consumption rate than the United Kingdom. The United States ranks in the middle with regard to alcohol consumption and the Soviet Union (if you can believe the figures) is in the lower third.

Most adults in the United States are light drinkers. About 35 per cent abstain, 55 per cent drink less than three drinks per week, and only 11 per cent consume an average of one ounce or more of alcohol per day.

Drinking patterns vary by age and sex. For both men and women, the prevalence of drinking is highest and abstention is lowest in the 21–34 year age range. Four to five times more males are 'heavy' drinkers compared to females at all ages. For ages 65 years and older, abstainers exceed drinkers in both sexes and only 7 per cent of men and 2 per cent of women are considered heavy drinkers.

The level of consumption varies markedly in different segments of the population. In the United States consumption is greatest in the North-east, lowest in the South. Young white males drink more than any other group in the US.

The proportion of adolescents who report drinking increases steadily with age, reaching 80 to 90 per cent among the oldest schoolchildren. By that time as many girls report having 'ever' drunk as boys.

Most alcohol is consumed by a small percentage of people: 70 per cent of the drinking population consume only 20 per cent of the total alcohol consumed; 30 per cent of drinkers consume 80 per cent of the alcohol; and 10 per cent consume 50 per cent.

24

Alcohol through the ages

These figures refer to overall consumption. In America and the UK this apparently has not gone up or down much in the last 150 years.

Overall consumption must be distinguished from alcoholism. Is the latter increasing?

There is some evidence it may be *decreasing*. The distinguished American physician, Benjamin Rush, in 1795 estimated that 4000 Americans died each year from 'over-indulgence in ardent spirits'. Since the population of the country was about four million, this gives a rate of 100 per 100 000. The officially recorded rate of death from alcoholism in the United States today is two per 100 000. Granting that Dr Rush's estimate is suspect, alcoholism in the United States may be less prevalent today than it was 200 years ago.

It's hard to say. There are several problems in estimating the prevalence of alcoholism. One is that few agree on the definition of alcoholism. Also, when a household survey is done, the alcoholics, more than most people, are not home. Neighbourhood bars are rarely included in household surveys.

A third reason to be sceptical about prevalent estimates is that axe-grinding is a potent factor in the production of statistics. Government officials spend much of their time trying to wring money out of reluctant legislators and often are caught in the dilemma of, on the one hand, wanting the prevalence of alcoholism to be low to show they are doing a good job and, on the other hand, wanting it to be high to inspire lawmakers to spend more money on the problem.

In the late 1960s, for example, the US Government announced that there were five million American alcoholics. Now it is said that there are fourteen million. This increase coincides with increased efforts by the Government to study and treat alcoholism. The connection no doubt is coincidental, but since the figures are fictitious anyway it does not matter. No one doubts that alcoholism is common.

Normal drinking

Throughout the ages (and throughout this book), a distinction has been made between normal and abnormal drinking. Before dealing at length with abnormal drinking (or alcoholism), a few words should be said about normal drinking.

How much can you drink and still be 'normal'?

Normal can be defined in several ways. It can be defined as drinking no more than 'society' deems safe and prudent, i.e. normal. Since societies vary in this regard, the definition is not very helpful.

According to another definition, normal drinking is drinking less than is required to produce medical, social, or psychological problems. The problem definition also has problems, as will be discussed in the next chapter.

Finally, attempts are made from time to time to separate normal from abnormal drinking in terms of quantity of alcohol consumed. A nineteenth-century British physician named Dr Anstie proclaimed that normal drinking consisted of drinking no more than three ounces of whiskey or half a bottle of table wine or two pints of beer a day (known for years as 'Dr Anstie's limits'). In 1979 a special committee of the Royal College of Psychiatrists in Great Britain proposed more liberal limits. The Committee announced that four pints of beer daily or 'four doubles of spirits' or a bottle of wine 'constitute reasonable guidelines for the upper limit of drinking'. Upper limits vary from person to person and many would support the more conservative position of Dr Anstie.

Section Two

Alcoholism

In my judgment such of us who have never fallen victims [to alcoholism] have been spared more by the absence of appetite than from any mental or moral superiority over those who have. Indeed, I believe if we take habitual drunkards as a class, their heads and their hearts will bear an advantageous comparison with those of any other class.

—Abraham Lincoln

He drank, not as an epicure, but barbarously, with a speed and dispatch altogether American, as if he were performing a homicidal function, as if he had to kill something inside himself, a worm that would not die.

—Baudelaire, writing about Edgar Allan Poe

5

What is alcoholism?

An alcoholic is a person who drinks, has problems from drinking, but goes on drinking anyway:

I am David. I am an alcoholic. I have always been an alcoholic. I will always be an alcoholic. I cannot touch alcohol. It will destroy me. It is like an allergy—not a real allergy—but *like* an allergy.

I had my first drink at sixteen. I got drunk. For several years I drank every week or so with the boys. I didn't always get drunk, but I know now that alcohol affected me differently than other people. I looked forward to the times I knew I could drink. I drank for the glow, the feeling of confidence it gave me. But maybe that's why my friends drank too. They didn't become alcoholics. Alcohol seemed to satisfy some specific need I had, which I can't describe. True, it made me feel good, helped me forget my troubles, but that wasn't it. What was it? I don't know, but I know I liked it, and after a time, I more than liked it, I needed it. Of course, I didn't realize it. It was maybe ten or fifteen years before I realized it, *let* myself realize it.

My need was easy to hide from myself and others (maybe I'm kidding myself about the others). I only associated with people who drank. I married a woman who drank. There were always reasons to drink. I was low, tense, tired, mad, happy. I probably drank as often because I was happy as for any other reason. And occasions for drinking—when drinking was appropriate, expected—were endless. Football games, fishing trips, parties, holidays, birthdays, Christmas, or merely Saturday night. Drinking became interwoven with everything pleasurable —food, sex, social life. When I stopped drinking, these things, for a time, lost all interest for me, they were so tied to drinking. I don't think I will ever enjoy them as much as I did when drinking. But if I had kept drinking, I wouldn't be here to enjoy them. I would be dead.

So, drinking came to dominate my life. By the time I was 25 I was drinking every day, usually before dinner, but sometimes after dinner (if there was a 'reason'), and more on weekends, starting in the afternoon. By 30, I drank all weekend, starting with a beer or Bloody Mary in the morning, and drinking off and on, throughout the day, beer or wine or vodka, indiscriminately. The goal, always, was to maintain a glow, not enough, I hoped, that people would notice, but a glow. When five o'clock came, I thought, well, now it's cocktail hour and I would

Alcoholism

have my two of three scotches or martinis before dinner as I did on non-weekend nights. After dinner I might nap, but just as often felt a kind of wakeful calm and power and happiness that I've never experienced any other time. These were the dangerous moments. I called friends, boring them with drunken talk; arranged parties; decided impulsively to drive to a bar. In one year, at the age of 33, I had three accidents, all on Saturday night, and was charged with drunken driving once (I kept my licence, but barely). My friends became fewer, reduced to other heavy drinkers and barflies. I fought with my wife, blaming her for *her* drinking, and once or twice hit her (or so she said—like many things I did while drinking, there was no memory afterward).

And by now I was drinking at noontime, with the lunch hour stretching longer and longer. I began taking off whole afternoons, going home potted. I missed mornings at work because of drinking the night before, particularly Monday mornings. And I began drinking weekday mornings to get going. Vodka and orange juice. I thought vodka wouldn't smell (it did). It usually lasted until an early martini luncheon, and I then suffered through until cocktail hour, which came earlier and earlier.

By now I was hooked and knew it, but desperately did not want others to know it. I had been sneaking drinks for years—slipping out to the kitchen during parties and such—but now I began hiding alcohol, in my desk, bedroom, car glove compartment, so it would never be far away, ever. I grew panicky even thinking I might not have alcohol when I needed it, which was just about always.

For years, I drank and had very little hangover, but now the hangovers were gruesome. I felt physically bad—headachy, nauseous, weak—but the mental part was the hardest. I loathed myself. I was waking early and thinking what a mess I was, how I had hurt so many others and myself. The words 'guilty' and 'depression' sound superficial in trying to describe how I felt. The loathing was almost physical—a dead weight that could be lifted in only one way, and that was by having a drink, so I drank, morning after morning. After two or three, my hands were steady, I could hold some breakfast down, and the guilt was gone, or almost.

Despite everything, others knew. There was the odour, the rheumy eyes, and flushed face. There was missing work and not working well when there. Fights with wife, increasingly physical. She kept threatening to leave and finally did. My boss gave me a leave of absence after an embarrassed remark about my 'personal problems'. At some point I was without wife, home, or job. I had nothing to do but drink. The drinking was now steady, days on end. I lost appetite and missed meals (besides, money was short). I awoke at night, sweating and shaking, and had a drink. I awoke in the morning vomiting and had a drink. It couldn't last. My ex-wife found me in my apartment shaking and seeing things, and got me in the hospital. I dried out, left, and went back to drinking. I was hospitalized again, and this time stayed dry for six months. I was nervous and couldn't sleep, but got some of my confidence back and found a part-time job. Then my ex-boss offered my job back and I celebrated by having a drink. The next night I had two drinks. In a month I was drinking as much as ever and again unemployed. That was three years ago. I've had two big drunks since then but don't drink other times. I think about alcohol and miss it. Life is grey and monotonous. The joy and gaiety are gone. But drinking will kill me. I know this and have stopped—for now.

A tree is known by its fruit; alcoholism by its problems. Theoretically, a person can drink a gallon of whiskey a day for a lifetime, not have problems, and therefore not be alcoholic. Theoretically. In fact, heavy drinkers almost always have problems. Sometimes they are mild. Alcohol calories may result in overweight—a cosmetic if not a medical problem. Things may be said while drinking that would not or should not be said other times. A minor traffic offence may have major consequences when alcohol is on the breath.

Problems, yes, but alcoholism? The verdict rests with the observer. A fundamentalist teetotaler may view any problem from drinking as alcoholism. Moderate drinkers may be more indulgent, saying in effect, 'These things happen. If they do not happen too often, it probably does not mean much.' But what is too often? Except in extreme cases—the Davids, about whom everyone agrees—there will always be controversy about who is and who is not an alcoholic. This is understandable; doctors disagree about who has heart disease if the case is mild.

'Alcoholism' in this book refers to the David type of alcoholism, granting that patterns of human behaviour are bewilderingly variable, even patterns of illness. Not all Davids, for example, reach bottom (in AA terms). Some stop drinking long before. Others drink, but with enough control to prevent the big problems from happening. The essence of the David type of alcoholism is a vulnerability to alcohol that sets him apart from other drinkers. By taking extreme measures, such as total abstinence, he may prevent alcohol problems; but if he drinks at all, the chance of developing problems is high, and this vulnerability appears to be lifelong.

How many people have this condition? It is not known. Population surveys show that about 70 per cent of adults in the United States drink. About 12 per cent (20 per cent of men, 8 per cent of women) drink 'heavily', meaning they drink almost daily and enough to be somewhat intoxicated several times a month. About 9 per cent have problems from drinking, mostly minor; another 9 per cent have had problems in the past. (There seems to be a considerable migration in and out of the 'problem-drinking' pool.) Among the problem drinkers are a subgroup called alcoholics. How many alcoholics are there? Nobody knows, but undoubtedly alcoholics like David exist in large numbers in all Western countries.

Is alcoholism a disease? The question arises frequently and is the subject of fierce debate among alcoholism experts.

A little historical background may help put the matter in perspective. The 'disease concept' of alcoholism is not new. It originated in the writings of Benjamin Rush and the British physician Thomas Trotter in the early nineteenth century and became increasingly popular with physicians as the century progressed. In the 1830s, Dr Samuel Woodward, the first superintendent of Worcester State Hospital, Massachusetts, and Dr Eli Tood of Hartford, Connecticut, established the first medical institutions for inebriates. *The Journal of Inebriety* was founded in 1876 on the 'fact that inebriety is a neurosis and psychosis'. In 1904 the Medical Temperance Society changed its name to the American Medical Association for the Study of Inebriety and Narcotics.

The concept of alcoholism as a disease lost favour in the early years of the twentieth century, but came back in vogue in mid-century, in part through pioneering studies at the Yale School of Alcohol Studies and the writings of E. M. Jellinek.

Still, many people resist. Calling alcoholism a disease, they say, simply gives the alcoholic a good alibi for self-indulgence.

What is alcoholism?

Maybe a comparison with a 'real' disease would help resolve what is essentially a semantic problem:

Is lead poisoning a disease? Lead poisoning is diagnosed by a specific set of symptoms: abdominal pain, headache, convulsions, coma. Alcoholism also is diagnosed by a specific set of symptoms (reviewed in the next chapter). Both lead poisoning and alcoholism are 'medical' problems, meaning that doctors are supposed to know something about them and possibly be of help.

One reason people, including doctors, have trouble viewing alcoholism as a disease like cancer is that alcoholism is associated with having fun, and fun is not usually associated with disease. (Where does that leave syphilis? Is sex less fun than drinking?)

The point is this: why or how a person 'catches' a disease is not relevant. If some 'self-indulgent' people *enjoyed* lead and ate it like popcorn, this would not change the diagnosis of lead intoxication. Diseases are known by their manifestations as well as their causes, and why alcoholics drink is irrelevant to the diagnosis of alcoholism.

33

6

The symptoms

The fashion today is to describe alcohol in terms of problems. This has the advantage that inferred mental states, such as 'compulsion' or 'craving', or terms such as addiction, themselves hard to define, do not have to be invoked. The World Health Organization and the United States National Council on Alcoholism base their definitions of alcoholism on problems—personal, social, medical, etc. Even so, there is still disagreement. How many problems? How serious must the problems be? With alcoholics like David, there is no difficulty—their problems are both abundant and serious. But in milder, less advanced, and less typical cases, there is controversy.

Psychological problems

The symptoms of alcoholism fall into three groups: psychological, medical, and social. Starting with those that are psychological:

1. *Preoccupation with alcohol*

The alcoholic thinks about alcohol from morning till night, and at night, if not too drunk to dream, dreams about alcohol. When to have the first drink? When the next? Remember the times that bars will be closed. Remember liquor stores are closed on Sundays. Prepare, prepare. Will they sell more than two drinks on the aeroplane? Take a flask. Do the Smiths drink? Find out before accepting their dinner invitation. This goes on and on, blotting out other thoughts, other plans.

It is obsessional in precisely the way psychiatrists use the

34

word. Obsessions breed compulsions, and when an alcoholic drops in a bar or liquor store, ever so casually, it is as compulsive as the neurotic washing his hands for the twentieth time that day.

2. *Self-deception*

But he must not admit it to himself. 'We are all victims of systematic self-deception,' Santayana said, and the alcoholic is a victim *par excellence*. People are victims of many things—cancer, lust, society—and can accept it. But, deep down, the alcoholic believes he is doing it to himself; he is the perpetrator, not the victim. And this he cannot accept, so he lies to himself.

'I can stop drinking anytime. Important people drink. Churchill drank. Today is special—a friend is in town. Nothing is going on—why not? Life is tragic—why not? Tomorrow we die—why not?'

As he lies to himself, he lies to others, and concealment becomes a game like the one children play when they raid the cookie jar and hope their mother won't notice.

3. *Guilt*

But he does know and can't help knowing. There are too many reminders. The wife's pleas and tantrums. The boss's 'friendly' advice. The dented bumper. The night terrors and night sweats. The trembling hands. The puffy eyes and blotchy complexion. The terrifying memory gaps. All spell self-destruction, and even the cleverest self-deceiver knows it.

4. *Amnesia*

Alcoholics have memory lapses when they drink and this is often attributed to guilt. It is said the forgetter does not want to remember. Non-alcoholics also have memory lapses when they drink, not so often or so severely, but non-alcoholics by

35

Alcoholism

definition drink less. Memory lapses—or blackouts, as they are called when alcohol is involved—are probably not due to guilt. More likely alcohol, in some people on some occasions, interferes with chemical processes that make memory—perhaps the most mysterious of biological phenomena—possible.

Precisely how it occurs is unknown, but the memory lapses are genuine. The drinker does things when he is drinking that ordinarily he would remember perfectly, but when he sobers up, usually the next day, he has no recollection of what he has done. Sometimes he realizes that he had a memory lapse. He is apprehensive. He checks to see if his car is in the garage. He looks for dents that weren't there before. His overriding fear is that he did something—broke a law, harmed someone—and punishment is at hand. He retraces his movements of the night before. 'Was I here, Joe?' he asks. Told that he was: 'What did I do? Was I drunk?' Reassured that he did nothing wrong and was no more drunk than usual, he goes to the next place where he might have been. Alternately, he may avoid all places and all companions he might have visited or been with during the forgotten interval, preferring not to know.

In truth, people rarely do things during blackouts that they don't also do when they are drunk and suffer no memory loss.

During blackouts, the person is conscious and alert. He may appear normal. He may do complicated things—converse intelligently, seduce women, travel. A true story:

A 39-year-old salesman awoke in a strange hotel room. He had a mild hangover but otherwise felt normal. His clothes were hanging in the closet; he was clean-shaven. He dressed and went down to the lobby. He learned from the clerk that he was in Las Vegas and that he had checked in two days previously. It had been obvious that he had been drinking, the clerk said, but he hadn't seemed very drunk. The date was Saturday the 14th. His last recollection was of sitting in a St. Louis bar on Monday the 9th. He had been drinking all day and was drunk, but could remember everything perfectly until about 3 p.m., when 'like a curtain dropping', his memory went blank. It remained blank for approximately five days. Three years later, it was still blank. He was so frightened by the experience that he abstained from alcohol for two years.

36

The symptoms

Some people forget and do not realize when sober that they have forgotten anything. Someone tells them and then they remember a little.

A 53-year-old member of Alcoholics Anonymous said that he had experienced many blackouts during his 25 years of heavy drinking. He could not remember his first blackout, but guessed it had happened about 15 years before. The memory loss had not bothered him, he said; he assumed everyone who drank had trouble with memory. Sometimes, however, it was embarrassing to be told he had said something or gone somewhere and not recalled it. Upon being told, he would sometimes remember the event and sometimes not. Occasionally, months later, something would remind him of the event and his memory would 'snap back'. Typically, he could remember some parts of a drinking episode and not others; a half hour might be blanked out and the next hour remembered. The forgotten parts appeared to have no more emotional significance than the remembered ones. 'It's like turning a switch on and off.'

Sometimes a curious thing happens when a person is drinking: The drinker recalls things that happened during a previous drinking period which, when sober, he had forgotten. For example, alcoholics often report hiding money or alcohol when drinking, forgetting it when sober, and having their memory return when drinking again. This is reminiscent of the 'state-dependent learning' described in the first chapter. Whatever the explanation, the mind does play odd tricks on drinkers:

A 47-year-old housewife often wrote letters when she was drinking. Sometimes she would jot down notes for a letter and start writing it but not finish it. The next day, sober, she would be unable to decipher the notes. Then she would start drinking again, and after a few drinks the meaning of the notes would become clear and she would resume writing the letter. 'It was like picking up the pencil where I had left off.'

5. Anxiety and depression

What goes up comes down, and alcoholic euphoria is followed by alcoholic depression with a kind of Newtonian inevitability. Anxiety and depression occur not only with hangovers but

37

intermittently during the drinking period itself, if the drinking is heavy and continuous. This sequence is common: a man feels bad for any reason (it's a grey day); he drinks, feels better; then he feels bad again, this time because the alcohol effect is wearing off; he drinks again, feels better again. And a vicious cycle is under way, based on alcohol's ability to alternately raise and lower spirits. This rollercoaster effect is probably chemical in nature, but the drinker only knows that alcohol, having raised his spirits, now lowers them, and that the best way to raise them again is to have another drink.

Medical problems

If this process goes on long enough, there are usually medical problems. They may take years to develop, and some lucky drinkers never are affected. Incredibly, a person may consume a ferocious quantity of alcohol, maybe a fifth or a quart of whiskey a day for twenty years or longer, and when he dies a 'natural' death, his brain, liver, pancreas, and coronary arteries appear normal. But the odds are strong that something will give. Here are some favourite targets:

1. *The stomach*

Gastritis, inflammation of the stomach's lining, is common. The symptoms are gas, bloating, heartburn, nausea. The cure is alcohol. Before-and-after pictures of the stomach prove it. Raw and inflamed from a night, or week, of heavy drinking, the stomach is miraculously restored to a normal appearance after a shot or two of alcohol.

Alcohol's role in producing stomach or duodenal ulcers is debatable. Ulcers are caused by hydrochloric acid and digestive enzymes. These are powerful enough to digest fish bones and the toughest beefsteak, but inexplicably do not digest the stomach itself. The mucous lining of the stomach somehow prevents it. When the protection is lost, ulcers develop. If alcohol, hot peppers, or pent-up anger produce ulcers at all, they must do so either by increasing acid production or by breaching the protective barrier. But alcohol, in strong doses, decreases rather than increases acid production. Its effect on the protective lining is not clear.

2. *The liver*

The word 'cirrhosis' comes from the Greek word for yellow–orange, probably because people with cirrhosis become jaundiced. Alcoholics are disposed to a type of cirrhosis called portal cirrhosis, or Laennec's cirrhosis.

In the first stages of cirrhosis, liver cells become inflamed and gradually die out. The liver swells up and can be felt through the belly wall, whereas usually it is hidden behind the ribs. New cells appear—the body incorrigibly bent on keeping things going—but with a difference. Previously the cells lined up in columns, forming banks for concentric canals through which blood coursed. The new cells form higgledy-piggledy, and the blood flow comes nearly to a halt.

The results are predictable. Blood backs up and seeps into the abdomen, which swells like a balloon, or it detours around the liver, engorging the paper-thin veins of the oesophagus. If the veins burst, fatal haemorrhage may result. The liver cells, formerly little factories with many functions, go on strike and their production of proteins, blood-clotting factors, and other vital constituents falls off. In men, the cells no longer suppress female sex hormones (the manliest man has *some* female sex hormones), so men's breasts grow, their testicles shrink, and they lose their baritone voices, beards, and hairy chests.

As the process continues, scar tissue forms and eventually the liver is like a small lumpy rock, incapable of sustaining life.

Cirrhosis is a leading cause of death in the United States, and most people with Laennec's cirrhosis are alcoholics. Most alcoholics, however, do not develop cirrhosis, and the connection between drinking and cirrhosis is still not understood.

Alcoholism

The risk of liver disease increases when certain drugs are taken together. Carbon tetrachloride and other halogenated hydrocarbons can produce liver damage alone, but when they are combined with alcohol the risk of liver damage is much greater. Acute and sometimes catastrophic liver disease has occurred in individuals who devote a Saturday afternoon to scrubbing their wall-to-wall carpets with a cleaning fluid while drinking a half a case of beer. Just recently it was found that acetaminophen, a widely used aspirin substitute, may produce serious liver damage when combined with alcohol over a period of time.

3. *Nerve fibres*

The long nerve fibres extending from the spinal cord to muscles often suffer degenerative changes in alcoholics. The fibres make muscles contract and maintain muscular tone; they also transmit back to the spinal cord, and thence the brain, messages from sensory receptors in muscle and skin. The degeneration of nerves results in muscular weakness and eventual wasting and paralysis. Pain and tingling are experienced, and there may be eventual loss of sensation. The cause of nerve-fibre degeneration in the alcoholic is not alcohol; it is a vitamin deficiency. High doses of B vitamins almost always restore the fibres to their normal state, if not given too late.

4. *Brain damage*

There is little direct evidence that alcohol alone causes brain damage. After many years of heavy drinking, most alcoholics, when recovered from their latest drinking bout, show little or no sign of intellectual impairment. Their IQs are normal, their thoughts logical, and their minds clear. If there is impairment, it is usually subtle, rarely persists, and can be attributed to factors other than loss of brain cells—poor motivation, for example, in taking the tests psychologists are forever giving alcoholics.

The symptoms

Computerized X-rays of the brain—CAT scans—have been applied to alcoholics in several studies. The results have been mixed. Some studies show a loss of brain tissue in alcoholics, others show no loss, and still others show loss followed by a return to normal! Rats, in one recent study, suffered loss of brain cells after prolonged alcohol intoxication. Intriguingly, the loss occurred mainly in regions of the brain associated with memory processes. In view of the frequent blackouts experienced by alcoholics, it is tempting to speculate that alcohol has a special affinity for these areas of the brain, but more study is needed to prove this.

But a small minority of alcoholics definitely suffer brain damage due to deficiency of thiamine, a B vitamin. The malnourished alcoholic gets too little thiamine, and if the deprivation persists and is severe, certain well-demarcated areas of the brain are destroyed. These areas are definitely involved in memory storage. Their destruction results in severe memory impairment. A German named Wernicke and a Russian named Korsakoff first described the disease. The patient with Wernicke–Korsakoff disease can remember the distant past fairly well, has a normal IQ, and seems reasonably bright; however he is unable to remember anything that happened to him a few minutes after it happens. The condition is devastating, and the chronic Wernicke–Korsakoff patient needs custodial care for the rest of his life. Thiamine, given early, may prevent a permanent defect. Fortunately, the condition is rare.

Alcoholics also are inclined to suffer degenerative changes in the cerebellum, the half-melon bulge at the base of the brain that regulates co-ordination. An unsteady gait results. Vitamin deficiency is believed to be the cause.

5. *Impotency*

MACDUFF: What three things does drink especially provoke?
PORTER: Marry, sir, nose-painting, sleep and urine. Lechery, sir, it

> provokes, and unprovokes; it provokes the desire, but it
> takes away the performance...
>
> *Macbeth* (Act II, scene iii)

Shakespeare names not three but four of alcohol's well-known actions, lechery being the most famous. By dilating blood vessels, alcohol 'paints' the nose; it makes people sleepy; and, one of the things a novice drinker first notices about drink, it makes him go to the bathroom.

It also increases sexual desire. More accurately, perhaps, it 'releases' sexual desire—the well-known disinhibiting effect of alcohol. But performance may be impaired. Drunken men have trouble achieving an erection or ejaculating. Whether sexual performance in drunken women also is impaired is hard to determine. Women have less to erect, and the female orgasm remains poorly understood.

Some alcoholics not only have trouble with sexual performance when drinking; the problem persists long into sobriety. Whether the cause is psychological or physical is not known, but it may contribute to a well-described syndrome: alcoholic conjugal paranoia. Husbands, without evidence, become convinced that their wives are unfaithful. They hound their wives, accuse them, search for anything to support their delusion: inspect underwear for semen spots, hire detectives, sniff blouses for aftershave lotion. The delusion is precisely that: a fixed false idea. It may be related to the husband's feelings of inadequacy about his own sexual ability and perhaps to feelings of inadequacy about life in general, in ruins from years of heavy drinking. Whether women alcoholics also develop alcoholic paranoia is not clear.

6. *Other medical problems*

'To know syphilis is to know medicine', William Osler said at a time when syphilis was untreatable and affected, or could affect, nearly every organ in the body. The same can be said of alcoholism. It can affect, or is alleged to affect, nearly every organ. Rare is the medical journal that does not occasionally

The symptoms

publish new evidence of alcohol's dangers: heart disease, muscle disease, pancreatitis, anaemia, cancer, not to mention the conditions described above. The list is long and growing. But are the reports reliable and is the culprit alcohol?

The problem in ascribing an illness to heavy drinking is that heavy drinkers differ from non-heavy drinkers in other ways. They smoke more. They often eat less. They often lead irregular lives—staying up all hours, never exercising, sleeping it off in doorways. How can these potentially harmful influences be separated from the effects of alcohol? It is difficult.

Moreover, the reports associating alcohol with a particular illness often are contradictory. At least one study reports that alcoholics have less heart disease, not more. Another claims that drinkers live longer than teetotalers, but the 'drinkers' studied were probably not alcoholics.

In conclusion, it is a fact that serious medical problems are associated with alcoholism, although why, how, and how many, remains unknown.

The alcohol-withdrawal syndrome

Alcoholics also experience a medical problem that, strictly speaking, does not come from drinking alcohol but from *not* drinking alcohol. This is the alcohol-withdrawal syndrome. It is commonly, but mistakenly, called the DTs, or delirium tremens. In medical usage 'delirium' means gross memory disturbance, usually combined with insomnia, agitation, hallucinations, and illusions. Most alcoholics do not experience delirium.

As a rule, alcohol withdrawal is a distressing but temporary condition lasting from two days to a week. The mildest symptom is shakiness, which begins a few hours after the patient stops drinking, sometimes awakening him during sleep. Morning shakes are inevitable if the drinker has been drinking enough. His eyelids flutter, his tongue quivers, but, most conspicuously, his hands shake, so that transporting a cup of coffee from saucer to mouth is a major undertaking.

Alcoholism

The cure for the shakes, as for all alcohol-withdrawal symptoms, is a drink or two.

After a day or two without drinking, the alcoholic coming off a bender may start hallucinating—seeing and hearing things that others do not see or hear. He often realizes he is hallucinating and blames alcohol. Not always, however. Sometimes the hallucinations are vivid, frightening, and as real as life.

Occasionally alcoholics have convulsions that resemble the *grand mal* seizures of the epileptic. Most alcoholics are not epileptic and have seizures only when withdrawing from alcohol. The seizures usually occur one to three days after the person stops drinking.

The most severe form of withdrawal involves delirium and justifies using the term delirium tremens, the 'tremens' referring to the shakiness. Delirium is ominous. It often means the person has not only withdrawal symptoms but also a serious medical illness, often of the type to which alcoholics, because of their way of living, are vulnerable: pneumonia, fractures, blood clots in the brain, liver failure. People occasionally die in delirium tremens, whereas death from milder forms of withdrawal is rare.

Many alcoholics are capable of withdrawing from alcohol on their own. They often do this by tapering off—gradually decreasing the amount they drink. Serious withdrawal symptoms, however, justify hospitalization so that tranquillizers can be given to make the alcoholic feel better, vitamins to prevent brain damage, and frequent medical examinations to exclude medical illness.

The DTs have been described brilliantly in fiction by, among others, Malcolm Lowry and Mark Twain. Lowry, in his novella 'Lunar caustic', wrote from personal experience how it felt to wake up in an alcoholic ward:*

* 'Lunar caustic' appeared in the *Paris Review* in the Winter–Spring issue of 1963.

The symptoms

The man awoke certain that he was on a ship. If not, where did those isolated clangings come from, those sounds of iron on iron? He recognized the crunch of water pouring over the scuttle, the heavy tramp of feet on the deck above, the steady Frère *Jac*ques: Frère *Jac*ques of the engines. He was on a ship, taking him back to England, which he never should have left in the first place. Now he was conscious of his racked, trembling, malodorous body. Daylight sent probes of agony against his eyelids. Opening them, he saw three negro sailors vigorously washing down the deck. He shut his eyes again. Impossible, he thought . . .

As day grew, the noise became more ghastly: what sounded like a railway seemed to be running just over the ceiling. Another night came. The noise grew worse and, stranger yet, the crew kept multiplying. More and more men, bruised, wounded, and always drunk, were hurled down the alley by petty officers to lie face downward, screaming or suddenly asleep on their hard bunks.

He was awake. What had he done last night? Nothing at all, perhaps, yet remorse tore at his vitals. He needed a drink desperately. He did not know whether his eyes were closed or open. Horrid shapes plunged out of the blankness, gibbering, rubbing their bristles against his face, but he couldn't move. Something had got under his bed too, a bear that kept trying to get up. Voices, a prosopopoeia of voices, murmured in his ears, ebbed away, murmured again, cackled, shrieked, cajoled; voices pleading with him to stop drinking, to die and be damned. Thronged, dreadful shadows came close, were snatched away. A cataract of water was pouring through the wall, filling the room. A red hand gesticulated, prodded him: over a ravaged mountain side a swift stream was carrying with it legless bodies yelling out of great eye-sockets, in which were broken teeth. Music mounted to a screech, subsided. On a tumbled bloodstained bed in a house whose face was blasted away a large scorpion was gravely raping a one-armed negress. His wife appeared, tears streaming down her face, pitying, only to be instantly transformed into Richard III, who sprang forward to smother him.

After a few days, the DTs go away. Lowry's patient 'now knew himself to be in a kind of hospital, and with this realization everything became coherent and fell into place. The sound of water pouring over the scuttle was the terrific shock of the flushing toilets; the banging of iron and the dispersed noises, the rattling of keys, explained themselves; the frantic ringing of bells was for doctors or nurses; and all the shouting, shuffling, creaking and ordering was no more than the complex routine of the institution.'

45

Alcoholism

Psychiatric patients are rarely dangerous, but delirious patients are an exception. They may be dangerous indeed, as was the case of Huckleberry Finn's alcoholic father, whose DTs were described by Mark Twain as follows:

I don't know how long I was asleep, but all of a sudden there was an awful scream and I was up. There was Pap looking wild, and skipping around and yelling about snakes. I couldn't see no snakes, but he said they was crawling up his legs; and then he would give a jump and scream, and say one had bit him on the cheek. I never see a man look so wild. Pretty soon he was all fagged out, and fell down panting; then he rolled over and over, screaming and saying there was devils a-hold of him. He wore out by and by, and laid still awhile, moaning. Then he laid stiller, and didn't make a sound. I could hear the owls and the wolves away off in the woods, and it seemed terrible still. He was laying over by the corner. By and by he raised up partway and listened, with his head to one side. He wails, very low:

'Tramp-tramp-tramp; that's the dead; tramp-tramp-tramp; they're coming after me; but I won't go. Oh, they're here! Don't touch me— don't. Hands off—they're cold; let go. Oh, let a poor devil alone!'

He rolled himself up in his blanket and went to crying. But by and by he rolled out and jumped up to his feet looking wild, and he see me and went for me. He chased me round and round the place with a clasp knife, calling me the Angel of Death, and saying he would kill me. . . I begged, and told him I was only Huck; but he laughed such a screech laugh, and roared and cussed, and kept on chasing me. Once when I turned short and dodged under his arm he got me by the jacket between my shoulders, and I thought I was gone; but I slid out of the jacket and saved myself. Pretty soon he was tired out, and dropped down with his back against the door, and said he would rest a minute and then kill me. He put his knife under him, and pretty soon he dozed off.

Social problems

In simpler times, it was said that marihuana smoking was a 'crime without a victim', but even then no one would have called alcoholism a victimless 'crime'. The victims of alcoholism are legion: spouses, children, other relatives, bosses, fellow workers, pedestrians, drivers, police, judges, physicians who get called late at night, taxpayers who often pick up the bill for treatment, and other innocent and not so innocent

46

people who cross the alcoholic's path. Here are some telling statistics.

1. The average city policeman spends one-half of his time dealing with alcohol-related offences. Nearly half of the men and women in prisons are alcoholic or, at any rate, heavy drinkers. Most murderers are drinking at the time they commit a murder, and so are most of the victims, although how many would be considered alcoholic is uncertain.

2. Between 20 and 30 per cent of male psychiatric admissions are alcoholic or have alcohol-related problems. About one-quarter of the men admitted to general hospital wards for medical treatment have alcohol-related problems.

3. Industry loses at least 500 million pounds a year because of absenteeism and work inefficiency related to alcoholism. Monday morning and Friday morning absenteeism, at least partly attributable to alcoholism, is so common that both industry and unions are considering a four-day working week (whereupon Tuesday morning or Thursday afternoon absenteeism will probably become common).

4. Alcoholics are about three times more likely to be divorced than non-alcoholics.

5. Alcoholics have a death rate at least two times higher than non-alcoholics. The most common causes, aside from medical diseases, are accidents and suicides. There are an estimated 25 000 deaths a year in the United States from alcohol-related automobile accidents. Studies indicate that most of the drinking drivers are not just social drinkers coming home from a Christmas party but serious problem drinkers, alcoholic by most definitions. About one out of four suicides in the United States is an alcoholic, usually a man over 35.

7

The course

When does alcoholism begin? Fixing the onset of a chronic condition is difficult. In cancer, when does the first cell become malignant? When does the first coronary artery narrow in heart disease? Cancer and heart diseases usually can be diagnosed only after they are far advanced, and the same is true of alcoholism. With some alcoholics, the alcoholism seems to start with the first drink, but if this happens, often it is not apparent except in retrospect.

Nevertheless, alcoholism has a 'natural history'. This means the condition tends to develop at certain ages, progresses in a more or less predictable manner, and terminates in more or less predictable ways. 'More or less' is an important qualifier, as there is much variation. Men and women vary; whites and blacks; Americans and French.

The 'typical' white male alcoholic begins drinking heavily in his late teens or early twenties, drinks more and more throughout his twenties, starts having serious problems in his thirties, is hospitalized for drinking (if ever) in his mid- or late-thirties, and is clearly identified by himself and others as alcoholic—a man who cannot drink without trouble—between age 40 and 50.

Men, with rare exceptions, do not become alcoholic after 45. There is an 'age of risk' for alcoholism, as for most illnesses, and if a man has no symptoms of alcoholism by his late-forties, he probably will develop none.

The illness ends by death from suicide, accident, or medical illness—or by cessation of drinking. Few alcoholics return to social drinking.*

---

* Whether alcoholics can return to normal drinking has been the subject of heated controversy. When the idea that they could was proposed in the late 1950s,

The course

Patterns of drinking are variable and it is a mistake to associate one particular pattern exclusively with 'alcoholism'. America's best-known authority on alcoholism, E. M. Jellinek, divided alcoholics into various 'species' depending on their pattern of drinking. One species, the so-called gamma alcoholic, is common in America and conforms to the stereotype of the Alcoholics Anonymous alcoholic. Gamma alcoholics have problems with 'control'; once they begin drinking, they are unable to stop until poor health or depleted financial resources prevent them from continuing. Once the 'bender' is terminated, however, the person is able to abstain from alcohol for varying lengths of time. Jellinek contrasted the gamma alcoholic with a species of alcoholic common in France. The latter has 'control' but is 'unable to abstain'; he *must* drink a given quantity of alcohol every day, although he has no compulsion to exceed this amount. He may not recognize that he has an alcohol problem until, for reasons beyond his control, he has to stop drinking, whereupon he experiences withdrawal symptoms.

A French alcoholic describes himself:

My name is Pierre. I am not an alcoholic. I do not know alcoholics. There are no alcoholics in France, except tourists.

I have drunk wine since I was a child. Wine is good for you. I drink it with meals and when I am thirsty. Since I was a young man, I have drunk three or four litres of wine every day. I also enjoy an occasional apéritif, especially on Sunday mornings and after work. I never drink more than this. I have no problems from alcohol.

Once, when I was in the Army, no wine was permitted. I started shaking all over and thought bugs were crawling on me. I think it was

---

the investigators making the proposal were attacked vehemently and had their lives threatened. Controversy goes on, with some therapists actively *trying* to restore alcoholics to social drinkers (a goal many recovered alcoholics would consider not only unfeasible but morally reprehensible).

The most recent round in the controversy occurred recently in the United States when the Rand Report said that treated alcoholics did about as well when they continued to drink as when they stayed completely sober. The report was based on the largest alcoholism treatment evaluation ever conducted.

Alcoholism

the Army food. My doctor says my liver is too large. My father and grandfather had large livers. It probably means nothing.

The American alcoholic stereotype has two choices—abstain or go on a bender. The French alcoholic stereotype does not go on benders, but cannot abstain.

Although these two types of alcoholism do exist, many individuals who do not conform to the stereotypes still have serious drinking problems. Among American alcoholics, one drink does *not* invariably lead to a binge; a person may drink moderately for a long time before his drinking begins to interfere with his health or social functioning.

Black alcoholics start drinking younger—often in their early and mid-teens. By twenty they may be floridly alcoholic and need hospitalization. They have withdrawal hallucinations more often than do white alcoholics and, for unknown reasons, are less suicidal in middle age.

This diversity in drinking patterns explains the current emphasis on *problems*, rather than a single set of symptoms, as the basis for diagnosing alcoholism.

The most common causes of death in alcoholics are suicide, homicide, accidents, and a variety of medical illnesses, including acute hepatitis, cirrhosis, pancreatitis, subdural haematoma, pneumonia, and alcohol-related heart disease. Apparently this increase in mortality occurs only with the very heavy drinkers we call alcoholic. Studies find the highest life expectancy among moderate drinkers, a somewhat shorter expectancy among abstainers and the shortest of all for heavy drinkers. This does not prove that alcohol prolongs life.*

---

* It is true, though, that man the tippler tends to outlive his cousins of the animal kingdom. Here is a little poem by 'Anon', a favourite of nineteenth century anthologies:

> The horse and mule live 30 years
> And nothing know of wines and beers.
> The goat and sheep at 20 die
> And never taste of Scotch or Rye.
> The cow drinks water by the ton
> And at 18 is mostly done.

50

The course

Whatever induces a man to drink moderately may be associated with characteristics that lead to a long life. However, a recent large-scale study found a positive correlation between moderate drinking and longevity, even when other factors (such as smoking, social class) are taken into account. This observation has gained support from other studies showing that drinkers (non-alcoholics) have less coronary artery disease than do non-drinkers and higher levels of high density lipoproteins (which are associated with reduced risk of heart disease). These findings should be viewed as no more than tentative; moderate drinking is not yet being prescribed to prevent heart disease.

Alcoholism has a higher 'spontaneous' remission rate than is often recognized. The incidence of first admissions to psychiatric hospitals for alcoholism drops markedly in the sixth and seventh decades, as do first arrests for alcohol-related offences. Although the mortality rate among alcoholics is higher than among non-alcoholics, this is probably insufficient to account for the apparent decrease in problem drinkers in middle and late middle life.

Will treatment of alcoholism improve the prognosis? Many believe it does, but mostly on faith. There is little hard evidence one way or the other. Regardless of treatment, most follow-up studies find that about one-third of alcoholics will be abstinent a year after treatment, one-third will be less impaired but still drinking, and another one-third will be unchanged or worse.

The dog at 15 cashes in
Without the aid of rum and gin.
The cat in milk and water soaks
And then in 12 short years it croaks.
The modest, sober, bone-dry hen
Lay eggs for nogs, then dies at 10.
All animals are strictly dry:
They sinless live and swiftly die;
But sinful, ginful, rum-soaked men
Survive for three score years and ten.
And some of them, a very few,
Stay pickled till they're 92.

8

Women and alcohol

'There is no there there', said Gertrude Stein, comparing Oakland to San Francisco. In reading the alcoholism literature one has the same feeling about women—there are no *women* there. Almost all studies of alcoholism deal mainly or exclusively with men.

Nevertheless, in the last few years some tantalizing distinctions have been made between male and female drinkers and alcoholics. The most talked about if not most important distinction arises from the woman's ability to have children. There is now impressive evidence that drinking and pregnancy do not mix.

Here are ten ways in which women alcoholics appear to differ from men alcoholics:

1. Women tend to become alcoholic at an older age. If men are not alcoholic by their mid-forties, they probably will not become alcoholic. This is less true of women.

2. Women alcoholics are more likely to have a depressive illness preceding or coinciding with heavy drinking.

3. Alcoholism in women is more serious. Women are harder to treat and stay sober for briefer intervals. The interval between the onset of heavy drinking and the start of treatment appears to be shorter for women. (Women are more likely than men to seek help for health problems in general, and to do so at an earlier stage, so this 'telescoping' in the development of alcoholism in women may have no connection with the illness itself.)

4. Women alcoholics more often have disruptive early life experiences, such as loss of a parent or other close relative, or psychiatric problems in the family. In several studies about half of women alcoholics reported a parent missing during their childhood, compared to about 15 per cent for male alcoholics.

Women and alcohol

5. Women alcoholics more often have alcoholism in the family. Many studies have shown a high incidence of alcoholism in a parent or sibling of women alcoholics (upwards of 60 per cent). Women alcoholics are more likely to have relatives who are clinically depressed or commit suicide.

6. Women alcoholics tend to use alcohol medicinally as a form of self-treatment. Male alcoholics tend to use alcohol (at least early on) recreationally and socially. Women alcoholics are more likely to use prescribed as well as over-the-counter medications. They are more likely to leave a doctor's office with a tranquillizer prescription. They are more likely to seek out solutions-in-medications, and apparently doctors encourage this tendency.

7. Women are more likely to cite a traumatic event as the cause of heavy drinking. The event may be a divorce, rejection by a spouse or lover, abandonment, the death of someone close, hysterectomy, miscarriage, or health problem.

8. Women alcoholics tend to be submissive as children, rebellious as adults. This is said to be less true of men alcoholics.

9. Men generally are introduced to heavy drinking by other men when they are young. Women tend to get involved in heavy drinking later in life, often through the influence of husbands or men friends.

10. Women are more likely to have a personality change when drinking; find unexplained bruises after a drinking episode; and drink before a 'new situation' (based on a study of members of Alcoholics Anonymous).

Some of these distinctions are pretty conjectural and probably some do not exist. But all have been reported in respectable scientific journals in the past ten years.

Items to be particularly sceptical about are six and eight. Six was obviously based on studies by *men*. Regarding eight, if every submissive child who became rebellious as an adult drank too much, the oceans could not contain enough alcohol to meet the demand. One wonders, too, about the bruises (item ten). Maybe men can't see their bruises because of those hairy legs.

Alcoholism

Some more information from the scientific journals:

More men are alcoholic than women. Some believe the gap is closing, but there is no direct evidence for this.* The best current estimate of a sex ratio for alcoholism is 3:1 (male: female).

With 'liberation' has come an increase in women drinkers. In secondary schools as many girls now drink as boys. This was not true several years ago.

But has there been an increase in heavy drinking among women? Probably not. Less than 10 per cent are heavy drinkers, meaning they drink almost every day and get intoxicated perhaps several times a month. Between 20 and 40 per cent of men fall in this category, with young men more likely than older men to be heavy drinkers.

Because more girls are drinking than apparently ever before it is commonly assumed that the rate of heavy drinking and alcoholism will automatically increase in women. This may not occur for one reason:

More women than men are physiologically intolerant of alcohol; after a modest amount of alcohol, more women experience dizziness, headache, nausea, or a sense of simply having enough. Since this 'protection' is physiological and probably genetically determined, presumably it will not

* The first British book on the subject, *Women and alcohol*, was published in the autumn of 1980 by The Camberwell Council on Alcoholism. It holds that alcoholism among British women is indeed increasing, based on the following kinds of evidence:

Since 1964 the number of men admitted to psychiatric hospitals in England and Wales with a diagnosis of alcoholism doubled; the corresponding number of women so diagnosed *trebled*. There also was a disproportionate increase in women's rates of convictions for drunkenness (including drunken driving), and for cirrhosis deaths and other forms of alcohol-related mortality. Agencies providing help for problem drinkers recorded a steady increase in women clients.

This may seem persuasive, but increases in treatment cases and arrests do not necessarily mean increases in the population. In recent years, alcoholism has become increasingly destigmatized and more alcoholics of both sexes are 'surfacing' in treatment facilities. Moreover, more treatment facilities exist, and there tends to be a correlation between opportunities for treatment and the number of people who seek treatment. To repeat, there is no direct evidence of an increase in female alcoholism.

disappear even though more secondary school girls drink now and then and society is more tolerant of drunken behaviour in women.

Men and women have different hormones, and hormones in women, if not men, seem to influence drinking behaviour. When drinking the same amount of alcohol, in proportion to body weight, women have higher blood levels of alcohol than men and these blood levels vary according to the phase of the hormonally controlled menstrual cycle, being highest in the premenstrual period. Many women say they drink more during the premenstrual period and alcoholic women more often give a history of premenstrual tension than do non-alcoholic women. Just how these hormonal shifts relate to alcoholism, if they relate at all, is not known.

The fetal alcohol syndrome

Women have heard for a long time that they shouldn't drink during pregnancy. The idea goes back at least to Biblical times. In Judges 13:7 an angel tells Samson's mother: 'Behold, thou shalt conceive and bear a son: and now drink no wine or strong drink.'

In early Carthage bridal couples were forbidden to drink for fear of producing a defective child. According to Aristotle, 'Foolish, drunken and harebrained women most often bring forth children like unto themselves, morose and languid.' In 1834 a report to the British House of Commons said: 'Infants of alcoholic mothers often have a starved, shrivelled and imperfect look.'

The Biblical injunction does not make clear *why* pregnant women shouldn't drink. The concern may have been that the child would become alcoholic. Plutarch said that 'Drunkards beget drunkards', reflecting a belief held well into the twentieth century that traits and habits acquired by parents would be passed along to offspring. There was also of course the theological view that sins of the fathers, and no doubt mothers, would be passed on.

Alcoholism

Only in the last decade has convincing evidence emerged that pregnant women should not drink, or drink much, for another reason: heavy drinking may produce fetal abnormalities. During this decade the term 'fetal alcohol syndrome' came into vogue. It has been widely publicized and has absorbed most of the resources in time and money devoted to research about women and alcohol.

Exactly what is the fetal alcohol syndrome?

It was first described with any precision in an obscure French gynaecological journal in 1968 and again, with much more publicity, in 1972 by two Seattle paediatricians. These reports led to an almost evangelical search for the syndrome in children of drinking women. After many conferences, large amounts of money spent on research, and passionate disagreement, a kind of consensus has emerged:

The fetal alcohol syndrome (FAS) has specific and non-specific features. The specific features largely relate to the head. An FAS baby has a small head. The baby has a short nose, thin upper lip, an indistinct groove between upper lip and nose (called the philtrum), small eye openings, and flat cheeks. These facial features are considered characteristic of FAS, although they are also associated with maternal use of certain drugs (particularly those prescribed for epilepsy).

The non-specific features are multitudinous. They include low birth weight, retarded growth as an infant and child, mental retardation, heart murmurs, birthmarks, hernias, and urinary tract abnormalities.

It now appears that between 30 and 50 per cent of women who drink 'heavily' during pregnancy have infants with one or more of these defects. The incidence of fetal abnormalities in children born of women who drink lightly or not at all during pregnancy appears to be about 5 to 10 per cent. (Abnormality is used here in a broad sense, referring to anything from a birthmark to missing limbs.)

The term 'possible fetal alcohol effects' has been suggested to describe these non-specific abnormalities. It has become increasingly clear that the specific facial characteristics of the FAS are fairly rare.

Some studies have failed to find the FAS in *any* of the offspring of heavy drinking mothers. In one study of 12 000 deliveries it was reported that five of 204 children born of heavy drinking women (2.5 per cent) had the FAS, and even in these few cases the examining doctors knew the mother had been a heavy drinker and may have been deliberately looking for FAS features. ('Seek and ye shall find.')

One thing, however, seems clear. Women who give a history of 'heavy' drinking during pregnancy have about a fifty-fifty chance of having a baby with some abnormality, and the abnormality most often reported is low birth weight.

There are two problems in interpreting this finding. One has to do with the definition of 'heavy'. The other refers to the fact that alcoholic women are often heavy smokers and often use other drugs suspected of causing fetal abnormalities; tend to have poor nutrition; fall down a good deal; and generally have a life style different from that of non-alcoholic women.

The definition of 'heavy' remains elusive. It ranges from two or more drinks a day to eight or more, depending on the study. Even heavy drinking women drink erratically during pregnancy, ranging from binge drinking to abstinence and moderate drinking. Timing is crucial in fetal development. In a matter of seconds early in pregnancy a virus or drug can determine whether a limb is formed or not formed; birth size relates mainly to events occurring in the last two or three months of fetal development. It is not surprising that the FAS has come to describe such a welter of observations.

How much a pregnant woman can drink without risk to the fetus is not known and perhaps never will be. Women are simply too diverse, and so are fetuses. To be on the absolute safe side pregnant women should not of course drink at all. Since for the first few weeks after conception many women do not know they are pregnant, this really means women should abstain from alcohol as long as they are able to have babies. In our society this is asking a lot.

Alcoholism

There are some sceptics who question whether alcohol alone, in whatever amounts, produces specific fetal abnormalities in the same way that German measles and thalidomide produce specific abnormalities. As mentioned above, alcoholic women differ from non-alcoholic women in many other ways than simply drinking more.

Take smoking. At least 70 to 90 per cent of alcoholic women smoke cigarettes. Women who smoke cigarettes tend to have small babies, whether they drink or not, so perhaps cigarette smoking and not alcohol is responsible for the small babies born of alcoholic women.

Because non-smoking alcoholic women are rare, this is a difficult question to answer. However, at least three studies suggest that alcohol abuse and cigarette smoking contribute independently to small size of the newborn. The best estimate at present is that alcohol abuse approximately doubles the risk of birth of a small infant, whether the mother smokes or not.

Another factor to consider is heredity. Birth defects run in families. So does alcoholism. Is it possible that in some instances a common genetic predisposition explains both? There is little evidence for this one way or the other. However, some reports about twins suggest this explanation may not be far fetched in all instances. Sometimes one twin shows signs of the FAS and the other does not; if alcohol is responsible, this should not happen.

There obviously is a great deal of uncertainty about the FAS and how often it occurs or whether it occurs at all. To what extent should women modify their usual drinking patterns because of concern about the FAS? Many women spontaneously reduce their alcohol intake during pregnancy because alcohol makes them ill. Should they reduce their intake to zero?

Investigators of the fetal alcohol syndrome met in 1979 and made the following recommendation: 'Observations of human babies and of experimentally treated animals have made it clear that a mother's heavy drinking can severely damage her unborn child. We do not know the exact amount or timing of drinking that causes these effects. We cannot say whether there is a safe amount of drinking or whether there is a safe time during pregnancy. We do know that heavy drinking can be damaging. Women should therefore be especially cautious about drinking during pregnancy and when they are likely to be pregnant.'

There are thousands of women in Alcoholics Anonymous and in alcoholism treatment facilities who have perfectly normal children and this does not seem to get much attention. Many more children of problem drinking mothers will have to be studied before the fetal alcohol syndrome can be defined with certainty. Meanwhile, caution obviously is the wisest course, both for women who drink and for investigators who make premature and poorly substantiated claims.

The question whether pregnant women should drink raises another: should women drink while breast feeding? There is certainly alcohol in the milk. If the mother is intoxicated while breast feeding, the infant will be intoxicated.

No one knows whether this will harm the infant. Newborns, like fetuses, are in a plastic stage of development. One would expect them to be especially vulnerable to environmental insults like alcohol. Not drinking for a few hours preceding nursing, and during nursing, is undoubtedly the safest course.

Section Three

Understanding Alcoholism

First the man takes a drink, then the drink takes a drink, then the drink takes the man.

—Japanese proverb

9

Risk factors

Between 65 and 70 per cent of Americans drink alcohol. About one in 12 or one in 15 have serious problems from drinking. There is no scientifically acceptable explanation why some develop problems and most do not. The ultimate goal in alcoholism research is to solve this mystery.

While the cause of alcoholism is unknown, a number of 'risk factors' have been identified. They include the following:

Family history

Alcoholism runs in families. Children of alcoholics become alcoholic about four times more often than children of non-alcoholics. There is evidence that they become alcoholic whether raised by their alcoholic parent or not. (Chapter 11 examines this evidence.) Whether 'hereditary' or not, alcoholism in the family is probably the strongest predictor of alcoholism occurring in particular individuals.

Sex

More men are alcoholic than women. The difference is about three to one. As discussed in Chapter 8, there is no evidence that the sex difference is changing.

Age

Alcoholism in men usually develops in the twenties and thirties. In women it often develops later. People over 65 rarely become alcoholic, regardless of sex.

Geographical

People living in urban or suburban areas are more often

alcoholic than those living on farms or in small towns. People in northern countries are more often alcoholic than those in southern countries. In France people living in the North are more often alcoholic than those living in the South.

Occupation

Statistics on cirrhosis indicate that individuals in certain occupations may be more vulnerable to alcoholism than those doing other types of work. Waiters, bartenders, dockers, musicians, authors, and reporters have relatively high cirrhosis rates; accountants, postmen, and carpenters have relatively low rates. There appears to be a high incidence of alcoholism in the military services. The group with possibly the highest alcoholism rate in the world may consist of Americans who won the Nobel Prize for Literature. Of seven Nobel Prize winners, four were alcoholic.

Whether particular occupations contribute to the development of alcoholism is not clear. Conceivably bartenders become bartenders because of the availability of alcohol on the job. Some reporters may choose their jobs because the hours and work conditions are favourable to drinking.

Racial background

In the United States, blacks in urban ghettos have a high rate of alcoholism; whether rural blacks have a high rate is unknown. American Indians are said to have a high rate, but this does not apply to all tribes, and the prevalence of alcoholism among Indians generally is unknown.

Orientals have low rates of alcoholism. Many Orientals are physiologically intolerant of alcohol, which may explain this partly.

Income

In Great Britain the distribution of alcoholism among social classes is believed to be bimodal; the highest rates are in the lower and upper classes, with the middle class having an intermediate rate. It is not clear whether the same is true of alcoholism in the United States.

Money obviously is necessary to buy alcohol, but in recent years alcohol in most western countries has been a bargain compared to most other commodities. The decrease in price of alcoholic beverages in relation to all consumer goods is exemplified by distilled spirits, which increased in retail price by only 20 per cent between 1973–1980, while consumer prices generally rose four times more rapidly.

(In countries such as Sweden, the price of distilled spirits is tied to the consumer price index so that a consistent relationship is maintained. United States federal taxes on alcohol have not changed since 1961.)

Whether increasing the price of alcohol results in a decrease of alcoholism is not known. Some countries have tried placing exorbitant taxes on alcohol to reduce alcohol problems, with equivocal results.

Nationality

The per capita consumption of alcohol in France and Italy is comparable, but alcoholism is less common in Italy. Estimates of alcoholism rates are usually based on cirrhosis figures and admissions to psychiatric hospitals for alcoholism. France has the highest cirrhosis rate in the world—considerably higher than Italy. It is interesting that Ireland has a relatively low cirrhosis rate, despite its reputation for rampant alcoholism.

Religion

Almost all Jews and Episcopaleans drink, but alcoholism among Jews is uncommon and appears relatively low among Episcopaleans. Irish Catholics in the United States and Great Britain have a high rate of alcoholism. Although fewer than 50 per cent of Southern Baptists drink, Baptists and members of other fundamentalist churches in the South appear to have a relatively high rate of alcoholism.

School difficulty

Alcohol problems are correlated with a history of school difficulty. Secondary school dropouts and individuals with a record of frequent truancy and delinquency appear to have a particularly high rate of alcoholism.

These are factors associated with alcoholism. Any ultimate explanation of alcoholism must account for them, at least in a broad way.

10

Alcoholism and depression

*Melancholy is at the bottom of everything, just as at the
end of all rivers is the sea . . . Can it be otherwise in a world
where nothing lasts, where all we have loved or shall love
must die? Is death, then, the secret of life? The gloom of an
eternal mourning enwraps every serious and thoughtful
soul, as night enwraps the universe.*
                                —Henri-Frederick Amiel (1893)

> *And malt does more than Milton can*
> *To justify God's ways to man.*
>   —A. E. Housman (1894)

God's ways have struck many people, including Amiel, as
pretty depressing. What is a good cure for depression? Alcohol,
Housman says, and through the ages people have agreed with
him.

But is it so? Does alcohol relieve depression? Will it relieve
serious depression, the kind psychiatrists see?

More importantly, does depression *cause* alcoholism? Are
alcoholics really just depressed people who drink to feel
better (and better, and better) until drinking becomes uncontrolled, a habit with its own propulsion, progressing
independently of the depressed feelings that caused it?

Some believe it. What is the evidence? Here are the questions
that need to be asked:

How many alcoholics have manic-depressive disease?*

Many alcoholics become depressed. Their depressions resemble

---

* Manic-depressive disease is a condition manifested by episodes of depression

67

the depressions seen in manic-depressive disease. The alcoholics become irritable and can't sleep. They feel melancholy and sad. They experience feelings of guilt and remorse. They lose interest in life and contemplate suicide.

Suicide, indeed, is a common outcome of alcoholism. Except for manic-depressives, alcoholics commit suicide more than any other group. One reason to believe alcoholism and manic-depressive disease are related is that, in Western countries, most people who commit suicide have one or the other illness. Many psychoanalysts believe that alcoholism and manic-depressive disease have the same origin; victims of both illnesses are orally fixated and, instead of feeling angry toward others, feel angry toward themselves. Aggression directed toward one's self is experienced as a feeling of depression. The ultimate act of self-aggression is suicide. Alcoholism has been called 'slow suicide'.

This is an interesting theory, but difficult to prove scientifically. Although the depression experienced by alcoholics resembles manic-depressive depression, there is a difference: when the alcoholic stops drinking, the depression often goes away. Alcohol is a toxin. In large amounts it produces depression, anxiety, irritability. The alcoholic feels guilty and for good reason: he *has* botched up his life and he knows it.

Based on most studies it appears that alcoholism causes depression more often than depression causes alcoholism. As noted, the cure for alcohol-induced depression is not antidepressant pills or electroconvulsive therapy but abstinence. (The toxic effects, incidentally, may last for weeks or months after a person stops drinking. Often several months pass before sleep becomes normal again.)

Chapter 8 tells how women alcoholics are different from men alcoholics. One difference is that they more often have depressions *preceding* the onset of heavy drinking. In women

---

which are prolonged, disabling, and often require treatment. Episodes of mania may or may not have occurred. As used here, manic-depressive is synonymous with 'endogenous depression', 'bipolar affective disorder', 'unipolar affective disorder', and melancholia.

Alcoholism and depression

more than men, a case can be made that alcoholism is sometimes a manifestation of depression. Women, as a group, start drinking heavily at an older age than men. In people who are drinking heavily it is hard to tell whether the depression or alcoholism came first. Since women become alcoholic at an older age than men, there is more opportunity for depressions to occur before heavy drinking occurs. Depression may promote heavy drinking in men as often as it appears to in women, but because men start drinking heavily at an earlier age, it is impossible to determine whether the depressions are a cause or consequence of the drinking.

How many manic-depressives are alcoholic?

This sounds like the same question as the one above, but isn't. If you study a group of manic-depressive patients, how many are alcoholic? Such studies have been conducted, with conflicting results. In one study, one-third of manic-depressives were alcoholic. In another study 8 per cent were alcoholic. Eight per cent is not much higher than the prevalence of manic-depressive disease (as broadly defined here) in the general population. A third is much higher. Which is correct? Nobody knows.

Do manic-depressives drink more when they are depressed?

Leaving aside alcoholic manic-depressives, some drink more and some drink less. Probably more manic-depressives cut down on their drinking when depressed than increase their drinking.

One investigator gave alcohol to hospitalized manic-depressives. A small amount of alcohol improved their mood. A large amount made them more depressed. The same is true of alcoholics. Bring alcoholics into an experimental ward, give them alcohol for a long period, and instead of feeling happy they feel miserable. Alcohol, it turns out, is a rather weak euphoriant compared, for example, to cocaine and amphetamines. The hedonistic explanation for alcoholism, contrary to popular opinion, has little support in science.

After giving alcohol to many psychiatric patients, including manic-depressives and alcoholics, Dr Demmie Mayfield at Kansas University reached the following conclusions:

If you feel bad, drinking will make you feel a lot better.
   If you drink a lot, it will make you feel bad.
   Feeling bad from drinking a lot does not seem to make people choose to stop. Feeling a lot better from drinking does not seem to encourage people to continue drinking.

Do manic-depressives drink more when they are manic?

Definitely. Many manics who ordinarily drink little or nothing start drinking heavily when manic. The explanation is not clear but it seems alcohol has almost a specific ameliorative effect on the manic mood. Manics often feel *too* high, uncomfortably high, and alcohol seems to reduce the unpleasant effects of the mania while amplifying the pleasant ones. Lithium, an effective drug for mania, has been given to alcoholics and *seems* to reduce the frequency of relapse, particularly if the alcoholics are depressed. More studies are required before it can be known definitely whether lithium is helpful for alcoholism.

Does alcoholism and manic-depressive disease run in the same families

If they *did* run in the same families, this would suggest a common genetic predisposition. There is evidence that both alcoholism and manic-depressive disease are influenced by heredity, but is it the *same* heredity?

The evidence is mixed. Some studies show an increase of depression in the families of alcoholics and of alcoholism in the families of manic-depressives. Other studies fail to show this. Those that show an overlap have resulted in a concept called 'depressive spectrum disorder'. In this still hypothetical

70

condition, alcoholism occurs on the male side of families and depression on the female side. There is some evidence, based on adoption studies (Chapter 11), that daughters of alcoholics suffer depressions when they are raised by their alcoholic parents but not when they are separated from their alcoholic parents and raised by non-alcoholic adoptive parents. This suggests that the depression seen in female relatives of alcoholics may be less influenced by heredity than by the environmental circumstance of being raised by an alcoholic parent.

Does antidepressant medication relieve alcoholism?

If it did, of course, this would suggest that alcoholism was caused by depression. The best studies, however, do *not* indicate that antidepressant medication is useful for alcoholism.

To summarize: Alcohol may make depressed people feel a little better, but not for long. It may, indeed, make them *more* depressed. The evidence that depression causes alcoholism is weak. Women, more than men, become alcoholic following or during a depression but the causal connection is still not established. Even if depression doesn't cause alcoholism, alcoholism certainly is depressing and most drinking alcoholics are depressed a good deal of the time.

11

Heredity

*We are as days and have our parents
for our yesterdays.*
　　　　　　　　　−Samuel Butler

Alcoholism runs in families. This has been known for centuries. As noted, Plutarch said that 'Drunkards beget drunkards' Aristotle said that 'Harebrained and drunken women have harebrained and drunken children'. The nineteenth century medical and religious literature is replete with references to the familial aspect of alcoholism. Clergymen blamed the 'sins of the father' for the transmission of alcoholism from generation to generation. Doctors attributed the transmission to deleterious effects of alcohol on the sperm or egg, a consequence of parental imbibing at time of conception.

Numerous studies in the twentieth century document the familial nature of alcoholism. About one-quarter of the sons of alcoholics become alcoholic and between 5 and 10 per cent of the daughters. The prevalence of alcoholism in the general population is around 5 per cent in men and 1 per cent or less in women. Having alcoholism 'in the family' increases one's chances of becoming alcoholic by a factor of four or five to one.

Not everything that runs in families is inherited. Speaking French runs in families and is not inherited. It is often hard to separate 'nature' from 'nurture' in conditions that run in families: the same people who provide our genes usually bring us up.

One way to distinguish between the influences of heredity and environment is to compare identical and fraternal twins. Characteristics controlled by heredity should co-exist in

72

identical twins (since they share the same genes) and differ in fraternal twins (whose genes are shared only to the extent that siblings share genes). In other words, assuming that large noses are inherited, both identical twins should have a large nose but one fraternal twin may have a large nose and the other have a small nose. If alcoholism is influenced by heredity, both identical twins would develop the illness more often than would both fraternal twins. Does this happen?

There have been half a dozen studies of alcoholism in which identical twins were compared to fraternal twins. In general, identical twins more often had similar drinking habits and alcohol-related problems than did fraternal twins, indicating a genetic influence. However, heredity could not totally explain alcoholism in the twins. In some pairs of identical twins, one twin was alcoholic and the other was not. If genes completely controlled development of alcoholism both identical twins should *always* be alcoholic.

Of course, no one expected this would happen. Environmental factors, such as cultural attitudes and the availability of alcohol, obviously are important. In few inherited disorders is there 100 per cent correspondence between occurrence of the illness in both identical twins.

Another way to determine whether heredity influences the development of a familial disorder is to study people who have been adopted. In the case of non-family adoptions, individuals are raised by different people than those who provided their genes.

The author and colleagues from America and Denmark conducted the first large-scale study of alcoholism in adoptees. It was conducted in Denmark because of easy access to adoption records.

First we studied a group of young Danish men who had a biological parent hospitalized for alcoholism but had little or no contact with the parent because they were adopted away early in life and raised by adoptive parents. We found that 18 per cent of these men were alcoholic at a young age (before 30). The rate of alcoholism in this group was four times greater than was found in a comparison group of adoptees of the same age and sex who did not have an alcoholic biological parent. Except for alcoholism, the adopted-away sons of alcoholics were no more likely to have a psychiatric disturbance than were adopted-away sons of non-alcoholics. They were no more likely to be non-alcoholic heavy drinkers. In this study, *just alcoholism* distinguished the adopted sons of alcoholics from the adopted sons of non-alcoholics.

We also studied sons of alcoholics who were raised by their alcoholic parents. They had the same rate of alcoholism as did the sons of alcoholics who were adopted by non-relatives in infancy and had no exposure to their alcoholic parent.

In addition, we studied daughters of alcoholics, both those raised by their alcoholic biological parents and those adopted away in infancy and raised by non-alcoholic adoptive parents. Both groups of daughters had high rates of alcoholism compared to the general population. A group of adopted women without known alcoholism in their biological parents also had a high rate of alcoholism, raising the possibility that adoption itself in some way promoted alcoholism in women. As was true of the men adoptees, the adopted-away daughters of alcoholics, studied in their mid-thirties, showed a high rate of alcoholism but no evidence of susceptibility to other psychiatric disorders.

Two other adoption studies have subsequently been performed, one in Sweden and the other in Iowa. Both studies produced essentially the same results as the Danish studies: an increased prevalence of alcoholism in adopted-away children of alcoholics with no evidence of an increased prevalence of other disorders.

Summing up the results of these studies, one might conclude as follows:

1. Children of alcoholics have an increased susceptibility to alcoholism whether they are raised by their alcoholic parents or by non-alcoholic adoptive parents.

2. Children of alcoholics are susceptible *only* to alcoholism.

74

They are no more likely to develop any other psychiatric illness than children of non-alcoholics.

From these studies the concept of 'familial alcoholism' has developed. This differs from 'non-familial' alcoholism in having the following features:

1. There is a family history of alcoholism.
2. The alcoholism develops at an early age (usually by the late twenties).
3. The alcoholism is severe, often requiring treatment.
4. Having alcoholism in the family only increases the risk of alcoholism, not of other psychiatric disorders.

The idea that alcoholism can be subdivided into two types —familial and non-familial—has generated some new research findings. It seems that about half of alcoholics have alcoholism in the family. Of those who have alcoholism in the family, about 90 per cent have *two* or more relatives who are alcoholic. (This is also true of other illnesses influenced by heredity, such as breast cancer and late-onset diabetes.) The younger the alcoholic at time of diagnosis, the more likely it is that there will be alcoholism in the family. Familial alcoholism tends to be particularly severe. Whether any alcoholic can ever return to normal drinking is a subject of controversy, but this possibility seems particularly remote with regard to familial alcoholics.

If alcoholism in some individuals is influenced by heredity, what is inherited? No one knows, but one kind of reaction to alcohol is definitely inherited:

Millions of people have unpleasant reactions to small amounts of alcohol. These may take the form of dizziness, nausea, or headaches. Adverse reactions to alcohol have been most studied in Orientals. About two-thirds of Orientals develop a flush of the skin and have palpitations and other unpleasant effects after drinking a small amount of alcohol. Oriental babies given small amounts of alcohol also develop a flush. The basis for the flush unquestionably is genetic. Apparently this response can be blocked by antihistamine drugs, suggesting the phenomenon may be allergic in nature.

Alcoholism

There is some evidence that a higher proportion of women than men have adverse reactions to small amounts of alcohol. There is a lower alcoholism rate in the Orient than in Western countries, and this is usually attributed to culture. Women have a lower rate of alcoholism than men and this also has been ascribed to culture. Culture may indeed be important in both instances, but obviously in Orientals, and perhaps in women, another factor contributing to the low alcoholism rate may be physiological and presumably genetic in nature.

Many people, in short, are born *protected* against becoming alcoholic. Conversely, those who become alcoholic are born *un*protected.

Is there more to the story than this? Are children of alcoholics vulnerable to alcoholism only because they lack an inborn intolerance for alcohol?

The story clearly is more complicated. People differ in their response to alcohol in other ways than having varying degrees of intolerance for alcohol. Some people get higher on alcohol than others. As will be explained in the next chapter, people who get higher may also get lower and this roller-coaster effect may explain why some people are more susceptible to alcoholism than others.

12

The addictive cycle

Live moderately because great
pleasures rarely go unpunished.
—Puritan moral

Any ultimate explanation of alcoholism must account for two features of the illness: *loss of control* and *relapse*.

Loss of control refers to the alcoholic's inability to stop drinking once he starts. Relapse is the return to heavy drinking after a period of sobriety, and it is the great mystery of addictions. Why, after months or years of abstinence, does the smoker smoke again, the junkie shoot up again, the alcoholic fall off the wagon?

Here is an attempt to show how inherited and environmental factors may combine to produce loss of control and relapse.

Some people experience more pleasure, or glow, from alcohol than others. How much pleasure a person gets from alcohol may be partly determined by heredity. The pleasure is short-lived and, in some people more than others, it is followed by a feeling of discomfort. The *degree* of discomfort may also be determined by heredity (Fig. 12.1).

Alcoholics learn that the discomfort has a simple remedy: another drink. Thus, the alcoholic drinks for two reasons: to achieve the pleasure and to relieve the discomfort. The same substance that produces the happy feeling also produces the unhappy feeling and is required both to restore the one and abolish the other. Nothing abolishes the unhappy feeling quite as effectively as the drug that produced it.

The unhappy feeling is called craving. To relieve craving the alcoholic will try anything—a chocolate bar, sex, tranquillizer,

77

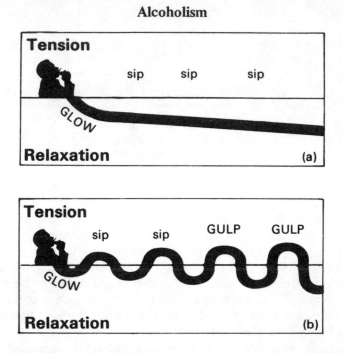

Fig. 12.1. Two different reactions to alcohol. According to the 'addictive cycle' theory, the normal drinker experiences a progressive glow, or relaxation, from alcohol (a). The alcoholic's glow is temporary, followed by a feeling of tension, or craving, that requires another drink for relief (b). These different responses to alcohol may be determined by heredity. (Reprinted with permission of the Schnick Institute.)

jogging, or prayer—but has learned that only alcohol gives complete and immediate relief from craving. After a time, the alcoholic drinks more to overcome the unpleasant effects of alcohol than to attain the pleasant effects.

Thus some people are 'born' to have higher highs and lower lows from alcohol than others. The highs and lows—the addictive cycle—may occur repeatedly in a single drinking session, and of course there is the monumental low that comes the next day known as hangover. The mind and body of the alcoholic 'learns' that the lows can be banished by another drink. The learning is experienced physically as

The addictive cycle

craving and psychologically as a preoccupation—literally an obsession—with having alcohol on hand at all times. Once the true binge drinker has started drinking, he often cannot stop until the high–low cycle has left him exhausted and he must stop.

But why start in the first place? Why does the binge drinker, who actually has come to hate alcohol and doesn't drink anything for months or years, one day start drinking again? It is not from ignorance; he knows what will happen. Why go through it *again*?

This brings up the problem of what is and isn't voluntary, which is a philosophical issue having to do with free will, and not a suitable topic for discussion here. Leaving aside free will, relapse can partly be explained by something called *stimulus generalization*.

The term refers to the fact that things remind people of things. For the drinker, the hands of a watch pointing to 5 p.m. (the stimulus) may remind him that, for years, he always had a drink at 5 p.m. (the generalization), and so he drinks. Acts of drinking become embedded in a maze of reminders. Every drinker has his own reminders, but there are common themes. Food, sex, holidays, football games, fishing, travel: all have nothing intrinsically to do with drinking but all commonly become *associated* with drinking and are powerful reminders. Physical feelings become reminders: hunger, fatigue. Moods become reminders: nostalgia, sadness, elation. Anything, in short, can be a reminder and *remain* a reminder long after a person has stopped drinking.

Reminders may lead to relapse. One day, unexpectedly, the 'recovered' alcoholic is flooded with reminders. It is 5 p.m. on Christmas Eve (which also is his birthday). The boss balled him out and he missed lunch. His alimony cheque to his wife bounced, but he learns he just won the Irish Sweepstakes. Suddenly he has an incredible thirst. As he passes a pub, a strong West wind blows him in the door—and a relapse occurs.

This is an extreme example. The relapse trigger may be subtle:

'For any alcoholic', Mark Keller writes, 'there may be several

79

or a whole battery of critical cues or signals. By the rule of generalization, any critical cue can spread like the tentacles of a vine over a whole range of analogs, and this may account for the growing frequency of bouts, or for the development of a pattern of continuous inebriation. An exaggerated example is the man who goes out and gets drunk every time his mother-in-law gives him a certain wall-eyed look. After a while he has to get drunk whenever any woman gives him that look.'

In either case, he probably will not be able later to say why he started drinking again. And maybe stimulus generalization is not the whole story. But it seems to explain a lot.

The idea of addictive cycles has been applied not only to alcoholism, but also to thrill-seeking, over-eating, and love. The theory holds that every 'addiction' eventually produces its opposite; pleasure turns to pain, and pain to pleasure.

Richard Solomon, a psychologist and leading proponent of this idea, believes that every event in life which has a strong effect also has an opposed process that fights it. 'At the start', he says, 'drugs are highly pleasant. You get a big "rush" and euphoria. But as tolerance builds up, the rush disappears and the threat and pain of withdrawal begin to take command.' He compares the addictive cycle from drugs to a runner's 'high' which, he says, is an example of pain giving way to pleasure. Parachute jumpers sometimes become extremely distressed when bad weather cancels their sport, reflecting, some believe, an 'addiction' to jumping.

Some animal studies seem to support the idea of addictive cycles. In experiments measuring the distress calls of ducklings, birds show far more distress when their mother is removed and returned at brief intervals than when removed for long periods of time. Frequent separations, in short, produce an addictive cycle in which the distress calls are the equivalent of withdrawal symptoms,

Such studies suggest that in its early stages any attachment is controlled mainly by pleasure, but late in the attachment the main control is the threat of separation and loneliness.

The addictive cycle

Although the leap to human behaviour is a long one, Dr Solomon sees the same mechanisms at work. 'The ecstasy and madness of the early love affair are going to disappear', he says, 'and when they do, it means that a withdrawal symptom has to emerge if you are denied the presence of your partner.'

According to the theory, the size of doses and the intervals between doses are crucial to addiction. The distress shrieks of ducks are prolonged at one-minute intervals away from the mother, but not at two or five minutes. A rat fed a food pellet every 60 seconds shows withdrawal symptoms (agitated behaviour, drinking too much water) after each morsel. But the symptoms disappear if the pellets are spaced several minutes apart. The implication: proper timing of dosage prevents addiction.

Why do people keep eating when their stomachs are full? 'Because we like to fight off withdrawal by redosing with a pleasurable taste', says Solomon. 'The better the taste of the food, the harder the withdrawal.' It make sense, he says, to eat tasty foods early in the meal and save bland ones for last, so the withdrawal will be easier. Better yet, eat only bland, uninteresting foods.

A weakness of the theory is that it seems inadequately to take into account the *strength* of addictive behaviour. It's hard to believe fat people would become thin merely by eating bland food at the end of meals. Still, who knows? Strategies for aborting the addictive cycle are being studied in various academic centres and may someday provide the basis for a rational therapy of the addictions, including alcoholism.

Section Four

Treating Alcoholism

Formula for longevity: Have a chronic disease and take care of it.

—Oliver Wendell Holmes

13

The treaters

Sometimes people recover from an illness without professional help. This is called spontaneous remission, 'spontaneous' meaning the remission cannot be explained. It happens in almost every illness, including alcoholism. Before treatment can be judged effective, it must be shown to be superior to no treatment.

Usually studies comparing treated and untreated groups are needed in order to show effectiveness. Some treatments are so effective, however, that such studies are not needed. Penicillin for pneumonia is an example. But it is a mistake to judge the effectiveness of a treatment by what happens to one, two, or a small group of patients. Even terminal-cancer patients sometimes recover 'spontaneously', and the history of medicine is a graveyard for treatments that were worthless but flourished because people tend to get over things anyhow.

There is no pencillin for alcoholism. Studies are needed. Some of the treatments discussed in the next chapter have never been studied; others have been studied, but not well. It may be a slight exaggeration, but only slight, to say that no study has proved beyond question that one treatment for alcoholism is superior to another treatment or to no treatment?

Nevertheless, alcoholics seek help and people try to help them. Uncertainty about the results of treatment has not and should not discourage this effort. Who is providing treatment? What treatments are available?

The providers include clergymen, social workers, psychologists, psychiatrists, other physicians, and people called alcoholism counsellors, many of whom are recovered alcoholics.* Most large cities in the United States have a branch

* The term 'recovered' alcoholic deserves comment. AA takes the view that no

85

of the National Council of Alcoholism listed in the 'phone book. Among other things, this useful organization maintains a list of alcoholism-treatment services.

Concerning physicians, two points of view are heard: they should treat more alcoholics; they should treat no alcoholics. The view depends on whether alcoholism is seen as an illness.

If it is, then it is generally agreed that physicians are less active in treating the illness than they should be. Psychiatrists are notoriously reluctant to see alcoholics. Many view alcoholics as people who don't pay their bills, miss appointments, call at all hours, and test the psychiatrist's patience by refusing to get better. Even when treating a patient with a drinking problem, some psychiatrists interpret the drinking as symptomatic of some other condition and ignore it.

Alcoholism is often ignored by other physicians as well. A survey of a large medical ward revealed that 25 per cent of the male patients had a serious drinking problem which may have contributed to their illness, but the hospital charts rarely mentioned drinking. Another study found that before some physicians suspect alcoholism, the alcoholic has to be dirty and unshaven. Until recently many general hospitals in the USA would not admit patients with a diagnosis of alcoholism. Alcoholics often take a dim view of doctors. Since the feeling is often reciprocated, this attitude is understandable.

Naturally, those who believe alcoholism is *not* a disease do not expect doctors to help alcoholics and indeed would prefer that they not try (except of course for medical complications, such as cirrhosis and delirium tremens). Some alcoholics reject any treatment that does not come from other alcoholics. 'How can anyone help an alcoholic who has not been one?' goes the reasoning. The same principle could apply to any condition. How can anyone treat schizophrenia or diabetes who has not been schizophrenic or diabetic?

one recovers from alcoholism; they simply stop drinking. Whether or not this is always the case, one should be cautioned against using terms that seem synonymous with 'recovered' but have different connotations. Terms to be avoided are 'ex-alcoholic' and 'reformed' alcoholic, both having a criminalistic flavour.

The treaters

Some feel they can, and do, with some success.

The real issue concerns not who treats alcoholics but who treats them best. Until social workers or recovered alcoholics can show they get better results than medical doctors, or vice versa, professional chauvinism seems ill-advised.

14

Specific treatments

One thing about alcohol: it works. It may destroy a man's career, ruin his marriage, turn him into a zombie unconscious in a hall-way—but it works. On short term, it works much faster than a psychiatrist or a priest or the love of a husband or a wife. Those things . . . they all take time. They must be developed . . . But alcohol is always ready to go to work at once. Ten minutes, half an hour, the little formless fears are gone or turned into harmless amusement. But they come back. Oh yes, and they bring reinforcements.
—Charles Orson Gorham

This chapter reviews what is available to help the alcoholic: psychotherapy, behaviour therapy, and drugs. It tends to be critical, but there is no choice if you respect evidence. I have my own method for treating alcoholism, and it seems to work, at least for a time. I've described it in some detail.

Alcoholics Anonymous, some say the best treatment of all, is discussed in Chapter 15.

Psychotherapy

There are many schools of psychotherapy, but they all have one thing in common: they involve two or more persons talking to each other, and one of the discussants is supposed to know more than the others about what is going on. He knows more because he has gone to college and received a degree or has some other special experience that makes him an authority on the subject, such as having been 'in treatment' himself or having himself been a victim of the illness being treated.

'Talking it out' or 'getting it off your chest' has long been

88

valued as a means of relieving certain forms of distress, such as a smouldering resentment or feelings of bereavement. The amount of relief thus attained, however, is often exaggerated, and sometimes, rather than feeling better for having talked about their problems, people feel worse; talking about the problems reminds them of them. At any rate, psychotherapists tend to attribute the success they believe they obtain to unique features of their particular school of psychotherapy.

Each school has a doctrine. Each doctrine, almost without exception, has a founder, or great man whose theories and writings are highly esteemed by his followers, so that schools of psychotherapy inevitably tend to resemble religions. The therapist is a votary and the patient a supplicant hoping to overcome his problems by *understanding* them. In psycho-therapist is a priest and the patient a supplicant hoping to religion. There is an assumption in psychotherapy which is sometimes denied but is almost always present—that understanding the nature and origins of a particular problem helps a person overcome the problem.

This has come to seem almost self-evident, but it is not clear why. A patient with cancer presumably would benefit little from understanding the cause of his condition. What we call understanding, in fact, is simply the point where curiosity rests. There is no area of inquiry where you cannot go a layer deeper if you are able to and so desire. Electricity is understandable as a 'flow of electrons' but what is an electron? An electron is an 'elementary particle consisting of a charge of negative electricity', according to Webster, which shows how understanding is frequently an exercise in circular reasoning. In psychotherapy understanding occurs when the patient agrees with the therapist about what is wrong with him. When the patient's theories about himself coincide with the therapist's theories, he is supposed to improve. Does he?

There is hardly any *scientific* evidence that psychotherapy for alcoholism or any other condition helps anyone. There have been a number of studies, but few have met even the minimal requirements for a scientific study. Yet thousands of people make their living giving psychotherapy and millions have received psychotherapy, many of them feeling they have benefited from it. They may indeed *have* benefited from it; after all, there is no evidence that psychotherapy does *not* work. But the burden of proof, as always in such matters, is on the proponents.

The schools of psychotherapy are too numerous to go into here. Most are identified by the name of their founder. Much of what is called psychotherapy can be subsumed under two headings: psychodynamic psychotherapy and transactional analysis.

Psychodynamic therapy is generally of two types—the classical type and the non-classical or 'watered-down' type. Both ultimately derive from the doctrines of Freud and his followers. The classicists (psychoanalysts) attribute mental illness to unconscious conflicts that originate in early childhood. Since drinking is an oral activity, alcoholism is assumed to arise from oral conflicts. Small babies are more oral than anyone, since practically their whole existence revolves around sucking a nipple. If the sucking does not go well, conflicts develop which, unless resolved in psychoanalysis, result in an 'oral-dependent' personality (dependent because tiny infants are exceedingly dependent on mothers). Alcoholics are said to have oral-dependent personalities. They not only drink too much, but if you go to AA meetings you find they also smoke a lot and drink gallons of coffee, as well as tending to be extremely talkative when given a chance. Alcoholics can overcome their oral dependency, but it takes a long time. They must first have 'insight' about their orality and, second, 'work out' their oral conflicts by being dependent for extended periods on their therapists. They are encouraged to believe this, despite the widely held view among psychoanalysts that alcoholism is exceedingly difficult to treat.*

* One reason psychiatrists in private practice find alcoholism difficult to treat is that they do not recognize it when it exists. A study of alcoholism-treatment programmes conducted by the Joint Information Service of the American Psychiatric Association and the National Association for Mental Health found that some

Specific treatments

Freud himself held that addictions were hard to treat because, at bottom, they were so pleasurable.

Another psychoanalytic explanation for alcoholism is that alcoholics are latent homosexuals. The reasoning is that since both homosexuality and drinking involve oral activity, both have origins in oral conflicts. It explains, too, why male alcoholics seek out the masculine camaraderie of barrooms; they can be with men while simultaneously denying their homosexual tendencies by engaging in heavy drinking, an activity associated with masculinity. Others hold that alcoholism is a form of self-destruction (which it obviously is) and has the same roots as depression. People have angry feelings toward others, cannot express them, and therefore become angry at themselves. Self-hatred is subjectively experienced as depression or leads to self-destructive acts such as alcoholism. Therapy consists of helping a person recognize his unconscious drives and motives, which results in a happier and more mature person who does not drink as much.

Many therapists who are not technically psychoanalysts nevertheless use concepts derived from Freudian theory. Any therapist who uses such terms as 'ego defence mechanism' or 'acting out' views abnormal behaviour, whether he realizes it or not, as a product of psychological conflict. This, at bottom, is what psychodynamic means. Although everyone has experienced psychological conflict, the idea that mental illness arises from conflict remains speculative.

A currently popular form of psychotherapy is based on the theories of Eric Berne and is called transactional analysis.

---

psychiatrists do not know about the drinking habits of their patients because the patient who does not volunteer such information may well not be asked. Several times the following dialogue was reported:

> *Staff member of alcoholism-treatment program to patient*: Have you previously had psychiatric treatment?
> *Patient*: Yes, from a psychiatrist in private practice.
> *Staff member*: What did he tell you about your drinking?
> *Patient*: Nothing. I never told him about it, and he never asked me.

(From R. M. Glasscote, T. F. A. Plaut, D. W. Hammersley *et al. The treatment of alcoholism*. American Psychiatric Association, Washington, DC (1967).)

91

Alcoholism

Dr Berne was an amusing writer whose ideas have much in common with Freud's. Instead of id, ego, and superego, he substitutes the terms child, adult, and parent. These three *dramatis personae* of mental life are constantly feuding, just as members of a family quarrel, and the quarrels sometimes take the form of abnormal behaviour. All people play games, and 'sick' people play games calculated to make them losers. The alcoholic punishes other people by punishing himself and is the loser in the end. Transactional analysis, or TA, makes alcoholics aware of the games they play and encourages them to find other games that are less destructive.

Transactional analysis lends itself somewhat more to group therapy than does psychoanalysis or psychodynamic psychotherapy. It is often said that group therapy helps alcoholics more than individual therapy does, but there is no evidence for this. Group therapy does have one advantage: it takes less of the therapist's time.

Anyone reading this who believes the theories of Freud, Jung, Adler, Sullivan, Berne, or any of the other founders of psychotherapeutic movements to be correct will no doubt be offended by the above or at least take strong issue with what has been said. This is unfortunate, but there is no avoiding it; if there is no acceptable evidence that something works, it would be unfair to the reader to pretend that there is. Single-case reports that patients have improved while receiving a particular therapy do not constitute acceptable evidence. As noted earlier, even terminal-cancer patients sometimes recover.

To show that a particular treatment is useful, three questions must be asked: Would the patient have recovered without any treatment? Would he have done as well or better with another treatment? Is the improvement related to non-specific aspects of a treatment? 'Non-specific aspects' include, in Peter Medawar's words, the 'assurance of a regular sympathetic hearing, the feeling that somebody is taking his condition seriously, the discovery that others are in the same predicament, the comfort of learning that his condition is explicable (which does not depend on the explanation being the right one)'. These factors are common to most forms of psychological treatment and the good they do cannot be credited to any one treatment in particular.

Behaviour therapy

There are two kinds of behaviour therapy with two different ancestries. One comes from Pavlov, who conditioned dogs. The other comes from B. F. Skinner, who conditioned pigeons. Behaviour therapy, in other words, is conditioning therapy by another name.

Pavlov found that if dogs repeatedly heard a bell before eating, eventually bells alone would make them salivate. And if you shocked the dog's foot every time he heard a bell, he would soon respond to bells in the same way he did to shock —by withdrawing the foot.

For many years attempts have been made to condition alcoholics to dislike alcohol. Alcoholics are asked to taste or smell alcohol just before a pre-administered drug makes them nauseated. Repeated pairing of alcohol and nausea results in a conditioned response: after a while alcohol alone makes them nauseated. Thereafter, it is hoped, the smell or taste of alcohol will cause nausea and discourage drinking.

Instead of pairing alcohol with nausea, other therapists have associated it with pain, shocking patients just after they drink, or they have associated it with the panic experienced from not being able to breathe by giving them a drug that causes very brief respiratory paralysis. Others have trained patients to imagine unpleasant effects from drinking, hoping to set up a conditioned response without causing so much actual distress.

Does it work? Some degree of conditioning is usually established, but it is uncertain how long the conditioning lasts. The largest study that involved conditioning alcoholics was conducted some 40 years ago in Seattle, Washington. More than 4000 patients conditioned to feel nauseated when exposed to alcohol were studied ten to fifteen years after treatment. Half were abstinent, which is an impressive recovery rate compared to other treatments. The patients who did best had booster sessions—that is, they came back to the clinic after the initial treatment to repeat the conditioning procedure. Of those who had booster sessions, 90 per cent were abstinent. Based on this study, the nausea treatment for alcoholism would seem an outstanding success. Why hasn't it been universally accepted?

One reason is that the results can be attributed to factors other than the conditioning. The patients in the study were a special group. Generally they were well-educated, had jobs, and were well off financially. They may not have received the treatment otherwise, since the clinic where they were treated is private and costs money. Indeed, the patients who did best, it turned out, had the most money. Studies of alcoholics have often shown that certain subject characteristics are more predictive of successful-treatment outcome than the type of treatment administered. These include job stability, living with a relative, absence of a criminal record, and living in a rural community. In the Seattle study there was no control group that did not receive conditioning therapy. It is possible that the select group of patients, many having characteristics that favour a good outcome, would have done as well without conditioning.

Furthermore, in conditioning treatments, motivation is important. Treatment is voluntary and involves acute physical discomfort, so presumably few would consent to undergo the therapy who were not strongly motivated to stop drinking. The Seattle study makes this point graphically clear. Those who came back for booster sessions did better than those who didn't, but another group did better still: those who *wanted* to come back but couldn't because they lived too far from the hospital. *All* of these people remained abstinent.

Other studies of the Pavlovian type of therapy for alcoholism—including chemical, electrical, and verbal conditioning—have been less ambitious and the results have been mixed. To the extent they seem to help, success may be attributed to factors unrelated to conditioning, such as patient selection, patient co-operation, and so on. Another factor also may promote at least short-term success. It is called the Hawthorne effect and refers to the enthusiasm therapists often have for any treatment that is new. The enthusiasm may be infectious, and patients who are enthusiastic themselves about a particular treatment may do somewhat better, for a time, than those who are neutral or unenthusiastic.

The same considerations apply to therapy based on the work of B. F. Skinner, called operant conditioning. There is a large scientific literature based on this work, but the basic ideas are simple. People behave like pigeons in the sense that they do things which are rewarded and avoid doing things which are punished. This has led to a type of treatment known as token economy. Anything a patient does that is believed good for him is rewarded (often literally with tokens which are exchangeable for food, money, and other desirable things). Anything he does that is bad for him is punished (usually simply by withholding the reward). In this manner an attempt is made to 'shape' the behaviour of patients in directions that are beneficial to them, with the hope that the new behaviour—abstinence or controlled drinking—will permanently replace the less beneficial kind.

Does this actually happen? Most treatments of this kind take place in institutional settings, and whether the new behaviour brought about in the institution 'sticks' in the outside world is not known.

One final word needs to be said about conditioning therapies. Alcoholics, by the time they seek professional help, have already suffered bitterly from their drinking, but this has not deterred them from continuing to drink. Being made to vomit or having their hand shocked by a friendly therapist is incomparably less excruciating than the physical and mental anguish that alcoholics normally experience: the morning heaves, the shakes, the crushing weight of conscience. There is a sizeable delay, to be sure, between the drinking and the anguish, and for conditioning in the literal sense to occur the delay should be shorter. But the effects of heavy drinking are so punishing that one would expect some kind of deterrent effect. After all, some people get sick from a pork chop and thereafter avoid pork chops. The need to drink must be compelling indeed, given the infinitely greater misery that comes from drinking. This is what addiction really means, as was movingly described by William James (who incidentally had a brother who was alcoholic):

> The craving for drink in real dipsomaniacs (drunkards) is of a strength of which normal persons can form no conception. Were a keg of rum in one corner of a room and were a cannon constantly discharging balls between me and it, I could not refrain from passing before that cannon in order to get the rum. If a bottle of brandy stood at one hand and the pit of hell yawned at the other, and I were convinced that I should be pushed in as sure as I took one glass, I could not refrain.

James then gives two case-histories:

> A few years ago a tippler was put in an almshouse. Within a few days he had devised various expedients to procure rum, but failed. At length, however, he hit upon one which was successful. He went into the wood-yard of the establishment, placed one hand upon the block, and with an axe in the other, struck it off at a single blow. With the stump raised and streaming he ran into the house and cried, 'Get me some rum! my hand is off!' In the confusion and bustle of the occasion a bowl of rum was brought, into which he plunged the bleeding member of his body, then raising the bowl to his mouth, drank freely, and exultingly exclaimed, 'Now I am satisfied.' [There also was the] man who, while under treatment for inebriety, during four weeks secretly drank the alcohol from six jars containing morbid specimens. On asking him why he had committed this loathsome act, he replied: 'Sir, it is as impossible for me to control this diseased appetite as it is for me to control the pulsations of my heart.'

To control 'this diseased appetite' with a few sessions of conditioning therapy seems a little like attacking an elephant with a pea shooter. However, one thing can be said in favour of conditioning therapy: it is inexpensive, probably does no harm, and arises from a scientific tradition that emphasizes evidence more than faith.

Specific treatments

Drug therapy

In Sears Roebuck mail order catalogues at the turn of the century two pages were devoted to drug therapies for morphine addiction and alcoholism, respectively. The drug being sold for morphine addiction consisted mainly of alcohol; a good part of the drug for alcoholism consisted of tincture of opium, a relative of morphine. Whether morphine addicts became alcoholics as a result of the treatment, or vice versa, is not known, but it illustrates the long history of giving one drug that affects mood and behaviour to relieve the effects of another drug that affects mood and behaviour. Substitution therapy has reached its pinnacle, perhaps, with the recent widespread, officially sanctioned, and possibly useful substitution of methadone (an addicting substance like heroin) for heroin. Heroin itself was introduced at the turn of the century as a 'heroic' cure for morphine addiction and was also believed to be useful for alcoholism. It has not done much for either condition.

Drugs are still widely prescribed to alcoholics. They mainly consist of drugs for anxiety, such as Librium and Valium, and drugs for depression. There are no studies indicating they offer long-term help for alcoholics. The anti-anxiety drugs have some effects similar to those of alcohol—they calm and relax—and are useful in relieving the jitteriness that follows heavy drinking, so that they may be useful in stopping a drinking bout. Whether they stop the *resumption* of drinking —the test of a drug's true worth in treating alcoholism—is debatable, and many clinicians feel they do not.

These drugs are sometimes used in excess by alcoholics, and sometimes in combination with alcohol. This may not be as harmful as it sounds since they have a low range of toxicity and few people become addicted in the literal sense of needing increasingly larger amounts and having serious withdrawal symptoms when they stop taking them. Nevertheless, they have obviously contributed little to the management of alcoholism, and some clinicians feel strongly that they should not be given to alcoholics for extended periods.

Alcoholism

Nor is there evidence that antidepressant medications are useful in the treatment of alcoholism, although some alcoholics do become seriously depressed and antidepressant drugs may then be indicated for their depression. Recently, lithium, a drug useful in the treatment of mania, has been given to alcoholics, and early reports indicate that some people benefit from it. Since early reports often indicate that a particular treatment is useful, only to be refuted by later reports, lithium therapy should be viewed with both interest and scepticism. One clinical observation that lends support to the possibility that lithium might help alcoholics is that people with manic-depressive disease often drink more when they are manic than when they are depressed.

From a theoretical viewpoint, it is interesting that anti-anxiety and antidepressant drugs do not seem to deter alcoholics from using alcohol. There is ample evidence that these drugs do indeed relieve anxiety and depression, and if alcoholics drink because they feel anxious and depressed, one would assume that the drugs would substitute for alcohol more than they seem to do. This brings up the old question considered earlier in this book, namely, are addictions specific? Are people who are vulnerable to alcohol-abuse only vulnerable to alcohol-abuse? Evidence presented in Chapters 11 and 12 suggests this indeed may be the case.

Other treatments that have been tried are LSD and large doses of vitamins, but there is no convincing evidence that they help.

Perhaps the drug most commonly prescribed for alcoholism over the past 25 years is one that has no effect on anxiety or depression or apparently anything else *unless* combined with alcohol. This, of course, is Antabuse.

The drug makes people physically ill when they drink. When it was first used in the early fifties, Antabuse got a bad name for two reasons. First, like most highly touted treatments, it was not the panacea its enthusiastic supporters had hoped it would be. Second, some people taking the drug died after drinking. It was later learned that the drug could be given in smaller amounts and still produce an unpleasant reaction when combined with alcohol, but death was exceedingly rare.

Partly because of the bad reputation it obtained in the early years, it has perhaps been underused since then. The more dogmatic members of AA view Antabuse as somehow incompatible with the spirit of AA, and many alcoholics resist taking the drug on the grounds that it is a 'crutch'.

Antabuse has not been entirely popular with doctors for another reason. Many still believe they must give an Antabuse 'challenge' test before prescribing the drug for indefinite periods. This test consists of giving the patient Antabuse for a few days and then giving him a small amount of alcohol to demonstrate what an Antabuse reaction is like. The Antabuse challenge test is no longer considered necessary or even desirable. Patients can be told what the effects of Antabuse will be and this will have the same effect. One awkward aspect of the challenge test is that some patients have no reaction when given the alcohol, simply because people react very differently to both alcohol and Antabuse and the cautious doses of alcohol administered are too small to produce an effect.

The main problem with Antabuse, however, is not that patients drink after taking the drug but that they stop taking the drug because they 'forget' to take it or convince themselves the drug is causing side-effects, such as impotency.* A way to obviate this problem, at least, temporarily, is described below.

* A large number of side-effects have been attributed to Antabuse, including impotency, rashes, and psychotic reactions. These occur so infrequently that it is not possible to know whether they are caused by the drug. Impotency, as explained in Chapter 6, afflicts not only intoxicated alcoholics but sometimes sober alcoholics. A small percentage of alcoholics may have rashes and psychotic episodes whether they are taking Antabuse or not. Clinicians inclined toward scepticism sometimes wonder whether side-effects attributed by the patient to Antabuse may in fact be motivated by a desire to stop taking the drug and start drinking again. Therefore, the issue of side-effects from Antabuse taken *alone* remains open to question. Combined with alcohol, of course, there is no question that Antabuse produces serious effects.

Alcoholism

Something that works, provided . . .

There is an approach to treating alcoholism that works every time, given one stipulation: the patient must do what the doctor says. In this case he must do only one thing: come to the office every three or four days.

Doctors cannot help patients, as a rule, who refuse to do what they say, so there is nothing unusual about the stipulation. Why every three or four days? Because the effects of Antabuse last up to five days after a person takes it. If the patient takes Antabuse in the office, in the presence of the doctor, they both *know* he will not drink for up to five days. They have bought time, a precious thing in the treatment of alcoholism.

This approach involves other things besides Antabuse, but Antabuse makes the other things possible. First it gives hope, and hope by the time the alcoholic sees a doctor is often in short supply. He feels his case is hopeless, his family feels it is hopeless, and often the doctor feels it is hopeless. With this approach the doctor can say, 'I can help you with your drinking problem' and mean it. He doesn't mean he can help him forever (forever is a long time) and it doesn't mean the patient won't still be unhappy or that he will become a new man. It merely means he will not drink as long as he comes to the office every three or four days and takes the Antabuse. Properly warned, he won't drink unless he is crazy or stupid, and if either is the case, he probably should not be given Antabuse.

On the first visit the doctor can say something like this:

Your problem, or at least your immediate problem, is that you have trouble controlling your drinking. Let *me* take charge; let me control your drinking for a time. This will be my responsibility. Come in, take the pill, and then we can deal with other things.

I want you to stop drinking for a month. [At this point the doctor makes a note in his desk calendar to remind himself when the patient will have taken Antabuse for a month.] After that we can discuss whether you want to continue taking the pill. It will be your decision.

You need to stop for a month for two reasons. First, I need to know

100

Specific treatments

whether there is anything wrong with you besides drinking too much. You may have another problem that I can treat, such as a depression, but I won't be able to find out until you stop drinking for at least several weeks. Alcohol itself makes people depressed and anxious, and mimics all kinds of psychiatric illnesses.

Second, I want you to stop drinking for a month to have a chance to see that life is bearable—sometimes just barely bearable—without alcohol. Millions of people don't drink and manage. You can manage too, but you haven't had a chance recently to discover this.

F. Scott Fitzgerald complained that he could never get sober long enough to tolerate sobriety, and at least this much can be achieved with the present approach.

It is important for the patient to see the doctor—or whatever professional is responsible for his care—whenever he comes for the pill. Patients as a rule want to please their doctors; this is probably why they are more punctual in keeping office appointments than doctors are in seeing them. In the beginning the patient may be coming, in part, as a kind of favour to the doctor.

The visits can be as brief or as long as time permits. The essential thing is that rapport be established, that the patient believe something is being done to help him, and that he stay on the wagon (he has no choice if he lives up to his part of the doctor–patient contract). Brief, frequent visits can accomplish these things.

The emphasis during the visits should be not on the pill but on problems most alcoholics face when they stop drinking. The major problem is finding out what to do with all the time that has suddenly become available now that drinking can no longer fill it. Boredom is the curse of the non-drinking drinking man. For years, most of the pleasurable things in his life have been associated with drinking: food, sex, companionship, fishing, Sunday-afternoon football. Without alcohol these things lose some of their attraction. Who can enjoy French cooking without wine, tacos without beer, or business luncheons without martinis? The alcoholic is sure *he* cannot. He tends to withdraw, brood, feel sorry for himself.

The therapist may help him find substitute pleasures—

101

hobbies, social activities not revolving around alcohol, anything that kills time and may give some satisfaction, if not anything as satisfying as a boozy glow. In time he may find these things for himself, but meanwhile life can be awfully monotonous.

Also the patient can bring up problems of living that tend to accumulate when a person has drunk a lot. People usually feel better when they talk about problems, particularly when the listener is warm and friendly and doesn't butt into the conversation by talking about his own problems. The therapist can help by listening even if he cannot solve the problems.

If he is a psychiatrist, he can also do a thorough psychiatric examination, looking for something other than drinking to diagnose and treat. Occasionally—not often—alcoholics turn out to have a depressive illness, anxiety neurosis, or other psychiatric condition.

One thing the therapist can do is help the patient accept his alcoholism. This is sometimes difficult. Alcoholics have spent most of their drinking careers persuading themselves and others that they do not have a drinking problem. The habit of self-deception, set and hardened over so many years, is hard to break. William James describes this habit with his usual verve and concludes that the alcoholic's salvation begins with breaking it:

> How many excuses does the drunkard find when each new temptation comes! Others are drinking and it would be churlishness to refuse; or it is but to enable him to sleep, or just to get through this job of work; or it isn't drinking, it is because he feels so cold; or it is Christmas Day; or it is a means of stimulating him to make a more powerful resolution in favour of abstinence than any he has hitherto made; or it is just this once, and once doesn't count . . . it is, in fact, anything you like except *being a drunkard*. But if . . . through thick and thin he holds to it that he is a drunkard and nothing else, he is not likely to remain one long. The effort by which he succeeds in keeping the right *name* unwaveringly present to his mind proves to be his saving moral act.

After a month of taking the pill and talking about problems, what happens then? The patient and doctor renegotiate. Almost invariably, in my experience, the patient decides to

102

Specific treatments

take the pill for another month. The doctor says okay, and
this is the first step in a process that must occur if the patient
is going to recover: acceptance of personal responsibility for
control of his drinking.

Proceeding on a month-to-month basis is a variation on the
AA principle that an alcoholic should take each day as it
comes. For years, alcohol has been the most important thing
in the alcoholic's life, or close to it. To be told he can never
drink again is about as depressing as anything he can hear. It
may not even be true. Studies indicate that a small percentage
of alcoholics return to 'normal' drinking for long periods.
'Controlled' drinking is probably a better term than 'normal'
drinking, since alcoholics continue to invest alcohol with a
significance that would never occur to the truly normal
drinker.

Many people, especially some AA members, reject the
notion that alcoholics can ever drink normally. If alcoholism
is defined as a permanent inability to drink normally, then
obviously any person able to drink normally for a long period
was never an alcoholic in the first place. The issue is really a
definitional one, and those few alcoholics who reported
sustained periods of controlled drinking in the studies were at
any rate considered alcoholic when they *weren't* drinking
normally. Most clinicians would agree that it is a mistake to
encourage an alcoholic to believe he can ever again drink
normally, but on the other hand telling him he can never drink
again seems unnecessary and may not be true in every case.

When does treatment end? The minimum period is one
month because that is the basis for the doctor–patient contract agreed upon in advance. Ideally, however, the treatment
should continue for at least six months, with the patient himself making the decision to continue taking Antabuse on a
month-to-month basis. Why six months? Because there is
evidence that most alcoholics who begin drinking again do so
within the first six months following abstention.

A general rule applies here: the longer a patient goes
without drinking at all, the shorter the relapse if a relapse

103

occurs. It takes time to adapt to a sober way of life. Both the doctor and patient should be prepared for relapses. Alcoholism, by definition, is a chronic relapsing condition, although relapses are not inevitable. It resembles manic-depressive disease in this regard and also has similarities to such chronic medical illnesses as diabetes and multiple sclerosis. When the alcoholic has a relapse, his physician often feels resentful. When his diabetic patient has a relapse because he failed to take insulin, the doctor tends to be more understanding. The reason for this inconsistency is not clear.

Three objections have been raised concerning the above approach to treating alcoholism. The treatment is said to be based on fear, namely, the fear of getting sick, and fear is held to be one of the least desirable forms of motivation. This is debatable. Fear may be the *only* reason some alcoholics stop drinking. There is evidence that internists have somewhat better success in treating alcoholics than psychiatrists do, and the reason may be that they are in a better position to frighten the patient. They have merely to examine his liver and tell him he may be dead in a year if he keeps on drinking. Innumerable alcoholics have stopped drinking because they were told something like this. Others have stopped because they were afraid of losing their wives or jobs. It is probably no coincidence that the hardest alcoholics to treat are those who have little to lose, those who have already lost their wives, jobs, and health. They have no hope of regaining these. All they have left to lose is their life, and, by now, living has little appeal. Probably the most effective alcoholism-treatment programmes are run by industries, where the patient is an employee and his job depends on staying sober. The quotation at the beginning of this chapter is from Gorham's fictional study of an alcoholic, *Carlotta McBride*. As Gorham says, alcohol works. It has worked for the alcoholic for many years. Unless he is very much afraid of *something*, he probably will not give it up.

The second objection to the approach outlined here is that the patient becomes too dependent on a personal relationship with an authority figure, the physician, which must end at some point. In the treatment of alcoholism, the goal is not so much a lifetime cure—although sometimes this happens—as it is to bring about improvement. If the patient stays sober for longer periods after treatment than he did before, the treatment has been at least a limited success. The physician in any case should discourage a dependent relationship. He can insist upon the patient taking the pill and staying dry for a month (realizing that a month is an arbitrary unit of time and any fixed interval will do), but after that the patient has to realize that he himself has the ultimate responsibility for the control of his drinking.

Finally, the complaint is heard that this approach does not get at the root of the problem; it does not explain how the patient became an alcoholic. This is true but, in my opinion, no one can explain how a person becomes an alcoholic because no one knows the cause of alcoholism. Doctors sometimes blame the patient's upbringing and patients often blame everyday stresses. There is no way to validate either explanation. There is probably no harm in telling the patient that his condition remains a medical mystery. And despite the evidence presented in Chapter 11 it is still premature to say that he *inherited* his disease.

However, if it is ever shown conclusively that some forms of alcholism are influenced by heredity, this would not make the prognosis less favourable or the treatment less helpful. Sometimes, when evidence for a genetic factor is presented, you hear the following: 'But if it is genetic, then you can't do anything about it'. It should be noted that adult onset diebetes is almost certainly a genetic disorder and there are excellent treatments for diabetes.

The most serious objection to the above approach in treating alcoholism is that it has not been studied and there is no evidence that it is better than any other treatment. For this, the writer apologizes and promises he will do whatever he can to correct the situation.

105

15

Alcoholics anonymous

'. . . Drop the anvil!'
—AA joke (see page 115)

Since its creation in 1935 by two alcoholics, this organization
has grown into a world-wide network of self-help services for
alcoholics and their families. It has many attractive features,
including three common denominators of psychotherapy
(and at no cost): the assurance of a regular sympathetic hearing, the feeling that somebody is taking one's condition
seriously, the discovery that others are in the same predicament. Unlike most talking therapies, AA expends little effort
in trying to explain why anyone is alcoholic. The term 'allergy'
is sometimes used, but usually properly bracketed in quotation
marks (alcoholism does not of course resemble conventional
allergies at all).

There is an old idea that alcoholics must become religious
in order to stop drinking, and it is true that Alcoholics
Anonymous has certain similarities to a religion and that
some of its members have been 'converted' to AA in the same
way they would be to other religions. Its 'twelve steps', for
example, have a definite religious flavour, emphasizing a
reliance on God, the need for forgiveness, and caring for
others.

Nevertheless, to the extent that it is a religion, AA is one
of the least doctrinaire and authoritarian religions imaginable.
Atheists can belong to AA as comfortably as believers. There
is no formal doctrine and no insistence that anyone accept a
particular explanation for alcoholism. AA gives drinkers
something to do when they are not drinking. It offers occasions
for the soul-satisfying experience of helping someone else. It

provides companions who do not drink. And it provides hope for those who need it desperately—the alcoholic and his family —and instant help for the man who wants to get back on the wagon and can't quite make it.

This sounds like a wonderful package of services, and AA is often credited with helping more alcoholics than all the other alcoholism treatments combined. There is no way of knowing whether this is true, since the kind of careful studies needed to show it have not been done. However, most professionals working with alcoholics agree that certainly nothing is lost by encouraging them to attend AA meetings and possibly much can be gained.

How does an alcoholic arrive at his first AA meeting? There are several routes.

In despair, alone or at the urging of family or friends, he may call the number in the phone book, locate a meeting and go by himself or be escorted. His doctor or clergyman may suggest it. He may be visited by an AA member in a hospital or prison, perhaps go to his first meeting in the institution.

'When he arrives, he is likely to be frightened, depressed, and still sick from withdrawal after his last drink', writes Margaret Bean in her book *Alcoholics Anonymous* (Insight Communications, Inc., New York, 1975).

If he comes on his own and speaks to no one, he will probably be left alone. If he approaches someone or asks for help, however, he will almost invariably get it.

Most people, at first, treat him with reserve, friendly interest and encouragement. The usual practice is for the veteran member to talk about his drinking problem but not push the newcomer to reveal his. Most members realize that the newcomer has lost his self-esteem, is overcome with guilt and remorse, and feels that his weakness is all too apparent. They do not expect him to reciprocate confessional stories. The initial transaction is the instillation of hope.

The new member is taken under the wing of some sympathetic person as a 'pigeon', or beginner. He is asked if he has admitted to himself that he has trouble with alcohol, and whether he has accepted his problem. 'Admitting' and 'accepting' are carefully distinguished as separate steps. He is urged to come to many meetings, preferably '90 meetings in 90 days,' because as a newcomer he needs them. He is taught that he should listen, keep his opinions to himself, ask questions when he does not understand, and observe and imitate successful members. He often is encouraged to give up all social contacts outside AA. The express reason for this is that he is in danger from them, because they were where he 'caught' alcoholism in the first place.

While a new member is not pushed to disclose details about himself, it is suggested that it would do him good to find someone he can talk with about his drinking. The idea is that he will find it a relief to confess all the things of which he is ashamed. For some AA members, AA may totally replace non-AA social activities.

All AA groups provide members with a protected environment in which they are treated as equal, regardless of the extent of their alcohol problem. They are freed from the fear that besets new relationships in conventional society, that one's alcoholic history will be discovered and one will be rejected because of it.

Long sobriety does confer status in AA, but there are safeguards against holier-than-thou attitudes, since at some point all members were stigmatized as alcoholics and no one is in a position to point an accusing finger. . .

Recovery is divided into three stages—physical, emotional, and spiritual. Physical recovery is the first step and the one in which Twelve Steppers are most active in the AA outreach system. A call comes for help from someone who is still sobering up. A worker at Central Service will talk with him on the telephone for awhile or contact a member on call for Twelve Step work and make immediate personal contact.

The Twelve Step worker usually gets a new member to a meeting within 24 hours if possible. He knows that the desire to drink is very strong in the early stages of physical recovery and encourages the newcomer to go to as many meetings as possile.

Meetings are either open—anyone who wants to come is welcome—or closed to non-alcoholics. A new member usually has a sponsor, the person in whom he chooses to confide early in his membership.

'Many AA members go to meetings with each other, see each other relapse and return, watch each other stay sober longer and longer', Dr Bean writes. 'Many apparently expect to continue to do so several nights a week for the rest of their lives. Sometimes their families sabotage them in their use of AA and sometimes support them. Most of them are deeply loyal and very grateful to AA.'

AA has two 'Bibles'. One is called *Twelve steps and twelve traditions*. The other is named *Alcoholics Anonymous*, called the 'Big Book' by members. The latter is a volume of anecdotal accounts of experiences with alcohol written by early members.

The *Twelve traditions* book describes the organization itself. It stresses that AA is not a reform movement, nor is it operated by professionals. It is financed by voluntary contributions from its members, all of whom remain anonymous. There are no dues, no paid therapists. All comers who want help are accepted as members. All groups are autonomous. AA does not endorse other enterprises or take sides in controversies. (AA has learned a lesson from the Washington Society, a self-help group of alcoholics in the mid-nineteenth century that floundered on internal dissention over antislavery and other issues.)

When Bill W., co-founder of Alcoholics Anonymous, was asked earnestly, 'How does AA work?' he was fond of answering, 'Just fine, thanks. Just fine.' Three chapters in the 'Big Book' (chapters 5-7) explain how AA works in detail. These are devoted essentially to the 'twelve suggested steps of recovery':

1. We admitted we were powerless over alcohol—that our lives had become unmanageable.
2. Came to believe that a Power greater than ourselves could restore us to sanity.
3. Made a decision to turn our will and our lives over to the care of God as we understand Him.
4. Made a searching and fearless moral inventory of our lives.
5. Admitted to God, to ourselves, and to another human being the exact nature of our wrongs.
6. Were entirely ready to have God remove all these defects of character.
7. Humbly asked Him to remove our shortcomings.
8. Made a list of all persons we had harmed, and became willing to make amends to them all.
9. Made direct amends to such people wherever possible.
10. Continued to take personal inventory and when we were wrong promptly admitted it.
11. Sought through prayer and meditation to improve our conscious

contact with God as we understood him, praying only for knowledge of His will for us and the power to carry that out.

12. Having had a spiritual awakening as the result of these steps, we tried to carry this message to alcoholics, and to practise these principles in all our affairs.

Note that only two of the 12 steps mention alcohol. More than a prescription for abstinence, the steps give a prescription for living. As one AA member stated, 'AA doesn't teach us how to handle our drinking; it teaches us to handle sobriety. Most of us knew before we came through the door of the first meeting that the way to handle our drinking was to quit. People told us so. Almost every alcoholic I know has stopped drinking at one time or another—maybe dozens of times! So it is no trick to stop drinking; the trick is how to stay stopped.'

Many AA members approach Twelve Step 'work' with an open mind and are prepared to be flexible. 'Greater Power', for many, stands for AA itself. God may be a symbol for the mystery of the universe rather than a traditional deity.

Last year an estimated 800 000 alcoholics attended meetings of 23 000 groups in 90 countries. Many friends and relatives attended Alanon and Alateen—self-help groups for spouses and teenage children of alcoholics. Many of course only go to one meeting.

How successful is AA?

The Rand Corporation in America recently completed the most extensive study of alcoholism ever made. Information was obtained on 85 per cent of 922 men who had received treatment in an alcoholism unit. They were followed over four years. The report found that alcoholics who *regularly* attended AA had a higher rate of long-term abstinence than all the other groups. About half were abstinent after four years. However, only 14 per cent of the patients were regularly attending AA at the end of four years. Patients had not been randomly assigned to AA groups and other forms of treatment. Conceivably, the small minority regularly attending AA after

110

four years represented a highly motivated group that would have done as well receiving some other treatment or no treatment.

Particularly in large cities, alcoholics may be able to choose from a variety of AA groups. Often the National Council of Alcoholism can help match the individual alcoholic to a group of his or her social class and general background. Whether this results in better attendance and more favourable results is not known, but many AA members believe it is worth trying.

Dr Bean writes: 'In view of the fact that all speakers adhere to a formula and everyone knows how it is going to turn out, meetings are surprisingly varied and entertaining. Speakers vary in education, charm, articulateness, age, and sex. Each tells a story: How he started to drink, lost control, and began to destroy everything in his life that had been important to him. Each has his own version of hitting bottom and—despairing, disbelieving, and full of revulsion and uncertainty—coming to AA. He then describes his recovery and how he has been able to cope with his life without alcohol.'

An AA member came to our medical school to talk with students. Her story gives the flavour of AA meetings around the world and passes on some good advice to young doctors-to-be:

Hi, I'm Pat—I'm an alcoholic. This is the way we introduce ourselves in an AA meeting and it seems appropriate to begin that way.

To begin with the vital statistics. I have been married to a professional man for 25 years. We have three sons. I have been sober for two and one-half years. I am a registered nurse. During the period of the alcoholism I was attending the university where I earned a bachelor's degree in sociology. After I became sober I returned to school and this semester I will finish a master's degree in social work. I plan to work in the field of alcoholism when I graduate.

My life before the age of 38 was wholly unremarkable. There is no alcoholism in my immediate family, but my paternal grandfather was clearly alcoholic. My parents had a stable marriage; I was neither neglected nor abused as a child. I had what one could consider a normal adolescence, I had no problems with authority, and made straight As in school. I was socialized to be a wife and mother; my nursing career was

111

strictly an insurance policy, not a career. It should be clear I was raised before the women's movement. It was a search for my own identity that precipitated the crisis leading to the alcoholism. Those of you who have seen the movie, 'Kramer vs. Kramer', can have some idea of how I lapsed into dysfunction. Except that I lacked that woman's courage to confront the problem directly and took the back door out into depression and alcoholism.

When I became depressed I didn't understand what was happening to me. I only knew that I was miserable and that there was something terribly wrong with me. I went to see a psychiatrist who started giving me antidepressants and tranquillizers. I took those drugs almost constantly until I entered an alcoholism treatment center where they took me off cold turkey and I went through withdrawal. I saw the psychiatrist on a weekly basis except when he was on vacation or I was. At the end of four and one-half years of traditional psychotherapy and drugs I was still depressed, alcoholic and addicted to the drugs as well.

It is always difficult for an alcoholic to identify that moment in time when you cross from normal to alcoholic drinking. I can see now that I was getting into trouble when I began using alcohol as medicine. I began to drink at bedtime to combat the insomnia that plagued me. I drank a lot to quell the fear and anxiety that overwhelmed me. The longer I drank, the greater the anxiety grew—a connection I was unable to make at the time. I also drank for all the reasons everyone else drinks —because I thought it made me feel better, any occasion seems more festive if you drink. I drank a lot to gain confidence in myself—something that has never been my long suit. I also used Librium for that purpose and I can tell you that in my drugged days this would be at least a 100 mg performance.

Let me establish my credentials by telling you that before I began my recovery I was hospitalized twice for detoxification, I made a serious attempt at suicide, I left my husband at one point only to have the drinking grow even worse and I returned. I suffered innumerable blackouts. The longest blackout I had lasted for 24 hours. I woke up on Thursday to find out it was Friday. I used to park my car in a blackout when I went to class and then couldn't find it when I came out. I hid bottles all over the house, and sometimes did that in a blackout and couldn't find them later. During the first year of my sobriety they kept turning up all over the house.

I was a binge drinker. I would have a period of weeks of sobriety or social drinking followed by several days of uncontrolled drinking. The binges grew closer and closer together. My husband learned to time them and could often tell when he could expect to return home and find me drinking again. During this time I was trying to stay sober on will power. My psychiatrist gave me Antabuse, but it didn't do any

Alcoholics Anonymous

good. Usually when I found it necessary to drink again I realized I had conveniently forgotten to take the Antabuse. And then I made the dangerous discovery that I could drink within two days of stopping the Antabuse and the reaction was tolerable. Toward the end my psychiatrist tried to get me to go to AA, but I refused. Someone might see me and suspect that I was an alcoholic—and that would have been the absolute end of the world! Besides, I kept asking, what could a bunch of ex-drunks do for me that a board-certified psychiatrist could not? The only thing my doctor told me was that it would give me someone to call in case I wanted to take a drink.

The turning point came when my husband came to the end of his rope. He sat me down for another of our many talks where we would both agree that I simply *had* to stop drinking and I would go out again and try it on will power. Only this time it was different—this time he was telling me what *he* was going to do. 'Alcohol is controlling your life and therefore it is controlling mine and *I won't have it*.' In desperation he turned to a friend of ours who is a nurse and she had found out about treatment centers and had gotten him some Al-anon literature. My doctor had never told him about that organization. My husband tried to get me to go for treatment but I did not want to go to a mental institution, so I threw myself on his mercy with pitiful tears and pleading—something that I was very good at doing. He gave in, but extracted a promise that if I took one more drink I would go to treatment. The week had not ended until I was drinking again and he carted me off to a treatment center. I tried to leave after I got there and he told me if I came home I would go back with a sheriff because he would commit me.

In forcing me into treatment my husband provided that last final ingredient for recovery from alcoholism—and that is hope. For the first time in my life I met recovering alcoholics and learned about AA.

Out of the fog of the final days of my drinking I can recall the expression on the faces of my family and psychiatrist. It was a look of infinite sadness. As though they were saying to themselves, 'She was such a nice person—too bad she's lost.' It was like being present at my own funeral. Their attitude reinforced my own feeling of hopelessness. My behaviour was perfectly understandable to them. I was an alcoholic. They seemed to know without my telling them all the helplessness, hopelessness, fear, and anger that raged inside me. And because they understood me so thoroughly I began to believe that perhaps what had worked for them could work for me as well.

There is a spiritual component to recovery from alcoholism. It is that moment of truth when the alcoholic says, 'I give up. I surrender. I will do *anything* to stop drinking and change my life.' This is commonly known as 'hitting bottom'. It is a very painful experience for the alcoholic. For now he must give up all the defenses that have been

113

protecting him from painful reality. You feel like you're standing naked before the whole world.

Those of us who recover in AA believe that a part of this surrender is a willingness to accept belief in a Power Greater Than Ourselves, whatever one conceives that to be. For me this occurred during the second week of my recovery. I was experiencing acute withdrawal from the Librium and I was virtually paralyzed with anxiety. I was terrified that I was losing my mind and would spend the rest of my life in a mental institution. And in that, the lowest ebb of my life, I got in touch with the finititude of my being. I gave up intellectualizing about who or what God might or might not be and prayer welled up from inside me, a simple 'Help me—for I cannot help myself.' And when I reached out, help was there for me in the form of the AA program and all the alcoholics who so lovingly taught me how to put it into practice in my own life.

I was in treatment for five weeks. When I returned home I was terrified that I would slip back into my old behavior pattern and start drinking again. But I attended AA regularly and tried diligently to work the program. And one day at a time I managed to stay sober. And the days lengthened into weeks and then into months and the day came that I realized that I not only hadn't taken a drink that day—I hadn't even thought about taking a drink. The obsession was leaving me. I can't tell you what an enormous sense of relief I felt when I finally realized I don't ever *have* to drink again.

And then I came to realize that I was experiencing life differently than I ever had before. As I have come to recognize the changes in my behavior and attitudes, I have realized that without the pain of the alcoholism I would never have opened myself up to the possibility of growth. I could have muddled around in depression and self-pity for the rest of my life if the alcoholism had not forced me to deal with it. Sometimes in AA meetings you hear an alcoholic say, 'I thank God I am an alcoholic.' The first time I heard that I hadn't been sober very long and I thought the man must have been brain damaged. But I understand now what he is saying. You also sometimes hear alcoholics say, 'I had to do everything I did to be where I am today.' That is for me the epitome of self-acceptance.

I want to take a few minutes to speak to you briefly about your own attitudes toward alcoholism. The medical profession taught *me* that alcoholics are hopeless. As a student nurse I hated alcoholic patients. They tried my patience when they were admitted drunk and took up my time that I felt better spent on patients whom I considered to be really sick. I learned this attitude from the doctors and nurses who taught me. A doctor who was teaching us said, 'I want to warn you girls about the alcoholics you will be taking care of on the wards. They can charm your socks off, but don't you be fooled—you can never get an alcoholic to stay sober.' In those days I believed everything doctors told me—I was to learn better much later. But in any case I had no reason to doubt him. I never saw anyone get sober either.

And so I ask you to stay very closely in touch with your attitudes as you begin to practise medicine. If you think alcoholism is a moral problem then you won't be inclined to intervene very actively in the disease process. By a moral problem I mean if you think the alcoholic can quit drinking by himself using will power, if he will only get his act together.

I believe alcoholism is a disease in the sense that it is something that happens to you—just as cancer or heart disease happens to you. I did not ask to become alcoholic. That was never one of my goals in life. But I was forced back into contact with reality one day and realized that I had become the victim of a process with a known symptomatology, a predictable course and a terrible prognosis. That process is called alcoholism.

We don't know what causes it, but not knowing what causes a disease has never before stopped the medical profession from treating it. I am reminded of a joke you sometimes hear around AA meetings. This drunk wanders down to the edge of a lake carrying an anvil. He's going to swim across to the other side. He jumps in and very soon he's drowning. Now on the opposite shore are all these people who want to help him. The ministers are yelling, 'We're praying for you, we're praying for you'. The doctors are yelling, 'We're doing research, we're doing research'. The AA members are yelling, 'DROP THE ANVIL!'.

16

Attacking the problem

Prevention of alcoholism is an impossible dream, people say, and maybe they are right. Thirty years ago prevention of polio was an impossible dream. People said it, and they were wrong. It is true that prevention of alcoholism is still at an 'iron-lung, avoid-swimming-pools' stage, but it may not always be that way.

What can any of us—the family, employer, doctor, or society—do to help prevent alcoholism or arrest it at an early stage?

What can the family do?

First it can recognize the problem when there is one. There often is great reluctance to do so. Wives sometimes get maternal gratification from caring for drinking husbands—it makes them feel superior, like head of the family. The children may prefer a tipsy happy daddy to a sour sober father. First the problem has to be seen as a problem—but then what?

Nothing is more frustrating for someone in the helping business—doctor, social worker, etc.—than to get a call from the spouse, 'John is drinking too much. What can I do?'

'Well, have him come see me.'

'But he *won't*. He doesn't think he has a drinking problem. I'm desperate. What should I do?'

Call the police? What can the police do? Usually nothing. Drinking is not a crime. Wife-beating is, and that is when the police may help (but usually not help with the drinking).

Nag? Nagging just provides another reason to drink.

Threaten? Well, yes, sometimes. If the last straw is really the last straw, it is probably a good idea to say so. Sometimes people do stop drinking because a husband or wife threatens to leave them. Coercion sometimes works. However, often it

116

isn't the last straw, but next to the last straw, and what then? If threats or importunings don't work, what will? Family life poses few problems as painful as this one. How the spouse handles it says a good deal about the spouse, and also about the role of the sexes in dealing with each other's problems.

A sociologist, Dr Jacqueline Wiseman, sums up a lot of experience with husbands and wives in the table on the next page.

There are infinite variations, of course. 'Happy families are all alike', wrote Tolstoy. 'Every unhappy family is unhappy in its own way.' In their own ways, husbands and wives play out the roles society and their own unique personalities assign to them, and usually there is not as much 'choice' as people like to believe. Advice, even from the wisest adviser, may be bad advice simply because family relations are tremendously complicated, played out intuitively by and large, and outsiders never know how it *really* is.

Advice to be tender or tough—to leave him or not—is usually best not given, and most people don't listen anyway.

Here are some general principles to remember:

1. The alcoholic must face the consequences of his behaviour.

The family often tries to protect him from these consequences and shouldn't.

Don't pick up the pieces. If he passes out, leave him there (if it's indoors, etc.). If he throws up, let him clean it up the next morning. If he doesn't remember how the window was broken, tell him later. Be matter-of-fact. Don't pretend it was funny. Don't say I told you so. (Blackouts are scary. Sometimes people stop drinking because of them. Don't let him forget he forgot.)

Don't buy him drink.

Don't call the boss to say he has the flu (a hard rule to follow when the family depends on the income).

Don't bail him out of jail—or anything else. Let *him* explain —not you. Let *him* apologize—not you.

Stop trying to control his drinking behaviour. You can't

Comparison of behaviour of wives and husbands of alcoholics*

Wives of alcoholics

1. Wife notices symptoms of alcoholism early. Does not go by official symptoms like morning drinking and blackouts but by antisocial behaviour, such as:
   - Stays out all night
   - Stops taking wife out
   - Is rough during intercourse
   - Starts drinking at work

2. Wife starts immediate campaign to get husband to stop drinking. Tries:
   - Logical discussion
   - Tears and persuasion
   - Nagging
   - Threats

3. Wife tries very hard to get husband into professional treatment. Often threatens to leave if he does not go. He often goes because he is so sick (physically)

4. Wife stays with husband through entire treatment:
   - Many for financial reasons—whether real or imagined
   - AA for the insurance
   - For love

5. Wife drives husband to detoxification; picks him up

Husbands of alcoholics

1. Husband notices much later:
   - Usually goes by official symptoms (often claims to know them because he is a former alcoholic himself)
   - Sometimes had to be told by friends (wife never had to be)
   - Only became really upset when wife started letting down on child care, house-work, etc.
   - May have noticed because wife embarrassed him in front of guests, etc.

2. Husband does nothing. Usually knows AA credo. Believes he can do nothing to help her stop drinking—that it is up to her to want to stop.

3. Husband does not urge wife to go into professional treatment as soon or as strongly
   - Worries about the cost (not covered by insurance)
   - Says that she doesn't like to leave home (a few suggest that she might try weekend treatment)
   - Is afraid that she will meet some other man and be unfaithful if the institution takes both male and female patients

4. Husband leaves wife after she slips once or twice after being institutionalized; looks for another woman (often looks while still married)

5. Husband often refuses to drive wife to detoxication centre, social worker has to call and beg him to come get her

* From Jacqueline Wiseman, *Alcohol and Women*. NIAAA Research Monograph No. 1, p. 112. Rockville, Maryland (1980).

118

anyway. You are as powerless in this regard as he is. Stop playing games. Stop hiding bottles. Stop pouring them down drains. Stop organizing the family routine around his drinking; shortening the cocktail hour won't help. Stop babying him. Allow *him* to be responsible for *his* behaviour. Love the sinner but not the sin.

2. Don't preach. It doesn't help.

3. Keep up hope. Many alcoholics just up and recover, with help or without.

4. Save yourself.

Finally, try the Yellow Pages. AA usually has a listing and so does Alanon. AA usually won't send someone to the house —the alcoholic must first ask—but the spouse can go to Alanon and the kids can go to Alateen. If there is a National Council on Alcoholism in town, it can direct you to these groups. A minister can usually direct you. A physician? Less often, sad to say.

The alcoholic is isolated and ashamed. The alcoholic's family is isolated and ashamed. The kids don't invite friends over because father may be drunk. Bowling and Saturday night bridge become things of the past.

Isolated, ashamed, and bewildered, the family thinks it has never happened to anyone else. It has. Alanon and Alateen are opportunities to find this out. They are opportunities to learn how others deal with the problems. They are opportunities to learn how you may be contributing to the problem yourself without knowing it.

Should the family directly confront the alcoholic—lay it down straight and simple? Confrontation has become a big word in the treatment field. Some favour it more than others. It seemed to work with Betty Ford. Jerry and the children descended on her one day and said she was drinking too much. They brought along the head of a nearby alcoholism hospital. He gave her a copy of the book *Alcoholics Anonymous* and suggested she substitute the word 'chemical dependence' in the book for 'alcoholism'. 'I was in shock', writes Mrs Ford in her autobiography. She cried. She was enraged. But she went in the hospital, stayed a month, and returned home free of her chemical dependence. Forever? In Mrs Ford's case, it seems quite likely.

Confrontation is tricky. It works in some families, fails in others. Alanon, Alateen, a good alcoholism counsellor, can help a family decide whether to try.

What can the employer do?

Every year millions of pounds are lost to business and industry because of employees drinking on the job, alcohol-related absenteeism, and ineffective performance because of hangovers. There is an old saying in America that you should never buy a car built on Mondays and Fridays, Mondays because of hangovers and Friday because of long lost weekends.

For the employer, humanitarian and economic motives combine to provide a strong incentive for action against alcoholism. The employer is in a unique position to take action.

First, by definition, the drinking employee has a job and therefore something to lose. Alcoholics with nothing to lose have the worst prognosis. Second, the employer can document poor job performance; he has an objective yardstick to go by and doesn't have to rely on pleading or moralizing. He can rely on something better: the hovering axe.

For these reasons company alcoholism programmes tend to be successful. Some claim a rate of improvement as high as 85 per cent.

First comes the confrontation. 'Frank, we think you are drinking too much. How can we help?' Often there is a company physician who has gone to alcoholism courses and knows something about the problem. He may talk with Frank, put him on Antabuse, send him to AA meetings, or get him into a treatment programme. There is an excellent way to tell whether this is working: Frank gets to work on time, stops chewing mints on the job, and his performance improves.

Attacking the problem

People stop drinking because they are afraid of losing something important to them: job, wife, health, life. Losing health and life may be low on the list. Losing the good opinion of others may be first. The author John Cheever, a recovered alcoholic, said he stopped drinking not because of his liver but because of social disapproval. After years of social disapproval he couldn't take it any longer. Gradually, grudgingly, he stopped.

The same thing has happened to many others, and the employer is in a good position to make it occur. Money and good opinion go together and the employer has some control over both.

What can the doctor do?

Like the employer, the alcoholic's doctor (if there is one) is in a good position to identify a drinking problem early.

Doctors are notoriously slow to take advantage of this. Sometimes the patient has to show up drunk, jaundiced, with his liver down to his pelvis, before it occurs to the physician to ask whether he drinks.

Why so unobserving? One reason is that doctors don't know much about alcoholism. The subject isn't brought up much in medical school. Doctors don't like to see alcoholics. They don't know what to do with them when they see them. Alcoholics let themselves go; they look a mess. They don't pay their bills. Their wives call in the middle of the night. Their breath smells. They *want* to be this way, so what can you do? If it wasn't alcohol, it would be drugs or something else. They are obviously unstable people. 'Stay away from my door' is the message sent out by many doctors, and alcoholics get the message.

When asked about their drinking, they say no, I don't drink much. No more than anyone else. A couple of drinks before dinner. Maybe some wine with dinner. That's it.

And maybe that is it. For many doctors the subject seems too personal, almost too embarrassing, to bring up. Sometimes there seems to be an unspoken agreement between the patient and doctor that the subject will not be brought up or, if it is, that the whole truth is too much to expect. The patient doesn't want to talk about his drinking habits and the doctor doesn't press him.

One problem is that doctors don't know how to ask. 'You don't drink too much, do you?' is easy to concur with by saying no, and 'Do you have an alcohol problem?' prompts an equally quick denial.

How well a physician obtains a 'drinking history' depends on tact and training, but the important thing is to be non-judgmental.* 'Do you drink?' obviously is the first question. For the drinker, 'How do you drink?' is a good second question, neutral and unaccusing. Two questions that may follow are, 'Have you or your family ever been concerned about your drinking?' and 'Has drinking ever caused problems in your life?' At this stage the alcoholic may begin to lower his defences and disclose a problem.

Often the physical examination discloses—or hints at—a problem before the patient does.

* Even the best doctors sometimes have trouble getting a good drinking history:

Q Have you a drink problem?
A I have no difficulty in swallowing liquids.
Q I mean, have you a problem with alcohol?
A No, I can get all the booze I want.
Q I mean, do you drink more alcohol than you should?
A Why? How much should I drink?
Q What I mean is, do you drink more alcohol than is good for you?
A That depends on how much is good for me. What quantity do you recommend?
Q (Sighs) Is alcohol affecting your behaviour for the worse?
A My friends don't think so, but my wife is inclined to fuss about it.
Q So your wife has a problem with *your* drinking.
A No problem at all. She is quite clear in her mind what is wrong.
Q Thank you! I will see you again next Thursday. (Slips off his elastic-sided shoes which have begun to feel uncomfortably tight). —B. J. Freedman.

With apologies to Jaroslav Hašek, author of *The Good Soldier Švejk, and his fortunes in the World War*. William Heinemann, London, 1922. Translated from the Czech by Cecil Parrot, 1973. Reprinted from the *British Medical Journal*.

Attacking the problem

Arcus senilis—a ringlike opacity of the cornea—occurs commonly with age, causes no visual disturbance, and is considered an innocent condition. The ring forms from fatty material in the blood. Alcohol increases fat in the blood and more alcoholics are reported to have the ring than others their age.

A red nose (acne rosacea) suggests the owner has a weakness for alcoholic beverages. Often, however, people with red noses are teetotalers, or even rabid prohibitionists, and resent the insinuation.

Red palms (palmar erythema) are also suggestive, but not diagnostic, of alcoholism.

Cigarette burns between the index and middle fingers or on the chest, and contusions and bruises, should raise suspicions of alcoholic stupor.

Painless enlargement of the liver may suggest a larger alcohol intake than the liver can cope with. Severe, constant upper abdominal pain and tenderness radiating to the back indicates pancreatic inflammation, and alcohol sometimes is the cause.

Reduced sensation and weakness in the feet and legs may occur from excessive drinking.

Laboratory tests provide other clues. More than half of alcoholics have increased amounts of a chemical called GGT (gamma-glutamyl transpeptidase) in their blood, which is unusual in non-alcoholics.

What can the physician *do* when he suspects a drinking problem? He can talk it over with the patient; this is often more productive than most physicians seem to believe. If the patient denies excessive drinking, the doctor can still suggest that he cut out alcohol entirely for a month or two. Perhaps he will sleep better, be less irritable, and get rid of the heartburn. In Chapter 14, there is a plan for helping someone abstain from alcohol which physicians may find useful.

Then, of course, the physician should know where to refer the alcoholic. Recent years have seen a proliferation of institutions for treating alcoholics and every family doctor should know those in his area.

Alcoholism

What can society do?

One can easily get the impression in our society that alcoholism is funny. Drinking and drunkenness are the subject of many cartoons in magazines and newspapers. Four million humourous greeting cards reflecting alcohol use are sold each year in the United States, the second most popular topic for cards after sexual behaviour.

The French novelist, George Simenon, believes this preoccupation with alcohol is peculiarly American:

> I did not become truly alcoholic with an alcoholic consciousness except in America. I'm speaking of a particular, almost permanent state, in which one is dominated by alcohol, whether during the hours one is drinking or during the hours when one is impatiently waiting to drink, almost as painfully as a drug addict waits for his injection.
>
> If one has never known this experience, it is difficult to understand American life. Not that everyone drinks, in the sense in which my mother used this word, but because it is part of private and public life, of folklore, you might say, as is proved by the large, more or less untranslatable vocabulary, most often in slang, that relates to drink.*

The French are *always* saying things like that about America. With the highest per capita consumption of alcohol and highest cirrhosis rate in the world, they are not in a position to feel superior.

The United States tried to prohibit drinking during the twenties and early thirties, but failed. Actually, Prohibition in the United States had some measure of success. The cirrhosis rate dropped. There were fewer alcohol-related admissions to hospitals. But, after 14 years, the 'noble experiment' ended for an obvious reason: people wanted to drink.

They wanted to drink to satisfy a need, as Berton Roueché explains:

> The basic needs of the human race, its members have long agreed, are food, clothing, and shelter. To that fundamental trinity most modern authorities would add, as equally compelling, security and love.

* George Simenon, *When I Was Old*. Harcourt, Brace, Jovanovich, New York (1971).

124

Attacking the problem

There are, however, many other needs whose satisfaction, though somewhat less essential, can seldom be comfortably denied. One of these, and perhaps the most insistent, is an occasional release from the intolerable clutch of reality. All men throughout recorded history have known this tyranny of memory and mind, and all have sought, and invariably found, some reliable means of briefly loosening its grip.*

But there is another reason why Prohibition is unpopular: it is unfair. The rich have never been denied alcohol; Prohibition invariably discriminates against the poor.

It also discriminates against minorities. This partly explains the chaotic, crazy quilt pattern of drinking laws in the United States. It is no accident that Mississippi and Oklahoma were last of the dry states, and in most of the South restrictive and sometimes bizarre laws still exist. These blossomed in the post-Civil War period out of the desire of Southern whites to deny alcohol to their former slaves.

In Oklahoma it was the Indians. Everybody knew the explosive effect of firewater on Indians, who, sober, were menacing enough.

The North also had restrictive laws. Here the foibles to defend against belonged to the newly arrived Irish, Germans, and Italians. These groups were known to be fond of alcohol and it was essential that they show up at the factory on time and with a clear head, meaning the saloons had to close early and be closed all day Sundays.

Country clubs, on the other hand, sometimes never closed.

Paradoxically, sometimes the rich and powerful encourage alcohol abuse in the lower classes. The eighteenth century gin epidemic in England came from a Government decision to sell gin for pennies to relieve a grain glut. Election day used to be the wettest day of the year for the unemployed in the United States whose vote could be bought for a drink.

Laws, of course, discriminate against the young who can't legally buy alcohol until a certain age. In at least one Southern state it discriminates against women—in a sense. Men can buy

* Berton Roueché, *Alcohol*. World Press, New York (1960).

125

alcohol at 18, but women have to be 21 *unless* they are married, when they can buy it at 16. (Girls there tend to marry young, and a married man is believed entitled to send his wife to fetch a bottle when he gets thirsty.)

What else can society do? From time to time support grows for measures like the following:

1. Ban advertising of alcoholic beverages.
2. Put warning labels on alcoholic beverages.
3. Increase taxes on alcoholic beverages.
4. Restrict availability of alcoholic beverages.

Some believe that alcohol advertising encourages alcohol abuse by glamourizing drinking and that it contributes to increased drinking among teenagers in particular. The beverage industry maintains that advertising at most induces people who already drink to change brands.

There is no evidence for either view. There never has been a scientific study of the effect of beverage alcohol advertising on alcohol abuse. Since alcohol abuse existed long before advertising, the mass media certainly did not create the problem.

Should containers of alcoholic beverages have a warning label? The idea is not new. In 1945, the following label was proposed by a Massachusetts Legislative Special Commission:

> *Directions for use: Use moderately and not on successive days. Eat well while drinking, and if necessary, supplement food by vitamin tablets while drinking. Warning: If this beverage is indulged in consistently and immoderately, it may cause intoxication (drunkenness), later neuralgia and paralysis (neuritis) and serious mental derangement such as delirium tremens and other curable and incurable mental diseases, as well as kidney and liver damage.*

The label was rejected. More recently the United States Congress considered adoption of a law requiring a more laconic label:

> *Caution: Consumption of alcoholic beverages may be hazardous to your health.*

126

Attacking the problem

Can alcohol abuse be discouraged by increasing alcohol taxes? Would it help to place a large tax on distilled spirits and maintain lower taxes on beer and wine?

These tactics have been tried in various European countries, with discouraging results. The per capita consumption of alcohol has usually not decreased, although some change in beverage choice may occur, at least temporarily. There is no evidence that alcoholism has declined as a result of higher taxes. Many believe that alcoholics are not deterred by the price of a beverage, and that massive price increases are unfair to light and moderate drinkers. This view was taken by a committee of the British House of Commons:

We do not recommend that alcoholic drink should, by the increase of taxation, be priced out of the reach of many more people. We consider that this step would unfairly penalize the vast majority of unaddicted drinkers, and do nothing to reduce the incidence of alcoholism amongst those who could still afford it, whilst tempting those who could not towards dangerous alternative sources of intoxication.

A certain result of a massive price increase would be the expansion of a black market in alcoholic beverages, probably involving organized crime and the illicit production of alcoholic beverages. Some indigent alcoholics would turn to non-beverage alcohol, despite its dangers.

Finally, would it help to make alcohol less available? There has been a world-wide trend towards liberalization of drinking laws as shown by the increasing number of sales outlets, longer hours for sales, even mini-bars to dispense alcoholic beverages in hotel rooms. Has this resulted in increased use and abuse of alcohol?

The evidence is inconclusive. In Scotland, where alcohol laws are more restrictive than in England, the rate of alcoholism is higher. In England the number of pubs has declined but convictions for drunkenness have increased.

In 18 states in the United States the Government operates and owns liquor stores. States with Government-owned stores tend to have lower consumption rates than those with privately owned stores. The explanation may be that states whose

127

Alcoholism

voters prefer Government-owned stores are, for whatever reason, less heavy consumers of alcohol. One study concludes that consumption and alcoholism rates are more closely related to urbanism and income than to availability.

Since none of the above proposals offers much hope, what can society do to combat its alcohol problems? Over the long run, only two measures are likely to be effective: (i) A systematic, extensive, low-keyed, public education programme based on the best available knowledge about alcohol and its *real* dangers. (ii) Scientific studies directed toward explaining why some people abuse alcohol while most who drink do not. Knowing the cause—or causes—of alcoholism offers the best hope for ultimately preventing the disorder.

Self-appraisal

The most widely used screening questionnaire for detecting alcoholism is the Michigan Alcoholism Screening Test (MAST). A score of five or more puts you in the alcoholism category. Although some clearly non-alcoholic individuals will score five or above, this is unusual enough to make the test useful for screening purposes. It is published here for readers who wonder, 'Am I? Am I not?'*

1. Do you feel you are a normal drinker? (By normal we mean you drink less than or as much as most other people.) (No, 2 points)
2. Have you ever awakened the morning after some drinking the night before and found that you could not remember a part of the evening? (Yes, 2 points)
3. Does your wife, husband, a parent, or other near relative ever worry or complain about your drinking? (Yes, 1 point)
4. Can you stop drinking without a struggle after one or two drinks? (No, 2 points)
5. Do you ever feel guilty about your drinking? (Yes, 1 point)
6. Do friends or relatives think you are a normal drinker? (No, 2 points)
7. Are you able to stop drinking when you want to? (No, 2 points)

* From M. L. Selzer, A. Vinokur, and L. van Rooijen (1975). A self-administered short Michigan alcoholism screening test. *Journal of Studies on Alcohol* 36, 117.

Attacking the problem

8. Have you ever attended a meeting of Alcoholics Anonymous? (Yes, 5 points)
9. Have you ever got into physical fights when drinking? (Yes, 1 point)
10. Has drinking ever created problems between you and your wife, husband a parent, or other near relative? (Yes, 2 points)
11. Has your wife, husband, a parent or other near relative ever gone to anyone for help about your drinking? (Yes, 2 points)
12. Have you ever lost friends or girlfriends because of your drinking? (Yes, 2 points)
13. Have you ever got into trouble at work because of your drinking? (Yes, 2 points)
14. Have you ever lost a job because of drinking? (Yes, 2 points)
15. Have you ever neglected your obligations, your family, or your work for two or more days in a row because you were drinking? (Yes, 2 points)
16. Do you drink before noon fairly often? (Yes, 1 point)
17. Have you ever been told you have liver trouble? Cirrhosis? (Yes, 2 points)
18. After heavy drinking have you ever had delirium tremens (DTs) or severe shaking, or heard voices or seen things that weren't really there? (Yes, 2 points)
19. Have you ever gone to anyone for help about your drinking? (Yes, 5 points)
20. Have you ever been in a hospital because of drinking? (Yes, 5 points)
21. Have you ever been a patient in a psychiatric hospital or on a psychiatric ward of a general hospital where drinking was part of the problem that resulted in hospitalization? (Yes, 2 points)
22. Have you ever been seen at a psychiatric or mental health clinic or gone to any doctor, social worker, or clergyman for help with any emotional problem, where drinking was part of the problem? (Yes, 2 points)
23. Have you ever been arrested for drunken driving, driving while intoxicated, or driving under the influence of alcoholic beverages? (Yes, 2 points)
24. Have you ever been arrested, even for a few hours, because of other drunken behaviour? (Yes, 2 points)

129

Index

131

Index

death rate 25, 47, 51, 54n
defining alcoholism 31–2, 34
dehydration 17–18
delirium tremens 43–6
Denmark 73–4
'depressant' alcohol as 16–17
depression 16, 37–8, 52, 53, 67–71,
    91, 98
'disease' alcoholism as 32–3
divorce 47, 53
doctors 86, 104, 121–3
driving and alcohol 47, 54n
drug therapy 97–9
DTs 43–6
duration of drinking, effect on behav-
    iour 12–13

effect, biochemical, of alcohol 7
Egypt, ancient 21
elimination of alcohol 8
employer, help from 120–1
'epileptic' seizures 44
Episcopaleans 65
Eskimos 20
ethanol 3, 6
ethyl alcohol 3, 6
euphoria 8–9
exercise 8
expectation and effect of alcohol
    14–15

'familial alcoholism' 75
family, help from 116–20
family history 53, 63, 70–1, 72–6
fashions for particular drinks
    23–4
fat
    in bloodstream 8
    in liver 7
fetal alcohol syndrome 55–9
Fitzgerald, F. Scott 101
food, effect of on absorption of alco-
    hol 11
Ford, Betty 119
France 11, 24, 49–50, 64, 65, 124
Freud 90, 91
fructose 8
fruit sugar 8
fusel oil 3

gamma alcoholics 49
gamma-glutamyl transpeptidase 123
gastritis 38
gender and alcoholism 24, 52–5
genetic factors 58, 63, 70–1, 72–6,
    77, 105
geographical variations 24, 64–5
    See also under individual
    countries
GGT 123
gin 11, 12, 22
Gorham, Charles Orson 88, 104
gout 7
guilt 35, 68

hallucinations 44, 50
halogenated hydrocarbons 40
hangover, cures for 8, 21
Hawthorne effect 95
heartburn 38
heart disease 43, 50, 51
hepatitis 7, 50
heredity 58, 63, 70–1, 72–6, 77, 105
history of alcohol 20–6
Holmes, Oliver Wendell 83
homicide 16, 50
homosexuality 91
hospital patients, alcoholism among
    47
Housman, A.E. 67

immune response, depression of 18
impotency 41–2, 99
incidence of alcoholism 25, 32
income 64–5
Indians, American 20, 64
    intolerance to alcohol among 14
insulin 8
intolerance to alcohol 14, 19, 54,
    75–6
intoxication
    period of 8–9
    rate of 12
    stages of 15–17
IQ and alcoholism 40–1
Ireland 24, 65
irritability 68
Israel 24
Italy 11, 24, 65

Index

James, William 96, 102
Jellinek, E.M. 32, 49
Jews 65
Journal of Inebriety 32

Keller, Mark 79

labelling of alcoholic drinks 4, 126
lactic acid 7
Laennec's cirrhosis 7-8, 39-40
laws, drinking
  in England 127
  in Scotland 127
  in United States 125-6
learning, effect of alcohol on 17
Librium 97
life expectancy 51
Lincoln, Abraham 27
lithium 70, 98
liver 6, 7, 18, 39-40, 123
  cirrhosis of 7-8, 39-40, 50, 54n, 64
longevity 51
Lowry, Malcolm 44-5
LSD 98

malnutrition 7-8
Mania 70
manic-depression 67-70
Mayfield, Dr Demmie 70
mead 20
Medawar, Peter 92
Medical problems of alcoholism 38-43
  of the brain 40
  impotency 41-2
  of the liver 39-40
  of the nerve fibres 40
  of the stomach 38-9
Medical Temperance Society 32
medicinal use of alcohol 53
memory, effect of alcohol on 17, 36-7, 41
men, drinking among 24, 48, 72, 73-4
  compared with women 52-5
menstrual cycle 55
Mesopotamia 20-1
methanol 3
mood, effect of alcohol on 14-17, 69-70
'moonshine' 23
morphine 8-9

mortality rate 25, 47, 51, 54n
murder 16, 50
muscle disease 43
muscular weakness 40

narcotic antagonists 8
National differences 23-4, 25, 65
  See also under individual countries
'natural history' of alcoholism 48-51
nausea 38, 54
  treatment by inducing 93-4
nerve fibres 40
'normal' drinking 25-6
  among ex-alcoholics 48-9, 75, 103
nose, red 18, 42, 123

obesity 31
occupation 64
onset 48, 50, 52, 63, 75
operant conditioning 95
oral fixation 68, 90
Orientals, intolerance of alcohol in 14, 19, 64, 75-6
Osler, William 42

palmar erythema 123
palms, red 123
pancreatitis 43, 50
paralysis 40
paranoia, alcoholic conjugal 42
parent, loss of 52
Pavlov 93
performance, effect of alcohol on 17
  sexual 42
personality changes caused by alcohol 15-16, 53
placebo effect 14
Plutarch 22, 55, 72
pneumonia 50
Poe, Edgar Allan 27
portal cirrhosis *see* Laennec's cirrhosis
pregnancy 52, 55-9
premenstrual tension 55
preoccupation with alcohol 34, 79
prevalence of alcoholism 25, 32
prevention 116-28
price of alcohol 65
prisoners, alcoholism among 47
prognosis 51, 120

133

Index

134

Index

135

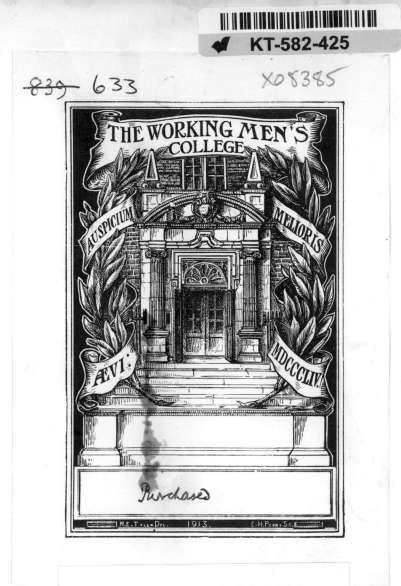

THE WORKING MEN'S COLLEGE

AUSPICIUM

MELIORIS

ÆVI:

MDCCCLIV

Purchased

R.E.Tyler Del.   1913.   C.H.Perry Sc.

WORKING MEN'S COLLEGE

LIBRARY REGULATIONS

The Library is open every week day evening (except Saturday), from 6.00 to 9.30.
This book may be kept for three weeks. If
not returned within that period, the borrower
will be liable to a fine of one penny per week.
If lost or damaged, the borrower will be
required to make good such loss or damage.
Only one book may be borrowed at a time.

RISE OF THE PUBLIC SCHOOLS

Rise of the Public Schools

A Study of Boys' Public Boarding Schools in England and Wales from 1837 to the Present Day

T. W. BAMFORD

NELSON

THOMAS NELSON AND SONS LTD
36 Park Street London W1
P.O. Box 336 Apapa Lagos
P.O. Box 25012 Nairobi
P.O. Box 21149 Dar es Salaam
77 Coffee Street San Fernando Trinidad

THOMAS NELSON (AUSTRALIA) LTD
597 Little Collins Street Melbourne

THOMAS NELSON & SONS (SOUTH AFRICA) (PROPRIETARY) LTD
P.O. Box 9881 Johannesburg

THOMAS NELSON AND SONS (CANADA) LTD
81 Curlew Drive Don Mills Ontario

THOMAS NELSON AND SONS
Copewood and Davis Streets Camden 3, N.J.

First published 1967
© 1967 by T. W. Bamford

Printed in Great Britain by
Thomas Nelson (Printers) Ltd, London and Edinburgh

Contents

Author's Notes

This study has been largely confined to public boarding schools for boys in England and Wales. Statements and statistics do not include girls' schools, or schools in Scotland, Ireland or overseas, unless specifically stated.

The 'seven', as they are usually referred to, consist of Charterhouse, Eton, Harrow, Rugby, Shrewsbury, Westminster and Winchester.

The 'nine' consist of the seven, together with Merchant Taylors' and St Paul's. The nine are often referred to as the 'Clarendon schools', since they were the subject of study by the Clarendon (Public Schools) Commission. While the seven are boarding schools, the other two are day.

It should be noted that in referring to certain events various dates may be used. With the Clarendon Commission, for example, any of the following years are permissible, depending on the context: 1861, 1862, 1863 and 1864 (1861 being the year in which the commission was set up and 1864 the year in which it reported. Evidence was taken at various times between these dates).

Readers should also note that the following terms are recognized alternatives:

Clarendon Commission/Public Schools Commission

Taunton Commission/Schools Inquiry Commission—Endowed Schools Commission

LIST OF ABBREVIATIONS

DNB: *Dictionary of National Biography*

PSC: Report of Her Majesty's Commissioners Appointed to Enquire into the Revenues and Management of Certain Colleges and Schools, and the Studies Pursued and Instruction Given therein; with an Appendix and Evidence, 1864. (The Clarendon, or Public Schools, Commission)

SIC: Schools Inquiry Commission, 1868

Acknowledgements

This book was started some years ago at the request of Professor A. V. Judges, and in the early stages parts were read by H. L. Beales and O. R. McGregor. I have used extensively the libraries of the British Museum and of the University and the Institute of Education at Hull. In particular I owe a debt to my former colleague W. R. Fraser for many suggestions and long discussions on educational themes, and to Professor W. O. Lester Smith for my first research exploration of this field and for continual encouragement thereafter. In a real sense, however, this book is the end result of a long-term study of public schools which began when my father introduced me long ago to the exploits of Landor, Butler, Byron, Hodson and other legendary schoolboy heroes.

Introduction

A few schools of the present day can be traced back over many centuries. To survive they have had to overcome religious and economic pressures, not to mention shifts in population, the threat of disease and varying degrees of popularity. In spite of these hazards, the records show that when the prospects were certain, if distant, masters were willing to cling on at all costs and face any adversity, even the sheer starvation which overtook Raphael Pearce, headmaster of Rugby, in 1651. Over the years abuses crept into every school. Often the whole purpose of the charity was forgotten and the money spent according to whim, gambling or cupidity. Some masters received their income for little or no work, while in other places the foundation took on the atmosphere of a family business, as happened at Eton. Above all, an assured income was essential for survival, and it is no coincidence that the main schools of the late eighteenth and early nineteenth centuries were the richest.

A vital factor in the character of a school lay in the quality of the individual master. The statutes of grammar schools usually prescribed an M.A. from Oxford or Cambridge, which means he would have been a classical scholar with little knowledge outside this field. It is not surprising, therefore, that these grammar schools concentrated on the classical education which befitted entrants to the old universities.

The term 'public school' was already in use in the early nineteenth century, if somewhat vaguely. As early as 1801 Dr Vincent tried to define which particular schools he had in mind when he was defending the kind of Christian education given in the public schools.

Are we to understand only Winchester, Eton and Westminster? or are we to extend our notion, as we ought to do, to the three other great schools in the Metropolis, to Harrow, Rugby, Manchester, Wakefield, and many more of equal magnitude in the north?[1]

If the 'three other great schools in the Metropolis' mentioned here are Charterhouse, St Paul's and Merchant Taylors', then

1. W. Vincent, *A Defence of Public Education* . . ., 1801.

this is very close to the modern grouping (see Appendix) and was reinforced nine years later in a pungent article in the *Edinburgh Review* which revived the controversy over discipline.

> . . . even if we include in the term of public school, not only Eton, Winchester and Westminster, but the Charter House, St Paul's School, Merchant Taylors', Rugby and every school in England at all conducted upon the plan of the three first. . . .

An official attempt to recognize these schools came soon after the battle of Waterloo with the long agitation by Henry Brougham which led ultimately to the creation of the Charities Commission. He wanted a wide approach to the problem and wrote an extremely successful pamphlet expounding his views and complaining of the large number of exceptions that were suggested, including the 'Universities and the Public Schools down to Rugby'.[1] His objections, however, were overruled and the Charity Commissioners were set up under Act of Parliament.[2] Here, under Provision XII, certain exceptions were made:

> That none of these provisions . . . shall be construed to extend to either of the Universities of Oxford or Cambridge . . . nor to the Colleges of Westminster, Eton, or Winchester, or to the Charterhouse, or the schools of Harrow or Rugby or any of them. . . .

The selection of these six schools for special treatment was no mere chance; they comprised a distinctive type, and some people argued that Shrewsbury should have been included as well. Certainly this Act set a precedent, for when in 1820 Henry Brougham introduced two Bills concerning endowed grammar schools it was suggested that the same six schools be exempt. At once Samuel Butler, the headmaster of Shrewsbury, protested. He wrote to Members of Parliament, and went to the extent of publishing a long and detailed letter to Brougham himself. In this he complained that Shrewsbury was no different in kind from the others—it was national in scope, amply endowed, prosperous and distinguished in its scholars and history.

It is evident by 1820 that seven particular schools were already being linked as a group. They were not by any

1. H. Brougham, *A Letter to Sir Samuel Romilly* . . ., 1818.
2. 58 George III, Cap XCI, 1818.

means equally significant, but they did have certain features in common in the terms already defined by Butler. They were endowed schools of some historical significance, with an education based on antiquity, in particular on Latin and, to a lesser extent, Greek language and literature. They were patronized essentially by the aristocracy and landed gentry, as well as by many who did not exactly fit into either category but who were rich enough to adopt the gentry's way of life and manners, and even to intermarry with them or mix with them occasionally at receptions and hunt-balls—without being fully acceptable to the uppermost stratum of society. The children of successful professional men in the Church, law and medicine were only found there occasionally, while the sons of middle-class parents, shopkeepers, farmers and the like were very rare indeed and the lower classes all but non-existent.

It is said that Eton recruited many poor boys in earlier days, and certainly thirty-eight entrants in twenty-eight years between 1753 and 1790 were of the tradesman class; but this small number, out of 3,000 or so, only emphasizes the rarity of the phenomenon, while the fact that Richard Porson was one of them indicates that there were probably good reasons for making exceptions in at least some cases. It is true, however, that a middle-class element did try to invade the schools, notably Harrow and Rugby, but this was an essentially Victorian occurrence.

By 1820 these seven schools had a national reputation and were recruiting boys from all over the British Isles, some attracting a few from overseas as well, though these travellers were almost invariably the sons of British exiles. The schools were primarily, if not exclusively, boarding, closely linked to Oxford and Cambridge, and in two cases—Eton and Winchester—these ties were very intimate indeed. In addition, they were supporters of the establishment, for the very fact that they had managed to survive throughout long periods of religious persecution meant that they were religious conformers and Anglican in spirit. These schools, therefore, were essentially variants upon the same theme.

While the seven had many points in common, they did not stand entirely alone in public estimation. Whenever historical significance, education, buildings or foundation problems were

considered, two or three day schools immediately came to mind, like St Paul's, Merchant Taylors' and Manchester Grammar. These also dispensed a classical curriculum in the manner of Eton and Harrow, but they lacked the essential qualifications of boarding and of catering specifically for the upper classes. St Paul's, for instance, only received 109 boys who might conceivably have belonged to the upper classes during the early nineteenth century up to the accession of Queen Victoria, and even this tiny intake showed a pronounced falling off towards 1837. This particular school was, in fact, dominated by the lower and middle classes. Moreover, the fact that St Paul's was a day school meant that it satisfied a local demand, more than four out of five of its pupils being Londoners in the true sense of the word. In spite of its eminence and its association with the cathedral, St Paul's was essentially different from the seven, and the same distinctions applied with equal or greater force to Merchant Taylors' and the grammar schools.

In the early years of the century these distinctions were not so keenly felt, and both St Paul's and Merchant Taylors' enjoyed great prestige and were included with the seven in books of reference or whenever educational issues were being discussed. Somewhat later, in 1861, this wider grouping was recognized officially when a Royal Commission under Lord Clarendon was appointed to look into the affairs of these nine and to make recommendations. These schools were thereby given undoubted public-school status, although it should be remembered that the day schools were different in kind from the other seven.

Public schools were guardians of the old tradition. For geographical and social reasons they lived in closed worlds, ignoring the significant developments in middle-class education being brought about by the numerous private day and boarding schools and academies. With one exception (Charterhouse) there is no real evidence that they were aware of the 'experimental' approach to education which was such a feature of the age from the late eighteenth century to 1837. All efforts, for instance, have failed to establish a solid relationship between the Hill family (see p. 65n. 3 and the public schools, in spite of the fact that the Hills were national figures subject to great publicity, that they and the schools had problems and friends

in common, and that at least one headmaster and one of the Hill brothers served on the same committee. For all the notice that was taken, Hazelwood, the Hills' school, might never have existed. The one exception to this general rule of ignoring other developments is quite extraordinary, in that it emanated from the lower classes and the efforts of Joseph Lancaster and Andrew Bell to solve the problem of illiteracy. This was the so-called monitorial system, with its horizons limited in the first place to reading, writing and arithmetic, although the technique of boy teaching boy was obviously capable of wide application, depending on the capabilities and ages of the boys concerned. It was both an experimental system and a device to cut down costs and educate the masses on the cheap. It enabled the churches to expand their schools rapidly and to incorporate them as part of their welfare work. In a sense these schools were on the receiving end of charity, so that at first sight there was little here likely to appeal to the middle- and upper-class schools. It is all the more surprising, therefore, that the monitorial system was introduced into Charterhouse by John Russell.[1] Perhaps it was the experimental nature of the system as much as the economy that appealed here, and at the beginning the results can only be described as wildly successful. The number of boys entering the school sprang from thirty-seven in 1816 to 167 four years later in 1820. Unfortunately this meteoric rise was followed by a steady fall to as little as seventeen (1832), the lowest entry-figure for this school at any time from the beginning of the nineteenth century. Apart from the long-fought battle over science, this was the only real case of lower-class influence on upper-class schooling for over a hundred years.

Even though the public schools comprised a closed community of separate institutions with a well-established style of education before the Victorian era began, there were already signs of outside rivalry owing to the breakdown of the Anglican monopoly in education. Until the late eighteenth century the children of Catholics, dissenters and others had to obtain what learning they could secretly or else sail across the Channel to a school on the Continent. This forced migration of youth had

1. See E. C. Mack, *Public Schools and British Opinion, 1780 to 1860*, 1938, pp. 224-8.

been a constant feature of education for centuries, although it was not entirely a one-way traffic. One of the more interesting and fortunate facts of history appears to be that, although the attitudes of the French and English governments to religion and education have wavered between one extreme and another, they have not adopted repressive measures towards the same minority groups at the same time, so that it has always been possible for a refugee, for a child seeking education or even for a whole school to find shelter across the water in one direction or another. About the time that England was relaxing her penal laws in 1778 and 1791, the French began their own persecution, and Catholic colleges which had operated overseas became exiled in their turn. Some of these escapes to safety were sudden and exciting—even to the clandestine burying of plate—and several colleges found their way to England to start afresh in what was, in spirit at least, their home soil. Stonyhurst (1794), Oscott (1794) Downside (1795), and Ampleforth (1802), among others, all started in this way, and the tradition has been carried into more recent times with the re-founding of Douai at Woolhampton after the passing of the 1901 law in France.[1]

Other religious groups also began their own classical boarding schools, inspired, no doubt, by the examples of Fulneck and John Wesley's venture at Kingswood in 1748. Mill Hill is only the first example (1807) of several schools in the new century, some of which came to provide a link with the new type of higher education offered by one or other of the two new colleges in London—King's in the Strand and the 'Benthamite Institution' in Gower Street. In this way a ladder was provided for Catholic, Jew, Nonconformist and atheist to a fresh and vigorous kind of university education.

All these non-Anglican ventures, of whatever denomination, were classical boarding schools, in part at least, but were small and negligible in the number of boys they dealt with. In no real or competitive sense were they comparable at this stage to the hard core of Anglican schools. Indeed, the reputation of the old schools was so great that many Nonconformists who could stomach an Anglican background and hide their own convictions preferred to enter their sons there rather than to patronize new places catering for their own beliefs. These new

1. See A. S. Barnes, *The Catholic Schools of England*, 1926, pp. 231–3.

schools were, therefore, symbolic rather than important. In effect they represented the embryonic phase of non-Anglican growth, and only much later in the century did the size of some become significant and their stature recognized.

In pre-Victorian England there were three distinct groups of schools providing a boarding education combined with the Classics. The first comprised the seven themselves, catering for the upper classes. The second consisted of a few schools for non-Anglicans which were destined to grow in importance later but which were negligible at this stage. Finally there is the unique case of Christ's Hospital. This was a boarding school of great renown, but its pupils were drawn exclusively from the ranks of the poor.

This was not by any means the limit of classical education in England, but the rest was either carried out in small groups at home, in rectories, in the houses of schoolmasters, or else in day grammar schools, of which the most famous were St Paul's, Merchant Taylors', Manchester, Reading and King Edward VI at Birmingham.

The use of this legacy in Victorian and later times, and the subsequent evolution of the public-school system, are the underlying themes of this book.

CHAPTER ONE

The Quest for Security and an Elegant Environment in the Old Schools

Every school in the early nineteenth century led a precarious existence, whether it catered for rich or poor. Public schools were no exception. The easiest and most dramatic way of demonstrating this fact is to examine the numbers of new pupils entering a school year by year, and we can take Harrow as a typical example (Figure 1).

It is clear from this figure that prosperity was by no means assured even for such a major school as this (and Harrow was not in any way an exception). Eton also felt similar waves of fortune in spite of its clientele and the nearness of the Court; its graph of intake shows the same erratic annual variations in intake between ninety-four and 207 for the period after 1804. This was a serious situation (though the minimum of ninety-four still ensured a substantial school), but the effect was mild compared with the catastrophic variations at Shrewsbury between nine (1807) and 104 (1826) during the same period.

Public schools were still on trial. By itself, historical significance was obviously not enough, and parents were not prepared to take a school on trust. All this is clear from the graph in Figure 1. Security did not exist. The gamble on next year's popularity dominated the schools and brought with it a whole host of problems. Headmasters on the crest of a large intake were forced to decide between a new appointment to cope with a pressing situation—which might, after all, only be temporary —or of managing larger and larger classes with an ageing staff. The vast numbers that Keate taught at Eton were as much a reflection of insecurity and cupidity as of outmoded teaching methods. It is no wonder that, in the early days, assistant masters were encouraged to take on extra duties such as private

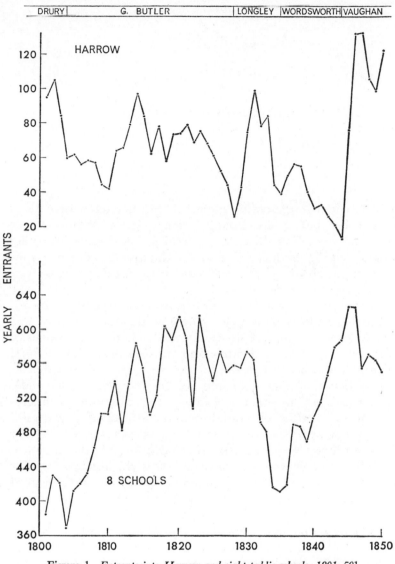

Figure 1. *Entrants into Harrow and eight public schools, 1801–50*[1]

1. The figures for the Harrow graph were calculated from M. C. Dauglish and P. K. Stephenson, *Harrow School Register 1800–1911*. There are difficulties, as in all school records. New names are occasionally added, and in this particular case the yearly numbers were adjusted from collective totals. For the sources of the combined graph of eight schools (the seven, with St Paul's), together with an overall discussion, see T. W. Bamford, 'The Prosperity of Public Schools, 1801–1850', *Durham Research Review*, III, no. 12, September 1961.

pupils and curacies to give them some personal stability in a bewildering situation, or that the governors of Rugby tried to buy their way out of despair by building new and impressive structures in the so-called Elizabethan or Tudor style.

On further examination, Harrow's progress is seen to be not entirely haphazard, but linked in part with the advent of a new headmaster. This is apparent in the examples of Vaughan, Wordsworth and Longley. A glance at Figure 2 shows a similar

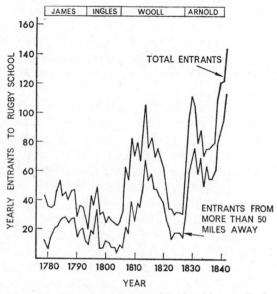

Figure 2. *Variants in the annual intake of boys to Rugby, 1779–1842*[1]

jump in the entrance figures at Rugby after the appointments of Ingles, Wooll and Arnold, while the same effect is seen in the cases of three later headmasters—Tait, Temple and Jex-Blake. The most spectacular instance is that of Vaughan at Harrow, and his achievement is similar to that of Samuel Butler, who found a mere handful of boys in the school on his arrival at Shrewsbury in 1798. In spite of their success in the early years of office, it is clear that none of these men brought real security and that their reigns were subject to periods of decline. Altogether, this phenomenon is seen as a major factor only at Rugby

1. Material extracted from *Rugby School Register*, revised and annotated by Rev. A. T. Michell, 3 vols., 1901–4.

and Harrow, though it did occur to a lesser extent at Westminster and Eton.

Insecurity was the chief feature of the nineteenth century, but it was an individual affair, each school being unique.[1] Only in one eleven-year period, from 1832 to 1842, was there a common depression. In that time the total number of new boys entering eight schools (the seven, with St Paul's) fell rapidly from a figure of 575 in 1830 to 412 in 1835 (Figure 1). The Victorian era began, therefore, with the schools in shadow and about to make a rapid recovery, so that by 1845 the common crisis was over. Even during depression some variations occurred between the schools, particularly in recovery, and indeed Shrewsbury hardly recovered at all until the later years of the century.

Explanations for the facts of insecurity and the common decline are not easy to find. Each school has plausible reasons for its own success or failure, but against the combined national picture they invariably fail. Social reform, brutality, unrealistic curricula, success in examinations, finance, cholera and disease, poor headmasters, inadequate buildings, the need for enlightenment—all these with other reasons have been suggested from time to time and been found unsatisfactory. Even such apparently obvious answers as the threat of Napoleonic invasion in the earliest years of the century and the social unrest from 1831 to 1842 are not entirely acceptable as explanations for a drop in numbers during those periods. One might expect the anxious parent to keep his son at home at such critical times rather than take the risk of him travelling long distances, but this supposition is not supported by any detailed analysis, or by the fact that the post-Waterloo troubles ending in the Peterloo massacre produced nowhere any noticeable effect.

The inter-relation of popularity and the distance of home from school has been studied most closely for Rugby, which was already a national school by 1800 and became increasingly so. It can be shown, for this school at least, that the variations in entry were really reflections upon the variations of the number of boys attending who lived more than fifty miles away. This is certainly true for the good and poor years of James,

1. For a discussion of insecurity and related problems, see the reference to 'Prosperity' on p. 2, footnote 1.

Ingles, Wooll and Arnold, as indicated in Figure 2. The number of boys from within a radius of fifty miles, excluding the town itself, tended to decline—the high-water mark being that part of the headmastership of Wooll between 1807 and 1814—and the pattern is generally erratic. Boys from the town of Rugby itself formed a complex group with at least three categories— sojourners, traders' children and the sons of professional people. The sojourners were the offspring of gentry families, temporarily resident in the town, and their numbers fluctuated broadly in the same manner as those from distant parts. Altogether it would seem that the relative popularity of the school was felt most keenly in those with distant origins, irrespective of whether or not they travelled long distances to school. It also follows that it was the national rather than the local reputation of the school which really mattered. For this reason it is very doubtful if anything of local significance could have affected the school seriously, and this explains the fact that happenings which appeared to people on the spot to be catastrophic had, in fact, very limited results. This leads naturally to an explanation, more difficult to verify, that nation-wide publicity was a root-cause of prosperity. There is some confirmation of this from detailed analysis of some national publications.[1] Periods when Rugby was subjected to considerable publicity (1807–10, 1816–18 and 1827–42) coincide with large entries into the school; similarly, periods of no publicity correspond roughly with poor entries (1800–6 and 1821–7). This is too striking a coincidence to be airily dismissed, yet it is somewhat surprising to find that it did not seem to matter whether or not the publicity was adverse. On this theory the mere appearance of the school in the news seems to have been enough, and if this supposition could be confirmed in other schools, particularly at Harrow, it might well have a considerable bearing on this whole question, besides having a profound bearing on the reputations of headmasters—to the point where revaluations would be necessary in many cases.

Uncertainty, and the corresponding nightmare of decline, dominated the life of all public schools until the final quarter

1. The publications analysed were—newspapers: *The Times, John Bull;* magazines: *Annual Register, Gentleman's Magazine;* Acts of Parliament and chancery cases; various books.

of the century. The search for some solution was continual and many new and adventurous headmasters were willing to apply one or more of the suggested remedies, provided they did not interfere with what was considered to be the school's proper role.

The schools, taken individually, were extraordinarily uniform in social content; each had a distinctive type of clientele and remained true to it.[1] Cross-sections of the intake at Eton in 1800 and 1850, analysed in terms of social class, are virtually the same. The main core of recruitment was the landed gentry— the aristocracy. Virtually no lower or middle classes were involved at all, and less than one boy in ten came from the professional ranks. Harrow was similar, but had a higher proportion of clergy, and this difference proceeded a stage further at Rugby, where the school relied on the landed gentry and clergy. The leading schools, from the earliest days of the century until mid-Victorian times at least, remained, as we have said, faithful to their clientele and did not alter the pattern of entry. This means that successive headmasters must have appreciated and preserved the situation. We know from correspondence and the queries of parents that Thomas Arnold deliberately did so to the exclusion of a higher proportion of the aristocracy, and the general situation described here would seem to infer that his actions were typical. The temptation to fill a school for the mere sake of appearances or economy was sternly resisted; even at the depths the headmasters did not contemplate dilution with socially inferior or incompatible children.

Of the schools studied in detail, the only exception to this was the day school, St Paul's. In the early years of the century it relied on the lower and middle classes, but slowly, with the years, the numbers belonging to these groups were cut drastically and professional parents began to dominate the scene. This changing situation shows that while the major boarding schools were content with their particular clientele, and loyal to it, St Paul's was not. Indeed, by analogy with human society, we have in this last school an institution that was socially mobile in an upward direction.

Looking at the public schools as a whole, it would be fair to

1. For the social content of the schools and a relevant discussion, see T. W. Bamford, 'Public Schools and Social Class, 1801–1850', *British Journal of Sociology*, XII, no. 3, September 1961, pp. 224–35.

say that, at the beginning and middle of the reign, the boys came from aristocratic, gentry or near-gentry homes, with minor additions from the clergy, and even less from the armed forces and other professional groups. Indeed, all but the gentry-titled-clergy, and those who adopted their way of life, can be ignored. In this connection it must be remembered that army officers commonly had gentry or aristocratic connections, while the more successful members of the clergy (those patronizing the schools) were, as we shall see, forced to adopt the same attitudes.

The gentry were still essentially landed and had their estates and mansions, although there were signs of change. Some began to have business interests; their children began to notice opportunities overseas and in some of the professions; but the typical member still did no work in the usually accepted sense of the word, had plenty of servants and lived on an income from property and investments.

Lower down the social scale were families of great wealth which had been amassed by hard work. There, work was often extolled as a virtue, and yet, if these men wished to rise into the 'upper ranks' of society by marriage or by style of life, this meant coming to terms with the virtues of leisure.

The ambitious merchant or manufacturer who exalted work valued idleness as a badge of status; it showed, as the saying went, that one was 'a gentleman of independent means'. But more important, even as he threw himself ardently into his work, he longed for a life of ease. Not of mere ease—*luxurious* ease. At the heart of the bourgeois dream was the ideal of gracious living, symbolized by the country house. The middle-class businessman longed to escape from drudgery in hideous surroundings into a world of beauty and leisure, a life of dignity and peace, from which sordid anxieties were shut out.[1]

In private life the gentry travelled a great deal in this country' and on the Continent, too, if the state of peace allowed it, and this habit sometimes became a semi-necessity as they wandered grimly about with some ailing member of the family. The energetic might become officers in the armed forces or help to run the country in Parliament or local government, but work was usually regarded as regrettably necessary for younger sons. The navy, army, the church and the law were generally considered to be reasonable occupations, in descending order of

1. W. E. Houghton, *The Victorian Frame of Mind, 1830–1870*, 1957, p. 190.

acceptability. Business slowly came to be recognized in the 1860s and 1870s, but entry into the other professions of medicine, engineering and the like was at most tolerated or dismissed as an eccentricity. All other occupations, to the gentry-minded, were unacceptable, and some, like trading or manual labour, regarded with horror. As we shall see from the analyses of old boys (Chapter 9), this situation showed little sign of change at least until the late-Victorian era. This does not mean that the landed gentry were not involved in the maintenance of their estates. Indeed, their horse-riding, their closeness to the land and personal involvement with the facts of life in the breeding of stock produced a welcome frankness and an un-Victorian attitude to life and sex during the century which shook the susceptibilities of more than one headmaster when views clashed at governors' meetings and elsewhere.

In practice this meant that schools in the top bracket were relieved of any responsibility of providing the basis for a living until during the second half of the century at least, and the actual pabulum of learning was of no practical importance, though the classical tradition was too firmly entrenched and universal to be discarded lightly. Only if the head of the household had a large family and limited funds was the possibility of a future occupation important. The schools were, in fact, a major influence of social pressure in the production of an old-fashioned conformity in those who patronized them.

STRUCTURE AND ENVIRONMENT IN THE OLD SCHOOLS

Of the main boarding schools, Eton and Winchester are the most famous historically; their buildings were from the outset intended not solely as schools but also as shelter for other men and institutions. At Eton:

> The main objects . . . were . . . the promotion of learning and religion and the relief of poverty. To promote learning, a home and a sufficient though frugal maintenance were provided for a limited number of men devoted to study, and a school was established in direct connection with a sister college in Cambridge, to which the scholars were to proceed: to advance religion, a noble chapel was erected, in which stated services were to be celebrated by an ample choir, and the Fellowships were confined to men of the clerical

order; while the claims of poverty were represented by the bedesmen, and recognized by requiring indigence as a condition for gratuitous education.[1]

The school, therefore, was only part of a cluster of other institutions, with close links not only with their own Fellows but with King's College, Cambridge. The over-all head was the provost and not the headmaster, and this additional step in the hierarchy tended to distribute power and spread the agony of responsibility in times of adversity. In theory at least, Eton was far more than just a little teaching world, and yet, because fellowships went by internal promotion, Eton tended to become a narrow, closed, almost self-perpetuating society.

The closeness of the two foundations of Eton and Winchester to colleges at university level ensured some degree of similar treatment in every phase of life. It brought a similar outlook among the staffs, with a personal security and freedom of thought and speech unequalled in any other school in the country and only comparable to that found in the universities. On the material side Eton was faced, from its foundation in the fifteenth century, with the necessity of providing adequate surroundings for learned men not engaged in teaching, and by 1747 the external view was already imposing enough for Canaletto to paint it from across the Thames.[2] A century later, the buildings were a mixture of the beautiful and the austere, and although the chapel may have dominated the scene, this was more than matched by the neighbourhood of the castle and royalty at Windsor, the treasures of plate, the unique library and the vast archives. These were unmistakably the haunts of the aristocracy, while the possession of an ancient impressive façade emphasized the fact that the school was equally distinctive and a fit home for aristocrats' sons. This was the ideal, and if other schools were less impressive, Westminster, at least, was at the heart of influence and power alongside the abbey and the Houses of Parliament, while St Paul's was built within the shadow of the cathedral.

Winchester and Eton, with sister colleges of common foundation at Oxford and Cambridge, embodied a similar architectural style that came to be associated with learning, dignity

1. PSC, I, p. 101.
2. The painting can be seen in London in the National Gallery.

and solidity, and which was copied extensively. This was perhaps inevitable, since both trustees and headmasters at all major schools were university products themselves and the aura of their colleges was woven into their judgement. It was natural, therefore, that, when the accumulation of ample funds at Rugby made a new school possible, they erected between 1809 and 1813 the well-known structure that still survives with its quadrangle and cloisters, turrets and battlements.

If we glance at the drawings and plans of other schools in pre-Victorian times,[1] it is clear that the scale and newness of Rugby were unique.[2] Very few others had any claims whatever to permanence or architectural merit. Most were small and insignificant, mere adaptations of the country-cottage tradition. Occasionally under the influence of successful headmasters and governors with different ideas on building, successive extensions had produced an incredible mixture of styles, as at Barnstaple and Canterbury. A local shop partly obscured the premises in the city of Salisbury, while the buildings at Manchester and Marlborough were more reminiscent of corn exchanges than of schools. If we ignore the funereal and the ones in bad repair, only a few are left with any pretence to quality and size: Sherborne, Gloucester, Tonbridge, Harrow, Shrewsbury, Charterhouse, Christ's Hospital, Merchant Taylors', St Mary Overies, besides those already mentioned, namely Eton, Winchester, St Paul's, Westminster and Rugby. It is difficult to find others to add to this list, although it must be confessed that the more readily available contemporary illustrations do not always do justice to the buildings. With two exceptions all these schools are members of the Headmasters' Conference at the present day, and it is evident that style of building and survival over long periods of time are linked and that both are ultimately related to the amount of money available. If we eliminate the seven major boarding schools and three others

1. Illustrations can be seen in various school histories. The outstanding source of pictures of the main schools is: R. Ackermann, *The History of the Colleges of Winchester, Eton and Westminster* . . ., 1816. A wider selection of school illustrations, but without the same artistic quality, is given in J. C. Buckler, *Fifty Views of Endowed Grammar Schools*, 1827.

   Comparative descriptions of the schools can be seen in Carlisle, *A Concise Description of the Endowed Grammar Schools of England and Wales* . . ., 1818.
2. For some details of the buildings at Rugby, see M. H. Bloxam, *Rugby, the School and Neighbourhood*, 1889, p. 4 *et seq.*

of historical significance—St Paul's, Merchant Taylors' and Christ's Hospital—there were less than half a dozen other school buildings in the country worth considering, and most of these were small.

Pre-Victorian critics were well aware of the position. The excellence of Eton, Winchester, Rugby and one or two London schools were taken for granted; the rest were usually passed over in silence. Only occasionally could they say anything positive, as in the case of Shrewsbury: '. . . a large and stately edifice of Grinshill stone, standing on two sides of a court . . .'.[1] On the other hand Carlisle found the buildings at Harrow quite unworthy: '. . . a building little calculated to call forth the admiration of the casual spectator by any architectural embellishment . . . this unambitious structure . . .'.[2]

The fact is that buildings of quality cost a great deal of money and the prosperity of the schools was too precarious, as we have seen, for any risks to be taken. Only with a substantial endowment could anything worth while be achieved, as at Rugby. Otherwise schools had to wait for more prosperous times in the late 1850s and after. Even then, the new demands of specialization, with laboratories and special classrooms, were resisted by headmasters simply on the grounds of cost.

Buildings, however magnificent, cannot be viewed in isolation. From the upper-class viewpoint they are not even perhaps the most important feature. Plenty of space was essential. The main street of the town of Rugby, for instance, may have been opposite the main gate, but all around and at the back was open country for miles: the thirteen acres of playing-field in 1837 was only the core. The school itself looked directly on to the close with its row of elms and its own particular history of rebellion and of the birth of a new kind of football. Beyond, all the fields and byways were open, with swimming and fishing pools a long way off. As a school specializing in the education of the gentry, it already had most of the trappings of the gentry's way of life. The buildings and site, however, although extensive, were new; to the sensitive mind they lacked both significance and historical tone. It worried Arnold: 'I envy Winchester its

1. Carlisle, op. cit., II, p. 385.
2. Carlisle, op. cit., II, p. 126.

antiquity, and am therefore anxious to do all that can be done to give us something of a venerable outside, if we have not the nobleness of old associations to help us.' [1]

Rugby, however, had the essentials—space, buildings and clientele. Without the space the clientele withered, and this, to some extent, explains the tragedy of the London schools. By the time of Victoria space was already limited and growth impossible, and all the metropolitan schools were trapped in cobbles and brick. Merchant Taylors' had virtually no playing-field at all of its own, neither had St Paul's, although it rented part of Kennington Oval for cricket in the summer. Strangely enough, the staffs in London hardly seemed to be aware that any problem existed. Perhaps the vision of gentry-like surroundings for top-class schools was new—and there are grounds for taking this view seriously—or perhaps, by 1860, they had lived with this situation for so long that their educational vision was dimmed. Certainly the fact that these schools recruited their staffs largely from their own old boys helped towards this parochial attitude and towards maintaining contentment with their own sub-standards. The High Master of St Paul's, the Rev. H. Kynaston, expressed this narrow point of view to the Royal Commission: 'St Paul's, being wholly a day school, the question of further accommodation in the way of playgrounds is of less consequence.' [2] Open space was for him merely ground to be used by the boys in play, and it is not without significance that he ran a school catering for the sons of the lower and middle classes. Such a sentiment could not possibly have emerged from Eton or Harrow, Winchester or Rugby, for it ignored absolutely the winds and fields of country life, and the lack of the sense of freedom derived from the open country which was the privilege of the gentry. In London even the five acres of Charterhouse were swamped on all sides. An official description of the third side lining those few green acres went as follows: '. . . partly separated by a high wall from Goswell Street, partly enclosed by a wall separating it from St Thomas's Church, and by a side of a factory for the manufacture of railway carriages, and by the wall of the fives court'.[3]

1. A. P. Stanley, *Life of Thomas Arnold*, 1901, p. 137.
2. PSC, II, p. 242.
3. PSC, II, p. 227.

It was past redemption. Nothing could make such surroundings a true haunt of the gentry.

There were similar problems at Westminster, and James Mure in 1862 gave his opinion about them:

I confess the greatest difficulty we experience is to . . . give it that appearance which would be more in accordance with the views of the present generation of what a great public school should be. If you could clear away everything between the school and the Abbey, and make the Abbey one side of a quadrangle of which the other three sides should be composed of handsome Tudor buildings . . . so as to make a clean appearance, like the colleges at Oxford and Cambridge, people would come to you and be so pleased with the appearance of it that you would have the school full almost directly.[1]

How much of the unpopularity of Westminster at this time was due to the built-up area and the uncomfortable presence of the lower classes is a matter of opinion, but certainly the school was at a low ebb throughout early- and mid-Victorian times, and so were the other London schools. The situation had changed drastically during the course of fifty years since post-Napoleonic times, when '. . . boarding houses were perfect pigstyes; yet the boys' fathers and mothers used to go and see them there, and they used to think nothing of it. Now nothing of that kind would be submitted to in the present day [1862].' [2]

However, it was not merely a question of tidying up dormitories. There had been a radical change in sensitivity and it was the whole school position which had driven away so many of the old aristocratic families from the London schools with a sense of shame. We repeatedly find the men-folk excusing themselves for not supporting their own school on the grounds that their wives objected to the London situation.[3] Health was also blamed. There was growing uneasiness about the relationship of slums, smells, poverty and disease, even before the work of Chadwick and others. This developed into general revulsion against overcrowded conditions. It may have been a fact, as the headmasters maintained, that children in London were in far better shape than their cousins in country schools, but no

1. PSC, ii, p. 426, Q. 919.
2. ibid.
3. An example of a man who argued from the point of view of the wives' objections was Sir James Graham.

one really took any notice. It was the rural atmosphere that
mattered rather than the facts, and some parents were outspoken enough to say quite plainly that Westminster was no
longer a suitable environment for their children and that they
had '. . . great objection to all the streets and courts around
the school'.[1]

Whatever the reason, there is no doubt that gentry and
gentry-like parents were loath to send their sons to London
schools in early- and mid-Victorian days. They were unpopular
throughout the period and everyone knew it. It had nothing to
do with staffing, character, boarding, the refinements of education—nothing in fact that was at all tangible. Without
anything specific to blame in the school itself, the only hope
seemed to lie in wholesale transportation. But even that was
not easy. Buildings, they soon discovered, suffered from one
immense disadvantage. The more solid and the more historic
they were, the more immovable they became, and the more
they anchored the school in impossible surroundings. As a
result arguments went on throughout Victoria's reign about
moving out into the country so that the schools could expand
and build new traditions.

In theory Westminster and Charterhouse had, as boarding
schools, a relatively free choice to go where they liked, while
the day schools, St Paul's and Merchant Taylors', had to stay
near the homes of their clientele, or as near to them as the
scientific revolution made necessary. By the 1860s boys were
already travelling by train and omnibus as much as two hours
a day to St Paul's, and this school was therefore affected by the
new developments, partly by the physical growth of London
proper, and partly by the apparent growth through increased
ease of travel.[2] A central site at the cathedral itself was
now only essential so long as they tried to scour all London for
their boys, a procedure which the growth of the city had, by
1860, made quite unrealistic. St Paul's was therefore torn two
ways. Space was important, but so too were its links with the
cathedral and all the nostalgia that the influential old boys felt

1. Rev. C. B. Scott in PSC, III, p. 444.
2. For the influence of the new mode of travelling in the metropolis and its
effect on the schools, see Rev. H. Kynaston's comments in PSC, IV, p. 92,
Q. 951 *et seq.* Also, see comments of Rev. C. Lane, ibid., p. 77, Q. 141.

for it. The story of the London schools demonstrates what a long and agonizing process this business was of shifting site. St Paul's only managed it in 1884, Charterhouse in 1872, Christ's Hospital in 1902 and Merchant Taylors' in modern times in 1933. Only Westminster remained true. In this last case the resistance of old boys and the attractions of Westminster Abbey and the Houses of Parliament were too strong even for the pressure of a prime minister—for at one time Lord Palmerston took an interest, selected his own ideal spot personally and led the school authorities to it by way of persuasion, only to meet with their blank refusal in the end.

London was not the only place to cramp its schools. Shrewsbury suffered in exactly the same way until Moss managed the transfer to the new buildings at Kingsland in 1882. The advantages of such a move were obvious, not only to the headmaster concerned, but also to parents caught in the eternal problem of choosing a school. The essence of this situation is to be seen in a delightful piece of fiction:

> I forgot, my dear, Shrewsbury's no longer in a hole; its moved. It's on a hill now, towering above the town and river. Just the very place: new buildings, old traditions. What could possibly be better? Shrewsbury's the place for him. I shall enter his name instantly—this evening.[1]

Before Victoria, appearances were perhaps not so important —the effect of the new buildings at Rugby on the number of entrants early in the century are an indication of that—but later on, changes of site were markedly beneficial. The effect of Charterhouse's removal to Godalming in 1872 was dramatic. In 1873 the number of boys was 268; three years later it was 500. Undoubtedly the accompanying publicity helped, but the result was none the less solid and to some extent explains the statement that '. . . in the interval between the retirement of Dr Russell (1832) and the removal of the school to Godalming (1872), Old Carthusians would do anything for their school except send their sons there'.[2]

The complex problems of site, buildings and acceptable surroundings are seen best of all in the cases of Harrow and

1. P. Cowburn, *A Salopian Anthology*, 1964, p. 209.
2. J. G. C. Minchin, *Our Public Schools, Their Influence on English History*, 1901, p. 39.

Eton. By the middle of the nineteenth century the growth of London was threatening the precincts of both schools, and twenty years later the situation became serious. In effect the schools met this challenge by sealing off the buildings with a green belt. In the case of Harrow, 220 acres were added in fourteen years after 1885 at a cost of £90,000. This development was expressed by C. Colbeck in 1898:

> The Harrow of the past, the Harrow of old memories, was a land of meadows and hedgerows. On whichever side it was approached it presented a delightful view of green slopes and red-roofed buildings, and above, the clustering trees of the Grove, the church spire, and the old school. Save for the houses on the western side, the eye looked straight upon a scene that was wholly rural. The romantic affection which gathers round an ancient public school is largely the outcome of local associations and is worth preserving at any cost. This is pre-eminently the case at places like Eton and Harrow. Both are national possessions. Both are inseparably bound up with the beauty and dignity of their surroundings. . . . A solid rampart has now been reared against attack on the London side.[1]

The same acquisition of an estate has taken place at every public school which has aspirations. Nowadays school precincts are an assortment of parkland, open space, school buildings and large houses, sheltering a sizeable community cut off from the outside world and with a secluded atmosphere suited to a life of elegance associated with the well-born and the well-to-do. A walk through these parts gives an impression of another, older world, reminiscent of a stately existence, of the studious calm and leisure to be felt in the cathedral close at Lichfield and elsewhere.

1. Quoted in E. W. Hewson and G. T. Warner, *Harrow School*, 1898, p. 155.

CHAPTER TWO

The Growth of the System (I):
Meeting New Social Demands by New Schools

The nineteenth century saw the growth of new boarding schools in the Anglican and public-school tradition. This growth had a remarkably sudden onset which happened, by chance, to coincide roughly with the accession of Queen Victoria, though it should be remembered that most of the schools had begun in a small way and built up gradually, while others, after a promising start, decayed or changed their status. The situation from the beginning of the century until half-way through Victoria's reign is shown in Table 1.

No less than seven Anglican schools which later achieved fame as boarding schools were born in the ten years 1840–9: Cheltenham, Marlborough, Rossall, Radley, Lancing, Brighton, Hurstpierpoint. This is very surprising, for whereas it is easy to understand the non-Anglican growth in the early years of the century since dissenters and others had previously been deprived of boarding accommodation, it is difficult at first sight to understand the significance of 1840 for Anglican development. The old-established public schools—Eton and the rest—were still suffering from a common depression and had plenty of accommodation to spare. Indeed, they were not really prosperous in terms of being continuously full for another twenty or thirty years after this date. This fact alone indicates that the old and the new schools were not competing for the same children, and that the new were formed in response to new social pressures which accompanied the steady growth of population owing to large families and increased health.

The early-Victorian period saw an acceleration of change in the pattern of life from an agricultural to an industrial society together with a steady movement from village to town—a

8

Table 1. *Foundation of public boarding schools by decades*
(England and Wales) 1800–69.[1]

	Number of public boarding schools founded			
	Church of England	Other denominations	Others	Total
1800–9	0	2	0	2
1810–19	0	2	0	2
1820–9	0	1	1	2
1830–9	0	1	1	2* (0)
1840–9	7	4	2	13† (9)
1850–9	5	0	0	5 (5)
1860–9	11	2	0	13§ (10)

* 1 school is now within the state system and 1 not within the 1962 definition as given in Table 20.

† 2 schools are now direct-grant, and 2 not within the 1962 definition as given in Table 20.

§ 1 school is now direct-grant and 2 not within the 1962 definition as given in Table 20.

migration that has never entirely ceased. Several new categories of highly competent men—engineers, scientists and managers —emerged to supervise these new developments and to begin their long struggle for social and academic recognition. Meanwhile the higher grades of the Civil Service and the old professions of the law, the church and medicine grew rapidly. The combined law and medical groups doubled in sixty years from the turn of the century to a total of 40,000 in England and

1. This table is based on the Victorian situation. For a comparison from the modern standpoint it should be compared with Table 20, p. 270. The corresponding figures from Table 20 are placed in brackets in the last column here. The differences are due to changes either in school independence or in lack of boarding growth in recent times. The table has been compiled from many sources, partly from publications listing public schools, partly from individual school histories, partly from SIC, etc. Schools with predominantly day scholars are not included. Schools which were essentially a reorganization at a particular date of some old foundation are also not included. No distinction has been made here between type of school at its origin, i.e. whether endowed, a private venture or proprietary, provided that adequate status was achieved. Other denominations include Quakers, Wesleyans, Noncomformists generally as well as Roman Catholics.

Wales. The clergy too had increased to over 16,000 by the same date (1861). Over-all figures like those quoted may give a general picture, but they should not blind us to the fact that they can be misleading, even if accurate on the face of it, for there is a general tendency to assume homogeneity in such a group so that the essential stratification is forgotten. The difficulties and complications of Victorian professional life and their effect on the public schools can be illustrated by concentrating on the complexities of one profession, taking the Anglican Church as our example.[1]

The upper ranks of the clergy resembled the aristocracy. Not only did many of them sit in the House of Lords, but archbishops and deans lived in palaces in affluence and luxury, any austerity coming from infrequently practised self-denial. They formed an *élite* with diverse ideals, since they were chosen by politicians who preferred radical or conservative members, as the case might be. Some were picked from the ranks of public-school headmasters, and one or two of these held great power in an advisory capacity to the government over a wide field covering education, welfare and all issues affecting the moral life of the nation.

At the next level down stood the rich livings, most of them at the disposal of the heads of leading families. Out of more than 11,000 benefices in England and Wales, over 6,500 were in the hands of private individuals. The colleges of Oxford and Cambridge accounted for almost 600, and schools, like Eton, for 146; the rest were at the disposal of the Crown and the bishops. The plums were kept for the favoured few, whether at Court, school or university. Within the family such livings were often reserved for younger sons, as in the case of the Stanleys, the Hares, Lawleys and Leycesters. Anyone lower in the social scale had to rely on friendship or to possess real ability coupled with the kind of restless, irrepressible energy shown by Charles Kingsley. As Miss Watt says:

> In those days a curate was not a sort of junior officer who would rise in time to higher rank. He was, as a rule, a permanently humble person who kept livings warm for younger sons, did the work of the pluralists' extra benefices on a small stipend, or kept the main

1. For some information concerning professional groups, see the reference given for p. 6 above, footnote 1.

parish going while the rector took his wife and family for a five or six months' tour on the continent.[1]

The lower ranks were haunted by an almost grinding poverty, seen bitterly at Haworth in the Brontës' day and in the novels of Trollope.

A sixth of the sons of the clergy found their way to the old public schools and represented, generally speaking, the wealthy apex of the pyramid, the 'family' rectories and deaneries, for education of this kind was clearly out of the question for the rest simply on grounds of cost. It is no wonder that any man with hopes of advancement cast an anxious and subservient eye on the numerous upper-class bestowers of livings. Knowing important rich people was essential, and this fact alone helps to explain the great value placed on school friendships as a means of entry into the 'right' circles. It is impossible to say how effective these friendships were in fact, but there is no denying that great hopes were, and still are, placed on them. Since only the upper ranks of the clergy could afford the public schools, the rest merely coveted the opportunities from afar, seeing chances slip by for their own children. In this way public-school education was seen as the background of influential people, and it followed that common youthful experience put patrons and protégés in touch with one another. The really important boys were at Eton and Harrow, and education in the same school was obviously preferable, but it was the public-school image as a type that was important, for similar schools produced similar products that spoke the same language. There was, therefore, a constant demand in the middle and late nineteenth century for cheap public-school education for the underpaid lower ranks of the clergy. The ambitions of the clergy in this respect applied equally to the other professions which were recognized by the upper classes, and where it was apparent that upper-class influence was very necessary for a successful career, as in the Civil Service, the law and the officers of the armed forces. It was this educational vacuum in the professional sphere that inspired the formation of both Cheltenham and Marlborough, if, as we shall see, in different ways.

1. Margaret H. Watt, *The History of the Parson's Wife*, 1943, p. 72.

The actual formation of schools, however, was only the second stage of a process which can be traced at least twenty years before the birth of Cheltenham. The first indications come with the appearance of a new kind of parent in the early 1820s. The most obvious cases concerned those families with a tradition of public-school education or a conviction of its worth, and who could no longer afford the fees or bear to be separated from their children. War widows are the most obvious examples, but there was plenty of tragedy otherwise in that unhealthy era, as in the all too frequent example of the tubercular father and healthy mother of many children that remained a haunting nightmare throughout the century. This situation was common enough for it to be said that the Victorians '. . . made a very serious business of widowhood. It was indeed a profession in itself, even before the seal of the highest example was set upon it.' [1]

These ladies with their bands of crape and pathetic burdens had grim determination and a high sense of duty. Many families were migratory by nature on account of the fathers' public service, either in administration or the army, at home or abroad. In one single case among many at Rugby, successive children in the same family had been born in the East Indies, Middlesex, Naples, Gloucester, Sussex and Rugby.

With such a background it is not surprising that widows and retired army and naval officers formed a mobile force that could, and did in many cases, move about the country with their children, living in temporary quarters wherever a suitable school could be found. Some were rich enough to buy and sell houses in the process, even to the employment of many servants, while others shared accommodation, and others again lived in rooms. Examples of all such were well known at Rugby, and it is said that the phenomenon was well developed at Bedford and elsewhere. No doubt it was widespread, though more evidence is needed on its nature and extent.[2]

These migratory folk who placed sons at Rugby were called sojourners by the townspeople. They began to arrive in 1821, and between them were soon accounting for eight to fifteen new

1. ibid.
2. T. W. Bamford, 'Public School Town in the Nineteenth Century', *British Journal of Educational Studies*, vi, no. 1, November 1957, pp. 25–36.

entrants each year. Perhaps the onset was connected with the changed situation after the Napoleonic Wars and the discharge of many officers. However that may be, in the twenty years from 1844 to 1863, 130 families arrived in the town for the specific purpose of educating their sons locally. Sending one child to the school was exceptional, involving about a third of the parents only; the majority sent two or three, while seven families sent five children each, and one family seven. In almost every case the pattern was the same, arrival and departure of the family from the town corresponding strictly with the children's career at the school. At one time admissions of this type had threatened to become a flood, but after 1830 cheap education on the foundation was possible only after two years' residence in the town. While this might have been irksome for many, at least it did ensure that sojourners had some claims to be considered inhabitants of the town, and gave the headmaster some warning of future pressures. With the boys came sisters and younger brothers with the result that private preparatory schools were set up for coaching. In addition, some professional men, like doctors and teachers (including one specialist teacher of the deaf), took up residence and began to practise their arts until their sons finished at the school and the fathers were able to move on again. Sojourning persisted in this area throughout the century, and indeed still persists in strange forms, although the foundationer element was radically changed in 1874 by a qualification period and a qualifying examination from a local 'lower' school.

Socially, sojourners embraced all groups from the professional upwards. For example, in one year (1850) two such entrants to the school were from a titled background, seven were gentry and thirteen from various professional groups.

From all this it would appear that in the early-Victorian period this migratory phenomenon was relatively new and represented not only a firm recognition of the value of public-school education, but a growing pressure for such education at reduced cost, and perhaps with the home influence as well. The fact that these people made the long trek to Rugby rather than patronizing a more convenient local grammar school indicates that the attraction was the aura of Rugby rather than the education itself. It is apparent from this that the social

attraction of Rugby was already significant by the 1820s, and for every sojourner there must have been a great many who watched their efforts enviously while themselves tethered to professional or family duties.

Mere demand for boarding education cannot produce new schools by itself. It may set people thinking and create a suitable climate for the production of a new venture, but fulfilment requires a great deal of planning and money. The old schools had started in a small way centuries before, helped by endowments often in the form of property which had grown valuable throughout the years and which had helped many a schoolmaster over hard times, and in some cases provided a growing reserve for expansion. To build a new school from scratch for any significant number of pupils in up-to-date buildings was a very expensive operation, and methods of raising money in the nineteenth century were variations on many themes of which four must receive attention if any understanding of the position is to be obtained.

In tune with developments in industry and commerce, the whole venture could be treated as a business operation by virtually floating a company and offering shares in the undertaking. Secondly, a school could be founded by public appeal as a national monument, akin to the manner in which Churchill College at Cambridge has been built in our own time. In addition, public benefactors, inspired by religion or social conscience, could continue the age-old tradition of founding schools, and in one celebrated case (Woodard) new business methods were introduced which combined successful advertising campaigns with subtle pressures to extract donations from rich individuals. Finally, as a fourth possibility, the vast number of educational endowments that existed all over the country could have been reorganized. Occasionally endowments increased rapidly in value, as at Dulwich, but such instances were rare. Usually the amounts were small and only in the mass did their total become significant. It did not require a great deal of imagination to see that by a system of coalescence and reorganization something more substantial and worth while could be achieved. This was the simplest and most promising scheme of all. On paper it was a simple matter to

juggle with the figures and create a new educational system on a national scale. This was a favourite theme for educational theorists throughout Victorian times, but it did not become a practical proposition until the later years of the century, and its consideration must be left to another context (Chapter 7). The real results in terms of school-founding came in the first instance from the other methods, and can be illustrated by reference to Cheltenham, Marlborough, Wellington and Lancing.

Cheltenham was in part a local venture. The sponsors enticed people to invest their money by giving them power—the power to select their own guinea-pigs. Like many similar schools of the period, it was run, in theory at least, as a business, although the crude realities of profit and loss were softened by the introduction of an impressive governing body called a Council. Proprietors had privileges. Each share carried with it the right to nominate one pupil, and a similar though more complicated situation existed at Marlborough, where two grades of governor existed with two different sets of rewards: at the lower level a governor could select one boy for the sum of £50, while for £100 he was raised to the rank of life governor with the privilege of filling one place in the school for life.

The success of Cheltenham does not surprise us now, for it was an ideal spot for a new venture of this kind, although whether the advantages seen in retrospect would have been quite so clear in 1840 is another matter. As a spa it was a fashionable meeting-place for the gentry and near-gentry, and a place of retirement for '. . . the old Indians, civil and military, the fleeting remnants of whose livers sent them to drink the Cheltenham waters'.[1] They were of the same species as the sojourners who brought complications to Rugby and elsewhere, but here, instead of travelling in search of education, good education was brought to their own doorstep. It is not surprising, therefore, that when the school opened in July 1841, 129 boys arrived, and that, of the 145 boys who entered in the first year, ninety-two were from parents who lived locally. Details given in the published register reveal that these local people were drawn entirely from the gentry and professional classes, including officers of the army and navy, with the Indian

1. A. F. Leach, *A History of Bradfield College*, 1900, p. 3.

contingent very prominent. Altogether three-quarters of those with known family backgrounds came from the professional ranks; tradesmen were excluded:

Had we admitted tradesmen in the first instance, we must have done so almost without limit, and in the confined circle of shops in Cheltenham, we should have had the sons of gentlemen shaking hands perhaps with school-fellows behind the counter, and a fusion of ranks taking place from which the gentleman of decided rank and property would derive even less inconvenience, possibly, than the clergymen of confined income or half-pay officers.[1]

This is frank, to say the least, and shows how Cheltenham managed to preserve its upper-class nature, and accounts in part for its rapid recognition as a public school.

From this early beginning Cheltenham developed rapidly with a national and yearly intake that fell below a hundred in two successive years only, 1844 and 1845. Even more significant than its success was the new role in education which it presented. It faced the fact squarely that in the new world the old standards and old ideas were outmoded, and that some of its sons would have to earn a living. The targets were those professions acceptable to the social standing of its clients. The main outlets were the army and the Civil Service, both at home and overseas, and, to a lesser extent, the law and the church. However, with the new discoveries in science many of these jobs were technical, based on a new mass of knowledge and insight that was not necessarily related to the nimble mind which was the goal, if not the achievement, of the old classical school. New languages had to be mastered, and new foundations laid for careers, with stiff examinations to pass. As Staunton expressed it: 'The reading of the higher classes being mainly guided by the Woolwich and Sandhurst examinations, which are to this department [of the school] what the University course is to a high Classical school.' [2]

Half the senior school was conceived in the classical mould of Eton or Harrow, and the other geared to a job of work. The sceptics sneered at the vocational side, but it would require a mind totally deadened by tradition to deny some romance and

1. Taken from a letter from the Honorary Secretary of Cheltenham College, quoted in G. P. Burstow and M. B. Whittaker, *A History of Brighton College*, edited by S. C. Roberts, 1957, p. 5.
2. H. Staunton, *The Great Schools of England*, 1865, p. 485.

cultural value to this 'military and civil side', when we read
the following: 'Extras—Sanscrit, Hindustani and Persian
languages. . . .' [1]

Cheltenham is a landmark, not only because it happened to
be the first of the major Victorian schools but because it combined great success with undoubted reputation, both for the
classics and the accepted career of government service. Its
excellent start was owing to the local resident pool of retired
men, some of them still young and others with a backlog of high
responsibility at home or overseas—erstwhile members of *élites*.

Marlborough, though more adventurous in some ways, was
essentially a copy of the old foundations. It was the brain child
of a clergyman who had the notion of creating a national
boarding school, equivalent to the seven, but far cheaper, so
that the ordinary clergymen would benefit. Two-thirds of the
school was to be reserved for the sons of the clergy at a cost of
30 guineas a year, with the lay element paying an extra 20
guineas in the hope that this would effectively subsidize the
lower rate of fees. It was poor economics and A. F. Leach
epitomized the situation exactly, if a little cruelly, '. . . the
Marlborough model, the barrack and caravanserai type, aiming
at cheapness by dint of a common life'.[2]

The site was chosen partly on account of its nearness to
Swindon, in the hope that it would develop, like Rugby, into
a nerve centre of the new railway system. More than 200 boys
arrived on the first day, and in four years the number on roll
had swollen to 500, a remarkable achievement for a school
without a large endowment and with financial ideas which
many claimed to be naïve. Even so numbers began to fall later,
and the school only recovered under a new direction and with
the introduction of a 'modern' side copied from Cheltenham.

Cheltenham and Marlborough are typical of the joint-stock
business method of starting a school. Technically they were
known as proprietary schools, and as such were, at first, carefully distinguished from the older, endowed variety. However,
it is not the technicalities so much as the nature of the clientele
that determines the reputation and status of a school, and the
more successful proprietary boarding schools soon obtained

1. ibid., p. 486.
2. Leach, op. cit., p. 3.

recognition. Indeed, the same general pattern seen at Cheltenham and Marlborough was followed at Brighton, Rossall,
Taunton, Epsom, Clifton, Malvern, Haileybury and elsewhere.
Business methods are still used, for the problem of capital and
investment still remains, but there is no doubt that the nineteenth century saw a climax to provisions of large sums of
money in this way without too many strings. It gave sufficient
scope for the headmasters to develop the schools as they wished,
and that was enough.

Paradoxically, the same freedom was not so readily given in
an outstanding case of a school which was to be raised by a
national appeal for funds. The Duke of Wellington died on
14 September 1852 and the question of a suitable memorial
arose. He had been such a mighty figure for so long that no one
doubted that an enormous sum would result from a public
appeal. It was reasonable, therefore, to think of the memorial
in somewhat grandiose terms, and the prime minister himself
took the matter in hand. The family of the duke was traditional
enough to want a bronze statue in every town in the country,
but this was vetoed at a royal discussion at Balmoral in favour
of a college devoted to 'the gratuitous or nearly gratuitous
education of Orphan children of Indigent and Meritorious
Officers of the Army'.[1]

This was a project which appeared to start with every possible
advantage. The Queen and Prince Consort were interested and
involved, and so were the prime minister and the government,
not to mention the opposition. The publicity concerning the
death and the pomp of the funeral was a long-drawn-out affair.
Yet, in spite of it all and the compulsory levy of a day's pay
from all ranks in the army, not to mention the writing of
100,000 letters, only £105,000 was collected, with a meagre
£5,000 to £6,000 after a second appeal. They could hardly
have raised less money for statues. For some reason or other
millions of admirers of the Iron Duke did not see in this school,
however worthy it might have seemed to the Prince Consort
and the upper classes, a fitting memorial for a great man.

The sum raised was nowhere near enough for the ideas the
sponsors had in mind. The education of girls had to be dropped,
the gratuitous or nearly gratuitous education drastically

1. D. Newsome, *A History of Wellington College, 1859–1959*, 1959, p. 9.

modified, and the scale of the buildings reduced. The building problem was particularly interesting. It was assumed that a memorial to a man of this calibre could not be skimped or made to look entirely functional, and yet, when all the other necessary allocations had been made, there was only £29,000 left. The government itself was none too helpful; it even appeared to be obstructive in refusing loans, in vetoing the use of Kneller Hall and being reluctant to negotiate a site in Chelsea. Altogether the organizers must have found the whole business depressing in the extreme. It is entirely to their credit that the buildings which eventually went up on healthy soil near the railway still look so magnificent and in keeping with the Prince Consort's opinion of officers as 'the gentry of the country'.[1] An architect with a critical eye might call the style 'flimsy baroque', but to the ordinary mortal it is impressive enough and shows the value of an endowment which does not have to be entirely husbanded for income and teaching.

Wellington is particularly interesting for the interplay which existed between the virtual founder (the Prince Consort), the commemorative figure (the Iron Duke) and the living representative of that figure (the second duke). The Queen and her Consort, together with the prime minister, virtually steamrollered their orphan school through against all opposition. The family of the duke, who were closest to him in sympathy, could not see that the care of orphans was a fitting tribute, and were not mollified by the sight of the building. This situation had all the ingredients of tragedy, for it is difficult to sustain the myth of a worthy memorial in the teeth of family bitterness. Only when Benson, the first headmaster, managed somehow to defy royalty without appearing to do so, and turn the school from a functional place of learning into a major public school, was the family reconciled. Benson had performed a miracle for them; they were grateful and genuinely sorry when he resigned after fifteen years. At the end of the ceremony marking Benson's farewell the duke took the headmaster on one side and tried to apologize for the poor speech he had made earlier in the day:

'Made a hash of it—Knew I should—Always do. . . . This is what I meant to say. . . . I and my family hoped that there would

1. ibid., p. 10.

be a fine monument set up . . . in every considerable town in England. And you can fancy what our feelings were when we found that it was going to be lumped together and a charity school built with it where scrubby little orphans could be maintained and educated. . . . By great good fortune the Governors found you and made you the first Headmaster and you have made the College what it is—not a mere Charity School—but one of the finest Public Schools in England—and I and my family are more than content at the result. There[digging Benson hard in the ribs with his elbow], that's my speech, that's what I meant to have said and so I say it to you—But Lord when I stood up to speak, it all ran out at my heels.' [1]

No man has ever received a more handsome tribute, yet this makes the whole problem of the purpose and fulfilment of endowments more difficult. One's sympathies are with the duke and his family, yet in the event their original viewpoint was wrong, although whether the general public, which had failed to subscribe, would have agreed is another matter. In the same way it is difficult not to sympathize with the Prince Consort, who, according to David Newsome, '. . . had little regard for the current system of education at the Public Schools. He disliked their classical bias, their lack of appreciation of the study of history . . . their complete disregard of the natural sciences'.[2]

Essentially the Prince wanted a sharp break with the past, while Lord Derby and Benson did not, and neither, in the outcome, did the second duke. Whether the Iron Duke himself would have agreed with any of them, or even preferred a school to statues, or for that matter have chosen something entirely different, we shall never know.

Wellington was unique. It was the only recent school with such royal interest, and the only significant one, apart from Framlingham, set up as a modern memorial.

If finance without recourse to joint stock made the founding of Wellington difficult but possible, then anything more ambitious would appear to be out of the question, yet Nathaniel Woodard performed this seemingly impossible feat several times.[3]

1. ibid., pp. 173–4.
2. ibid., p. 70.
3. For Woodard generally, see Sir J. Otter, *Nathaniel Woodard, a Memoir of his Life*, 1925; W. B. D. Heeney, *The Established Church and the Education of the Victorian Middle Classes. A Study of the Woodard Schools, 1847–1891* (D.Phil. Thesis for the University of Oxford), 1961.

There was nothing of the John Lyon or William of Wykeham about this new man. He was not content with one school, even though it might be of the calibre of Harrow or Winchester or Wellington; nothing less than a vast organization of schools arranged in a triple hierarchy would satisfy him, and he was successful enough to see several of them started before he died and to see one or two admitted into the jealous company of the old endowed schools.

It is a little uncertain when the national picture matured in Woodard's mind, but there is good evidence to suggest that he started by trying to cure a local social problem as early as 1847 and worked up rapidly. This issue concerned the ignorance of the people of his parish of Shoreham, and in particular the failure of sea captains to understand the art and science of navigation. From this beginning his ideas developed quickly and within two years he had founded two schools—Lancing and Hurstpierpoint—with many more to come. They were merely the first instalment of a plan based essentially on the fear that Christian civilization was threatened. These ideas were the driving-force behind his thinking from the start, but they are perhaps best expressed in a letter to Bishop Fraser on 13 June 1871, twenty years later:

> Somehow or other we must get possession of the Middle Classes, especially the lower section of them, and how can we so well do this as through Public Schools. . . . Education without religion is, in itself, a pure evil—nothing more or less—and engenders the opposite form of selfishness to that which is the curse of an evil aristocracy. Secular education makes Communists and Red Republicans. . . . Unless the Church, therefore, gets possession of this class at whatever cost, we shall reap the fruits, in some day of distress, of an universal deluge. . . .[1]

This could well be a quotation from Thomas Arnold, except that the religious thought underlying it was Anglo-Catholic.

The scheme was grandiose. Christian education in England was to be controlled by 125 senior fellows divided into five regions of twenty-five senior fellows each. These were to be responsible for organizing three grades of public boarding schools, as well as providing whatever day schools were necessary.

1. Otter, op. cit., pp. 240–1.

Woodard was primarily concerned with the middle classes. The regeneration of Anglicanism in England was to be achieved through them, and the lower classes were ignored since they were devoid of power and therefore not of prime importance as an instrument of national salvation. In the first place he also ignored the upper classes, since they already possessed their own Christian boarding education; indeed it was largely a copy of that particular kind of education that Woodard was trying to create for boys lower down the social ladder. Unfortunately, when we try to define the social terms—upper, middle, lower— a little more precisely, we are at once faced with a difficulty in that Woodard's own view on the composition of the various classes appeared to vary from time to time. Thus, royalty, the nobility and the landed gentry were excluded in the early scheme, and yet noblemen came to be included later. In this way he widened the scope at the top of the social pyramid and, presumably, the catchment rose accordingly beyond the strict confines of the middle class. In a similar way, at the lower section of the middle class, he included quite small tradesmen, mechanics, clerks, pedlars and hawkers. This makes heavy inroads into the lower classes, and it would seem that Woodard was not concerned so much with the niceties of sociological classification as with the kind of person likely to rise in society and hence become a potential nucleus of Anglican strength. In this way he was concerned with the creation of 'cells' of influence. Having regard to these difficulties, his three grades of schools were geared to three social levels within a rather broad and fluctuating framework.

The top grade was for the rich, for the sons of gentlemen and professional men including clergymen. The next was for superior tradesmen, the semi-professionals and farmers. The third and lowest grade of school was to be designed for small tradesmen, farmers and artisans undergoing social mobility. We shall see later that echoes of the three divisions outlined by Woodard are to be found in other educational schemes, and especially in the recommendations of the Taunton Commission.

The profits from the top-grade schools were to help out finances elsewhere and keep the whole system self-supporting. On paper the plan was solid if meagre, and logical too, provided we are willing to accept the Victorians' callousness in

their attitude to the lower orders. A top-grade school of 300 boys, charging £30 per annum a boy, should make a yearly profit of £2,000, and a second grade of 200 boys at £14 each, a 'positive margin' of £300.[1] Woodard worked from the example of cheap existing schools and based the calculations for his own lower school on the diet sheet of the London Orphan Asylum. On these assumptions the scheme would support itself once the buildings were provided, and for these he relied on the generosity of the upper and middle classes.

A provost was to be in charge of each of the five regions, with Woodard himself the reluctant provost of the south. His headquarters were at Lancing, and this school was destined, therefore, to be a kind of mother to a very large number of offspring and a meeting-place for all involved in the plan. This explains the dual nature of the school and the creation of the cathedral-like chapel which appears to conflict with an otherwise parsimonious approach. Needless to say the fulfilment of a policy of this magnitude needed drive and devotion, and it is not surprising that the south was the only really successful region for many years, with boarding schools at Lancing (1848), Hurstpierpoint (1849) and Ardingly (1858). Unlike Cheltenham and Marlborough, however, these did not spring at once into the public-school category, in spite of the classical curriculum, for neither the clientele nor the cost were restrictive enough and they had a slow uphill fight for recognition.

Again we are reminded of the character of Arnold. The grand scheme worked out in meticulous detail is typical Arnold, and so is the practical attempt to solve a serious social issue. Woodard also had the same religious drive and impatience of criticism, the same quarrelling nature. There, however, the similarity ceases, for Arnold would never have agreed to the principle of cheapness since this would have resulted in a lower standard of staff and teaching. Woodard was not a teacher and had no claim to magnetic personality. Even so, like Arnold, he managed to hold the friendship of great and influential men like Gladstone and Salisbury. He used them unmercifully as publicity agents, as main attractions at collection meetings, and

1. For the charges and profits in the various grades of school, see B. W. T. Handford, *Lancing, A History of SS. Mary and Nicholas College, Lancing, 1848–1930*, 1933, p. 22.

even as sources of wealth. He was unrivalled in the practical combination of financial skill coupled with ruthlessness and continual success in extracting money from the same person time after time.

By the normal standards of starting schools, Woodard was enormously successful, though his achievement fell far below his own ideas. He failed to provide able provosts at the other four centres he had continually in mind. Time was against him. In the words of Matthew Arnold:

> Mr Woodard proposes to establish one great school in Sussex, where he has got two already. What sort of a provision is this for that need which is, on his own showing, so urgent? He hopes, indeed, that 'if the public will assist in raising this one school, it will lead to a general extension of middle class education all over England.' But in what number of years? How long are we to wait first?[1]

To some extent Woodard's failure arose from his own narrowness of outlook and complete lack of touch with reality. He persisted in his idea of church–state and the supremacy of Anglicanism to the end, even when it was quite out of date and clear to everyone else that that particular hope was dead. On the other hand his first eye was on his schools, and he was prepared to swallow other Christian views for the ultimate good of his society. He had enough sense also to see the shallowness of the Tractarian conquest and the necessity for a broad religious face to the world—his acceptance of Nonconformist pupils is proof of that, and so was his choice of Augustus Hare as a team-mate.

Woodard was not the only Victorian to have such national schemes in mind. Most educational men of repute had their dreams, and if one combines all the various possibilities of school foundation that existed, with the various kinds of education suitable for boys and girls, then parallels can be found in plenty. Sewell[2] of Radley is a case in point, but the nearest perhaps was the Rev. J. L. Brereton, with another triple grading of schools. The three divisions here were remarkably similar to those of Woodard, and based similarly on geography and social class. The lowest grade was the poorest and the most numerous with one school for each set of parishes, the second with one school

1. Matthew Arnold, *A French Eton*, 1892 ed., pp. 53–4.
2. For Sewell, see A. K. Boyd, *The History of Radley College, 1847–1947*, 1948.

4

for each county, and the first grade was the most exclusive with
one school to serve several counties. This plan, based as it was
on national need and the details of the social system, has
obvious links with Woodard even if it was a little later in time
(1858). Brereton's panacea for foundation, however, was essentially that of Cheltenham, namely the selling of shares with a
5 per cent dividend—a solution that Woodard would not have
considered.

All this activity did not pass unnoticed. Woodard was both
liked and hated, and his actions, like the law of Newton,
produced inevitable reactions. Some people imitated his ideas,
while other schools, like Trent College, were set up in deliberate
opposition.

Looking back it is clear that any grandiose scheme based on
the church was doomed before it began. Not only was the
influence of the church itself in decline, but it faced the long
probing of charities which had started with Brougham and was
the subject of constructive criticism by a succession of men
through Lytton Bulwer[1] and Temple to Matthew Arnold.
These made state intervention and a massive middle-class
'secondary' network inevitable, as we shall see.

In these various ways, as exemplified by joint stock (Cheltenham), Wellington and Woodard, a large number of new schools
were born. Between the accession of Queen Victoria and 1869
no less than thirty-one classical boarding schools were founded,
and this figure does not include independent day schools or old
endowed grammar schools which had acquired new energy and
life. This does not mean that thirty-one new names were added
automatically to the public-school list, for schools have to grow
and there is a natural resistance to the recognition of any new-
comers, if only to prevent dilution. Any addition to the ranks—
even of a single school—meant some slight modification to the
definition of the very term public school, and added a little
vagueness. In every case there were social implications as well,
and the fact that the recent upstarts were new schools meant
that the old insistence on antiquity and tradition was threatened.

By 1870—or rather 1868, since 1869 was a fallow year—the
first rush of Victorian expansion in public schools was at an end.

1. See E. L. Bulwer, *England and the English*, 1836.

The next decade, 1870–9, only saw four new boarding schools which have since acquired recognition compared with the thirteen set up in the 1860s.

The middle 1860s would therefore be a convenient halting-place for a review of the position, especially since a commission appointed by the government to investigate public schools had just reported.

The Public Schools, or Clarendon, Commission—either name is used indiscriminately—was set up in 1861 and reported in 1864. Since it was only empowered to investigate the nine schools specifically mentioned in its terms of reference, this long report in four volumes conferred a superior and unchallengeable status upon Eton, Harrow, Winchester, Rugby, Westminster, Charterhouse, Shrewsbury, St Paul's and Merchant Taylors'. In this investigation these nine were compared with several others and particularly with Cheltenham, Marlborough and Wellington as boarding schools, and a few more like the City of London and King's College School. It is impossible to read these volumes without coming to the conclusion that the Commissioners believed that at least Cheltenham, Marlborough and Wellington were already established in the same bracket as the nine. In this they not only reflected public opinion but helped to form it, and the new influence was seen immediately in Staunton's *The Great Public Schools of England* published in the very next year (1865). It included the following significant statement:

> The original scheme of this volume comprehended no more than the ten Great Endowed Schools of England [the nine plus Christ's Hospital]. In compliance, however, with the request of many persons interested in the subject, it has been thought proper to append a brief account of the four chief Modern Proprietary Schools, Cheltenham, Marlborough, Rossall and Wellington, and of one more Foundation, Dulwich College, which, from the rapidly increasing wealth of its endowment, is surely destined under wise administration, to become one of the grandest educational establishments in Britain.[1]

Hitherto the term 'public school' had been reserved by many for the ancient endowed schools, but this simple classification was already out of date and was widening to include some successful new schools giving not only a classical education but

1. Staunton, op. cit., p. 481.

also having a parallel vocational bias in the so-called 'modern' sides. More important perhaps than any other single factor was the boys' social class. Before 1850 the gentry and aristocracy in schools outside the seven could be ignored; after that date they were beginning to patronize the new establishments. At Cheltenham the landed gentry was present from the beginning, and a member[1] of a peer's family entered with the very first batch in July 1841. Before 1865, seven boys inheriting titles are recorded in the register. Clearly Cheltenham had already become socially acceptable, as had Wellington, and no doubt Marlborough.

This social element was really the distinguishing feature of these public schools. Other factors, such as boarding or the classics, were not diagnostic, and it should be kept continually in mind that the schools we are considering were only providing a small part of the total classical boarding education in the country as a whole.

In 1865 about 25,000 boys in England and Wales were receiving a classical education. We can be fairly certain of this figure since the Taunton Commission was sitting at this time and the provision of each school was itemized and the nature of the instruction checked by inspectors well briefed in the efforts of headmasters to veil the truth and hoodwink the Commission. These 25,000 boys were engaged in classical, as distinct from semi-classical and elementary, education, and were almost equally divided into boarding and day scholars. The details, by type of school, are shown in Table 2.

No less than 209 endowed grammar schools were involved in giving a classical education, not to mention forty-six major proprietary schools, apart from a host of others where the classics were taught to smaller numbers. Investigating all these in detail, apart from accepting the work of inspectors at the time, would be a titanic task, and all we can say is that many were striving for recognition as public schools but that most of them fell short.

In following the general growth of the present system it would be easy to pick out from the list of 255 those which have since become successful, but within the context of a particular period that process would not only be unfair to individual schools but

1. The future Viscount Molesworth.

Table 2. *Scholars receiving a classical education in about the year 1865.*[1]

	Boarders	Day	Total
Endowed grammar schools with some boarders	9,300	7,080	16,380
Endowed grammar schools, day only	0	2,800	2,800
Proprietary (classical only) schools	3,350	2,680	6,030
Total	12,650	12,560	25,210

would give a totally inaccurate picture. At the same time some arbitrary criteria must be adopted to distinguish one from another. The educational implications will be considered later, but in our present context it seems reasonable to suggest that for any claim to public-school stature, even in embryo, the school must provide a classical education and be expensive enough to exclude the lower and lower middle classes at least. As for size, schools were generally much smaller in 1865, and a minimum of eighty boarders might be considered a serious enough attempt to provide an adequate background, or at least a core on which the school might build. Acting on this basis, and ignoring the seven, we have to include nine old grammar schools and sixteen more recent establishments (including five sectarian), catering altogether for over 4,000 boarders (Anglican) and almost 700 non-Anglicans.[2] These figures should be

1. The material in this table was calculated from the individual school details given in SIC, 1868. Since the material was checked by inspection, the distinctions given in the report were accepted. There were, however, one or two matters which call for comment. The position of Marlborough is a case in point. It should be noted that the proprietary schools included Haileybury, Taunton, Clifton, Cheltenham, Rossall and others. The Commission distinguished carefully between classical, semi-classical, non-classical and elementary types of curriculum. It also noted schools which were in abeyance or defunct, or those in which the funds had been passed over to some other non-classical (e.g. national) school.
2. In addition there were three classical boarding schools with either specialist functions or socially inferior clientele which are therefore ineligible, at this stage, for our consideration: Christ's Hospital, Royal Naval School (New Cross) and Canterbury Clergy Orphans.

compared with the 2,500 boarders at the seven major boarding schools. Clearly, with twenty-five schools hot on their heels, the monopoly of the seven was over, upper-class education having already entered a new phase by the time the Public Schools (Clarendon) Report was published in 1864.

This new situation meant that new voices were being heard, voices important enough, as we shall see, for the initiative to be taken out of the hands of the old schools.

CHAPTER THREE

Changing Attitudes to Religion

In the years before the first Reform Bill the stability of the country was threatened. The lower orders had begun to organize themselves and to fight for their rights. Bloodshed and violent revolution were expected by many. At the same time the Church of England was itself in turmoil; its power was crumbling away, for its monopoly had gone and its main religious competitors were now recognized by Parliament. It may still have had strongholds, but the population in the towns was lost to apathy and dissent. Only a major revival could have restored the greatness of the church, and to anyone who believed in its sanctity the situation was perturbing indeed. The years immediately before Victoria produced several attempts to counteract the drift and rebuild the church. One was associated with Thomas Arnold[1] and another with Keble and John Henry Newman.

Arnold saw an answer to the economic, moral and religious problems of the nation in a strengthening of the idea of church–state with a reduction of meaningless dogma and a broadening of basic principles to include dissent. John Henry Newman wanted an intense religious revival, with an accent on the holiness of the church and a repudiation of state interference. Meanwhile the politicians were forced to accept radical views on parliamentary reform as expressed in the Reform Bill of 1832, and to interfere more and more in church affairs through their involvement with Ireland. From the public-school point of view the campaigns of Arnold, Newman and Woodard were important, and to a large extent interwoven.

1. For the background of Arnold's religious views, see R. J. Campbell, *Thomas Arnold*, 1927; C. R. Sanders, *Coleridge and the Broad Church Movement*, 1942; A. P. Stanley, *Life and Correspondence of Dr Arnold*, 1844; T. W. Bamford, *Thomas Arnold*, 1960 (with bibliography).

Arnold was appointed to Rugby in 1827 and died in 1842, so his work overlaps the beginning of the Victorian era. His views on church reform were given to the world in two pamphlets, the second of which, entitled *Principles of Church Reform*, came out in January 1833, only six months before John Keble's sermon in July which precipitated the Oxford Movement. The sequence of events is no mere coincidence, for the new work was forthright and typical of a trend in thought that was religious treason for those who believed in the historical sanctity of the church. Keble was shocked; he broke off his intimate friendship with Arnold and the sermon at Oxford was the first shot in his counter-offensive. In a very real sense Arnold both helped to create and, ultimately, to defeat the religious issue that dominated the nineteenth century. It is indicative of his enormous energy that he was able to accomplish all this while he was also teaching boys and running a school.

Arnold based his religion squarely on the life and example of Christ without any of the frills that man has since added. The trappings and organization of the church and pronouncements by leaders in the past, however eminent, were therefore subject to logical analysis and, if necessary, to rejection. Added to this simplicity of approach to a religious and moral basis of life was a passionate nature which involved him in the contemporary scene and produced urgency and a driving force through his fear of rebellion and social unrest. As a supreme rebel himself he was sympathetic to lower-class objectives, but also frightened of their ignorance, their power and sheer destructiveness when led by mob orators. This was a haunting fear that literally kept him awake at nights, and was only balanced by his great hope for a revival of the idea of church–state, with every citizen involved in the struggle for the good life. The leaders of the movement he visualized could only come from the church on the one hand and the upper classes on the other. The church had to be broadened and its outmoded tenets, like the Thirty-Nine Articles, revised or removed so that a common front could be made with dissent. The church would then become a natural binding force between prince and pauper. As for the upper classes, they had to accept their responsibilities as leaders. They were the most educated and cultured section of society;

they must set the example. It was to this end that he worked in his school at Rugby, hoping that the boys, drawn largely from upper-class homes, would respond to his challenge. In the interests of the nation it was his duty to place the ideal of service constantly before them.

He preached and demanded a consciously overt kind of Christianity, likely at times to be heavily charged with emotion to an extent quite alien, even incomprehensible, to us now. This pouring out of exaggerated sentiment was also to be found in his letters and particularly in the pulpit, where the words would occasionally be so interlinked with human passion and remorse (as, for example, in recalling the agony of the Cross) that his reserve would be on the brink and he would break down and weep openly in front of the entire school. If he did not expect anything quite so extreme in return, he was thankful when it happened, as in the case of Spencer Thornton,[1] and at all times he expected the right attitude. Not only must a boy be earnest, truthful and sincere, but obviously and clearly so, the purity and the struggle showing on his face. The deep, still countenance which clouded feelings was suspect and marred any true apprehension of kinship between master and pupil.

The purpose and the ideal end of education was the good, open and full life coupled with a manly spirit. Manliness here was the conquest of weakness, weakness in the moral rather than the physical sense, and although this may possibly show on the playing-field it must certainly be apparent in work and character. The struggle to self-fulfilment should be a conscious one, with the realization that temptation had been met and conquered. Above all, it was an overt struggle, something to be proud of. This internal battle was an integral part of the over-all concept of original sin in which all headmasters of the period fervently believed, though few others took it to quite the same logical excess. It was based on the idea that in all of us there is an innate urge to sin inherited from our parents, an urge permanent and fixed that no amount of effort can remove. The only hope was to build an acquired sense of good sufficiently strong for original sin to be effectively buried beneath it. Sin to the Victorians was not passive but active, always eager to

1. See Bamford, op. cit., p. 54.

break from its bonds and show itself. Indeed, in some people the amount of inherited sin was so great that it swamped all efforts at rehabilitation and condemned generation after generation. In Arnold's own words, '. . . no convict [deported] or convict's child should ever be a free citizen, and that even in the third generation, the offspring should be excluded from all offices of honour or authority . . .'.[1]

Arnold was lucky in the environment of Rugby in the 1830s and 1840s, for it was only to be expected that the impact of a religious figure would be felt most in a school which had a special interest in educating the sons of the clergy. As was seen earlier, Rugby was the school which catered most for this particular section of the community, and the percentage of clergymen's sons varied from 15 to 22 per cent for successive decades in the first half of the nineteenth century.[2] At the other extreme was Eton, with a maximum of 5 per cent. Harrow lay between these two extremes, together, no doubt, with the other boarding schools. Rugby was therefore most likely to be sensitive to a religious revival, and Eton least. It is not surprising, too, that Marlborough, with Cotton and Bradley as successive headmasters, and a majority of clergymen's sons as inmates, was successful in developing within the Rugby pattern.

Arnold himself was a considerable religious figure and Rugby in his time might well have been more susceptible to religious influence than any other school, yet this does not necessarily prove that an educational revolution occurred there. This is an important matter which, together with the influence of Rugby, will be considered later. However, there is little doubt of the importance of Arnold the man. The school occupied only a part, and indeed a minor part, of his mind. He is reckoned as one of the founders of the Broad Church Movement together with his friends Julius Charles Hare and Hull, as well as the outstanding figures of F. D. Maurice and Charles Kingsley, but this again was only part of his effort, as was his tilt with Newman. His main aim was to produce a synthesis which would resolve all social and religious problems within the confines of the state.

1. Letter to Sir John Franklin, 20 July 1836, in Stanley, op. cit.
2. See pp. 215–16.

THE OXFORD MOVEMENT AND ITS INFLUENCE ON
PUBLIC SCHOOLS

Newman himself placed the beginning of the Oxford Movement at John Keble's sermon against state interference in church affairs on 14 July 1833. The agitation that followed resembled a religious crusade with a small nucleus of energetic and devout men stressing the apostolic succession, the religious powers of priests, and the ultimate supremacy of the church in spiritual and moral matters. They wrote articles, issued tracts, stirred up the dons and endeavoured to show their preoccupation with spiritual values by their liking for ceremonial.

Unlike the Broad Church Movement, the inspiration of the Oxford Movement owed little or nothing to the public schools in any positive sense, for the key men at the heart of the crusade —John Keble and John Henry Newman—had no acquaintance with them. Only at the slightly lower level of discipleship did this background exist, for both Pusey, a late convert, and Hurrell Froude were Old Etonians. What effect this education should have had on their religion is a matter of opinion, for Eton was hardly in favour of the developments that occurred, although, as a rebel, the authorities would no doubt have considered Froude to be a true son of the school. Certainly neither Pusey nor Froude were moulded into a set pattern, particularly not Froude. According to Geoffrey Faber:

> He loved paradox, slang, exaggeration. Solemnity was a bubble to be pricked whenever opportunity offered. The hearty 'muscular Christianity' of a later day would have been a perfect target for his disrespectful irony.[1]

Froude, at least, was a rebel by nature and not by education. None the less it would be interesting to know how far education of a specific kind exerted an influence on these men.

From the very beginning Arnold was in conflict with the whole movement. With its accent on the importance of the priest, its asceticism and essential effeminacy, it was as far removed from him and from the public-school spirit as was possible, and hardly in mental accord with the schoolmasters of the day, with their emphasis on manliness coupled with godliness and the necessary tolerance of the youthful desire for

1. G. Faber, *Oxford Apostles*, 1954, p. 195.

exercise and hero-worship. They were also outside the public-school spirit in their extreme policy of denigrating their opponents on personal grounds in an effort to spread their influence. This was one of their less pleasant attributes, and when their anger turned on R. D. Hampden, Arnold replied in kind and wrote his explosive article 'The Oxford Malignants' for the *Edinburgh Review* in 1836, the year before Victoria came to the throne. This article not only stirred Arnold's own trustees so that they all but demanded his resignation, but added fire to the religious controversy and laid bare the expediency and political manoeuvring of the Newmanites. It helped to crystallize the points at issue, and the vituperation that followed served its purpose in rallying forces against Newman and Pusey. Thereafter the movement and the men who followed its practices were watched with the utmost suspicion, and the ground was prepared for the outcry against Tract 90 in 1841.[1]

The Oxford Movement collapsed with the conversion of Newman to Roman Catholicism in 1845. The forecast of Arnold and others that this would be the logical outcome of his attitude was only too true. Many followed his example, and those left behind carried on in agony for some years, possessing a sense of guilt, almost as though they were traitors—as indeed Arnold had branded them. This was the situation with George Moberly of Winchester.[2] He had been friendly and sympathetic to the work of Keble, Pusey and Newman, and even wrote a letter of approval on Tract 90. The Oxford Movement left a bitter taste. Educationally it was unpopular, to say the least, and Moberly knew it. It is doubtful if the usual Anglo-Catholic accusations against him, like that of encouraging the boys to fast, were true, yet there is no doubt that he tried hard to deny his own bias and to smother any possible Catholic impressions. In the words of Charles Wordsworth, who served under him, 'Though personally a friend of the leaders and especially of Keble, he

1. Tract 90 appeared in February 1841, and in it Newman tried to show that the Thirty-nine Articles of the Anglican Church stemmed directly from the Roman Church before the Reformation. The Roman Church had changed since and the Thirty-nine Articles were thereby in conformity with Catholic doctrine, and it was possible for a Roman Catholic to subscribe to them.
2. For Moberly generally, see C. A. E. Moberley, *Dulce Domum*, 1916.

kept himself aloof no less than I did from Tractarianism as a party movement.' [1]

In spite of this it was usually claimed that the unpopularity of Winchester, and the falling off of numbers in Moberly's time, were largely due to his religious views. Such a conclusion, though evidence of strength of feeling, must be treated with some reserve as representing a complete picture, since the popularity of any school, as we have already seen, is often a puzzling and complex problem.

Moberly's term of office at Winchester was only an interlude in the history of the school; he had not the stature of Arnold to stand outwardly by his principles and win through. The relationship of these two men is one of the minor ironies of education, for Moberly was the man who clinched Arnold's fame by writing such a convincing, if debatable, account of his contribution to public-school reform in Stanley's biography. [2] The choice of Moberly for this task is strange, for Stanley was intimate with both men and knew that their views on any matter of importance were incompatible. The net result was that this friend of Newman and Pusey became the chosen instrument for projecting their bitter opponent into the hall of fame.

A more interesting case of the effect of Tractarianism is that of Nathaniel Woodard, whose efforts to form an educational empire have already been noted. [3] He had been at Oxford from 1834 to 1840, the years when the Oxford controversy was at its height, and became a confirmed disciple of Keble, Pusey and Newman. But while he accepted the tractarian ideal, he wanted it to be combined with the church–state principle of Arnold, if differently based, and his prime purpose in founding schools was to bring the middle classes into allegiance with the Church of England. The boarding-school atmosphere was a means whereby middle-class children would desert their immoral and debased practices and become a stabilizing core to English life. As a tractarian, Woodard believed in the sanctity of the church, in the priests' special powers, in fasting, in confession, in ritual and in display. At one time fasting was encouraged in his

1. F. B. How, *Six Great Schoolmasters*, 1904, p. 69.
2. Stanley, op. cit.
3. See pp. 29–34.

schools, to be replaced later, after protests, by sparse food on
Ash Wednesday and Good Friday, including rice, bread and
cheese for dinner. More significant than the fasting was the
moral side and confession. A clergyman was specially employed
to act as spiritual guide and friend to the boys, seeing each one
eight or more times a year to discuss their personal difficulties.
The boys were also encouraged to confess their sins. Confession
was not compulsory and was only done with parental permission, yet it was common enough according to contemporary
accounts. With his other tractarian views, illustrated by his liking
for plainsong and Gothic architecture, it is not surprising that
Woodard was constantly attacked and that he found it necessary
to deny that he was in favour of advanced religious views being
practised as part of school life. As a result of one storm he even
went so far, in March 1853, as to hold an inquiry to establish his
innocence. The evidence, however, is against him; he may have
managed to convince himself and others on technical grounds,
but the fact remains that he was a tractarian at heart, eager to
promote the cause, except perhaps for excessive ceremonial.

Woodard was in a perpetual dilemma. He insisted on the
supremacy of the Church of England, and yet his own views
were on the edge of Anglican belief. Anyone who agreed to
compromise on this he treated as a traitor, and he therefore
quarrelled bitterly with old friends like Gladstone and Lord
Lyttleton. His Roman practices were unpopular with many
and he had to be careful about them. At the same time it would
seem that educational zeal, and perhaps economy, were
overriding factors in many cases. Thus, he managed to
cultivate friends in the opposite camp like Julius Hare and
Bishop Thirlwall. Similarly, he accepted the money of dissenters
for his schemes, while his school at Ellesmere achieved some
popularity among Welsh Nonconformists.[1]

Moberly and Woodard illustrate the difficulties of transfer-
ring the Oxford Movement to education. A tractarian public
school operating in the heat of the 1840s and 1850s appears to
have been an impossible ideal, and Woodard added to his
difficulties by trying to cope with at least three social strata.
This meant that none of his schools was 'public', except in a
narrow boarding sense, and that they had no chance of entering

1. For Woodard's problems, see Otter, op. cit., and Heeney, op. cit.

the exalted ranks until the screening procedure for entry was altered. Even so the beginnings of any successful institution are significant, and Woodard had his imitators, as we have seen, although only one or two, like Bloxham, were connected with the Oxford Movement.

The affair of Newman and his supporters was rightly called the Oxford Movement, and those schools with strong Oxford connections were far more deeply involved than those with allegiances to Cambridge. On this ground alone one would have expected Eton to be rather aloof and indifferent, with Rugby more deeply involved, even apart from Arnold's intimate association with Oxford, which lent local fire to the dispute.

There are grounds for believing that the religious issue has been overstressed taking the schools as a whole. The fight of Newman and Pusey against the more orthodox church had all the elements of high drama. With so much accent on the religious theme it is easy to fall into the trap of assuming that everyone was equally devout: 'One is tempted, reading the lives of Newman and his associates, to suppose that introspective piety and the baffled pursuit of learning occupied the minds of all the intelligent young men.' [1]

It is salutary to realize that in the late 1850s and early 1860s, only a third of those at Oxford and a fifth of those at Cambridge came from the seven major schools. The contribution of ideas from any individual was, therefore, thinly spread indeed. Besides, the majority of those who went up to Oxford and Cambridge were not careerists and scholars, but the sons of the upper class, far more interested in life and the gentlemanly pursuits than in religion, and for many undergraduates it was this select section of university society that set the tone rather than the studious religious element. Moreover, there is a tendency to assume that the Oxford or Cambridge contingents were true representatives of the schools. This is by no means the case. Only a third of the boys who left the seven major schools went to university at all. The mass of children left without proceeding to higher education, and any sweeping generalizations based on this minority must clearly be treated with

1. Faber, op. cit., p. 55.

reserve. It is also dangerous to judge a school or a headmaster on the strength of contingents alone. It is true that Arnold had a particularly impressive quartet in A. P. Stanley, C. J. Vaughan, W. C. Lake and A. H. Clough, though it has to be remembered that the reputation of not all of them has stood the test of time, that they were not all contemporaries and not even all at Oxford, while Lake was technically as much a product of Wooll as of Arnold. In any case, such a contingent is not unique. Prince Lee, at Birmingham, a follower of Arnold and usually regarded as an unsuccessful headmaster, produced an even more impressive list with one archbishop (Benson) and two bishops (Westcott and Lightfoot) besides noted classicists.[1]

RELIGION AND THE SCHOOLS

It must be stressed that the schools were at no time indifferent to religion. The school chapel dominated the public-school scene at the beginning of the nineteenth century no less than at the end. And in some cases where it was absent, a separate building was unnecessary in view of the proximity of parent churches, as at St Paul's and Westminster. Those without this symbol rapidly repaired the omission. Clergymen, church services, confirmation, prayers and the Bible in Greek were all part of the tradition, and on this common backcloth were impressed all the differences and exaggerations that one would normally expect in a series of independently evolving schools at a time of social, religious and political crisis. Although some people complained of a casual attitude to religion, there were quite as many who were more than satisfied and even complaints that far too much religion was being forced upon the younger generation.[2]

All headmasters were, in fact, agreed on the paramount significance of the chapel; it would have been strange otherwise, considering that they were all clergymen. The generation of Keate, Wooll and Samuel Butler was quite as devout as that of Arnold's contemporaries which followed, but their religion was not overt or pressed to the limit of embracing all behaviour as a facet of sin. They thrashed with a will when confronted

1. For Prince Lee's achievement as a headmaster, see D. Newsome, *Godliness and Good Learning. Four Studies on a Victorian Ideal*, 1961.
2. See Bamford, *Arnold*, op. cit., p. 185.

with the stupidity of boys, no less and no more than their successors, but in doing so they did not consider themselves to be instruments of God's justice. This is the real issue. If they coupled morals and religion in a general way, they also saw the moral ideal as incorporated in the upper-class way of life as did the later headmasters. They all assumed that morals were layered in the same way as social classes and equated the two in a rough fashion. Certainly they considered that the middle and lower classes had entirely different standards from the upper, and that these were mutually incompatible. From the very nature of the school in their charge they had to be true to the upper-class way of life, and perhaps, the different values that were thrust upon them so intensely brought in time the view that the middle classes had no real sense of truth or honesty. This view persisted right through to the middle and late years of the century. Henry Hayman put the matter plainly: 'I will venture to say that there is little of that honorable love of truth which distinguishes English Public Schoolboys, to be found in the homes of the lower middling classes.' [1]

Even a man as radically minded as Temple was saying the same in the 1870s and 1880s, while this theme was at the very root of Woodard's fear for the future of the country and made him so energetic in founding schools. At these levels home life and school life did not mix, and Hayman argued that a boy from a lower-middle-class home who found himself in a public school would have to stay on throughout the holidays, earning his keep as a matter of duty by odd jobs and manual work to prevent any possibility of a relapse in his home environment. In this view upper-class standards at home and at school were essential, and accordingly upper-class boys were the best possible material for moral regeneration. Flogging was remedial and religious; it scourged the body in remembrance of the penalties of sin. It reminds one all too vividly of the spirit of the Inquisition, and with it went a corresponding brutality, at times approaching bestiality, as we shall see.

It is this combination of religious fervour and sadism that has brought charges of hypocrisy against the great headmasters. But it is to be remembered that they were consistent and logical,

---

1. H. Hayman, *Can We Adapt the Public School System to the Middle Class?* 1858.

5

if mistaken. For many of these men the very sight of the body itself was sinful. John Percival took this to the limit of farce by making the boys at Rugby lengthen their football shorts and tie them with elastic bands over their knees, on the grounds that the mere sight of bare flesh might be an incentive to vice.[1]

All schools were from the earliest days of the century dominated by religion, but there were differences between the early and late years, to be seen typically in attitudes to such matters as disobedience and lying, laziness and deceit, sex and masturbation, cruelty and theft. When the early headmasters were confronted with these lapses of character they tended to treat them as human failings. Some of the later headmasters were more apt to treat them as lack of religious consciousness, for they regarded all errors in human conduct as facets of sin and evidence of evil.

This contrast is seen most vividly in the difference between the pre-1830 headmasters and Arnold. The earlier men may well have been religiously minded, but by Arnold and Woodard standards they were clearly half-hearted. Alternatively, we might argue that the earlier ones had a normal 'healthy' approach while our two examples took religion to excess. It is certainly difficult to imagine a pressure more intense than that on the sensitive boy in the sixth at Rugby from 1828 to 1842, or that in a Woodard school with its accent on confession, moral uplift and the like. Indeed, Woodard took great satisfaction in the number of his products entering holy orders.

At the watershed between the attitude of the old and the new stood the years represented by Arnold and the Oxford Movement. The influence of the Oxford Movement on existing schools was negligible, as we have seen, and Arnold was the only educational figure of stature in that period. It became customary to associate every significant change with him. Thus he is said to have improved the moral tone of the school, to have cured bullying and atrocities, to have brought about a truly religious attitude in the boys, to have revolutionized the organization and cured disciplinary troubles. Moreover, Rugby is supposed to have acted as a focal-point from which these

1. For this anecdote, see O. F. Christie, *A History of Clifton College*, 1935, pp. 34–5.

benefits spread to the other schools. But such claims are too sweeping to be accepted without a close look at the evidence.

THE INFLUENCE OF ARNOLD AND RUGBY

When we try to assess how far the influence of Rugby spread outwards we are at once in difficulties, for we know far less about every other school and the usual assumption that Arnold's reputation brought about a revolution must be treated with reserve. Certainly it is difficult to see how he could have influenced many of his contemporaries, since the early Victorian headmasters had received their formative experiences twenty or thirty years back in the schools and universities of Napoleonic and post-Napoleonic Britain in an atmosphere that was far too cynical and radical to produce conformity in their products, or easy conversion to new ideas in later years.

Of the great schools, Eton was certainly not impressed. Hawtrey was no convert and the experience of Balston's two brothers at Rugby made that headmaster resist any of the Arnoldian ideas as being superficial. We also have the evidence of a pupil, Brinsley-Richards, writing of his schooldays at Eton in 1857–64: 'I fancy the sermons we heard had no appreciable influence in shaping our lives. I say this with my mind rather full of what Mr Thomas Hughes has written about Dr Arnold's preaching; and also with reminiscences of what I have heard other Rugbeians tell of Dr Temple.' [1]

At Shrewsbury Kennedy was impervious; he had his own idol in his old teacher, Samuel Butler, and was too absorbed in classics and scholasticism to pay undue attention to religious aspects such as this.

As for Winchester, Arnold himself went to school there, and it was the headmaster of that school (Moberly) who wrote such kind things about him. One would normally assume from this that Winchester was influenced by Arnold, but the school historian, J. D'E. Firth, emphatically denies this inference:

Nor does Winchester owe anything much directly to Arnold, except in the general sense in which all the schools were influenced by this seminal mind of his age. Moberly, indeed, sent Dean Stanley a graceful tribute of gratitude to be inserted in the biography of his hero; but words from his pen are never less to be taken at face value

1. J. Brinsley-Richards, *Seven Years at Eton*, 1883, p. 245.

than when he dipped it in honey. The facts appear to warrant no more than this, that Moberly had, before taking office, visited the Arnolds and had been impressed, and that his own pessimistic temperament had kindled to the encouragement given that some improvement might be effected at Winchester. Wordsworth expressly stated that his own efforts owed nothing, directly or indirectly, to Arnold. . . . The unbridgeable theological gulf between Arnold and the two Winchester Masters makes Wordsworth's account easily credible.[1]

From our knowledge of the characters of the men involved, and the insularity of an ancient school, there can be no doubt about this.

In the same way there is no evidence that Charterhouse and Westminster were involved in any Arnoldian 'new look'. Indeed, of all the major schools only Harrow appears to have been infected, through C. J. Vaughan, and yet recent revelations about this headmaster place a big question mark over everything happening there.

The position at Rugby itself is by no means clear. It would be naïve in the extreme to say that Arnold set a pattern in religion that was followed thereafter. Between the advent of Arnold and the end of the century there were eight headmasters, the seven others being Tait, Goulburn, Temple, Hayman, Jex-Blake, Percival and James. All these were highly independent men, more likely to change things when they arrived rather than preserve the old. Indeed, we know that the legacy of Arnold himself was diluted at once by his successor, Tait, and that similar drastic changes occurred on the resignation of Temple. The fact is that all these men were devout clergymen, just as Arnold's predecessors had been. It is true also that the peak in religious intensity under Arnold within this school was never reached again. Of those who followed him, Temple and Percival were nearest. Both these men were radicals in certain ways, and Temple a passionate reformer. With Temple, too, emotion and passion were closely linked, and he would weep openly in front of his victims when performing the unpleasant task of flogging boys. There is no doubt that of all headmasters anywhere Temple came nearest to Arnold in width of vision and fundamental ideas, but he had not quite that spirit of

1. J. D'E. Firth, *Winchester College*, 1949, pp. 144–5.

martyrdom and religious obsession that exhausted Arnold and eventually killed him. By comparison, the reigns of Tait, Goulburn, Hayman and Jex-Blake were religiously far less intense, almost placid.

The degree of religious emphasis was therefore highly inconsistent at Rugby itself, occurring in short significant bursts rather than generally over a long period.

Even for Arnold's own period the legend of the aftermath conflicts with the facts. It has been shown quite conclusively by an analysis of every single boy under him at Rugby that he did not at any time succeed in bringing about a moral revolution. Moreover, he never claimed this for himself, and indeed expressly stated the opposite. Troubles with discipline, morality, bullying and the rest continued throughout his reign, and, if anything, were worse at the end than at the beginning, though the small school left by Wooll in 1828 and the advent of a new headmaster undoubtedly helped the initial situation. As with all men of stature, others have created a legend around him, and in this case his reputation was built by a few pupils who were fascinated by the man and watched his painful conflict with his governors, the newspapers, the church and the politicians of his day. In their eyes he was not appreciated and the attacks were false. It was these boys who spread his fame, notably A. P. Stanley and Thomas Hughes, while the reputation of his son, Matthew Arnold, helped the process.

Rightly or wrongly, Rugby obtained a reputation as a centre for religion of a politico-social-liberal type. It is no coincidence that, of his three immediate successors, two became archbishops of Canterbury, A. C. Tait and Frederick Temple, while another master, E. W. Benson, who served under Temple at Rugby, also assumed that office. These were not the first of the Victorian archbishops to have been headmasters of public schools, for that honour belongs to the Harrow headmaster, C. T. Longley, while the Etonian master, John Bird Sumner, also attained that office, but the connection of the other three with Rugby, and therefore with Arnold, is quite remarkable and shows the lasting nature of his reputation and influence. There is no evading the conclusion that the public schools were a prime influence on the church when so many ex-headmasters were directing policy from the highest level within the church itself. There

was also another and less obvious way in which the schools
guided religious policy, by producing boys who were to become
leading politicians, some of whom, by virtue of their office,
were to possess the power of appointing bishops and archbishops.
In some cases old boys—or even the parents of old boys in one
or two documented instances—formed pressure-groups designed
to secure the elevation of their old heads.

These headmasters were positively anti-tractarian, and it is
significant that they are easily the most famous, perhaps because
elevation came more easily that way.

The probable answer to the whole question of religious
development in the schools generally is that no single pattern
persisted anywhere. The overall effect was a mass of different
approaches, with each school being unique and having a
pattern of its own, moulded on the whims of successive heads.
Even so, there appears to be a distinct difference between the
first years of Victoria and the last; the early attitudes were
quite outmoded by the last quarter of the century. This is seen
in many ways: in the gradual decline of religious influence and
in the changing attitudes to manliness.

EVIDENCES OF RELIGIOUS DECLINE AND RELATED THEMES

One of the more astonishing facts about the Victorian public
schools was the gradual loss of the prestige of religion in spite
of the outward piety of the times and the grip of the headmasters. As we shall see later, fewer and fewer boys from the
major schools entered the church, while the clerical collar lost
its dominating influence with a growing insistence on lay staff.
In the early years all masters were clergymen: in Arnold's
Rugby the only one outside the ministry was that remarkable
teacher, Bonamy Price.

The character of the staffs and the schools began to change
with the appointment of laymen who were not sufficiently
attracted to the church to become clergymen. The new outlook
was foreshadowed at Cheltenham from the very beginning, but
the change occurred in the old schools at least ten years later.
The first significant number of lay appointments for Eton,
Harrow and Rugby occurred in the 1850s, but not till 1870 for
Shrewsbury. In each case the change appears to have occurred

quite suddenly, as though owing to a change of policy. At Harrow it occurred in about 1853, at Eton in about 1856 and Rugby in about 1859,[1] but the significance of these dates is obscure at present, and they do not correspond with the appointment of new headmasters and a consequent change of policy. The 1850s were a significant turning-point for at least some of the older schools, and it is probably not without significance that changes were also occurring in attitudes to sport and the utilization of the boys' leisure time. Both trends were in full swing long before the schools began to tackle the aridity of the curriculum and the advent of science.

The replacement of staff, however, was a gradual process, and it was a decade or two before the number of clergymen began to thin out. By the last quarter of the century the situation had completely changed. If we take the twenty-two leading schools listed in Table 3, then, by 1886, 73 per cent of the masters were not in orders, while four years later this had risen to 80 per cent. The position as it was by 1893 is shown in the table. The belief in the churchly headmaster was obviously still firm in the boarding schools, but it is also clear that the headmasters in the appointment of staff had little faith in the quality of their own cloth. Presumably the care of the boys' souls had given way to the care of their minds and bodies. The insistence on having clerical heads with lay staff produced an absurd situation both for ambitious young men thinking of a teaching career as well as on the quality of the headmasterly ranks. By the 1880s and 1890s the governing bodies were appointing heads from 20 per cent or less of the available pool and were therefore unnecessarily restricting their choice and appointing less competent people. The figures in Table 3 also show that there was a clear distinction between boarding and day schools. In abandoning the clerical headmaster, as all have today done in principle, the main public schools did not inaugurate reform but followed the example of their day brethren.

The period of religious dominance in those schools, like Rugby, where we know it existed in practice, brought its own reaction through its effect on those boys who took it seriously.

1. These changes are deduced from details in the school registers.

Table 3. *Clerical and lay masters and headmasters in 1893
in twenty-two day and boarding schools.*[1]

Type	Name of school	Masters			Headmasters	
		Lay	Clerical	Total	Lay	Clerical
The Seven	Eton	47	10	57	–	1
	Harrow	32	6	38	–	1
	Rugby	24	6	30	–	1
	Winchester	18	7	25	–	1
	Westminster	12	4	16	–	1
	Charterhouse	24	9	33	–	1
	Shrewsbury	17	5	22	–	1
New boarding	Cheltenham	35	6	41	–	1
	Marlborough	29	7	36	–	1
	Wellington	21	9	30	–	1
	Haileybury	19	8	27	–	1
	Clifton	35	7	42	–	1
Old boarding	Repton	14	6	20	–	1
	Uppingham	23	9	32	–	1
	Sherborne	9	5	14	–	1
Day	St Paul's	28	4	32	1	–
	Merchant Taylors'	15	9	24	–	1
	City of London	35	4	39	1	–
	University College School	30	2	32	1	–
	King's College School	20	2	22	1	–
	Dulwich College School	35	5	40	1	–
Lower-class boarding	Christ's Hospital	20	9	29	–	1
	Total	542	139	681	5	17

The more renowned examples seemed to have curtailed that
stage of development known as youth, and to step straight from
childhood into the serious contemplation of an adult. 'Bearded
sages'[2] was the way some people at Oxford saw these products.

1. Figures taken from C. Dukes, *Health at School*, 3rd edition, 1894, pp.
43–4.
2. See *Reminiscences and Opinions of Sir Francis Doyle, 1813–1885*, 1886.

There can be little doubt that some of them were old before their time; the example of Stanley alone is sufficient to establish this, while both Clough and Lake regretted their lost and wasted opportunities. It was the rediscovery of youth, in the way that Dickens preached, that separated the ideas of the old headmasters from the new. Even in the immediate post-Arnold period there are traces of change, for Cotton was clearly a man with feet in both camps.

Boys are immature, growing organisms needing vigour, activity and action; discussions, moral issues and exaggerated introspection are no substitute, and are in many ways irrelevant. Religion was not for everyone, neither was the old spirit of scholasticism. There was in fact no one way to the good life. Much of the change is linked with the attitude of boys and masters to games and team spirit. Boys had always played to win—Tom Brown is sufficient evidence of that—but in the early years it was a glorious extempore achievement. Later, winning became a serious preoccupation, even for many masters, and for many of the boys the only thing about the school that mattered. A feverish fight developed for perfection in muscular activity, the desire to win going hand in hand with a nonchalant superficial air of not caring about the result. The ideal became not only a complete concealment of the emotions, but the masking of them with a false façade, i.e. the stiff upper lip. This was the new manliness, extolled as such. It amounted to a change-over from the old loosely governed, emotionally enthusiastic and romping play to the serious professional approach under the eye of expert coaches. The pressure was for greater and greater skill producing more and more glorious results, until the time given to it outstripped the simple ideas of playing the game as a game. But amateurism remained an ideal with headmasters and staffs, while professionalism became a word of contempt, in spite of the fact that the opposite corresponds more closely to their scale of values. Professionalism was not understood, and was linked in the minds of the staff with that lower-class expertise seen in the coaches that the boys employed.

The old headmasters had been as keen on games as were the newer variety, but the issues had not seemed so vital. No moral questions were involved. In the last analysis it is they who were

not so concerned with results and who were the true sportsmen, rather than the new advocates of upholding the school honour and putting a brave face upon it all. David Newsome puts this point perfectly:

> The doctrine of the stiff-upper-lip was no part of the public-school code of the Arnoldian period. This gradually came in with the manliness cult of the 1870's and 80's. For it would never have done for Empire builders and games players to exhibit their emotions.[1]

The schoolmaster became more of a kindly father than the stimulator of a conscience. He was also compelled to become an exponent of the new manliness, and be 'one with the boys', and this did not always blend with a clerical way of life.

From the schools' point of view the new approach was linked with the cure of indiscipline, as we shall see, but there were undoubtedly connections with wider and deeper issues. The old certainties were being destroyed, both socially and intellectually, with the development of science and scientific viewpoints. One could easily explain the outburst of religious education and its aftermath as a sidelight on the war between religion and secularism which was taking place both before and after Darwin. Newman's was one answer, Arnold's and the Broad Church's another. We meet the same problems in corresponding dilemmas of our own time—like the choices between individual liberty, bureaucracy and totalitarianism.

1. Newsome, *Godliness and Good Learning*, op. cit., p. 83.

CHAPTER FOUR

The Victorian Boy at School

Travel on a national scale did not begin until the opening of the London–Birmingham line in 1838, so the railways and the Victorian age grew up together. Until then only seven public boarding schools of size served the sons of Anglican gentry, all of them in the southern half of England and only two, Shrewsbury and Rugby, actually north of London. This is an astonishing fact in an age of infrequent coaches, when a journey from Edinburgh to London took almost two days if all went well, while bad roads immediately off the main routes delayed travel interminably. It was impossible to begin a term knowing for certain that every boy would be in his place at a precise hour. In many cases several days' grace had to be allowed either way, and many boys had exciting tales to tell of adventures in transit. It is true that a servant sometimes went with the child, and occasionally, at Eton, stayed with him in the school, but this was not invariably the case, and the seemingly careless way in which parents entrusted young children, often only seven or eight, to coach drivers and inn-keepers is evidence not only of their confidence in law and order, but of the familiarity of road travel for this kind of child. It confirms our reading of Jane Austen, Maria Edgeworth and Anna Seward. One result of these difficulties was the usual system of two terms a year—with holidays at Christmas and summer—giving way slowly to the neater short-term system which relied on the accuracy of the railway time-table.

In the early days of railway building boys of all kinds and ages, rich and poor alike, hung over the barricades and watched the laying of tracks with an interest that was the rightful due of a new way of life. But the schools themselves reacted to this

new means of transport in surprising ways. Eton wanted to seal
it off altogether with a ten-foot wall, while in 1848 they compelled the company of a nearby line to patrol it in case their
boys happened to stray. This last decision was only the beginning of a farce that dragged out for almost forty years, until
1886 in fact.[1] Arnold personally welcomed the railway, for the
good it would do society at large, but he tried to shield his boys
from it—without success. At Rugby, while the excavations for
the tunnel at Kilsby were hampered by flooding for so many
months, it was a favourite pastime to steal away at night,
remove a freshly laid brick, sign it on the back and replace it.
A useless activity, perhaps, but adventurous and akin to the
adult urge to bury samples of modern life beneath new buildings
for posterity to discover. It was the early Victorian equivalent
of eel-baiting and night-lines which had occupied so much of
the time of Rugbeian fags fifty years before. If the resistance of
the old schools to the railways lingered on, the newer foundations embraced the new invention by placing themselves nicely
with a divining-stick on suitable places of the network, at
Marlborough, Wellington and Cranleigh.

It is obvious that the railways provided a convenient mode of
travel, and it is usually said that they had a profound effect on
the boarding schools:

> With the coming of the railways boarding schools were more in
> demand, and men who had themselves been educated at a local
> grammar school sent their sons to Rugby or Shrewsbury, or to a
> new foundation like Marlborough. The grammar schools suffered
> accordingly.[2]

However, the argument that the development of the railways
was a factor vital to school prosperity must be treated with
some reserve, for prosperity is a complex problem, as we have
seen, and the awkward placing of the schools in the pre-railway
era and the long journeyings of the boys is rather discouraging
for this theory.

Most schools were in 1837 still fashioned in the age-old style
of a barrack-like dormitory and a lofty schoolroom on the scale
of a modern assembly-hall. Here each master sat with the boys

1. For Eton and the railway, see E. L. Woodward, *The Age of Reform,
1815–70*, 1949, p. 44.
2. M. L. Clarke, *Classical Education in Britain, 1500–1900*, 1959, p. 88.

of his form on benches curving around him, the senior master nearest the fire.[1] There were groups in each corner, with others filling the gaps as necessary at strategic points along the sides. Class teaching in the modern sense was rare and individual tuition the rule. The boys had their work set, and the master called each one up in turn to be tested on it. With luck he might possibly get through each boy in the normal period of an hour, but more often he only covered a fraction of the class.[2] With a methodical master boys could anticipate whether they were likely to be called or not, and consequently whether they needed to do their prep or could afford to read novels instead. This system of teaching was all but universal, though nearing an end. The need for class teaching and some degree of privacy was already apparent, and as new schools were built separate rooms were provided, particularly for the writing master, the sixth and the older boys. Not till the second half of the century was there further specialization as the need arose for exercise, the display and use of apparatus, and work benches and special fittings.

Whether a boy entered a small or a large class was entirely a matter of chance. On a wave of prosperity classes were huge, being correspondingly small in days of depression. The variations were a necessary part of school life. Headmasters were used to this situation and there is no evidence that staff were sacked in lean times at the major establishments, in spite of statements to the contrary. Fewer students meant better and easier teaching, and although the boys may have benefited the teachers did not, for small classes involved a smaller income for the school and corresponding reductions in salary. The staff, therefore, had a vested interest in prosperity. All this had important repercussions on class size, for the evidence shows that a school could shrink or distend with almost boundless elasticity, as though the modern conception of a school full to capacity did not exist. The narrow curriculum helped, for all men were similarly qualified, or very nearly so, and this made the problem of erratic numbers easier. In an emergency the headmaster would take the whole school, or call upon a local

1. For typical pictures of classrooms of the period, see Ackermann, op. cit.
2. For a description of a similar situation at Sedbergh in the 1850s, see J. M. Wilson, *An Autobiography, 1836–1931*, 1932.

private tutor or clergyman to help out, as in the case of Herbert Hill, who used this *entrée* as a stepping-stone to the headmastership of Warwick School.

In the 1830s and 1840s boys were generally time-tabled for twenty-six to thirty hours a week, with a series of possible extra options.[1] The classics, with relevant ancient history and geography, occupied from eighteen or nineteen of these hours at Harrow to twenty-one at Rugby. Mathematics was at a low ebb; it was ignored altogether at Harrow, given two or three hours at Rugby and left as an option at Eton and elsewhere. Any idea of a balanced curriculum did not exist. Apart from Rugby, where it was compulsory, French was optional, though sometimes stressed and taught by refugees, since it was held that only a national could do justice to the language.[2] English had no real place on the time-table—one formal hour at Harrow and little or none elsewhere, although everything depended on the approach, since Arnold and others like him insisted that lessons in classics were, by the very nature of things, lessons in English also. In addition to the time-tabled programme, a great array of possible options was theoretically open to the boys, including French, German, Italian, fencing, drill, natural philosophy, music and dancing, but they were unmistakably frills and headmasters took no responsibility for them whatever. At least three-quarters, and in some cases four-fifths, of the time was spent in class on Latin and Greek and the direct ancillaries that went with an understanding of them. This is an undeniable fact, for we have a series of articles written by the schools themselves at the very dawn of the Victorian age, giving details of their courses of study. This one-track situation continued more or less unchanged for almost thirty years, right through

1. For details of time-tabling, see various articles issued in the *Quarterly Journal of Education*. Also *The Miscellaneous Works of Thomas Arnold*, 1845.
2. The influence of refugees and other foreign gentlemen on modern-language teaching can be seen in the names of 'extra masters' at Harrow in the first half of the nineteenth century: M. Butticaz, M. Briad, M. Jacques W. Marillier, M. Amable J. Ruault and M. Pierre M. G. Ruault. Similar examples could be given for Eton, and for Rugby from the early eighteenth century onwards. The tradition persisted. When Cheltenham was started in 1841, among the first appointments in 1841 were the following men from overseas: J. A. Drieu (French), J. Duprez (French), J. Lindwart (German), and F. L. Murgeaud (French). Many arguments on the suitability and limitations of such men are to be found in PSC. Music and fencing were other avenues open for refugees.

to the time of the Public Schools Commission at least. If we take the seven old boarding schools in 1863, classical masters outnumbered all the others by more than two to one (actually in the ratio 75:35).[1] This fact alone shows what little scope there was for extra study by the boys. Certainly anyone who hated Horace and Ovid had a miserable time.

It is true that there were signs of change by 1863, but the invasion of the classical stronghold by other disciplines is a complicated story that belongs elsewhere. All that need be said here is that classicism was the dominant theme and that other studies were despised. Headmasters tried to evade this issue where they could, as in the case of the headmaster of Eton itself when questioned by the Chairman of the Public Schools Commission in 1862:

LORD CLARENDON: Do you think that it [French] is a matter that a boy should be required to learn?

HEADMASTER [Balston]: He ought to learn French before he came to Eton, and we could take measures to keep it up as we keep up English.

CLARENDON: What measures would you take to keep up French, and I may also add, what measures do you now take to keep up English at Eton?

HEADMASTER: There are none at present, except through the ancient languages.[2]

This attitude was not confined to Eton, but even dominated many of the new schools, in spite of the introduction of new ideas from Cheltenham and elsewhere. At Lancing, we find it expressed as late as 1885: 'It [the modern side] consisted at first of one despised form, the members of which were debarred from entering the sixth. . . . It existed. No one had the least wish for it to exist and it was a sort of parasite. . . .'[3]

Although the waves of prosperity did, as we have seen, affect class numbers seriously, it is still a most surprising fact that the larger and more successful the school, the larger the size of class. Out of nine schools investigated by the Public Schools Commission, only three possessed any classes with thirty-five or more pupils, and these were Eton, Harrow and Rugby. Indeed, in fifteen out of twenty-two forms at Eton that number was

1. The ratio of classical and other masters has been deduced from staff-lists.
2. PSC, I, p. 85, Qq. 3529–30.
3. Handford, op. cit., p. 142.

exceeded. Correspondingly the largest class at Shrewsbury had twenty-one.[1] In view of Shrewsbury's outstanding scholastic success during this period, it would be tempting to correlate size of class with the academic achievement shown in examination and scholarship results, but a thorough investigation of this important point from several related and even unrelated aspects would first be necessary. What is clear, however, is that the much vaunted smaller class, which many claim to be one of the virtues of present-day education in public as against state schools, was certainly not the case in the last century, and was far less so with the major schools of Eton, Harrow and Rugby than with the lesser breed. Parents were indeed paying more money for less attention.

If class sizes have changed, the organization of teaching has not. Then, as now, setting was the rule. Under this scheme subject-matter was divided into order of difficulty, and a boy progressed from one set to another by passing the appropriate test or examination, usually at the end of a term or a year. If he failed he was kept down, and if he suddenly acquired great mental powers he could climb through the forms of the school with extraordinary rapidity. Such a boy was A. P. Stanley, and his example was common enough throughout the century and beyond. In 1861 we have the advantage of precise figures on this point.[2] A difference in age of three years for boys in the same class was very common indeed, and six years not unknown. In one form of fourteen boys at Shrewsbury, a boy of ten years five months sat down with another of sixteen years eleven months—a difference of six and a half years. By the modern standards of the state system, the youngster would be looking forward to the eleven plus, while the older boy would either be in the sixth or have left altogether. Bodily, too, one would be a child and the other almost a man. Similar cases of six-year differences could be quoted for Harrow and Rugby. Size of class had nothing to do with this arrangement, but there are other important by-products of such an arrangement which remain to be considered, such as the psychological and sexual relationships of the boys involved.

1. Details of class sizes deduced from information in PSC.
2. Details of the structure of school classes deduced from Tabular Analysis, no. 3, PSC, ii, p. 504.

Whatever its origin, the sixth was already firmly established in the early nineteenth century, so well established, in fact, that the rest of the school had to be geared to fit in with it. The general growth in the size of schools meant that there were already far too many class-divisions for a neat numbering from one to six, and the more logical attempts to systematize the period of a boy's development failed. Brighton,[1] at its formation, tried the experiment of numbering up to six in the lower school, and down from one (the highest form) in the upper. A little earlier, at Cheltenham, they decided to reverse the numbering throughout, so that the uppermost shelf was numbered one, and the lowest relegated to its rightful number in logical sequence.[2] But custom was against them all, as against Beaumont with its Catholic tradition, and they had all reverted to the usual practice by 1889. With a large number of divisions all kinds of devices were introduced to indicate intermediate grades, apart from the more usual labelling: upper, middle, lower; *alpha, beta, gamma*; A, B, C, etc. The Remove was already widespread by mid-Victorian times, as was Shell, not to mention more exotic names like the powerful concept of 'The Twenty' at Rugby. Elsewhere a wide variety of other names are to be found, such as 'Direct', 'Naval', 'The Seventh', although the strangest names of all were undoubtedly those two forms at Eton—'Sense' and 'Nonsense'.

Like the sixth, prefects have been traditional for centuries, though often called by other names—monitors and praepostors among them. But nowhere did they go to the extremes of the old Jesuit schools with their Senators and Emperors of the East and West, or even to the Silentiaries, the Judge and other dignitaries of Hazelwood.[3]

Prefects were senior boys selected for their so-called powers of leadership. In some cases recruitment was limited to the

1. For Brighton, see Burstow and Whittaker, op. cit., p. 10.
2. For Cheltenham, see A. A. Hunter, *Cheltenham College Register*, 1911, Preface.
3. For Hazelwood, see R. Hill, *Public Education: Plans for the Government and Liberal Instruction of Boys in Large Numbers as Practised at Hazelwood School* (2nd edition, 1825). There was a jury system here, where the jury decided on guilt and punishment. The school was, in fact, run as an adult society in miniature and had its own institutions.

6

sixth. In day schools, like St Paul's and Merchant Taylors', their powers were strictly limited, but at the other extreme, seen typically at Rugby, prefects were virtually minor members of staff with flogging and fagging powers.[1] They were supposed to act as moral organizers, responsible for discipline outside the classroom, reporting to the headmaster only when matters got out of hand. This was the role that Arnold and his followers required, and was due as much to the traditional view of a boy's right to freedom from adult control as to acute problems of staff shortage.

Apart from expulsion, flogging was the major punishment, although the solitary confinement which Arnold is said to have tried to introduce would have been frightful in the extreme.[2] Flogging is difficult to define precisely, for the word was often used in Victorian times to cover all forms of corporal punishment, from simple caning to sheer atrocity. Severe punishment was usually administered only by a headmaster or lower master, and there appears to be something of a strong positive correlation between eminence and a strong right arm, for all the great headmasters were renowned floggers—Keate, Arnold, Butler, Benson among them, although the record is apparently held by Moss of Shrewsbury with eighty-eight lashes.[3] The precise choice of weapon and the passion of delivery were clearly important, for eighty-eight from one of the others is unthinkable; in a white heat they would certainly have reduced the boy to insensibility, if not worse.

An infinite variety of implements could be brought into play, depending on the circumstances. For simple offences they relied on sticks, rods or canes; for the severest cases split canes, thongs or a tightly bound mass of switches specially and freshly made up each day. Occasionally the weapon was weighted with lead, or else, for extra effect, the ends were left supple and pliant to lick around the edge to the tender regions where the sting was really felt. Misdemeanours were dealt with contemptuously in private, but major offences became a public spectacle with the entire school looking on. At Eton and elsewhere there was an elaborate ceremonial whereby a boy knelt over a special stool

1. Prefects in some schools still have powers of corporal punishment.
2. Minchin, op. cit., p. 201.
3. For Moss, see G. F. Lamb, *The Happiest Days*, 1959, p. 145.

with trousers pulled down, while a boy on either side—one senior and one junior—held up the corners of his shirt in distaste to lay bare the flesh while the master wielded the birch.[1] This last procedure was still common in mid-Victorian times, and so was the system at Christ's Hospital where the boy was held firmly by the wrists and spreadeagled over the back of one man while another was free to use all his strength for the rod. Occasionally masters lost their tempers altogether, with results that fell little short of naval atrocities. It is not the fact that they reduced the back of the boy to a lacerated mass of scored meat and congealed blood that appals us now, although that happened frequently enough, but the fact that the boy was then cast back into the daily routine as though nothing had happened. In one case a friend spent part of the night by the bedside of the victim easing the shirt off the back and in pulling out 'at least a dozen pieces of birch-rod, which had penetrated deep into the flesh'.[2] He would have been in further trouble if he had used his condition as an excuse for drowsiness or failure to concentrate the next day. Christ's Hospital may have been the extreme example, brutality persisting there until the 1870s, but early Marlborough ran it very close indeed. The surprising fact, of great interest psychologically and sociologically, is that so few boys retaliated in kind. Undoubtedly many of the victims must have dreamt of murder—they certainly had enough justification—but the only known instance recorded, apart from those taking vengeance after they had left, was really due to another cause—when J. M. Wilson was stabbed in the shoulder on 6 November 1882.[3]

The most common minor punishment was 'lines', now so out of fashion, although it lingers still under a dozen different disguises and is even excused on educational grounds as 'spelling', 'corrections' and 'hand-writing'. Even in the mildest schools the minimum punishment was five or ten lines, to be copied out from a classical author in the best copperplate, but with a string of bad luck these penalties could mount up horribly, be doubled, or even redoubled. Imagine the state of mind of a boy faced with 500 lines to be written out to a close

1. For a painting of Etonian flogging, see *Change—A Revue of Eton in the Last Hundred Years*, 1932.
2. Lamb, op. cit., p. 152.
3. Wilson, op. cit., pp. 117–21.

deadline, or of young Cathcart of Wellington who managed to amass the penalty of 1,500 lines in a single week.[1] Ultimately, when the situation became quite impossible, a kindly master might resort to corporal punishment to clear the debt. Henry Hayman at one time did this as a matter of course, on Saturdays,[2] while the 'black book at Charterhouse' acted as a kind of cumulative record and clearing-house.

Flogging was an official punishment and rare for any individual boy. Fagging, on the other hand, was continuous and compulsory, a kind of bondage.[3] Outside class a junior was likely to be pounced upon for almost any task—cleaning shoes, making fires, sweeping up, shopping. He might be posted as a general lookout to warn of the approach of authority, or be sent out fishing or poaching. Cooking was a normal chore, and so was warming beds by lying in them. On suitable occasions he could be forced to play football, or act as a kind of retriever on the cricket field. The position varied from school to school and from one part of a school to another. Two juniors sitting side by side in class could be subjected to entirely different kinds of treatment. With a kindly prefect it was all no doubt a kind of game, and much enjoyed, but with an angry, spiteful one life became quite intolerable. There is plenty of evidence on both scores. In day schools, like St Paul's and Merchant Taylors', the need for servants or servitude did not exist and neither did fagging, while it appears to have been generally mild at Shrewsbury, but severe at Winchester and Rugby until the late 1860s at least. Apologists—of which Arnold was perhaps the most important—elevated the prefect-fagging system into 'something approaching a philosophy of education, as well as a Christian attack on evil'.[4] Another apologetic approach defined fagging as:

> . . . a power given by the supreme authorities of a school to the boys of the highest class or classes in it, to be exercised by them over the lower boys, for the sake of securing the advantages of regular

1. Newsome, *A History of Wellington College*, op. cit., p. 161.
2. Leach, op. cit., p. 131.
3. For some details of a fag's life, see Lamb, op. cit. For a typical factual contemporary account of fagging, see G. Melly, *School Experiences of a Fag . . .*, 1854. The more romantic and classic account, based on fact, is Thomas Hughes, *Tom Brown's Schooldays*.
4. A. B. Badger, *The Public Schools and the Nation*, 1944, p. 46.

government amongst the boys themselves, and avoiding the evils of anarchy—in other words, of the lawless tyranny of physical strength.[1]

These are brave words, but, as far as the records go, there were few instances of humanity to emerge from this situation, and the most significant occurred, paradoxically, in those who were excused fagging altogether—as in the celebrated case of the young boy who was publicly thanked and excused fagging for life by the prefects for attempting to save a comrade from drowning.

It is easy to ridicule fagging, but it should be remembered that the Public Schools Commission of 1864 supported it in a mild way, although it is difficult to find anyone else who did so outside the ranks of prejudiced teachers. The list of critics from 1837 onwards is long and continuous, both from those with experience and those with moral objections, from Thackeray to Staunton and Clement Dukes.[2]

Expulsion was the ultimate weapon. The swift sudden chopping and the dark lonely journey in the cab to the nearest station is the vision that comes immediately to mind, but that was only the most drastic form of removal. More frequently a boy who was stagnating and making no progress just drifted away at the end of term in a kind of enforced retirement or superannuation. Some schools, like Eton, disliked a system of removal for scholastic inertia. Having accepted the boys in the first place, it seemed ethically wrong to eliminate their mistakes as easily as this, and certainly it was an admission of failure. None the less the Commission of 1864 supported the opposite standpoint, and incorporated that view as General Recommendation xxv:

No boy should be suffered to remain in the school who fails to make reasonable progress in it. . . . A maximum age should be fixed for attaining each stage; and any boy who exceeds this maximum without reaching the corresponding stage of promotion should be removed from the school.[3]

1. G. Long, 'On the Discipline of Large Boarding Schools', *Quarterly Journal of Education*, 1836.
2. For criticisms of fagging and a general analysis of the whole background of public schools to public opinion, see E. C. Mack, *Public Schools and British Opinion, 1780–1860*, 1938, and *Public Schools and British Opinion Since 1860*, 1941.
3. PSC, i, p. 54.

It is a hard doctrine in tune with the spirit of the time, for this was the era of 'payment by results'. It enshrines the famous dictum, '. . . the first, second, and third duty of a schoolmaster is to get rid of unpromising subjects . . .'.[1]

Anyone who knows anything about the great headmasters of the nineteenth century could not possibly claim that they (with the exception of Thring) were excited over, or vitally concerned, with the lesser brethren. They were anxious to get rid of the dross, not reclaim it. They paid lip-service to the weaker members, even extolled the virtues of the average boy, but their eyes went to the Stanleys and the Kennedys. In a similar way, from at least the eighteenth century, headmasters have been extremely lax with boys of brilliance. There is a soft spot for the potential genius, and one could argue from actual examples in the case of a single headmaster, like Arnold with his pupils Vaughan, Lake and Clough, that the brighter the lad the softer the spot. 'What struck me was the way in which Arnold referred to them [Stanley, Vaughan and Lake] in matters of criticism . . . looking towards them with such respect shown in the very tone of his voice, and always getting a good answer.' [2] How natural and human this is; and anyone who has taught at all knows how impossible it is to resist the subtle flattery of such excellent response to one's teaching. It is difficult not to make excuses for the brilliant boy who transgresses and to dismiss the case on the grounds of eccentricity, or even to question the whole basis for the misdemeanour and blame something else. Somehow it seems right to argue with the bright, but not with the stupid. It has always been the same. Well before the Victorian period there were too many stories of Landor, Byron and Samuel Butler, corroborated by too many witnesses, for them all to be inventions. Eccentricity coupled with a sense of intellectual dash and humour has always appealed to masters, and Eton has maintained a great reputation for it. A typical case concerned a boy in the 1860s who grew a beard and then bolstered up his case by a long disputation with the headmaster, in Latin, on the meaning of the statutes. Finally, with all patience gone and on being ordered to shave, he sent the bill for two razors to the Provost.[3] This is breath-taking bravado

1. Stanley, op. cit. (teachers' edition, 1901), p. 110.
2. Said by J. L. Hoskyns.
3. Brinsley-Richards, op. cit., p. 349.

and typical of the kind of insolence that was, and still is, excused as a necessary by-product of potential genius.

The ordinary boy could not rely on such latitude. Punishment for him was almost inevitable, and only by chance could he escape the hook:

> Saturday, June 6th, 1846. . . . About 2 o'clock a son and heir was added to the Doctor's [Kennedy] family. Bells rung. The Doctor graciously announced an amnesty of penals and punishments of all sorts.[1]

Sometimes the absurdity of ordinary punishment produced an impasse only soluble by expulsion. A boy of thirteen might easily get a flogging for a semi-serious offence, and once over everyone concerned would promptly forget about it. The same remedy, however, could not be applied to a fully grown youth of seventeen or eighteen who was virtually a man in the sight of his fellows. Whether the headmaster was lenient or severe, the situation was distasteful and the example for lesser boys unfortunate. Removal was the simplest way here.

Expulsion with a capital E was the automatic penalty for stealing, riots, flagrant defiance and sexual offences—and still is. Although individual cases of these so-called crimes are recorded, the overall picture is scanty in the extreme, for schools have been secretive and no reliable figures, as far as can be traced, have ever been published. This means that the reputation of some headmasters as great expellers must be treated with reserve. Not only is there the danger of confusing removals with expulsions, but the fact that we have more details, for instance, of Arnold's victims than those of anyone else may merely mean that we know more about him than we do about others. An expulsion register or two would be a gold-mine of information, and would certainly throw a great deal of light on nineteenth-century schools.

Sexual indulgence was never excused—the mere fact that boys could then talk with some knowledge and authority, becoming centres of lewd conversation, was enough. The headmasters of Eton, Harrow and Winchester were agreed at least on this, and supported Benson without reserve in a quarrel with his governors over the expulsion of three boys for having had sexual experience with a servant girl in the holidays. The fact

1. Cowburn, op. cit., p. 141.

that 'the eldest of the three contracted a shameful disease' [1] no doubt strengthened Benson's hand, but it did not alter the principle at all. The same penalty was the reward for homosexuality whenever it was discovered. We know that this was widespread, and indeed still is, but the extent and intensity of it is mere conjecture, for the Victorian pall on sex applied consistently even in memoirs, in contrast to the frank reminiscences of more recent years. There are plenty of meaningless phrases, such as 'immorality', 'evil', 'laxity', but nothing precise. Only very rarely indeed do we have enough evidence to describe a situation in terrifying detail: 'It was the common practice [at Harrow under Vaughan] for every good-looking boy to be addressed by a female name; he was regarded either as public property or as the "bitch" of an older boy.' [2]

Perhaps the sexual indulgence of Vaughan himself contributed to this a little, but it is tempting to think that the situation was common in view of a great deal of indirect factual evidence, like Benson's preoccupation with the problem of placing wire entanglements on top of the dormitory cubicles, not to mention his orders about going to bed:

> While they [the young boys] are undressing, steward and matron to walk up and down in the middle of the dormitory and report any boy who goes out of his own dormitory to another. . . . Door of cubicles as at Eton to be incapable of fastening on inside, but may be locked on outside, every door to be commanded by a master key.[3]

Similar precautions over lavatories were common, presumably with the same problems in mind. In some schools privacy was quite impossible because there were no doors at all, and no shielding walls either. In one establishment at least the rows of closets were on public display over a wide arc of building and countryside—a situation not unknown in recent times.

Open speech on sex was taboo, not only in school but throughout life; tracts on the social evils of sex indulgence were couched in words that would not offend the most sensitive

1. Newsome, *Wellington College*, op. cit.
2. Phyllis Grosskurth, *John Addington Symonds*, 1964, p. 32.
3. Newsome, *Godliness and Good Learning*, op. cit., p. 45.

spirit, and so vague that it almost needs a suspicious mind nowadays to realize that they are about sex at all.[1] There was a difference of attitude here between different levels of society. The upper classes viewed it all with amused tolerance, or even open defiance (as in the private lives of many eminent men), or in the 'carpeting' of Benson for his attitude to the episode of the three boys and the servant girl. The lower classes also followed their own code, while in between the schoolmaster-clergyman belonged to that particular layer destined to become the spearhead of the Victorian obliteration of sex.

Even if we ignore the mere spectacular side of crime and punishment, life at a public school was not for the weak. There were few comforts, and conditions were primitive. At Shrewsbury, in the 1870s, H. W. Nevinson declared that '. . . education was a natural process which all decent people went through, like washing; and their ideas upon it were unscientific as was our method of "swilling", when we ran down naked from the bedrooms to sheds in the back yards, sluiced cold water over us with zinc basins, and then came dripping back to dry upstairs'.[2]

Life was tough in other ways as well. In 1866 Marlborough spent £31·6 per boy on board, and Rossall £29·7. A specimen dietary at Rossall consisted of the following:[3]

Breakfast: Tea or coffee, or bread or milk, bread and butter
Dinner: Beef and mutton, pudding or pastry daily   } *ad libitum*
Tea: As breakfast
Supper: Bread and cheese or meat occasionally

This is hardly an exciting diet, even if it is filling. One would expect it to be near the minimum, and yet this standard should be compared with that at Hurstpierpoint, where the estimated

1. For a general note on sex problems, see Lamb, op. cit., pp. 43–5. Sex is a serious problem in schools at all levels and of all types. Most of it is treated as private and information is correspondingly difficult to get. Without this 'secret' information it is difficult to judge any particular situation, and it is easy to ridicule the precautions when one has no responsibility.
2. Cowburn, op. cit., p. 184.
3. The information on the dietary can be found in SIC, i, Appendix III, pp. 28–35.

cost was over £10 less (actually £18·1 per annum), and even
this was not the lowest limit. At Christ's Hospital, in Lincoln,
a poor-boys' school, the cost of boarding was only £11·2, two
and a half times less than that outlined above! It is not
surprising that the Assistant Commissioner had reservations:
'They [the boys] are said to enjoy good health, but do not grow
up very big and vigorous.' [1]

The callousness behind this attitude is one of the least
attractive elements of the Victorian scene, and this aspect of
school life, and its relationship to the cupidity or zeal of the
masters working for profit, and other relevant matters, needs
deep consideration.

A boy had to attend at meals, prayers, classes and bedtime.
Otherwise, at most schools, he could do what he liked and go
where he pleased, if he could only evade fagging duties.
Organized games in the modern and late-Victorian sense did
not exist, although, as we shall see, there was a system of
matches organized by the boys. Walking, fishing, poaching,
hunting, fighting and generally chasing one another were
favourite pastimes at all seasons of the year. It was common to
find boys many miles from the school gates at one or other of
several ale-houses forming traditional turning- or focal-points.
They indulged in an extraordinary range of hobbies from
model-making to natural history, chemistry and ballooning.
The older boys were encouraged to use their initiative and be
adventurous. Some organized games, kept their own records
and accounts, employed professional coaches at cricket. Others
plunged into the latest enthusiasm to catch their fancy—play-
writing, acting, producing magazines—all taken up and discarded in interesting but unexplained cycles. Some schools had
developed their own specialisms, like the rowing at Eton or the
long-standing tradition of promoting public race meetings and
hunts—taken at Rugby to the extent of keeping a secret pack
of foxhounds. All this was regarded by headmasters from Wooll
and Butler to Vaughan and Benson as highly meritorious, and
this attitude, which also ensured that boys could enjoy their
sins in private, prevailed until the 1860s at least, in spite of
external pressures to change it. The close watch over boys and
the introduction of the busy life did not come till later, although

1. ibid., p. 28.

masters always intervened to shield their charges from 'evil influences' whenever they considered moral virtue to be at stake.

Socially, the boys were divorced from cultural contamination with the lower and middle classes, and thereby cut off in sympathy from a true appreciation of science and industry. In a similar way the boys were denied any sight of awkward passages in standard authors and texts. The Victorian school may have been grossly immoral in some ways, but outwardly it was the temple of Thomas Bowdler, the expurgator of Shakespeare. Dickens and Ainsworth were specifically condemned by most headmasters,[1] and so were the 'yellow novels' to be seen on railway bookstalls,[2] although, as always, boys with outside contacts managed to outwit authority and secrete a few copies. In all this things have hardly changed. Dickens may have been replaced by D. H. Lawrence, or even some newer and less honoured name, temporarily under a cloud, but the spirit remains.

As a result of their freedom over many years, Victorian youth in all the public schools inherited a code of rights covering the use of its leisure, whether it was in sports and games, fighting, fishing, hunting, fagging or dramatics. Both juniors and prefects defended these rights against all-comers, even the headmaster, and the famous riots and rebellions almost always occurred over an alleged abuse of rights, seen typically in the Arnold episodes over fishing, the rebellions against Keate, and Tait's trouble with school bounds.[3]

Undoubtedly the playing-field itself offered the greatest scope for the exercise of freedom. By the time of Queen Victoria's accession Eton, Harrow and Winchester had been playing one another at cricket for a dozen years, and the heroes of schoolboys were not the open scholars, so beloved of headmasters, but the giants of the cricket and football field. Officially games were an incidental. They were not an integral part of the school curriculum, and apart from fencing and dancing, extra fees

1. Almost all the headmasters of whom we have knowledge condemned the modern novelists of their time. Arnold was particularly vehement.
2. For 'yellow novels', translations from Dumas, etc., see Newsome, *Wellington College*, op. cit., p. 119.
3. See Lamb, op. cit., pp. 81–8. Detailed accounts of many uprisings are given in school histories or in biographies of the headmasters, particularly the more recent assessments.

were not usually charged for them, except where special coaches were engaged. Masters encouraged and watched,[1] but essentially they were not involved; they might even play by invitation, as so many of the staff did at Eton in the 1850s and 1860s, but that was all. They did not interfere. Arrangements were usually in the hands of the heads of societies, and Edmond Warre calculated that at Eton nearly £1,300 a year passed through their hands and about £100 was spent on balls for fives alone.[2] In many ways this old system was more like the modern university than the modern school.

In some form or other cricket and football were almost universal by 1837, and so were athletics and cross-country running, although local circumstances curtailed one or other of these in some places, as at Harrow, where the farmers successfully objected. Altogether a vast array of other sports was carried on, from boating to boxing, single stick, swimming, fives, racquets and quoits. Some schools with a long-standing tradition, like Eton with its wall game, had games peculiar to themselves, while others invented new forms with special rules, as in the outstanding example of a new variety of football developed at Rugby.[3] Although there is a good deal of mist over the details, it would appear that this game, which in time became identified, almost universally, with manliness and the public-school spirit, was started by a son of one of the very first sojourners, a boy named William Webb Ellis. In 1823, in a kind of rebellion against his fellow-players and the existing rules, he picked up the ball and ran forward with it. It may well be significant that this was done by a member of a despised section of the community, and the episode might easily be interpreted psychologically and sociologically if more was known about it. Whatever the urge may have been that started this heresy, Webb Ellis opened up what was virtually a new game with great possibilities, a kind of legalized toughness, and Rugby football became popular and soon attracted royal interest.[4] For a long time this particular version was only one

1. Sometimes, as at Shrewsbury, the headmaster himself provided the playing-field.
2. For the money spent on sports at Eton. see PSC, III, Qq. 5393–4.
3. The game of Rugby football in the early days had very different rules from the game played today.
4. A royal interest in Rugby football originated with Queen Adelaide on 19 October 1839.

of many varieties, and perhaps the most exclusive types were played at schools with mixed and lonely traditions—like Stonyhurst,[1] where they retained their own particular brands of cricket and football until the 1880s, although the more orthodox version of cricket had been introduced alongside the old in 1860.

The use of leisure has always been immensely important. The old headmasters considered that the freedom of a boy to use his leisure as he wanted outside the classroom and beyond the master's eye was not only a right but essential to a growing independent spirit. This is captured in the school books of the period. In *Tom Brown* wandering, games and exercise were hardly a minor part of a boy's education, and so it was at every public school.

Sport, particularly cricket, was taken very seriously indeed by the boys, and professionals were employed to develop standards. At Rugby no less a person than John Lillywhite was taken on in 1850 and the game was revitalized not only at the school but throughout the neighbourhood.[2] No one interested in cricket could fail to be stirred by the announcement that on 5 and 6 April 1852 a match would be played between teams consisting of 'First Ten (with Lillywhite) *v.* Next Nine (with Wisden and Martingell).' This particular phase reached a climax with a three-day match in 1854 between an England XI *v.* Twenty from the Rugby Club and School.

The situation was expressed by Staunton in 1865: 'If at Eton work is not so vigorous as it might be, play is certainly not neglected . . . the captain of the boats is the greatest man in the school, and next in rank to him stands the captain of the elevens.'[3] Sport was part of leisure in those days; it belonged to the boys, and was necessary for developing individuality and the democratic spirit. There was something quite distasteful about the man in authority who must interfere, who could not sit back and leave the boys alone. Vaughan expressed this as well as anyone, saying that he had no wish to supervise children

1. For details of Stonyhurst, etc., see A. S. Barnes, *The Catholic Schools of England*, 1926, p. 168.
2. For some of the details of Lillywhite, see the local newspapers of the time, and also *The Scores of the Cricket Matches Played at Rugby School from 1851–1858*.
3. Staunton, op. cit., p. 36.

if it meant following the '. . . boys into their hours of recreation and rest, avowedly as spies, coercing freedom of speech and action, or reporting to their superiors what such observation has gleaned'.[1]

These remarks were used by Vaughan in 1854 as justification against taking on more masters or ushers, and the same spirit applied to the relationship between prefects and the rest of the school.[2] They were meant to be leaders, not policemen.

This freedom may have been one of the glories of public-school life, but it also had its undesirable side, as the schoolboy novels tell. It guaranteed privacy and therefore provided the perfect environment for gang warfare and sexual perversion. It gave ample opportunity for the bully to make the life of the timid very unpleasant indeed. Many have assumed that Arnold started a reform that abolished these abuses and that it spread from Rugby to the whole network through the influence of colleagues and pupils, as though a mere change in moral outlook was enough.[3] Unfortunately, as we have said, bullying, at times very severe, continued right through his reign and, on the evidence of Melly[4] and many others, into that of his successor, Tait, and beyond him too. The same was true of the other schools, and even of the new, of Marlborough and of Wellington. Claims to the contrary run counter to all the facts, and to the common sense of the situation. While the principle of 'boy freedom' was paramount, any other claim shows a lack of knowledge of children.

This was a time when the 'trades-unionism' of boys was displayed in its most exaggerated form. All boys, whether prefects or not, were subject to the code of secrecy, of 'not splitting' to a master or parent. This particular allegiance was, and still is, far stronger than any imposed moral law, so that only the grossest abuses which could not be concealed or cases where

1. C. J. Vaughan, *A Letter to Viscount Palmerston on the Monitorial System of Harrow School*, 1854.
2. Typical of Vaughan's critics at the time was 'Anti-Monitor', *Remarks Addressed to the Rev. Dr Vaughan in Reply to His Recent Letter to Viscount Palmerston*, 1854. This work illustrates the contemporary ignorance of internal matters in the schools, as illustrated by the remarks on Thomas Arnold.
3. For bullying, etc., at Rugby under Arnold, see T. W. Bamford, 'Discipline at Rugby under Arnold', *Educational Review* (November 1957), x, no. 1, pp. 18–28.
4. For Melly see Melly, op. cit.

actual physical harm was involved were ever reported. There are indications that this phenomenon was complex and manifest at many levels. It could apply to a whole school and also include the headmaster. In one instance, when one boy split on the sexual perversion of his headmaster, he was ostracized, even though he, the boy, had already left.[1] In a similar way the real facts about a school did not leak out for forty or fifty years— until the 'memoir' stage, in fact—parents being kept in the dark by their own children. Two friends could have their secrets and be loyal, and the same applied to a class, or a team, or a house. Such bonds could not be shaken by a mere show of authority or by force or reason. Arnold himself never fully appreciated these points, and even tried to force boys to 'tell' when he thought it their duty to do so. We have evidence that many boys faced with this problem preferred to be expelled.

This code also explains what is otherwise a puzzling feature to the assiduous reader of biography. Continually we meet with an account of excesses which the boy suffered in the junior school, to be followed by the claim that the school was cleaned up when he became a prefect.[2] These statements are too frequent not to be accepted as sincere, and yet they overlap, showing that excesses were continuous in the lower reaches. The answer would seem to lie in the fact that life appears differently to those in authority from those who are not, and that a boy's code of honour and secrecy acts as a barrier against authority—including prefects no less than parents and masters.

All this is typical of the early and mid-Victorian periods, but, by the end of the century, there is no doubt that the worst excesses were eliminated, almost certainly as a result of increased organization at the expense of boy freedom. The old principle of respecting a boy's character and allowing it to develop in private as he wished gave way to a regulated existence, with the boys' leisure ruthlessly time-tabled and supervised. This applied particularly to the playing-field and the new spirit of competitive games.

It would be absurd to suggest that we know precisely when this change occurred, and it is in any case certain that the

1. Grosskurth, op. cit.
2. For three typical examples of 'cleaning up' in Arnold's day, see Bamford, 'Discipline at Rugby', art. cit., p. 27, ref. 7.

timing was different in different schools, if only from the obvious fact that the headmaster was responsible for any change of emphasis, and change could only occur, in practice, after prolonged pressure or with a change of headmaster. The generation of heads in the 1850s and 1860s were of the old school and before any drastic change had come about. To the boys it was a revolution; to the masters it was largely another set of duties—a twenty-four-hour shift. The older generation had never frowned on games and exercise. Many of them had themselves been too keen and successful at sport for that. Balston is a case in point, and so too were Butler and Wordsworth of Harrow, not to mention the other Wordsworth of Winchester[1] and David Williams[2] earlier. These men revelled in exercise for its own sake, but there is no evidence that they took over sport and used it as an organized and official part of supervised education. The number of runs scored at Lord's had not yet been felt as a vital matter affecting the honour of the whole school—except at boy level—although the increasing publicity of these occasions in the newspapers was undoubtedly a factor for change. The incomplete evidence that we have would indicate that the new approach came slowly, in the 1860s and 1870s. At Rugby in 1859 there was one fives court, one small pavilion and little else; twenty years later, there were nine courts, two pavilions and a gymnasium, besides a new swimming-bath and a rifle corps. By 1880 the era of specialization in sport and leisure had obviously arrived.

As for the start of the change, there is little doubt that the consistent appointment of lay staff from the middle and late 1850s or beyond (as we have seen earlier each school had a different starting-point) helped the process. The accent on the chapel remained, but the official combination of vigour and the Christian spirit, with both geared to educational ends, became popular as muscular Christianity. By the 1860s some masters, even at Eton, were thinking of sport as an essential part of the educational machine (1865):

An assistant master who has taken an active interest in what may be termed the physical education of Eton, bears testimony to the

1. For Charles Wordsworth and the relationship of games to public schools, see Newsome, *Godliness and Good Learning*, op. cit.
2. See How, op. cit., p. 46.

beneficial effects, not only physical but moral, of a keen participation in athletic sports. It diminishes, in his opinion, the class of idlers and loiterers—a class by common consent most mischievous, to whom too many temptations are offered by the street and little shops of Eton, and is an antidote to luxurious and extravagant habits, to drinking and vice of all kinds.[1]

At Winchester, key dates appear to be the end of the triangular contest of Eton–Winchester–Harrow at Lord's in 1854 and the resumption of the Eton–Harrow match in 1858. The pride of many Wykehamists was hurt, and they wanted to see the new spirit of athleticism introduced so that the honour of the school could be restored. They took the growing and popular view that games provided the basis for everything that was beneficial to the individual and his country—moral character, co-operation, consideration, patriotism and the rest. The stirring events of empire in the 1850s, with the Crimean War (1854–6) and the Indian Mutiny (1857–8), undoubtedly helped, and so did the railways and the schoolboy stories, headed by *Tom Brown's Schooldays* (1857), though the real influences may well lie far deeper. In the case of Winchester, we also see the importance of the headmaster as an instrument, or, in this case, a counter-instrument, of change—for Moberly fought a strong and successful rearguard action.

The full complexity of this issue, as seen across the whole range of schools old and new, has still to be realized. The long-term result, however, was an over-regulated life, seen typically at Wellington somewhat later:

There were few activities for boys to indulge in legally, outside the manly pursuits which the community deemed permissible. . . . Morning school at seven began the day, followed by the long hours of ordered activity which were so arranged, as Harold Nicholson has shown, to give to the authorities the satisfaction of knowing not only what any given boy should be doing at any particular moment, but, 'exactly what the said boy would be doing at 3.30 p.m., six weeks hence'.[2]

It is difficult not to agree with the view that the energies of the boys were drained on the playing-field, and their passion for hero-worship and gang formation caged within the concept of the House. This is put another way by G. F. Lamb:

1. Staunton, op. cit., p. 36.
2. Newsome, *Wellington College*, op. cit., p. 264. The same general trend for Rugby can be seen in A. G. Butler, *The Three Friends*, 1900, Introduction.
7

One reason for the tremendous emphasis on 'healthy games'—compulsory cricket or football several times a week, and no slacking —has been the master's desire to leave no room for anything else. 'My prophylactic against certain unclean microbes was to send the boys to bed dead tired,' the headmaster of the United Services College admitted to his most distinguished Old Boy.[1]

The new accent on organized games produced its inevitable reaction, seen as early as 1858 in the review of Fitzjames Stephen, while school doctors were continually trying to pacify the fears of parents:

The attitude taken up by many parents with reference to games at school is simply intolerable. . . . When the question of school games is under discussion, the parent frequently urges the objection that the boy is too delicate to take part. But when the same boy is examined for 'Life Assurance', a marvellous 'bill of health' is presented, with the absence of every hereditary taint.[2]

With the takeover of sport went several other associated changes. If we look at the pictures of games in early and mid-Victorian periods, there is a general atmosphere of makeshift and abandon. There was any amount of toughness, even brutality, but it was all less organized and gives the impression of great fun, and of great terror, too, judging by the way fags tried their best to evade the occasional turnout. The modern exaggerations of team spirit, fighting for the school honour, colours, ties, tassels and the rest did not exist. Arthur Ponsonby stresses this point particularly well:

Compare a photograph of a group of schoolboys of today [1912] with one of only forty or fifty years ago. The comparison is instructive. In the latter boys will be seen lounging about in different attitudes with a curious variety of costumes. If it is a football eleven they will be in varied and strange garments, with their trousers tucked into their socks, some bareheaded, some with ill-fitting caps and old shrunken shirts, others perhaps neater, but each one individual and distinct. The group today consists of two or three rows of boys beautifully turned out with immaculate, perfectly fitting clothing. In the football eleven each will wear a cap, shirt, shorts, stockings of precisely the same pattern. They stand and sit so that the line of the peaks of their caps, of their folded arms, of their bare knees is mathematically level. And even their faces! You can hardly tell one from another. . . . Now no one will say that this

1. Lamb, op. cit., p. 45.
2. Dukes, op. cit., p. 289.

can be accounted for by the improvement in the tailor's art and an artistic desire for regularity in the photographer. It is, without doubt, an outward and visible sign not only of the love of the appearance of smartness, but of the stereotyping and conventionalizing effect of our modern educational system. This stereotyping . . . constitutes perhaps the strongest indictment that has to be brought against our Public Schools.[1]

And the same may be said of the masters, but that is another story. Again we have a significant change which, to judge by the actual photographs of teams and masters, began to take place in the 1860s in many schools.

If we collect the evidence on the changes of attitude in the Victorian era to manliness, to the staff in orders, to boy freedom, to games, to uniformity, we find that there is evidence of a new look in the 1850s, but that it was another twenty years or more before it was firmly and generally established. Undoubtedly some of these changes were related, but which were the seminal elements and which the important outside influences are, at the present time, a matter of some doubt.

From 1870 or thereabouts, at a conservative estimate, there was a subtle but organized drive by authority to sublimate the boy's self to a team; and this way of life, which resembled nothing so much as a human anthill heaving for a common purpose, was elevated by its supporters into a major principle of education. This attitude was progressive and reached its zenith in the 1910s and 1920s, although in recent years there has been a marked tendency to play down team games, so that we are, in some ways, moving back to the early pre-Victorian ideal of individualism.

Alongside this change on the playing-field have occurred similar and complicated changes in the curriculum. The narrowness of the classics gave way to an assortment of nine or more disciplines, including manual skills, the exploration of which properly belongs elsewhere.

1. Arthur Ponsonby, *The Decline of the Aristocracy*, 1912, pp. 207–8. The corresponding prim precision to that described by Arthur Ponsonby for boys is seen in the attitudes of masters, as shown by photographs between the middle and late Victorian periods. Two typical illustrations are to be seen in Boyd, op. cit. (1) the older, careless, haphazard and individualistic attitudes of Warden Sewell and Fellows (1857), facing p. 85; (2) the more stylized, symmetrically arranged picture with the men in neat rows seen in Warden Thompson and Masters (1893), facing p. 224.

In time boys became old boys. With luck they might be thrust into an adult, neutral situation, but if they passed on to the university, or to some other scholastic or training institution, they were likely to be pitted against boys from other schools. A normal, tough youth will ride this without much difficulty, but the sensitive lad without worldly experience will be all too aware of his weakness and ignorance, and will experience again all the agonies of his first day at school, except that this time the basis of his insecurity will have changed from the problem of a socially acceptable parental background to the socially acceptable school. This was the situation that L. E. O. Charlton faced when he was projected into Sandhurst in the 1890s:

> . . . the Etonian was . . . the aristocrat of the little college world. This pride of place may have been grudged by those from Harrow or Winchester, but the cadets who came from the Haileyburys, the Radleys, the Wellingtons or the Tonbridges had no illusions on the subject and were in consequence able to regain their balance of self-esteem only by assuming an air of lofty disdain towards the ignoble fry from the Brightons, the Lancings or the Epsoms.[1]

The half-way house between the school and the adult world is the Old Boys' Society. At once this brings us face to face with a fascinating sociological phenomenon of the first magnitude, with an immense literature almost wholly devoid of objectivity and analysis. Pride of school is an age-old feeling, and documentary accounts of the gatherings of old boys stretch back into the eighteenth century at least, with all the usual varieties of celebration and remembrance, drinks and dinners, poetry and lampoons, speeches and back-slapping.[2] It is easy to see why a school should keep in touch with its products, if only to judge teaching skill in the acid test of the successful and happy adult life of its pupils, but what is not quite so easy to explain is the well-developed homing instinct of some old boys. It would be farcical to suggest that the vast numbers on the rolls of the societies are stirred by a common urge that may or may not be fulfilled, but this unexplored field might well produce significant evidence on the influence of education at various levels. It

1. L. E. O. Charlton, *Charlton*, 1938, p. 53.
2. Accounts of some early meetings of old boys were given in the *Gentleman's Magazine*. For another aspect of school solidarity through old boys, see Chapter 11.

might also throw light on the influence of the old boys, individually and collectively, on such matters as the reaction of the school to social and cultural change, the significance of success, the development of pressure-groups. Whatever theories are advanced, from Freud to opportunism, to explain the apparent fact of old-boy solidarity, at least it is abundantly clear from the evidence of any single speech-day that some men, at any rate, need to revisit old battle-grounds.

Records show that the old boy who carries admiration and nostalgia far enough to entrust his own child to the same process he went through is a minority man, especially in the past, although both Westminster and Eton had the reputation of serving many families over many generations in the eighteenth and early nineteenth centuries. In a matter of this kind we would expect each school to present a different story, except perhaps for those at the summit, like Westminster, in the old days, and Eton, but the only known details appear to come from **Rugby** and **Winchester**. At Rugby it would seem that father–son continuity was non-existent until the time of Wooll (1807 onwards), as though boys before Wooll were loth to send their own sons through the same ordeal.[1] The percentage of boys sending the next generation only reached ten in 1853, and a similar situation existed at Winchester until 1880.[2]

1. For a summary of Rugby continuity, see Bamford, 'Discipline at Rugby', art. cit., p. 26, ref. 32.
2. For Winchester, see T. J. H. Bishop, *Origins and Achievements of Winchester College Pupils 1836 to 1934* (Ph.D. thesis for the University of London, 1962).

CHAPTER FIVE

The Public Schools, Science and Industry

By the time Victoria came to the throne in 1837, Britain was already an industrial nation. Its future lay with the products of science and, by inference, in a healthy approach to science in at least some of the young. It is not surprising, therefore, that the roots of science teaching lie far back in the eighteenth century, or even earlier for schools specializing in such crafts and skills as navigation.

For some of the public schools science began in the 1770s, if in a casual kind of way. Several men who had specialized in presenting the wonders of science in a practical manner began to travel about the country, spending three or four weeks in one place and then moving on.[1] They stayed at local inns and gave a whole series of lectures in each locality, covering a wide range of subject-matter: electricity, pneumatics, astronomy, hydrostatics, optics, galvanism, and related aspects of biology and the human sciences. With a school near by the series would be delivered in duplicate—one set for the local gentry and intelligentsia, at the cost of a guinea per person, and a second series for the school. Each lecture covered a theme with suitable demonstrations and experiments as the main attraction. With such an ambitious programme, an extensive and bulky amount of diagrams, apparatus and mechanical models had to be carried around the country in a special coach as part of the luggage. In those early days audiences were almost totally devoid of knowledge. Some of the instruments were beautiful and the demonstrations ingenious and dramatic, so that an atmosphere of wonder was created, like that caught in the

1. A typical scheme of work for the travelling scientist, as it applied to a public school, can be seen in an advertisement—of the handbill variety—kept in Rugby Public Reference Library.

celebrated pictures of *The Air Pump*[1] and *The Orrery*[2] by the
contemporary painter, Joseph Wright of Derby.

With the blessing of the headmasters of Eton, Harrow and
Rugby any boy who could manage the fee obtained an idea of
the range of science, even if these visits were rare and only once
in every two or three years. This long-standing tradition,
associated with the Walkers and Deane Franklin, was broken
for Rugby by a personal feud[3] between Arnold and D. F. Walker
in the very year that Victoria came to the throne, so that the
new era there was celebrated by the extinction of science rather
than by its encouragement. This was only five years before
Arnold died, and five years, too, before the visit of the chemist,
Justus von Liebig, to England. It was, in effect, the last stand
of total reaction, for lower down the social scale science was
already being taught theoretically and practically in some
grammar schools, and appeared generally in some form or other
in the curriculum of academies all over the country.

In 1849 a new approach was made at both Eton and Rugby.
S. T. Hawtrey began to arrange weekly lectures on natural
philosophy by eminent men of science of the calibre of Tyndall
and Baden Powell. Attendance was voluntary and cost 2*s*. a
week for each course. It was serious to the extent that written
work was handed in, and a fair coverage of science was achieved
in a few years, one man supervising the content and avoiding
any serious overlap.[4] The same system of visiting lecturers was
used at Winchester from 1857 as a direct result of pressure from
the Oxford Commission. This was a compulsory course for all
boys in the school, and was held in the summer term. It would
seem, therefore, that Winchester has the technical distinction of
being the first of the great schools with compulsory science, even
though it was held at the highly unpopular time of Saturday
afternoon, and in spite of some very harsh things which have
been said about the techniques: '. . . [the teacher's] meagre
apparatus was stored in so damp a cupboard that his experiments usually broke down'.[5]

1. Tate Gallery.
2. Joseph Wright Collection, Derby Art Gallery.
3. See Bamford, *Thomas Arnold*, Chapter 11.
4. A good deal of the S. T. Hawtrey story can be deduced from PSC.
5. *Report of the Committee to Enquire into the Position of Natural Science . . .*,
1918, p. 5.

It was a pity that Winchester did not accept the advice of the Commission and elect three Fellows specially for this purpose; had they done so, then Moberly, the headmaster, would have gone down in history as the father figure of science-teaching rather than a great obstructionist.

Meanwhile, at Rugby, a famous scientist-physician, William Sharp, arrived in the town as a working medical sojourner,[1] placed his sons at the school and began to practise. In the same year, 1849, Sharp gave his first lectures at the school, but how far these were successful it is impossible to say now. Two or three years later the work was taken over by Berdmore Compton, to be followed by Henry Highton and, especially, J. M. Wilson, in 1859.

These men were quite exceptional; Highton was awarded medals for telegraphy and Wilson worked on double stars. They stood on the frontiers of knowledge and explored in a way that very few masters attempt today. Perhaps they felt themselves to be pioneers, and it was this that made the difference. Their achievements were entirely a personal triumph, for they had little encouragement except from the locality, and until 1861 only the most modest start on a science curriculum had been made. No corner could be found for it on the premises at Rugby, and the experiments were performed out of sight, in the cloakroom of the Town Hall a hundred yards away down the road from the school, with the apparatus locked up in two cases so that the townspeople could use the space for other purposes at night.[2] At the end of 1861, two sets of boys, forty-one in all, were each involved for two hours every week. The master concerned, Wilson, only did this as a sideline, for he was employed more as a mathematics than a science master, since fourteen hours were spent on the study of algebra, Euclid and trigonometry compared with four on natural philosophy.[3] It was a miserable amount, even if it did mean that science was at last on the official time-table.[4]

1. William Sharp was a typical instance of a professional sojourner. Other professions included teachers, magistrates, solicitors, officers of the armed forces.
2. At the time the Town Hall was a multi-purpose building.
3. For science at Rugby, see Wilson, op. cit., and also J. M. Wilson, *Notes on the Early History of the Rugby Natural History Society*.
4. Details of Wilson's time-table, subject-matter, etc., from PSC, II.

This is easily the most favourable account that can be given for the main schools, since Rugby was the forerunner among them in science teaching. This fact alone indicates the appalling lack of recognition given to this subject in 1861—the year in which the Clarendon Commission was appointed. Fundamentally, the schools and the rest of the country were different worlds. It is as though the English heritage did not exist. Newton had died over 130 years before, the Industrial Revolution was more than a century old and the heroic age of industry associated with Boulton, Watt and Murdock was already more than fifty years in the past. England was rapidly being covered with railways, and the great scientific and industrial spectacle of the Hyde Park Exhibition was a ten-year-old memory. All this had had no effect on the schools whatsoever, and they were still pursuing the same line that had suited an out-of-date agricultural society dominated by landowners. At first sight this would appear to be conservatism carried to the point of blindness. On the other hand, the fact that several schools were involved under highly independent headmasters makes the common approach to this issue appear to show something more than sheer obstinacy. To say the least, they were educated and intelligent men, and their attitude needs to be explored to do them justice.

THE ATTITUDE OF THE SCHOOLS TO SCIENCE BEFORE THE CLARENDON REPORT

The argument that the schools were not reflecting the national picture is only strictly applicable in a situation where the needs of the clientele and the nation coincide.

The landed gentry, with large estates and assured incomes, stood for apparent solidity in a shifting world; they did not yet need to change their way of life. In the public mind science was linked with industry, and this obscured its respectability in upper-class (landed) eyes. This does not mean that the gentry did not admire it, or even invest in it, but rather that industry was not for them. Like the rest of the world they were awestruck by the march of science; they goggled at the giant machines of the Great Exhibition, but this was only the admiration of a spectacle. The landed gentry, at this stage, would no more have countenanced their sons going into a manual occupation

because they admired the processes and the products than they would have welcomed a daughter on the stage because they enjoyed the theatre.

In spite of this, it was true that a few members of the gentry and aristocracy had always been interested in science, more perhaps in the eighteenth than the nineteenth century. Some, like Bacon, Boyle and Cavendish, are numbered in the first rank. But the reputation of these few spread over the centuries should not blind us to the fact that they were highly exceptional, and when it is realized that, at a very conservative estimate, there were over 21,000 adult men in the upper classes in 1840 alone, it is clear that a scientifically minded adult member of the gentry was a very rare specimen. This fact can easily be checked by an analysis of the careers of old boys in the registers in a similar manner to that attempted later, in Chapter 9.[1] They all tell the same tale, and confirm the generally held view of men like J. Hooker,[2] that even a superior profession like medicine was beyond the pale.

Virtually none of the products of these schools was going to compete with others in industry, while science was not required for the accepted professions of scholastics, the law and the church, and only for certain specialized sections of the army could a special case be made. Even those who were to be involved in government at national or local level, with the power of making decisions which affected industry, were not handicapped at all by an ignorance of mathematics and science. They reached their goal without knowledge of any kind beyond the classics, on the theory prevalent at the time that the real needs of an administrator were a well-trained mind and a character that nurtured the power of decision—features that were supposed to be well developed by the public schools.[3] As Mr Jowett expressed it to Sir Charles Trevelyan in January

1. A convenient source of adult old boy interests in the first half of the nineteenth century, but a little early for us perhaps, comes from Eton, where the number entering science and medicine was negligible compared with the very large number concerned with Parliament and the law. See R. A. Austen Leigh, *Eton College Register, 1753–1790*, 1921, pp. 601–8.
2. For J. Hooker's views on recruitment for medicine, see PSC, IV p. 386, Q. 113 *et. seq.*
3. The relationship between the public schools and the ideal background for work in administration is discussed from several points of view in later chapters.

1854: '. . . it will not do to frame our examination [for the civil service] on any mere theory of education. We must test a young man's ability by what he knows, not by what we wish him to know.'[1]

Any relevance to the work to be done by the man in the future was ignored, and indeed was rendered highly unlikely by the weighting of the marks. This principle still seems to be the official view a century later, so we can hardly ridicule belief in this doctrine in the middle years of the nineteenth century.

It follows, from the schools' point of view, that potential future employment was not so important as the development of the child's wits and character. That this process was best developed by the classics was as self-evident to the upper-class Victorian as the axioms of Euclid and the training quality of an ancient language was only one phase of an attitude which worshipped most things classical. The architecture of the Greeks and Romans was copied, their literature supreme, and only on the Acropolis at Athens was the true spirit of democracy to be found. An ideal way of life was a combination of the classical virtues of antiquity with the moral and spiritual attributes of Christianity. The way to the first lay through a study of ancient literature and culture, and to the second through the Bible (preferably in Greek) and the church service. This was the opinion of every Anglican headmaster of any significance— except perhaps Wilson—up to the 1890s, although most of them had to yield slowly to outside pressures in the introduction of other subjects.[2]

It would be wrong, however, to assume that the Anglican headmasters were anti-science as such. The hard core of Thomas Arnold,[3] Hawtrey and Moberly were not unsympathetic. Arnold was notorious for his view that the development of industry was a godsend and the one hope for the emancipation of the lower classes:

> Those unsightly chimnies and that disfiguring smoke are a most wholesome balance to the palace, and the garden, and the woods of Wentworth. Were it not for them, England would be no better

1. A Bain, *Practical Essays*, 1884, p. 75.
2. The wider view of the curriculum held by non-Anglicans is seen typically in the works of Lant Carpenter.
3. For the relationship between Arnold and science, see Bamford, *Thomas Arnold*, chapter 11.

than Russia or Poland—we should be the mere serfs of a territorial aristocracy.[1]

It is quite true that he stopped the only science-teaching in operation at Rugby, but that was probably a political matter and a clash of personalities rather than a serious curricular dispute. Although fundamentally a classicist, he had personal sympathies with science, as is shown by his flowers, his interest in rocks, his hopes for the future, his visits to the British Association and his scientific friends like Buckland. It would be very difficult to find a contemporary anywhere who appreciated the social importance of the industrial upheaval more than he did. However, he did not see it as the hope of education and relate the ethos of science and industry to the school in the way that Sanderson did fifty years later. Education and industry were separate in Arnold's mind, and as an educational engine he knew the classics to be supreme as an inculcator of moral value:

> Physical science alone can never make a man educated; even the formal sciences [grammar, arithmetic, logic, geometry], valuable as they are with respect to the discipline of the reasoning powers, cannot instruct the judgement; it is only moral and religious knowledge which can accomplish this.[2]

There are signs, however, that Arnold began to change his mind later, and one of the question marks over the early Victorian era is the influence this man might have had, had he not died prematurely in 1842. However that might be, the refusal to confuse education with material progress was common throughout the century. It is seen particularly well in Arnold's son, Matthew, who saw education as the inculcation of culture. If one agrees with Matthew's definition of culture as activity towards perfection and social usefulness, and attained through an appreciation of the best thoughts and sayings, then, by his argument, we are back to Athens.

Like Thomas Arnold, Hawtrey,[3] at Eton, had scientifically minded relatives, and was so fascinated by the wonders of the 1851 Exhibition that he set it as a subject of a Latin Prize Essay! Important though Arnold and Hawtrey may be, they

1. ibid, p. 119.
2. T. Arnold, *Lecture to Rugby Mechanics' Institute.*
3. See F. St J. Thackeray, *Memoir of Edward Craven Hawtrey*, 1896, p. 106 *et seq.*

are only threshold Victorians, and the most crucial case of all was that of George Moberly, the headmaster of Winchester, with a reputation as the hard reactionary and enemy of science.[1] Although he resisted the subject as a serious part of the curriculum, he was none the less interested enough himself to attend every one of the lecture series at Winchester and to check the attendance of his boys. Even so, the real purpose of school was the training of the mind to provide a useful general basis for life; liking a subject, even if it were important, was not a sufficient reason for placing it on the time-table. This point is perhaps best illustrated in the examination of George Moberly himself by the Public Schools Commissioners on 30 May 1862:

LORD DEVON: Are the physical sciences not of value as a discipline of the mind?
MOBERLY: I hardly know what their value is. I do think it is very desirable that young people and old people should know these things. I think they are matters of accomplishment and knowledge which everybody should know something of. But as a matter of education and training of the mind, which is our particular duty as instructors, I do not feel the value of them. . . . I think with respect to physical science, there are three points of view. . . . First there is the actual learning. The learning of anything is in itself a good; while listening to a lecture on any subject of natural philosophy you are getting information. . . . Secondly, there are the practical applications of science; and thirdly, above all, if a man is pursuing a science practically and experimentally, so as to be making discoveries, and carrying it forward to greater heights of perfection than were attained before, then he is indeed exercising the highest faculties a man can have. But boys in school will not be pursuing science experimentally, they can only be taught what other people have done, they will only get such knowledge secondhand. They cannot do what the leaders of science have done, they can only be told of the results they have arrived at, without being able to test their accuracy, or to follow them up in any practical way. . . .
LORD DEVON: Then the difficulty [of a boy being original] is one which arises with regard to all subjects which are being taught?
MOBERLY: Yes . . . but the difference I think is this: a boy who has learned grammar, has learned to talk and to write in all his life; he has possessed himself for ever of an instrument of power. A man who has learned the laws of electricity has got the facts of science, and when they are gone, they are gone for good and all. . . .[2]

1. For Moberly's defence of his own actions, see PSC, III, Q. 481 *et seq.*
2. PSC, III (Winchester), Qq. 506, 511 and 512.

Moberly had some of his facts wrong, as in his statement concerning the practical work done by boys, but if we can ignore these shortcomings, his attitude does partly represent the crux. Whereas the proponents of the 'discoverer' approach have often overstated their case, as Moberly suggests, this kind of objective argument, which appeared so valid to the non-scientist, is typical of the attack on any subject of the curriculum. It is the spirit that is important. In the last educational analysis, the facts of science are no more and no less important than are the facts of the Peloponnesian War.

The headmasters were in a very strong position. Apart from the security of their office, they were supported by almost every educated person of note whose opinions mattered to them. They looked on their conservatism as a positive virtue, as though they were conscious of holding England together by their adherence to the old values. Arnold's view of industry was advanced, and the more usual outlook damned it as the producer of social chaos and unrest, while the new science, as exemplified by Buckland, Lyell, Huxley, and Darwin's *Origin of Species* (1859), was spreading doubt and agnosticism. The complaints of the scientists, and those who knew the industry of the Continent sufficiently well to be concerned for Britain's position as a major industrial nation, were outside their range of contact. Continental scares did not worry them anyway. The current lessons of France and Germany could not obliterate their reputation for revolution and unrest, while their scientific developments were not particularly relevant at the social level of the gentry-aristocracy with which they had to deal. Their isolated position and involvement with the conservative forces—Arnold and Temple were the great exceptions—protected them from criticism of their curricula by the radicals, free-thinkers, Nonconformists and Unitarians who maintained an insistence on a broad interpretation of education. Whatever parents and others might say of discipline and brutality, they were, by and large, satisfied with the pabulum of classics, and this was widespread even at a slightly lower social level than that catered for by the seven, as the Taunton Commission found out (see Chapter 7). No less a person than Gladstone made his views public:

... what I feel is, that the relation of pure science, natural science, modern languages, modern history and the rest to the old classical

training, ought to be founded on a principle. . . . I deny their right to a parallel or equal position; their true position is ancillary, and as ancillary it ought to be limited and restrained without scruples. . . .[1]

This may be taken as typical of the traditional upper-class viewpoint, and it is with this that we are here concerned. On the 'Arts' side, critics of the classical régime were few and were usually allied to one of the radical causes, as shown by the words of Charles Kingsley in 1859:

> The time devoted at our schools, whether Public or Private, to Latin or Greek, is a Laputism on which our great grandchildren will look back, I believe, as we do to the witch mania. It is astonishing that lads should be set to waste seven to ten years in acquiring the merest rudiments of Classics to be forgotten as soon as they leave. . . .[2]

Those words were part of a letter which began as follows:

> My Dear Dean, I will tell you categorically why I send my boy [Maurice] to the Wellington College
> (1) Because he will not be stupified with Latin and Greek
> (2) Because there are no traditions there
> (3) Because it costs £100 instead of £300
> (4) Because it is under the Superintendence of the Prince Consort[3]

When it is realized that Kingsley sent his other son, Grenville Arthur, some years later to Harrow, it is clear that even he could not avoid contradictions.

A further problem connected with the introduction of science to the public schools was the more practical one of staffing. An all-classical school was easy to run. Time-tabling was no problem at all, and the fluctuations in ratios of masters and pupils a matter of simple adjustment. Moving into a field of complex specialisms, of which science was one, made the understanding of new qualifications difficult for the old headmasters. This difficulty was often stressed as a major stumbling-block, and certainly there was a formidable problem so long as the schools insisted on a high-quality Oxford or Cambridge, if not a public-school, background together with church and classical links. With these self-made requirements it was difficult enough to maintain a small course, let alone

1. PSC, II, p. 42.
2. Newsome, *Wellington College*, op. cit., p. 80.
3. ibid., p. 81.

expand it. Temple complained of these difficulties, and so did
Moberly, who went further and protested that a scientist
really ought to live in a scientific community so that he could
meet and talk to his fellows, and that this was not possible in a
small provincial town like Winchester. Perhaps Moberly
was overstating his case, for these objections would wholly
vanish with three scientists on the staff—yet he was trying at
the same time to defend a decision not to appoint three of
them at once.

The difficulties over staffing were clear. The schools supplied
very few science candidates for the universities to work on, and
in one sense they could hardly complain, therefore, that the
universities had no surplus of first-class science graduates to send
back to them. On the other hand, the universities themselves
did not encourage the new subjects:

> If the colleges offered scholarships and exhibitions to acknowledge
> and encourage the study of science at school, then the teaching of
> science would at once be naturalized in most of the schools which
> contribute many men to the universities. Up to the present time
> Oxford has taken the lead in this; Christchurch, Balliol, Merton,
> Magdalen and New College all encourage science more or less.
> And their recognition of it, though very small, has been most useful.
> But at Cambridge very little is done. . . . Hence all the abler boys
> at school are in fact heavily bribed to study either classics or mathe-
> matics, even though their genius is for natural science. And from
> this want of recognition of science by the colleges generally, and
> from a belief that it is founded on a well-grounded disapproval of
> science as a part of early liberal education, and from some distrust
> of it as a possible disturber of classical tradition, schools naturally
> hang back from taking the step of incorporating natural science
> with their course of study.[1]

That was the opinion of J. M. Wilson in 1868, a man
supremely well qualified to summarize the position. It was, in
fact, a circular situation that persisted well into the twentieth
century.

This shortage has led some people to think that scientists of
good quality did not exist.[2] This is not true. There were plenty

1. J. M. Wilson in *Essays on a Liberal Education*, edited by F. W. Farrar,
1868, pp. 288–9.
2. That there were plenty of first-class scientists available is shown by the
fact that industry and the technical branches of government had no
difficulty in recruiting them. One important matter was remuneration
and the status that went with it. Very few, if any, would have been

of 'first-class' men available, many of whom would certainly have jumped at the opportunity, but they were not eligible since they had not passed through that particular set of arbitrary sieves which the schools demanded. Their education had often been a little unusual, but that was all. They had gathered their science in one of the ways already open elsewhere.

A little science was taught in some non-Anglican boarding schools and in many grammar schools, like Ilminster and Newcastle upon Tyne.[1] But the true home of science in its educational aspects lay in the workshops themselves, with the apprentices, in London University, in the new colleges, in the professional schools of medicine and in the host of commercial academies that catered for the professional middle classes in every town and city. These academies were run for profit and, of necessity, gave the customers what they wanted. The upper classes might have jeered at the telescopes, globes and electrical machines that often adorned their halls to impress parents, but these items were, in some at least, effectively used—beautiful copper-plate work-books of the period that still survive are ample evidence of that. The experimental or progressive schools of the period also indulged in science. Hazelwood included it in its curriculum twenty years before the Victorian era, while Bruce Castle took on the first full-time teacher of chemistry in a school in 1833.[2] A very few of the new schools, like Cheltenham, may have included some science for officers of the new army, but that did not really affect civilian needs, except in the special case of inspectors. The other sources of science, which had carried the burden for so long, were still quite capable of holding their own.

It is clear that, until 1880 at least, English science owed nothing whatever directly to the inspiration of science teaching

acceptable to the schools on the' irrelevant' grounds that their education was not sufficiently stylized. Had the schools been willing to consider these people, then undoubtedly they could have had their pick on grounds of finance alone at at least the top three schools. This matter is to be considered again later.

1. Among the obvious sources for the curricula of grammar schools are school histories like that of Ilminster. Newcastle upon Tyne is typical of other sources. For the curriculum of the Free Grammar School there in 1838, see Consultative Committee of the Board of Education Report on Differentiation of the Curriculum for Boys and Girls . . ., 1923, p. 5.
2. Information from J. L. Dobson.

8

in the old public schools. England would have been in a parlous state if it had had to rely on them for progress. Somehow the Victorian achievements had been won in spite of the schools which catered for the ruling classes, and the perturbing feature was not that science needed the few recruits the public schools might offer, but that they took no active part in the leadership in this extremely important field.

This lack of a national contribution and direction from the top schools, coupled with their denial of status to the subject, were at the root of the agitation against them over science.

THE PRESSURE ON THE SCHOOLS

The attack on the schools took several forms. Their obstinacy over the curriculum was an obvious educational battleground that brought in scientists, radicals and royalty against them. Others were concerned that the schools were failing both in their duty to the nation and in their duty to educate the upper classes as leaders of the nation, while a third attack arose inside the schools themselves.

Over the science question there was a sharp gulf between the classically minded and the rest. Those who had not succumbed to the public-school ethos and spirit, or who had not experienced it, could hardly understand why the schoolmen laid such stress on one particular form of learning to the exclusion of others. Most successful scientists knew little of the classics and cared less. The fact that many of these men were eminent by any standard, even the most rigid standards of Moberly, appeared to provide living evidence that classical superiority was a myth. Faraday put this problem as well as anyone:

I am not an educated man, according to the usual phraseology, and, therefore, can make no comparison between languages and natural knowledge . . . but that the natural knowledge which has been given to the world in such abundance during the last fifty years . . . should remain untouched, and that no sufficient attempts should be made to convey it to the young mind growing up and obtaining its first view of these things, is to me a matter so strange that I find it difficult to understand.[1]

Many people had been making the same point since the early part of the eighteenth century at least, and the arguments had

1. PSC, IV, p. 375, Q. 6.

been kept alive by such men as George Combe,[1] and elaborated by Herbert Spencer,[2] T. H. Huxley[3] and others.

Scientists were agreed. Science should be taught in its own right. Any other view was incomprehensible, and in particular they condemned the fashionable and fanciful notion that a study of the classics was a good preparation for science. There was, in their view, no evidence that the mind was a single weapon to be forged or sharpened. It may be that the belief in a faculty that was common to all activities of the mind and that could, therefore, be trained by a narrow approach, was generally accepted at the time (the 1860s) and only questioned later, as many maintain; but it is refreshing to see W. B. Carpenter stating the actual position so clearly in 1862:

. . . the use of the physical sciences is to train a class of mental faculties which are ignored, so to speak, by a purely classical or a purely mathematical training or by both combined . . . mathematical training exercises the mind most strenuously in a very narrow groove. . . .[4]

As for the basic motives, Faraday explained what he and others thought might be the underlying reason for the classical scholar's rejection of science:

It [the classics] does not blunt the mind . . . but it so far gives the growing mind a certain habit, a certain desire and willingness to accept general ideas of a literary kind, and to say all the rest is nonsense and belongs to the artisan. . . .[5]

The science conflict, as Faraday indicated, was partly a struggle of social class and attitudes. Work with the hands was considered by most people to be menial. Those at the top did not soil their hands for money, but relegated this to others. Yet science of the type stressed by the pioneers of the nineteenth century, who were often obliged to make their own apparatus, was essentially of a practical kind, with an insistence on the fact that there were other elements to the beauties of nature than mere juggling with words, whatever the language. The scientific viewpoint was comprised of observation, questioning,

1. See A. Price, 'A Pioneer of Scientific Education, George Combe (1788–1858)', *Educational Review*, xii, no. 3, June 1960.
2. See H. Spencer, *An Autobiography*, 2 vols., 1904.
3. See C. Bibby, *T. H. Huxley*, 1959.
4. PSC, iv, p. 364.
5. ibid., p. 377.

craftsmanship, knowledge and theory linked with continual change. While the old headmasters might have accepted the more novel aspects, they drew the line at the spirit of craftsmanship, which smacked too much of the artisan. This point, seen specifically in Hayman, is reflected by Huxley's success with working-class audiences:

> I am, and have been, any time these thirty years, a man who works with his hands—a handicraftsman. I do not say this in the broadly metaphorical sense in which fine gentlemen, with all the delicacy of Agag about them, trip to the hustings about election time, and protest that they too are working men. I really mean my words to be taken in their direct, literal, and straightforward sense. In fact, if the most nimble-fingered watch-maker among you will come to my workshop, he may set me to put a watch together, and I will set him to dissect, say, a blackbeetle's nerves. I do not wish to vaunt, but I am inclined to think that I shall manage my job to his satisfaction sooner than he will do his piece to mine.[1]

This is the typical scientific attitude, expressed with panache. Can anyone imagine a similar challenge coming from a member of the upper class? This is the heart of the matter, for the main exponents of science were manifestly not from the top drawer in breeding or attitude. It is true that a surprising number of public-school men did achieve a certain standing in the literary field of science, but they were exceptional, as we shall see later. If we restrict the consideration to social class and eminence in science in the middle and later part of the century, then only Lord Rayleigh came undoubtedly from the upper-class group; all the rest were lower, middle or professional class in origin. A mere handful—Rayleigh, Herschel the younger and Darwin —had actually been to a major school, and in the first two cases this had been a most fleeting experience, while Darwin's stay at Shrewsbury was hardly an advertisement for the success of the classics. The rest were, at most, educated at small grammar schools or private academies—Whewell, Owen, Joule, Maxwell, Tyndall, Lyell, Davy, Hooker, Airy, not to mention the giants of industry represented by the Stephensons, the Brunels, Swan, Trevithick, W. B. Armstrong and the rest[2]. Some indeed, like

1. Bibby, op. cit., pp. 99–100.
2. The following is a summary of the scientists' education:
    Lord Rayleigh was at Eton at ten, "but stayed only one half ", and a large part of that was spent in the sanatorium. Sir John Herschel was only a few months at Eton.

Faraday himself, were hardly educated at all. The achievements of these men were triumphs of individual initiative and true education as distinct from the work of the classroom, but their combined story held an essential weakness which the headmasters did not fail to exploit. Success in adult life was no proof that science was a suitable school subject, any more than any other adult accomplishment, whether it be in philosophy or economics, banking or the stage. At the same time, there remained a suspicion that the scientists' views were socially biased; they were ignorant and had no direct experience of what actually went on in the schools. Moreover, the headmasters could soften any criticism by pointing out how they had employed eminent scientists for odd lecture-series in the past, and by engaging in abstruse educational and philosophical arguments they were quite capable of winning.

The attack from scientists was only one of many outside pressures. Other onslaughts could not be dismissed so easily, since their cases often rested on material that could not be obscured by a dialectical and sociological fog.

Influence of the highest social prestige came from the royal family itself. Ever since Charles II at least, the ruling house had acted as the patron of science, and one or two members had passed beyond this vague approval to indulge themselves a little or to form valuable collections of scientific instruments. The only one, however, who tried to use his influence in any positive way was the Prince Consort, and it is significant that he was not an Englishman. With his Germanic background he had no reverence for the classical tradition. His view of the ideal school was one giving a real and functional end to the educative process, so that the boy was prepared to take his place in the world instead of moving on immaturely to the university. In his view education could not be meaningful in the existing situation; the schools should not allow the boys to leave and learn about life without some preparation.

On the wide field of science and industry, the Prince Consort's unique view of the German scene enabled him to judge the

At grammar schools: Whewell, Owen, Maxwell (Edinburgh), Davy, W. J. Hooker, Airy, Armstrong.

At private schools and academies: Lyell, Thomas Young, J. W. Swan, Robert Stephenson, Brunel the younger.

wastefulness of the English concept of progress whereby research
and new ideas were largely limited to the employees of individual firms. As a result he tried to sponsor high-level academic
work and research, while his part in the 1851 Exhibition and
the subsequent developments at South Kensington for scientific
and industrial education is too well known to need elaboration
here.

In his private life, Albert invited eminent men of science, like
Henslow and Owen, to lecture to the royal children. He sent
the Prince of Wales to the science facilities that Eton had to
offer, and also to the Faraday lectures at the Royal Institution.
If only Edward had shown the slightest interest we might well
have had a scientific king and a cultural revolution. That,
however, is conjectural. We are on more solid ground when we
consider the more practical side to his ideas. He continually
tried to press the cause of science in schools. When the problem
of a monument to the Duke of Wellington arose, he used his
influence at once in favour of a school, and the committee
produced their idea of the instruction to be given, with the
prince's views very much in evidence:

1st: What is usually understood by a good English and Classical
    education.
2nd: Those branches of scientific knowledge which have special
    application to the Arts, Commerce and Industry of the country.
3rd: The modern languages.[1]

This scheme bears a striking resemblance to the modern
curriculum and has far more of the spirit of the commercial
academy than the public school. Certainly Albert's ideas have
worn better than the views of the acknowledged experts of his
own day at school and university.

His whole influence is difficult to assess. Many people did not
like his Germanic background, his contempt for the classics and
his defence of the lower classes and industry. Socially he was
important, but his opinions could safely be ignored, and he met
only with great frustration in a campaign that very few really
understood or appreciated. In spite of every obstacle he persisted, as at Cambridge:

Prince Albert, though equipped with the prestige of a Prince
Consort and a Chancellor of the University, had to exercise all his

1. Newsome, *Wellington College*, op. cit., p. 31.

tact and influence before the possessors of power there could be convinced that reform was needed.[1]

From his supreme position of social prestige, and his nearness to Eton, one would have expected him to be at his most influential in the public-school field. In fact he was even less successful there than elsewhere. Benson, as the headmaster of Albert's brain-child, could not ignore him or avoid his presence or the pressures, but he still managed to evade carrying his wishes into effect.

The Prince Consort's fears were basically the same as those who were anxious about our national survival. Whatever may have been the position of England in the late eighteenth and early nineteenth centuries, there was no lack of industrial competitors overseas by the time Victoria came to the throne. This fact was demonstrated fourteen years later at the Great Exhibition, where the foreign exhibits made a brave show and proved that the English monopoly had gone for ever. A period of intense competition was foreshadowed, and to men who knew the Continent and were concerned for the future of British industry the position was bleak, if not alarming. They saw that a definite change was needed in the industrial pattern. The old-fashioned secrecies which had been such a feature of the iron, steel and manufacturing industries were no longer applicable in a scientific age. Many of the new ideas were in fact coming from the continental academic approach to research through universities and polytechnics, for which there were few parallels in Britain. In the 1830s and 1840s there was virtually nowhere in Britain for a man to learn the various branches of science at high level and get a training in research. Unless such a man could afford to build his own private laboratory and employ his own technicians to exploit his ideas—as one or two did—he had to go to the Continent. Few people were worried about this situation. Outside the ranks of the radicals it was difficult to find anyone who appreciated the subtleties of the problem; industry itself was complacent, and many good scientists—Lyon Playfair among them—could not get suitable jobs in Britain, even when they had had German training. In spite of this lack of enthusiasm the Royal College of Chemistry

1. Report of the Committee . . . to Inquire into the Position of Natural Science . . ., 1918, p. 6.

was founded in 1845, and its extraordinary success was without question due to Prince Albert's managing to persuade August von Hofmann to take control. In spite of this, the venture was in continual difficulties, which could be met as long as the Prince was there, but became intolerable after he died in 1861, so that many chemists in Britain left and Hofmann went to Berlin. In the short life of this college new industries were born, and yet the advantages that had been so carefully built up were allowed to disperse. Although other ventures were rising in London and elsewhere, this lapse and the general lack of interest were appalling. All this was happening at the very time of the Public Schools Commission, when Moberly and other head-masters were arguing as though education in science was an abstract question. They showed little sign of responding to an urgent educational and national need in the way that one might reasonably expect of the country's leading schools. It was their loftiness that angered the critics both before and after the Clarendon Commission. Meanwhile the need for a new approach increased, and subsequent exhibitions here, on the Continent and elsewhere only went to confirm this view. Scientists like Huxley and Playfair campaigned continually on the need for technical development.[1] The *Quarterly Review* took up this theme in 1867:

> England, at least as far as the natural and experimental sciences are concerned, seems in danger of sinking to the condition of what in political language would be called a third- or fourth-rate power. Our greatest men are perhaps still greater than those of any other nation; but the amount of quiet, solid, scientific work done in England is painfully less than that done in Germany, less even than that done in France.[2]

The agitation over science and industry was sound and lively[3] but there is still some doubt concerning the educational level at which the campaign was aimed—at least by some men. This

1. One of Lyon Playfair's arguments was the relatively poor showing of the English exhibits at the Paris Exhibition.
2. *Quarterly Review*, 1867, p. 487.
3. One of the scientific organizations with a pressure-group technique was the National Association for the Promotion of Technical and Secondary Education. This was composed of important politicians, scientists and public figures dedicated to the cause of scientific education and its advance-ment by legislation. Their main aim was the creation of an organized

is to be seen in the crucial decision which faced any man on the question of educating his own sons. Isambard Kingdom Brunel sent two sons to Harrow; the four sons of Sir Bernhard Samuelson went to Rugby. A son of Huxley was at University College School, and Playfair's son was at Cheltenham. As for grandchildren, they were commonly to be found at Eton. It is realized that the education of children is a complex matter often depending on the character of the child himself, but it is clear that some found the need for science only one factor among many.

A different but related fear concerned the future welfare and position of the upper class. The upper section was still essentially landed, with connections with many *élite* groups in government, administration and the armed forces. While these *élites* were perhaps significant for ownership and power in an agricultural society, England was no longer an agricultural nation in the old-fashioned sense. The new developments were rapid, and there appeared to be no limit to the powers of the new science. In the words of E. L. Woodward:

> The Archbishop of Canterbury, in the opening prayer [to the 1851 Exhibition], was humble before God, yet he assumed a considerable knowledge of the Divine plan. He seemed to know what songs the sirens sang, and, if he could not himself bind the sweet influences of the Pleiades, at least some Fellow of the Royal Society would be able to tell him how it was done.[1]

This knowledge was taking prestige away from the upper classes and placing it in the hands of the new middle- and

system of secondary education, and to this end they promoted many Bills in parliament designed to give school boards additional powers for secondary education (i.e. for the lower classes). This was connected with the ladder from elementary to secondary schools. These attempts failed, but their efforts were ultimately successful in a different direction—in getting secondary education attached to the newly-formed local authorities (1888) in the Technical Instruction Act of 1889. This agitation, therefore, was responsible in some measure for producing a conflict, since it introduced competition and suspicion between the central authority and those responsible for operating education locally—i.e. between the school boards, the county councils, the Education Department and the Department of Science and Art. This conflict within the main (state system) stream of education was not resolved until after the Cockerton Judgement and the 1902 Education Act.

1. E. L. Woodward, in *Ideas and Beliefs of the Victorians*, 1949, p. 62.

professional-class lords of science, business and technology. To
this extent the supremacy of the upper classes was threatened,
and their life in rural mansions, geographically remote from
the scene of activity, did not help; they no longer represented,
understood or even noticed the life of those below them. Their
power was slipping and might easily come to rest elsewhere.
Baden Powell, the Professor of Geometry at Oxford, had seen
this as part of the class struggle as early as 1832:

> Scientific knowledge is rapidly spreading among all classes except
> the Higher, and the consequence must be, that that class will not
> long remain the Higher. If its members would continue to retain
> their superiority, they must preserve a real pre-eminence in
> knowledge, and must make advances at least in proportion to classes
> which have hitherto been below them.[1]

The same thoughts were clearly in the minds of some of the
Commissioners inquiring into public schools thirty years later
in November 1862. H. H. Vaughan obtained a 'yes' from Sir
Charles Lyell to this question: 'And whether it [knowledge of
the material world] does not also tend to put a certain amount
of power into the hands of the middle classes, which the upper
classes have not?'

Of parallel significance was the particular danger that the
clergy would lose their influence and become isolated from the
masses:

> H. H. VAUGHAN: In a political point of view, is . . . [it] not only an
> unhealthy but also a dangerous state of things . . . that the material
> world should be very much better known by the middle classes of
> society than by the upper classes?
> SIR CHARLES LYELL: Certainly, and I think it is particularly so in
> reference to the teaching in this country by the clergy. . . . In
> order to bring their knowledge more into unison with that of the
> artisans, it is particularly desirable that a certain portion of
> science should be taught. . . . I think it . . . desirable that the
> clergy should have some initiation into these things.[2]

The fears expressed in these thoughts were common, and had
been widely discussed in Arnoldian circles thirty years before,
if not earlier.

1. Baden Powell, *The Present State* . . . *of Mathematical and Physical Studies* . . .,
1832.
2. PSC, IV, p. 374, Qq. 78, 81 *et seq.*

All the pressures so far mentioned were external to the schools and could finally be ignored by headmasters. There were, however, pressures within the school gates, from boys and teachers on the staff, besides the reactions of their colleagues at Oxford and Cambridge.

Whatever masters might think, many boys found the new machines and the new speeds exciting enough. The engine-driver replaced the charioteer in the dreams of youth, and teachers were forced to realize that the imaginations of boys wandered to the railway track rather than to the Parthenon. Everywhere boys' studies were littered with models and trophies, with fossils, and often, too, with the impedimenta of simple pieces of apparatus to produce smells, fumes and bangs. They were aided and abetted by sympathetic masters like Stephen Hawtrey at Eton or Wilson and Hutchinson at Rugby, or even in preparatory schools by men like T. L. and Matthew Bloxam.[1]

This, of course, did not apply to every boy, or even to the majority, for the embryo scientist had to be both an enthusiast and a pioneer in the scholastic world, where all the temptations of scholarship, prestige and headmasterly approval were against him. But it could cater for some of the boys who found the classics dry:

> The exclusive study of language at school weakens the fibre of those who have genius for it, fails to educate to the best advantage the mass who have fairly good sense but no genius for anything, and obscures and depresses the few who have special abilities in other lines. . . .[2]

On the other hand, science, even where it was introduced, was not a panacea, and the wisest teachers realized this from the beginning, as in the delightful words of J. M. Wilson in 1868:

> Suppose then your class of thirty or forty boys before you, of ages thirteen to sixteen, as they sit at their first botanical lesson; some curious to know what is going to happen, some resigned to anything; some convinced that it is all a folly.[3]

1. T. L. Bloxam kept a preparatory school in the town of Rugby. He was helped by his brother, Matthew, a solicitor and noted antiquary. Exhibitions of work done and of the boys' hobbies were held locally. Some of the results were extraordinary.
2. Wilson, in *Essays on a Liberal Education*, op. cit., p. 243.
3. ibid., p. 272.

Such an approach did lead to a significant, but tiny, split within the school at Rugby before the publication of the Clarendon Report in 1864.[1] However, the greatest single shock to the schools, far greater than the scares of social class or national supremacy, or the needs of boys, was a partial capitulation at Oxford and Cambridge. Continual pressure through the pages of the *Edinburgh Review* and other publications as well as from critics within, like Prince Albert, Whewell and Mark Pattison, brought about a Royal Commission in 1850 which undoubtedly hastened the process of reform at university level. An honours school in natural science began at Oxford in the same year, 1850, and at Cambridge in 1851. The subject had now the trappings of respectability, and a boy who had studied science at school could now continue with it to a higher level. It is, however, true to say that the new ventures at the universities were not received with rapture, and the colleges, especially in Cambridge, were very slow to catch the spirit. The influence was a personal one; the circular argument had now been broken in theory, and those public schools who denied these studies to their boys were denying something which their senior colleagues had accepted. The headmasters were thrown on to the defensive, and successfully resisted the pressures until the public schools were investigated by the Commission appointed in 1861.

THE CLARENDON REPORT AND DEVELOPMENTS

The evidence given to the Clarendon Commission showed the heads in defiant mood, if very conscious of the arguments against them; it may even have stirred one or two, like Temple, into a more serious frame of mind. The story of the Clarendon Commission and its origin rightly belong elsewhere, since ostensibly they were mainly concerned with revenues and management, but they found plenty to say and discover about the teaching. Their eleventh general conclusion was:

The teaching of natural science should, wherever it is practicable, include two main branches, the one comprising chemistry and physics, the other comparative physiology and natural history,

1. It is a most interesting fact that, when offered time-table space for science, the masters at Rugby chose botany as the vehicle, although they themselves were more qualified in mathematics and physics.

both animal and vegetable. A scheme for regulating the teaching of the subject should be framed by the Governing Body.[1]

However that might be, the dominant impression of the evidence was the obstinacy of the headmasters and the sad realization that, in the last analysis, it was their opinion which counted. This fact angered many intellectuals inside and outside the schools, and the collection of comments by the more radical schoolmasters and their colleagues at the universities, entitled *Essays on a Liberal Education*, was brought out in 1868 as a counter-blast. Harrow and Rugby were involved. In these essays the narrow view of classical education as liberal education was dissected in various ways. The content and treatment of the classics were found to be wanting, and Henry Sidgwick questioned their sufficiency:

> But the very exclusions and limitations that make the study of language a better gymnastic than physical science, make it, on the other hand, so obviously inferior as a preparation for the business of life, that its present position in education seems, on this ground alone, absolutely untenable.[2]

He advocated a curriculum of greater width, like that in vogue today, while others championed the teaching of English, or compared the English tradition with the superior situation in Scotland. It was left to J. M. Wilson to demonstrate the power and educative value of science with actual examples, showing science as a source of inspiration for the mind. All this was a most efficient answer to Moberly and the rest, and it made an impact in the very year that Parliament completed the work of the Public Schools Commission in the Act of 1868.

By this statute the ancient regulations were replaced. Strange names appeared on the governing bodies, and Eton, for the first time, found itself ruled from without rather than from within. Many people objected, like Wasey Sterry: 'No great commercial business, no large landed estate could possibly be managed by a body of absentees, however excellent and brilliant they might individually be.'[3]

But the fact was that the old system had not worked either, and the new system enabled prominent institutions to nominate

1. PSC, I, p. 53.
2. Sidgwick, in *Essays on a Liberal Education*, op. cit., p. 133.
3. W. Sterry, *Annals of Eton College*, 1898, p. 341.

men to protect broad and vital issues. One of the new governors
was to be a scientist, a Fellow of the Royal Society in fact, and
at one time a man as radical as T. H. Huxley filled this post.[1]
   The first battle of the subjects was really over; science had
won a foothold at last, although victory was not absolute. In
the words of Maxwell Lyte: 'Physical science was introduced
as one of the regular subjects of study for the Fifth Form in
1869, and for the Remove in the autumn of 1875.' [2]
   It was a slow beginning, and the internal resistance can be
gathered from the difficulties that Huxley experienced. Moreover, the definition of science was apt to be one-sided, and not
in the spirit of the Public Schools Commission's recommendation, or the pioneer efforts of Wilson and his colleagues. Those
branches of science nearest to mathematics—mechanics, applied
mathematics and physics—were the favoured group, probably
because of their relationship to the long-established non-
scientific and wholly theoretical mathematics. The biological
side was ignored, in spite of the express mention of 'comparative
physiology and natural history, both animal and vegetable'.
This aspect represents yet another side to the schools' delaying
tactics, but it is not a matter that can be pursued here.
   The final solution of the science problem, both in its real
acceptance and its spread, had to wait for a new century and
the bitter experience of two world wars. It is clear, however,
that the first break-through was brought about by legislation
and the influence of science within the governing bodies. It was
really a situation parallel to that seen in the foundation of
Cheltenham, the first of the new boarding schools, thirty years
before, where at least ten professional men sat on the Board of
Directors and brought in a curriculum 'fitted to life' in a manner
that would have been dear to the heart of the Prince Consort,
although it was really a screen for entry into the specialized
field of army officers, that old preserve of the upper classes.
   By 1890 the relationship of science to the big public schools
had gone through a series of stages. The travelling scientist-
showman had given rise, after an occasional fallow period, to
timid experiments with outside experts and members of staff,
until the Commission of 1864 and the following Act forced the

1. Bibby, op. cit., pp. 172–6.
2. M. Lyte, *History of Eton College*, 1899, p. 544.

schools to tackle the problem boldly. The schools had openly resisted change as long as they could, in spite of the partial example of Cheltenham, and they continued to resist it for another sixty or seventy years, as we shall see. On a broad view, the schools had reluctantly followed the successful science teaching found elsewhere in the good commercial academies and grammar schools, which had, hitherto, provided some of the education necessary for technical and professional growth. Even with an accepted place for science in the curriculum, two further stages in the drift away from the classics were still theoretically possible—first, that of making science, or at least the spirit of science, replace everything for which the classics had stood, and secondly to rely on the new lessons of industry as the mainspring for education itself. These are antitheses of the old ideal and they existed already in the curriculum of many lower-class and middle-class schools as a practical fact, in some cases with a long tradition. Whether this was education or vocational training has always been a matter for argument by the denigrators, and certainly the basic philosophy was not entirely accepted. In the public-school sector, however, there came, with the appointment of Frederick William Sanderson to Oundle in 1892, a man who raised the spirit of industry and science to the level of an intellectual and educational ideal.

SANDERSON[1] AND THE SCIENTIFIC AND INDUSTRIAL SPIRIT

Sanderson made the trek from being a poor boy in a village school through the arduous apprenticeship of student teacher and student of theology at Durham[2] to the position of 11th wrangler at Cambridge. Whether his beginning among lower-class elementary schools, associated with the dirt and machine

1. For information about Sanderson, see the standard school history and also H. G. Wells, *The Story of a Great Schoolmaster*, 1924; Anon., *Sanderson of Oundle*, 1923.
2. Sanderson was a student teacher in an elementary school in the village of Tudhoe, County Durham. The tradition of these schools was of a practical nature and, in the better ones, of a serious approach to science in one or more of its forms. It was common to relate the nature of the neighbourhood to the science, etc., where this was relevant. How much of this applied to this school we do not know, but clearly since it formed a background for Sanderson in his formative years, this could be a matter of the highest significance in tracing the origin of his ideas.

environment of the Durham coalfield, affected his outlook, is not easy to say, but certainly he carried a love of science on to Dulwich and then to Oundle. The governors had already decided to alter the nature of the school and find a man who would introduce science as a major development: Sanderson was therefore given a free hand.

His main aim was to eliminate the spirit of competition, since it 'destroys the creative inventive life—and is the seat of unrest'. [1] Schoolmasters had been confusing the needs of discipline and the needs of education. The quiet classroom, the supervised prep, the praise of lonely individual work and its precise marking, were specially designed to preserve the myth of fairness, whereas in fact they bore no relation to true education at all. They only simplified the teacher's task and established a competitive place-order. The immature mind cried out for help, and yet help could only come through authority which often did not understand. For one boy to help another was reviled as cheating and dishonesty. A boy might just as well have been a hermit for all the help he received in his studies from the rest of the school. It was, and still is, a system which extols jealous competition as a virtue and an incentive, and as a guarantee of efficiency, while the teacher had the impossible task of forcing the weaker brethren to struggle on alone in a frantic effort to perform the miracle of catching up. Sorting them out into sets of ability or achievement only intensified the process. The boys in the intellectual foothills saw the higher peaks above them, while those already in a favoured position could not rest and had to avoid the shame of relegation. For Sanderson competition was the root-evil, and efficiency was not only quite out of place in education, but irrelevant, since other qualities were more important. Co-operation, for instance, was a far more significant concept, and it intrigued Sanderson to think how co-operation had been crushed by competition, except perhaps in some games. He saw science as the great hope of the future:

> The newcomer Science, and with it industry . . . must take a prominent and inspiriting place in school, and in every part of school work. It is not sufficient to say that Science should be taught in schools. The time has gone by for this. . . . Science is essentially creative and co-operative, its outlook is onward towards change,

1. *Sanderson of Oundle*, op. cit., p. 276.

it means searching for the truth, it demands research and experiment, and does not rest on authority. Under this new spirit all history, literature, art and even languages should be rewritten. . . . Classrooms are places where boys go to be taught. They are tool-sharpening rooms—necessary, but subsidiary. For research and co-operative work the large halls are needed. Spacious engineering and woodworking shops, well supplied with all kinds of machine tools, a smithy, a foundry, a carpenter's shop, a drawing-office— all carried on for manufacturing purposes. . . . There will be a corresponding spacious literary and historical workshop with a really spacious library. . . .[1]

There is something of Wilson and T. H. Huxley here, with the insistence on the creative spirit of boys and recourse to their own work rather than authority. There is here, too, the spirit of research applied to the whole curriculum, arts as well as science. What was somewhat new, however, was the spirit of industry, both for its own sake and for the manufacture of some object of use to the community. Others, like Hayman, had considered similar work suitable at a lower social level, but beneath the dignity of the sons of the rich. For Sanderson it was not a matter of the relative position in society; the social usefulness of the operation was the initiation, the incentive, the purpose and the educational value of the entire operation. A vice, for instance, requires an assessment of the precise need in terms of priority, cost, location, strength and fitting, with a corresponding accuracy in designing and drawing the individual parts. Wooden patterns follow and sand moulds are made. Finally, the parts have to be cast in iron and machined to the limits of tolerance or appearance required. This sequence of operations involves a complex knowledge of the different technologies and a corresponding idea of the work of the others involved. A boy, for instance, who made one of the patterns would have worked from one of the drawings, probably prepared by someone else. His own construction work would be scrutinized by his fellow-workers and tested in the nature of the final product—any flaw in his own work would be revealed automatically. This sequence—analysis of need, design, drawing, pattern making, moulding, casting, machining, finishing, assembly—required many hands and minds, each one co-operating with others. This example is not fanciful, for workshops

1. ibid., pp. 276–7.

9

specializing in each of the operations outlined above were in fact started at Oundle and the details of the work undertaken are impressive. Industry, in this view, was entirely based on co-operation, and as such was the hope of mankind, provided interunion jealousy and the conflict of labour and capital could be eliminated.

It was claimed that these ideas were not incompatible with academic standards; a boy following them was not handicapped in the scholastic race. This is a vital point; no method, however brilliant, can survive which condemns the bright boy to the frustration of denied ambition. It was claimed that the work-shop method actually helped mathematics:

> . . . the experiments, tests, measurements, designs, which form the regular part of the work in the shops involve the use of a wide range of mathematics, and in carrying them out it will be found that a boy will learn his mathematics as he learns the use of tools by constantly applying them. It is true that the number of mathematical questions or examples he will in this way get through in the hour or two hours 'lesson' may be very few, but the questions arising in a concrete and visible form will make a more vivid and abiding impression on the mind, and both the methods and results will become an integral part of his being.[1]

The benefit was not limited to one subject. In the words of Sanderson:

> . . . with an education of this kind based fundamentally on science, a capable boy will leave a secondary school with a good knowledge of science and its application, with a research attitude towards history and modern problems, and with a good working knowledge of two, or three, or even four languages.[2]

Whether these claims are pedagogically sound is not really our concern, although an adequate analysis is still required. What is important is the different approach it represented in the public schools. In addition, he had a vision of the school as a local centre. In this perhaps the peculiarly intimate relationship of town and school at Oundle, which is still obvious to the visitor, affected Sanderson's viewpoint, for he did not see the school as the closed entity, as so many of the headmasters have done, but as in every way part of the locality. The problems of

1. F. W. Sanderson, 'Practical Mathematics at Oundle School', Board of Education Special Reports on Educational Subjects, xxvi, 1912, pp. 412–13.
2. *Sanderson of Oundle*, op. cit., p. 281.

local industry and agriculture were as much a part of school life as was classroom work, and Sanderson's aim was to make the school a real focus of community interest.

With the accent on science, on industry, on manual perfection and involvement with surroundings, Sanderson was as far from the nineteenth-century public school of the traditional type as it was possible to be, and indeed his ideals have not yet been accepted. With all his revolutionary outlook, it is refreshing to find that he could be reactionary too. He had one quality at least in common with Keate, Benson and all the great names: 'He thrashed hard and clumsily in a white-heat of passion.' [1]

Sanderson died suddenly and dramatically in 1923, so that it is impossible to estimate his success as a schoolmaster, for his pupils—the good and the bad—have still to write their memoirs. None the less, there is no doubt that he is a very considerable figure, in spite of the fact that he found difficulty in conveying his ideas to paper.

Without apparently having owed anything to John Dewey, there was a great deal of similar thought at the root of Sanderson's work, together with the ideas of T. H. Huxley, Herbert Spencer, Henry Armstrong, and much that resembled the project method also, but more soundly conceived. What precisely he owed to any of these we do not know, but the workshop procedure was essentially British, and stems, if anywhere, from the lower classes and the example of trade and science schools.[2]

It is tempting to think that the elementary schools were a direct source of inspiration for Sanderson from his early years as a student teacher among the coalfields. If future work confirms this view, then it displays a peak of lower-class influence on the public schools.

The solidity of Greece and Rome represented the cultural goal of the old headmasters; the restless spirit of science and industry was no less a driving force and philosophy of life for Sanderson.

1. ibid., p. 34.
2. The relationship of Sanderson to various other practical approaches to education presents a difficult problem. A parallel system in America, based somewhat on Dewey, can be seen in S. Tenenbaum, *W. H. Kilpatrick*, 1951. There is no evidence of any connection, and threads in this country could easily be traced back to the eighteenth century.

CHAPTER SIX

Masters and Headmasters

The staff of public schools in Victorian times presents a bewildering variety of masters, headmasters and 'extra' masters. The term 'usher' was already obsolete, and in so far as it referred to a person appointed 'to look after the boys in playtime' [1] it had never really applied to the public schools.[2] Such an office was held in supreme contempt; it inferred spying on boys in their leisure time and was an abuse of freedom.

In the early years of Victoria's reign, 'extra' masters were concerned with the frills of education—anything outside the serious study of the classics which the school would allow and for which parents were willing to pay.[3] These masters lived on the fringe of school society, tolerated, even sometimes encouraged, but essentially an inferior breed, lacking the security of a full staff member. French, German, Italian, Spanish, Writing, Dancing, Drawing, Fencing—all these came within the province of the extra master, although writing was rather different and often relegated to a poorly paid calligrapher, who was, perhaps, the nearest thing to an usher the public schools ever had. Even so, the names of extra masters and writing masters were usually to be found on the printed lists of staff, swelling the numbers

1. *A Cyclopedia of Education*, 1913, entry under 'Usher' (written by A. F. Leach).
2. The term usher was, however, used right up until this century in legal phraseology.
3. Extra masters, particularly of modern languages, were often refugees from the Continent, and sometimes aristocratic in origin. Their relationship to the staff proper and to the locality forms a fascinating sociological phenomenon. An example was Marc-Marie Emmanuel Wratislaw, who started a family that came to be prominent in Rugby, even dominant at times, for over 150 years. Extra masters were often left, rather curiously, on staff lists long after they had ceased to teach, as in the case of dancing masters at Rugby. See also note on extra masters given on p. 62.

and giving a spurious indication, not only of size and prosperity, but also suggesting a breadth of study which appealed to many parents and helped to counteract criticisms of narrow specialization.

The status and treatment of extra masters varied from school to school. At Eton a boy choosing an extra subject would be charged 10 guineas a year for two or three hours' tuition a week. The eighty pupils of Mr Tarver,[1] the French master, brought in a yearly sum of £840. This was a considerable income for the 1860s, and some of these specialists managed to build their own little empires and employ many assistants to help out. This was the age of lucrative 'perks', not only at the extra-master level but throughout the scholastic profession, at school and university alike. Every single minute of duty, or item of equipment, not laid down in the contract was carefully noted and paid for in a manner that would make the most rigid trade-unionist green with envy. Even a headmaster like Arnold did not despise the private student. This tradition is still a feature of the educational scene at the present day, not only in the same province of private teaching, but throughout the field of examinations.

One development of the nineteenth century was the slow elevation of the extra master to full status of master as subjects other than the classics were gradually recognized as part of a liberal education. If we exclude the special case of French at Rugby, where the master was considered a member of staff, this emancipation was essentially a Victorian phenomenon. It is an interesting case of social and scholastic mobility that was often combined with an extraordinary pattern of petty restrictions and snobbery seen at its best in the case of mathematics at Eton.

Stephen Hawtrey was appointed mathematical master at Eton in the same year that Victoria came to the throne, and at once began to organize the subject as a business, setting the scene for change.[2] He obtained a forty-year lease on a site in the college, and built at his own expense a mathematical school in the form of a rotunda, consisting of a theatre with desks so

1. For information about Mr Tarver, see PSC, I.
2. For information concerning Stephen Hawtrey, see the standard books on Eton, and PSC, II, pp. 154 *et seq.*

designed that it could easily be transformed into a hall for
lectures in experimental science to an audience of 350. With his
uncle as headmaster, he was now, in 1851, able to persuade the
college authorities to introduce mathematics as a compulsory
subject. Three hours a week was the time allotted, and although
his request for a fee of 6 guineas a boy was reduced to 4 guineas,
they did agree to increase the mathematics staff to seven to cope
with the extra work. Mathematics was now on the brink of
becoming a respectable subject, its usefulness later increasing,
in 1856, with the formation of the Army Class. With this
change, which happened, by chance perhaps, to coincide with
the year of the Great Exhibition, Hawtrey himself became
recognized officially as one of the staff, equivalent in status to
the classical masters, but leaving the rest of his mathematical
colleagues outside the fraternity, subject to a host of restraints
that kept them deliberately and unmistakably on the underprivileged side of the fence.[1] The seven assistants earned, on an
average, a little under £400 each, compared with the £1,700–
£1,800 of the classical masters.[2] Their work was strictly limited
to subject-matter; they could not discuss welfare or moral
questions with the boys even if they were in orders. They were
forbidden to wear white neck-cloths or even gowns in chapel,
no matter what degree they held; they could not meet the
headmaster as other masters did, while outside the classroom
itself they had 'less authority . . . than is entrusted to some of
the boys'.[3] No wonder the mathematical masters, and others,
too, ascribed all failure in mathematics to the one simple issue
—how could one expect serious study from the boys when the
masters were treated as inferiors? Yet mathematics was at least
semi-respectable; its logical basis was obvious; it had an ancient
lineage stretching to the Greeks, and university approval. Its
treatment was princely compared to that meted out to French,
German, Italian and all the other frills.

Quite as important as intellectual blindness was the attitude

1. For the treatment of mathematical masters, see the evidence given by
S. T. Hawtrey, E. Hale, C. O. Goodford, E. Balston in PSC, III. There is
also a good deal of material on this subject in PSC, II, since printed Q. 11
deals with fees in the extra subjects, Q. 21 with collections and apparatus,
etc.
2. For the salaries of assistants, see PSC, I, p. 82.
3. PSC, II; evidence of E. P. Rouse and H. Brandreth.

of the favoured staff.[1] Classical masters held modern-language men in some contempt. They made no secret of the fact and showed their scorn openly to the Public Schools Commission. The headmaster of Eton, the Rev. C. O. Goodford, when asked point-blank for his rating of the relative value of classics, mathematics and modern languages, rather surprisingly put his thoughts into mathematical form and answered with the proportion, 15:3:1.[2] With the boys taking their cue from the masters, it was hardly likely in such an atmosphere that serious work was possible in anything but Latin and Greek. It is astonishing to us now that in an adventurous, scientific and empire-building age, boys should not only have been content to spend so much of their life on the classics but should have sneered at other subjects as though they were lower-class migrants in upper-class preserves.[3] This social comparison is not too fanciful, for mathematics and modern languages were linked in the mind with the non-gentry problem of finding a job. This is a most interesting point and somewhat against our expectations, for the cold treatment given to the new subjects is the reverse of what common sense would suggest in view of the hobbies of the boys individually and the glamour of the Empire. Few boys took these extra subjects seriously. It is possible that there was a difference in attitude with age, but the normal assumption that children are rebels at heart and less conscious of their status in life than adults has little to support it from the example of upper-class Victorian youth of public-school age. Rebels did exist in plenty—occasionally the whole school would erupt—but it was a rebellion against any infringement of privileges or restrictions on freedom. Youth was not concerned —to the point of rebellion anyway—with the demand for something new, and there is much truth in the remark of Sanderson that boys have only one characteristic in common, their dislike for any change.

Even the small degree of recognition given to extra masters was denied to those who brought a professional grace to the

1. For the attitudes of staff in the various schools to modern languages, see PSC, II, answers to printed Q. 11 (III).
2. PSC, III (Eton), Q. 2584.
3. There are interesting parallels between these extra subjects of the nineteenth century and the attitudes adopted towards them and the corresponding non-examination subjects of today.

games and cricket fields, quite as elegant in its own way as the intellectual polishing of Greek and Latin. These men dwelt in lower-class lodgings, in that social no-man's-land between the writing master and the domestic servant, yet in retrospect there is no doubt at all that these rather despised experts were the most romantic, colourful and dashing sights at the schools. A glance at the picture of those at Wellington reveals the typical style and stance of top-flight sportsmen.[1] It relegates the appearance of a corresponding group of masters to the lifeless state of a dusty museum-piece. It is tempting to ascribe this contrast to the deadening conformity of an intellectual autocracy, for the professionals stood outside the official world, since they were not employed on the same terms and only held their positions by virtue of their influence with the boys and the private organization on the games side. The social relationships of these aspects of the world of sport in the schools merits some attention.

THE MASTERS

The task of a master in a public school was to teach the classics to the sons of the upper class and to those who were being educated with them. He had to be acceptable both to the parents and to the headmaster on academic and personal grounds, and his background was a matter of some importance. The school and university education of masters appointed at five major schools in the nineteenth century is shown in Table 4.

An Oxford or Cambridge degree was all but essential, with a bias for each individual school towards one university or the other. Eton, Harrow and Shrewsbury favoured Cambridge; Rugby and St Paul's, Oxford. These preferences may merely reflect a close connection in foundation, as at Eton, or else a carefully built and nurtured relationship, as in the case of Samuel Butler and Cambridge. In this way a place was prepared for the majority of the boys who reached the sixth. The influence was two-way. The universities obtained frank opinions of schoolboys as potential students and, in return, the heads of colleges gave advice back on good schoolmaster material. We know that this friendly network approach to appointing staff,

1. The picture of the 'Sportsmen' at Wellington can be seen in Newsome *Wellington College*, op. cit.

Table 4. *The education of masters appointed to five major public schools in the nineteenth century.*[1]

			Masters appointed to				
			Eton 1801 to 1862	Harrow 1801 to 1899	Rugby 1801 to 1899	Shrewsbury 1801 to 1900	St Paul's 1801 to 1900
Education of master at	School	Eton	55	5	6	1	1
		Harrow	0	15	2	0	1
		Rugby	0	11	35	2	3
		Shrewsbury	0	7	6	21	1
		St Paul's	0	3	2	3	13
		Winchester	0	5	8	0	1
		Charterhouse	0	3	1	2	1
		Westminster	0	1	1	0	2
		Other public schools	1	15	25	9	20
		Grammar schools	6	17	21	10	17
		Private schools and at home	0	2	1	4	2
		Elsewhere	0	1	0	0	0
		Scotland, Ireland, abroad	0	2	7	1	3
		No information	12	17	10	26	10
	University	Oxford	8	32	77	21	41
		Cambridge	66	65	44	50	29
		Other universities	0	3	2	1	4
		No information	0	4	2	7	1
		Total	74	104	125	79	75

1. The following sources have been used: for Harrow, Dauglish and Stephenson, op. cit., pp. 899–911; for Shrewsbury, G. W. Fisher, *Annals of Shrewsbury School*, 1899, pp. 472–9; for Rugby, Michell, op. cit.; for St Paul's, R. B. Gardiner, *Admission Registers of St Paul's School*. The material was checked and expanded by reference to Venn for Cambridge, to *Alumni Oxoniensis*, to other school registers, to school histories, to D.N.B., etc. This material is part of a longitudinal study of social mobility in public-school staff.

was common, but the evidence indicates that it was not the only method. There was also a tendency in all schools to select staff from among their own old boys in amounts varying from 17 to 74 per cent (Table 5). In many ways these percentages reflect the degree of scholastic inbreeding in the schools. It was clearly quite unrealistic to expect any significant changes at Eton (or, indeed, at Winchester) before 1870 at least, while one would expect that Harrow and St Paul's would be most receptive to new ideas, with Rugby and Shrewsbury lying in between. The preference for old boys is not really surprising; headmasters knew these candidates intimately, and there was no need to

Table 5. *Old boys on the staffs of five major schools in the nineteenth century.*[1]

School	Period	Staff: total appointed	Number who were O.B.s	Percentage of own O.B.s
Eton	1801–62	74	55	74
Harrow	1801–99	104	15	14
Rugby	1801–99	125	35	28
Shrewsbury	1801–1900	79	21	27
St Paul's	1801–1900	75	13	17

wonder in their case what lay unwritten between the lines of the testimonials. Apart from the inbreeding phenomenon, no school appears to have been particularly favoured as a scholastic pool, although the achievements of St Paul's and Shrewsbury were remarkable for small schools, and this may have been, in the case of Shrewsbury, a tribute to the celebrated teaching of Butler and Kennedy. For reasons given later it was certainly not due to any other member of the staff.

Apart from the old-boy situation, the most surprising thing was the apparent readiness of these schools to take on men who had been educated at public and grammar schools outside the favoured seven. This feature was largely a post-1850 phenomenon. At Rugby, for instance, of the forty-six masters from this source shown in Table 4, only five were taken on in the first half of the century, and none of the thirty-seven was taken on

1. Sources as for Table 4.

by St Paul's. Until 1850, therefore, those schools were educationally inbred, though thereafter there was a corresponding widening of the selection. The change in the character of recruitment in mid-century coincides with several other happenings in education concerning public schools. We have seen that about this time there came a change of heart over the necessity for appointing clergymen, that public schools began to increase rapidly in size and number and that, similarly, there was increased prosperity in the grammar schools.[1] These events helped to create a larger source of supply for the schools to pick from.

It is often a cause for complaint that teachers are not men of the world, that the sequence school–university–schoolmaster is no suitable preparation for anyone preparing boys for adult society. There is much truth in this, and the 74 per cent of Etonian staff recruited from old boys carries the situation to a farcical extreme. The boys must certainly have found more worldly wisdom and knowledge at home than at school. However, this particular case is not quite as simple as the bare figures would indicate, for on top of educational isolation were piled other problems of hierarchy and literal inbreeding.

The situation at Eton arose from the tradition of selecting staff from collegers who had passed on to King's College, Cambridge. Headmasters were also selected from this group, and by another tradition some ultimately became provosts. By Victoria the whole staff had thereby accumulated a common background and narrow outlook. Common culture and upbringing were not the only, or indeed the most effective, devices for unity. Many of the masters were related to one another by marriage or descent, and this can sometimes be traced over hundreds of years. Two diagrammatic family trees are shown to illustrate this point (Family Linkage 1). Those members holding official posts at Eton, whether as assistant masters, headmasters, fellows, vice-provosts or provosts, are indicated by an asterisk (*). Even these extensive ramifications are incomplete and by no means tell the whole story, for several related women ran boarding houses, and all those members of families holding high educational positions elsewhere have been omitted.

1. For these changes, see Chapter 3 above, pp. 54–8, including Table 3.

Sometimes these relationships had important consequences in the struggle for promotion. When Hawtrey, the provost of Eton, died in January 1862, and the Queen appointed Goodford in his place, a fight for the headmastership developed between W. A. Carter, with a father and an uncle among the Fellows, and his brother-in-law, Edward Balston, who possessed the added and significant advantage of being linked with the Dupuis family. Balston was successful.[1] Within the closed society of a public-school staff, this kind of situation is not surprising, and less extravagant examples of under-counter manoeuvres can be given for each of the other schools, as we shall see.

The fact that so many of the staff at Eton were old boys might lead to the assumption that they were gentry-aristocratic in origin. Nothing could be further from the truth. The masters at Eton were drawn from the collegers, and this fact, combined with extensive intermarriage, would suggest that they came from middle-class and professional stock, and this is confirmed by an analysis of the background of the masters, not only at Eton but elsewhere. The staffs of the schools formed isolated intellectual reservoirs, middle class–professional in origin, geared to the needs of the gentry and aristocracy.

The relationship of staff and pupils is generally of major social interest. All masters have to come to terms with their social environment. In the top schools of the Victorian era they were surrounded by boys drawn from the nobility and gentry, especially at Eton and Harrow, while they themselves were distinctly lower in the social scale. This raises many issues. How far, for instance, is it the responsibility of a school to adopt and preserve upper-class standards, and how far should the social class of the boys determine that of the teacher, to the extent, logically perhaps, that teachers in upper-class schools should be drawn exclusively from the upper class, or at least should adopt a similar way of life? The answer to this problem is not simple, for it requires subtle distinctions between values and traditions, truth and propaganda. The difficulties can be understood more easily through the converse problem of teachers in workhouse schools. Should they be paupers too, or at least live as paupers? The Victorian solution at one time

1. For some of the details concerning Balston's election, see Balston, op. cit.

'amily Linkage 1. *Two relationships among the staff at Eton (incomplete)*[1]

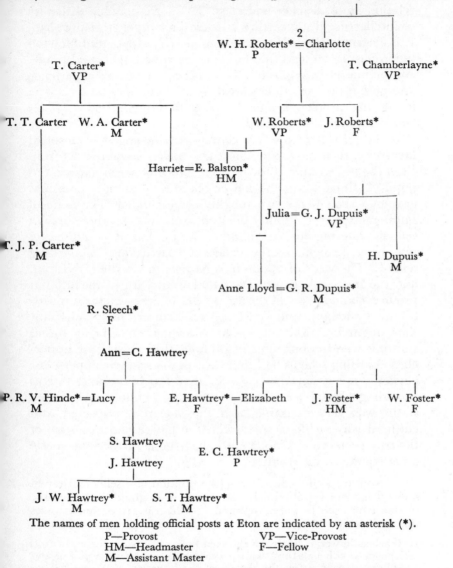

The names of men holding official posts at Eton are indicated by an asterisk (*).

P—Provost VP—Vice-Provost
HM—Headmaster F—Fellow
M—Assistant Master

1. The family relationships shown here have been deduced from the sources mentioned above for Table 4 (p. 121). Additionally, standard works on Eton were consulted, together with the following biographies: Thackeray, op. cit., and T. Balston, *Dr Balston at Eton*, 1952. These trees are by no means complete and could easily have been extended.

almost demanded this.[1] What, in fact, is the ideal social relationship of teacher and class? The corresponding difficulty of intellectual distance throws some light upon this problem. It is clearly impossible for any master with a potential Newton in his class to pretend that he is on the same intellectual plane. All the master can do is to rely on his character, his experience and perhaps on his wider knowledge. In one way, at least, the intellectual problem is much easier in that intellectual attitudes and values are not involved.

If the schools of the last century are arranged in a social hierarchy, then the further one's eye travels down the list from Eton the less striking is the social distance between master and pupil. Ultimately, in the newer boarding establishments and grammar schools the two roughly corresponded. The issue of pupil–master acceptability does not usually arise, therefore, in schools catering for the middle classes, but it could easily become acute higher up the social scale, particularly in boarding schools. The visits of upper-class parents to see their children, and the inevitable entertaining that went with it, meant that teachers could not avoid the acceptance of upper-class standards of life, thought and custom, no matter how reluctant they might be.[2] The inevitable consequences of being found wanting were serious, and it followed that masters at upper-class boarding schools had to be acceptable to their upper-class clientele, not as social equals, for that was impossible, but as providing a suitable environment. On any count, unquestioned status was very desirable, and this meant a respected and cultured way of life coupled with the power and expertise of the true profession. Arnold would have gone further and made an adequate status essential:

. . . you are well aware that it [the position of a schoolmaster in society] has not yet obtained that respect in England, as to be able to stand by itself in public opinion as a liberal profession; it owes the rank which it holds to its connection with the profession of a

1. Teachers in workhouses were expected to live like paupers and, in fact, *with* paupers, although they had separate rooms. Wages were pitiful, and sometimes, depending on the reports of the inspector, they received no wages at all for a year.
2. We know from personal documents that upper-class parents did in fact often visit the children in schools. In Rugby there was also a school for the deaf, catering for upper-class children, and in this case there were special arrangements for such visits.

clergyman, for that is acknowledged universally in England to be the profession of a gentleman. . . .[1]

In his view a master had to be a clergyman not only because of the boy-soul entrusted to him, but also because it gave him social respectability. Arnold also demanded the gentry way of life, with travel and a superior kind of establishment with plenty of servants and a seat in the country—in his own case in the Lake District, at Fox How, near to Wordsworth. As soon as he arrived at Rugby he set about providing the means for all this in a school where adequate provision on the required scale had been lacking. His own income soared to well over £4,000 per annum,[2] and his house-masters enjoyed an income considerably in excess of £1,500. This prosperity, which began in the first years of Victoria, was maintained: twenty years later, in 1862, the thirteen classical masters at Rugby received an average of just over £1,000 each, the highest amount being £1,617.[3] This rate of salary was rather less than that found at Eton, and a little more than that at Harrow. These three were far ahead of the field, with Winchester well below and the others lower still. The anomalies in this situation were brought out strongly by the 1864 Commission:

It must be admitted, we fear, that at several of the Schools . . . in our review, the Assistant Masters are as a body under-paid. . . . The total emoluments of the five masters, who with Dr Kennedy constitute the classical and mathematical staff at Shrewsbury, hardly amount altogether to the annual sum of which a young classical assistant at Eton commonly finds himself in possession within a few years after he has entered on his duties; and this sum is nearly half as much again as the whole income of the Head Master of Westminster or of the Charterhouse.[4]

When we consider that many of the boys in the two or three top schools came from the richest families in the land, with plenty of money for sports, extra subjects and special coaching, it meant that extra money was there for the taking. A house-master at one of the three major schools was very well off indeed, and accustomed to receive handsome presents as well, while the headmaster's life could be luxurious if he wished,

1. Stanley, op. cit., letter dated 19 March 1839.
2. Bamford, *Arnold*, op. cit., p. 222.
3. PSC, I, p. 263.
4. PSC, I, p. 48.

equivalent in style to the surrounding gentry. No wonder that
many of them retired early in life on a comfortable income from
their savings, helped in many cases by a well-paid and less
arduous church appointment, which to the Etonian had a fair
chance of devolving upon him by right.

The same happy picture is not to be found anywhere else in
the public schools except at headmaster level. There was a vast
gulf between assistant masters in all other schools and their
brethren in the top three. In the middle of the century, £150
to £250 a year was considered quite enough for them, and this
range lasted for sixty or seventy years, right up to the First
World War. From this narrowly financial viewpoint, Eton,
Harrow and Rugby—these three and no more—were remote
and in another world. The difference was so great that it almost
appeared as if two systems existed and that injustice based on
them as a yardstick was irrelevant.

The real terror of the assistant master in the 'ordinary'
boarding school was not so much lack of money as uncertainty.
His future and security depended entirely on the whim of the
head, or even of several during the course of time, for the joy
of teaching under one man could be destroyed utterly by his
successor. At Wellington, Wickham (1873–93) had tried to raise
the salary of two of his assistants to £700 and £550 per annum
respectively,[1] but the next headmaster, Bertram Pollock (1893–
1916), considered this excessive and £200 to £250 quite high
enough for an excellent man. In a similar way, while Wickham
nurtured his staff, Pollock despised them. He said in the hearing
of one member, 'If all the staff were to resign today I could
easily supply their places tomorrow.'[2]

If this could happen at Wellington with all its publicity and
royal connections, how much more easily could it be effected
elsewhere. We have chapter and verse for some of these abuses
now, but it is astonishing how such secrets were kept hidden
from the outside world. In this way many a headmaster built a
great reputation on a façade, and the staff, far from puncturing
it, as honesty would demand, helped to support it and suffered
injustice and shame in silence. That insecurity and exploitation
existed on a vast scale cannot be doubted, or that it continued

1. See Newsome, op. cit.
2. ibid., p. 267.

into Edwardian times at least. Cyril Norwood and Arthur Hope reported on the situation in 1909:

The majority of the Public Schools of the early Victorian foundations pay their men such stipends as £125 resident, or £150 non-resident . . . rising to £180 or £200 respectively after, say, four years service, and in some cases going on until the maximum of £250 or £300 non-resident is reached after ten years service.[1]

Until at least the First World War the gulf between the few traditional upper-class schools and the rest persisted, and although the newer variety rapidly increased in reputation, their success was, in a very real way, built at the expense of the assistant masters:

A certain well-known day school, when it moved to a more suitable site a generation or two ago, expended so much money on its new building . . . that it not only exhausted its available endowments, but ran so heavily into debt that its masters have till recently been paid the average salary of £150 p.a. non-resident. . . . A great Public School of Royal foundation has also lately been adding to its premises by reducing salaries that were already a caricature of payment.[2]

The truth is that impressive buildings cannot be built without sacrifice, and the more imposing the structures the greater must be the sacrifice. It was claimed, for instance, that at one school where the chapel was particularly imposing, nearly all the men were paid a mere £100 a year resident.

These accusations were not lightly made, but came from men with intimate knowledge. Apart from Cyril Norwood, the critics included F. B. Malim,[3] so that two of the most distinguished public-school men of our own century were represented.

In spite of the plight of the assistants the headmasters never suffered. The usual situation was for the head to receive ten times the salary of the assistant, and, as one example, it was stated categorically that at Tonbridge only one master earned more than £200, while the headmaster received at least £5,000.[4] The sacrifices at all these schools were borne entirely by the assistant staff and underlings.

1. G. Norwood and A. H. Hope, *The Higher Education of Boys in England*, 1909, p. 229.
2. ibid., pp. 227–8.
3. *Year Book of Education*, 1932, p. 221.
4. Norwood and Hope, op. cit., p. 235.
10

In all schools but those at the very top the relationship of the headmaster to his staff was clearly one of master and servant, in spite of so-called democratic procedures and masters' meetings. The idea that these menials were colleagues of the head cannot be sustained, and only becomes credible by regarding the school as an institution divorced from the normal criteria of society, or else by seeing masters as inspired by the missionary spirit for the benefit of the headmasters. One can only wonder at the conscience of heads who could allow such a situation to develop and take advantage of it. Also one might well ask what was the purpose of having governors at all, peppered as they were with such an impressive façade of bishops, nobles and well-known men, when gross abuses went on unchecked.

Whatever view one takes of the ethics or of the sociological interpretation of the situation, the facts meant that assistant masters had to wait many years for the luxury of marriage and the scramble for promotion was fierce indeed. There was little hope of a post at one of the top schools, for at the turn of the century they employed about two hundred masters all told, and Oxford and Cambridge produced that number of brilliant scholars and mathematicians every two years. The rest had to go to the poorly paid schools of the type we have just described, and hope for better days or the chance of a boarding house. Unfortunately, the turnover was not as great as might be hoped: 'It is not everyone who can get a boarding-house; and those who do, naturally, try to make the fat years swallow up the lean, and stick to it as long as they can.' [1]

No wonder that many got tired of waiting and drifted out of teaching altogether. Nothing illustrates this more vividly than a study of length of service—the time-lapse between the appointment of a master and his resignation. At Eton, Harrow and Rugby, twenty, thirty and forty years' continuous service were not uncommon. At Eton the situation was complicated by the creation of Fellows. If this possibility is included as service to the school and foundation, then the time was extended to fifty or sixty years for some men, and in one case (John Wilder) the period was sixty-eight years. When it is remembered that the long-service men at Eton were also educated there, it

1. W. H. D. Rouse, 'Salaries in Secondary Schools', *Contemporary Review*, August 1900, p. 277.

is evident that Eton had absorbed their lives completely, in spite of pluralist church appointments. The evidence indicates that these three schools were exceptional and that this kind of longevity was rare, although every school has had its 'Mr Chips'. Even within the seven, Shrewsbury does not show it at all and we can suspect that the same situation also applied to one or two of the others. This contrast is seen in Table 6, which deals with the appointments to Harrow and Shrewsbury in the years

Table 6. *Length of stay of masters appointed to Harrow and Shrewsbury, 1800–59.*[1]

Years at School	Percentage of masters at:	
	Harrow	Shrewsbury
0–9	36·6	77·8
10–19	21·9	13·3
20–29	4·9	6·6
30–39	26·7	0
40–49	7·3	0
50–59	2·4	2·2
Number of staff involved	41	45

1800–59. No less than 36 per cent of the staff at Harrow stayed on for thirty years or more compared with 2 per cent at Shrewsbury, and in the case of one of these men at Harrow, his service extended into the twentieth century. Similarly, 78 per cent at Shrewsbury left in less than ten years, and 58 per cent in less than five. This only applied to assistants, for two headmasters, Butler and Kennedy, covered the entire period.

Taking a realistic view, Shrewsbury provided no career in itself for any member of staff except the headmaster. Undoubtedly the prosperity of the school, poor pay and prospects

1. Sources as for Table 4, p. 121. The change in length of service is a most interesting phenomenon and one which has important and obvious relationships to the social climate, to security and to the stature of headmasters. Undoubtedly this matter dovetails into other school-social phenomena that need to be explored.

affected the attitude of the staff, and it was not until the mid 1870s that new appointees began to stay longer at Shrewsbury. The influence of success is also seen at Harrow, where, in the period mentioned, there was no real tradition for longevity of service until the years of C. J. Vaughan.

In spite of all that has been said, a young graduate in a lesser public school was more fortunate than his fellow in a preparatory school, who might earn anything from £40 to £80 per annum, and, in exceptional cases, £20 or £30 more. For him there was virtually no hope, unless he possessed capital. The preparatory school was indeed a last refuge, and those who remained were devoid of spirit, as Eric Parker realized when he traced the fate of sixty assistant preparatory-school masters known to him in 1898:

> Four of these have got schools of their own, and eight have become curates. Among the others are a barrister, a solicitor, a gold-digger, a professional tenor, a bookmaker and a grower of tomatoes. Two are out of work and cannot find any; one poor old man shot himself; twenty-four only remained as they were, and fifteen have completely disappeared, leaving no trace.[1]

Perhaps the public schoolmaster was never reduced to circumstances like this, but the sense of injustice was greater.

We are left with a complicated picture of the assistant master from the earliest Victorian times up to 1914. The situation in the three top schools, with one or two later additions, was very satisfactory indeed, with every prospect of promotion, security and an old age of leisured ease in a vicarage. The classical masters at the great schools had everything—good salaries, a real sense of participation, undeniable status and great freedom. The situation at Eton was so good that staff became rooted. At Rugby only restless men with a taste for power were tempted to go elsewhere, and they could use their financial sacrifice in moving as a powerful moral weapon to obtain better conditions, as Benson did.[2] In four or five other schools the situation was tolerable, but outside this very small circle the situation was deplorable, with very poor pay, a life of subservience and, for the realist, very little to look forward to.

1. E. Parker, 'Preparatory School Assistant Masters', *Longman's Magazine*, xxxi, 1898, pp. 330–46.
2. Newsome, op. cit.

HEADMASTERS[1]

It is a tradition of English life that the Headmaster is an autocrat of autocrats, and the very mention of the title conjures up in the minds of most people a figure before which they trembled in their youth and with which they have never felt quite comfortable even in mature life.[2]

That was an Edwardian view in 1909, when the absolute power of the Victorian head had somewhat declined. Sixty years before it had been said of Arnold:

We have heard it regretted that a man who should have been in his proper place swaying all the Russias, or sitting on the throne of the Antonines, should have been thrown away on the hopeless task of reclaiming a public school.[3]

If not all headmasters were Arnolds, at least many people saw the head of a Victorian public school like that, and this explains how so many rose to the highest offices in the state. The clerical garb, the Victorian passions, the classical basis and gentry background brought a certain unexpected virility into their lives. They all travelled a great deal—long, arduous journeys by coach and train, both in this country and on the Continent. The image of the headmaster buried in the books of his study to the exclusion of all else is largely a myth; it applied perhaps to Samuel Butler, although he too was often to be seen on the other side of the country in Cambridge, but he was a rarity, and even his arch-disciple, Kennedy, was partial to croquet. At the other extreme were David Williams, Edward Thring, Balston and Christopher Wordsworth, all of them renowned muscular heroes of the playing-field. A few had their own particular hobbies, like G. G. Bradley's mad rushes across country on a horse or Temple's extraordinary passion for

1. The first source of material about any headmaster is the relevant school history or histories, e.g. Shrewsbury for Kennedy and Moss. These sources have not usually been mentioned here. Only rarely have headmasters been the subject of biographies. Other obvious sources of information are *D.N.B.*, Venn and *Alumni Oxoniensis*. It is also particularly valuable to consult the works of their scholars. Usually one amasses the information slowly, bit by bit over the years, and much of it is often common to many sources. Some of the most exotic stories of headmasters have been omitted since they rest on hearsay—only if they were confirmed or 'eye-witnessed' have they been credited.
2. Norwood and Hope, op. cit., p. 213.
3. *Edinburgh Review*, 1845.

climbing trees. Balston had a choice, if small, collection of paintings, while Hawtrey mastered languages and built up a library of connoisseur quality. Many had their minds on other things and other places, as in Arnold's yearning for the Lakes, or James Robertson's love for Switzerland, where he had climbed with Whymper.

All headmasters developed eccentricities that most men without such power dare not show, and sometimes these affectations took unexpected turns. Thus Moss's studied and abysmal ignorance of sports shows that it was not even necessary for a popular master to take an interest in matters closest to the hearts of boys. Some carried their eccentricity to extraordinary lengths. Kennedy almost always forgot the time, and without much exaggeration it can be said that he was never early for a lesson and was frequently as much as half an hour late. Bradley, when he was not engaged in riding or watching games, raced pigeons and used to give any chance visitor a basket of them on leaving to be released at Didcot or Exeter. Such aloof and solitary heights of individualism, if not absurdity, undoubtedly helped to endear these men to the boys far more than the careful watchfulness of a man like Benson, who insisted on testing the ice first himself, with the inevitable result that he fell in.

Some headmasters came from large families. Edward Balston was one of ten, and so too was H. M. Butler, while Frederick Temple was one of fifteen. In many cases the headmaster's house itself sheltered large families. Benson and Percival had six children, H. M. Butler eight, Arnold eleven, and Moberly twelve. Bachelors like Temple and Pollock were rare, and the boys were thereby denied the gaiety that was otherwise provided by a wife and daughters. This colourful fringe to public-school life was always immensely popular, and in many cases softened the harshness of the regimen, so that the headmaster's wife and not the headmaster was almost invariably the most popular person on the campus.[1] Some, like Mary Moberly, were beautiful, others, like Mary Benson, were remarkably intelligent—Gladstone thought her 'the cleverest woman in

1. It is difficult to find a headmaster's wife who was not preferred by the boys to the husband. It is rare to find the wives of assistant masters as formidable as Mrs Buckoll.

Europe' [1]—but undoubtedly the most astonishing wife of all was Josephine Butler. As the wife of George Butler, the Principal of Liverpool College, she had always been interested in social affairs, but after the tragic death of her daughter she became, throughout the 1860s and 1870s, an active propagandist and case-worker on behalf of prostitutes. Those who were ill, dying or lacking a refuge, she cared for personally in the attics of her own house in Liverpool.[2] As headmaster of a public school, even a new one, George's life must have been extraordinarily difficult. He must often have been in the position of entertaining influential men and women downstairs when inconvenient callers arrived and drew attention to the proceedings on the upper floors. Yet he supported his wife unreservedly in her campaign. One cannot pretend that social reform on this level is the duty of a headmaster's wife, yet, looking back, the work of George and Josephine Butler makes the lives of other and more famous headmasters appear weak and almost colourless by comparison.

Headmasters stood between the schools and the outside world, both as shields and as spokesmen. This is not to say that they represented truly the views of the masters, let alone the children, but that theirs was the only voice to carry weight, and the only one in the last analysis that mattered.[3] To a large extent the same is still true.

At Eton and Winchester the power of the headmaster was limited by someone of higher authority. Elsewhere, among the old public schools, trustees and governors were generally of no account, in spite of the fact that in theory they controlled the destiny of the school and had sanctioning powers and control over finance and endowments. In practice, whatever ideas they had counted for little unless the headmaster agreed; the business of running the school was entirely his. They could be obstructive, but that was about all. In effect, the governors' main duty was, and always has been, to provide the environment in which the headmaster could work. They could not

1. E. F. Benson, *As We Were.*
2. See A. S. G. Butler, *Portrait of Josephine Butler*, 1954.
3. Headmasters had always been autocrats, and a powerful example was set by Richard Busby of Westminster at the time of the Restoration.

interfere, and even the private life of the head was sacrosanct —a precedent that was set and fought for by Arnold himself in the years immediately before the Victorian era, when he refused categorically to answer straight questions put to him by the trustees about his fight with Newman over the Oxford Movement. They could dismiss him, but they could not demand satisfaction. This stand of Arnold and others was amply reinforced by the Public Schools Commissioners for all the main schools in 1864. In their view: 'The Head Master should have the uncontrolled power of selecting and dismissing assistant masters; of regulating the arrangement of the school in classes or divisions, the hours of school work. . . .' [1]

It is difficult to imagine anything stronger than this, and it is no wonder that, as far as internal matters were concerned, governing bodies at worst were only minor nuisances unless a matter of school survival was involved, and at best merely rubber stamps. Many hardly took an interest in the school. At Harrow, 'Their meetings were quarterly, and their minutes show that it often happened that no business could be transacted for want of a quorum.' [2]

This apathy was not really the result of pressure of other work, for busier men found plenty of time at other places. The eminence of the governing body made no difference to the power of the headmaster. At Wellington, the new school was launched by one of the most illustrious groups of national celebrities that one could imagine. The Prince Consort, for one, knew precisely what he wanted, and yet even he was frustrated by a man of no social consequence whatever.

Everything in the public-school system worked to the same end. Not only did the head represent the school as a functional organization, but everything from correspondence to invitations was channelled through him. He was the ultimate power. Advancement for any of his staff without his active help was impossible, for he signed their testimonials.

THE APPOINTMENT OF HEADMASTERS

At Eton and the Roman Catholic schools promotions were internal adjustments, but the usual practice, in theory at any

1. PSC, I, p. 53.
2. E. Graham, *The Harrow Life of Henry Montagu Butler*, 1920, p. 149.

rate, was for the headmaster to be appointed from outside by the governors or trustees on the general principle that new blood was necessary. Since this was the greatest single decision they ever had to make, it might be thought that the matter would be sifted carefully by everyone concerned, but in fact the real decision was usually delegated to a small committee of two or three, often indeed left to one man, with the rest agreeing to the nomination later. This procedure had the effect of eliminating apparent competition, and the selected man typically received the offer in a letter waiting for him on the breakfast table. This happened to Benson, Percival and Wilson in the last century, and to F. B. Malim and W. W. Vaughan in this. This process, common enough when trustees existed, was almost invariably the case with new schools where the founder was all but omnipotent, as with Bradfield or the Woodard ventures, and was often accompanied with all the prejudice and absurdity that such power brings. A typical case occurred in 1860, when the Warden of Bradfield, Thomas Stevens, appointed S. P. Denning. A. F. Leach gives the following account:

It is said that his application was the first of several scores that were opened by the Founder. When he read the words 'Stephen Poyntz Denning', he said, 'This is an omen. "Stephen appoints Denning." So he shall' and he opened no more of the applications.[1]

Sometimes headmasters with dominant personalities had built up such a spirit of omnipotence over the years that they virtually managed to nominate their own successors in the manner of Cotton of Marlborough and Butler of Shrewsbury.[2] In many ways, however, nomination was unfair, and on the rare occasions when objections to this procedure were made,

1. Leach, *History of Bradfield College*, op. cit., p. 95.
2. One is always tempted to look for subtle or direct influences when coincidences occur in men who follow one another as the heads of the same institution. This, of course, is justified, but it is also theoretically possible to have an impressive succession of heads, related in some way to one another and yet appointed by chance and fairly. This applies to all institutions, not only schools. A good example comes from the comment on p. 189 of Sedbergh School Register: 'It is somewhat curious that of the five Principals of St Bees Theological College, four have been Sedberghians, and the present Principal is connected by marriage with one of his predecessors.' Corresponding sequences are clearly capable of statistical investigation, though the analysis of the various possible relationships would be complex.

the result had been acute embarrassment, as in the instance of J. M. Wilson.[1]

Not everyone accepted an invitation to apply, in spite of the advantages. Thus when Tait resigned and wrote to Temple with such an offer, Temple refused. Eight years later the vacancy occurred again on the resignation of Goulburn, and Temple thought that he would apply now, though the going was more difficult. Having scruples about reading the nice things other people might say, he got someone else to collect his testimonials. At this time Temple was at the Education Department in Whitehall, and on 9 September 1857 he listed the criticisms against him and assessed his chances:

> I have just had a list of the accusations made against me in the ears of the Rugby Trustees:
>
> 1. I am a Puseyite.
> 2. I am a Rationalist.
> 3. I know no Greek.
> 4. I have no experience in teaching.
> 5. I am not a gentleman.
> 6. I failed at Kneller Hall.
> But I think I shall succeed for all that.[2]

It is not surprising that he did succeed when three of his supports were Lord Lansdowne, Lord Russell and Lord Granville, backed up, among others, by Lingen and Sandford, both of them, like Temple, Balliol men. These men knew Temple and liked him, but even if they had not, the way of the world is such that one lukewarm testimonial from an eminent man of this calibre is worth a dozen enthusiastic statements from unknown people.

Influence is always important and usually decisive, especially that of the more intimate kind. Thus the election of Ridding to Winchester was a foregone conclusion. He was second master at the time, just as his father had been before him; the Warden was a great-uncle; two of the Fellows were relations; he had actually been born at Winchester, and the retiring head was his father-in-law.

When the post really went to open competition, the resulting scramble revealed an effort that passes all belief. When C. J.

1. See Wilson, *Autobiography*, op. cit.
2. E. G. Sandford, *Frederick Temple*, 1907, p. 178.

Vaughan resigned from Harrow in 1859, he made a point of not influencing the governors directly—indeed, if any rumour of the real reason behind his resignation had by chance leaked to one of the governors, he was very wise not to do so—but he did use all his skill and experience in directing the campaign of the man he wanted to follow him. He wrote to Henry Montague Butler on 26 September:

My own impression is that it would be wise to delay any formal announcement of yourself for a little time longer, and to let it come rather as an act of compliance with the expressed desire of others, than of personal choice. . . . Your warm friends here—Farrar more particularly—would do well to hold back. . . . They may run a risk of provoking hostility. . . .[1]

Altogether Butler submitted thirty-one testimonials. One of them was signed by William Whewell and twenty-five Fellows or ex-Fellows of Trinity. The rest came from a wide variety of important people—two bishops, two deans, an archdeacon, three professors, the headmaster of Westminster, Lord Macaulay, two Fellows of St John's, and so on. In spite of all this backing, the committee voted evenly between Butler and another candidate, Alfred Barry, who presumably had made an equal effort to get elected, and only personal pressure from Farrar on one of the voters turned the scale in time for the second meeting.

And Butler was only twenty-six! This kind of massive support at such an early age indicates the supreme importance of personal influence. Harrow had a tradition of young headmasters. In addition to Butler, Vaughan was appointed at twenty-eight, Wordsworth at thirty and Longley at thirty-five. This preference for youth was not universal. C. J. Vaughan may have been appointed at twenty-eight, but his kinsman, W. W. Vaughan, was elected to Rugby at exactly twice that age, fifty-six.

It should not be thought that Butler's effort was exceptional in any way. His thirty-one testimonials were somewhat meagre by the standard of the sixty-five printed in book form that Jex-Blake compiled when applying for Haileybury in December 1867.[2] Moreover, each one of these sixty-five was up to date,

1. For Vaughan's interest in his successor, and for the quotation, see Graham, op. cit., p. 121.
2. The Jex-Blake testimonials can be seen in Rugby Public Reference Library.

especially prepared by the writers for this one occasion. In the event it was an appalling waste of effort since the authorities preferred another candidate, E. H. Bradby.

Influence was undoubtedly important in obtaining a major post, but the evidence of H. M. Butler, Jex-Blake and others shows that not a little stamina and self-esteem were required as well, though few men went to the extent of Edward Thring's travelling round the country and pressing his own claims in person.[1]

In spite of their power, headmasters were well served by their staffs. The same kind of irrational loyalty that prevented, and prevents, boys from telling the truth to staff and parents stopped the staffs themselves from complaining to the outside world. They suffered in silence and resigned rather than air their grievances in public. Any potential rebel was dismissed. The situation, seen occasionally in state grammar schools, of a kind of running warfare between headmaster and staff hardly occurred unless both had legal rights, as at Sedbergh, or at Shrewsbury under Samuel Butler. United action against authority was rare and usually concerned money or security, as at Bradfield in 1880, when the headmaster himself and half the staff resigned because they had not been paid. Rebellion for other reasons was almost unknown, or at least unrecorded, although one case at Rugby is important in many ways, and most instructive for its bearing on the relationships of the head and the assistant staff and the refusal of the masters to accept the man chosen by the governors.

The man concerned was Henry Hayman.[2] When Frederick Temple accepted the bishopric of Exeter, the staff had assumed that his successor would be some well-known figure, with a name familiar to at least most of them. The appointment of Hayman, however, was a complete surprise. He was an unknown quantity with no claim to distinction in any field. He only had a second-class degree, and his experience at

1. See G. R. Parkin, *Edward Thring*, 1900, p. 52.
2. For sources of the Hayman story, see Wilson, *Autobiography*, op. cit. (which shows staff attitudes); R. C. Carrington, *Two Schools*, 1962, pp. 47–8; B. R. Wise, 'Rugby in the Seventies', *Cornhill Magazine*, October 1914, pp. 507–18; correspondence relative to the Rev. Dr Hayman's expulsion of P. O. Westfeldt of New York; *Rugby Advertiser*, issues of 16 and 23 April 1870, 18 and 25 March, 1 and 8 April 1871, *et seq*.

Charterhouse, St Olave's, Cheltenham and Bradfield was hardly that of a serious contender for one of the three or four greatest schools in the country. Several of the staff he would be controlling had a far better claim, on paper, notably J. M. Wilson, while Hayman could hardly be compared with Arthur Sidgwick or Henry Lee Warner. Altogether they regarded his appointment as an insult and took up a hostile attitude at once. Copies of the testimonials he had submitted for the post were obtained, read with minute attention to detail, and found to be misleading or inaccurate in certain particulars.[1] As a result, A. W. Potts, the master of The Twenty, who was about to leave Rugby in any case to take up the headmastership of Fettes, went down to Bradfield on behalf of the staff, saw Hayman and expressed serious doubts on the worthiness of his documents. To avoid unpleasantness all round, he suggested that the easiest plan would be for Hayman to withdraw his acceptance of the post and remain at Bradfield. Altogether it must have been a fascinating interview, with contempt very apparent and with both sides treading the delicate line between blackmail and bluff. An Old Rugbeian, Sir Stafford Northcote, also took a hand and saw Hayman as well, but it was no use, for he had already handed in his notice, and there was nothing now that could stop his translation to Rugby.

The trouble over Hayman's testimonials concerned both quantity and quality. In all he submitted thirty-seven letters in support of his application. This was twenty less than Jex-Blake, one of the staff at Rugby, had thought necessary when applying for the lesser school of Haileybury only three years before. In addition, only two of Hayman's were up to date; the rest may have been written by such important men as three bishops, six professors, a dean, headmasters and others, but they were two or three years old and therefore quite obviously designed for another purpose. The fact that Hayman had not bothered to produce new documents was taken as further evidence of incompetence and as a slight on the dignity of the school. In this way an extraordinary situation developed in which the previous headmaster, Temple, took a prominent part. He joined forces with the staff and the old boys. Legal advice was taken

1. For Hayman's testimonials, see the copy in Rugby Reference Library. There are also many references in school histories, e.g. Graham, op. cit.

and every move in the game scrutinized in the hope of some
overplay that would serve as an excuse for winkling this man
from Arnold's seat. In self-defence, Hayman and his lone
supporter on the staff, Burrows, adopted the same tactics. In
this battle Hayman could only play for time, for Temple and
the rest were far too strong. The new head found the whole
educational world against him, so that when the Rev. James
Robertson was dismissed from Rugby in 1871 the affair became
a public scandal. Robertson was immediately offered a post at
Harrow through the personal intervention of Temple, and went
on later to the headmastership of Haileybury. In this cat-and-
mouse display the misery was prolonged over three long years
until Burrows gave in his notice, and the disposal of the
boarding-house that he ran gave the staff the pretext which
they wanted.

It had been the custom to give this lucrative sideline to the
next senior man, but Hayman passed over the obvious choice
and gave it elsewhere. The assistant staff appealed to the
Governing Body, and in preparing his defence Hayman discovered that a previous headmaster, Goulburn, had passed over
a man named Shairp in a similar way many years before.
Shairp had since become a professor at St Andrew's, and it was
his reply to a request from Hayman for information that caused
the trouble. Shairp confirmed that he had been passed over,
but in telling this story to an old friend at Rugby he was
reminded that Goulburn, on being told the custom, had
immediately cancelled the decision and offered the house to
Shairp, who declined it. Shairp accordingly wrote a second
letter to Hayman, and sent copies of the correspondence to
C. T. Arnold. In this difficult situation Hayman was foolish
enough to send a copy of only the first letter to the Governors,
with the inevitable result that 'the second [letter was] placed
in the hands of one member of the Governing Body by Charles
Arnold. . . . This was fatal. It was told us that the Bishop
[Temple] said he would never speak to Hayman again.' [1]

Hayman was promptly dismissed, and in spite of an appeal
to the courts the dismissal stood. Many saw the old headmaster
as a kind of political martyr, and in many ways he was so.
Unfortunately the defeat at Rugby was not the end of his

1. Wilson, op. cit., p. 78.

troubles, but only the beginning, since one misfortune followed
another until late in life.

J. M. Wilson, who was an active participant in this affair,
summed it up as follows: 'The real blame lay, in my judgement,
solely with the old Trustees of the School, who so hated Temple's
Liberalism that they resolved at any cost to appoint a man of
their own party who was in no single respect fit for the post.' [1]

This may well be true, but the scandal brought credit to no
one. There is no doubt at all that Hayman was given no chance
to make good and that there was a conspiracy against him from
the very beginning, fomented in a most unchurchly way by the
retiring headmaster, Temple. As for the school, the boys
watched the spectacle in delight. They played off one party
against another, encouraged Buckoll to draw biblical parallels
in Esther, attended public meetings and hissed and jeered
everyone without discrimination.[2] The town took sides and a
subscription fund for Hayman was started. Altogether this was
a most exciting and unique period, and although, looked at one
way, it boils down to a fight between one man and the rest,
with all one's sympathies for the lesser opponent, it is a little
difficult to sympathize all the way with the complex, pompous
figure of the headmaster with his gigantic eyebrows and
alarming sniff, who never spoke simply if a complicated phrase
could be used, and to whom 'Put out the lights!' became
'Adumbrate the scintillation!'

Just as Tait had to change many things after the death of
Arnold, so now the situation left by Temple was not easy for a
lesser man. The difference between Tait and Hayman was that
Hayman lacked skill in persuading others. Even so, the staff
were very lucky in the outcome. They would have more than
met their match if the new man had been an equally unknown
Thring or Temple, Benson or Pollock at the outset of their
careers.

One cannot help feeling that the real problem lay in the fact
that Hayman was unknown and outside the headmasterly
cliques of the nineteenth century. In spite of the men who had
written testimonials for him—and some of them had hardly

---

1. ibid., p. 79.
2. For the attitude of the boys, see the *Rugby Advertiser* references already
given and others subsequently.

been enthusiastic to say the least—he had few really important strings to pull, while it is evident from reading the lives of other headmasters that they were often well connected before their elevation.

THE FAMILY CONNECTIONS OF HEADMASTERS

At one extreme the connections of headmasters with other important people were family ties. Even ignoring the obvious cases to be found at Eton, which have already been dealt with since they also concern masters and Fellows on the foundation, some families did manage to collect a goodly share of the plums. George Butler, headmaster of Harrow, was the son of a school proprietor, and the father of three sons who were respectively the heads of Harrow, Liverpool College and Haileybury. Only slightly less exalted is the example of the Gilkes family, while another outstanding father-and-son combination were the Temples, Frederick and William, not only as heads of public schools but also as Archbishops of Canterbury. At Winchester George Moberly was followed by his son-in-law, George Ridding. Brothers filling headships at different public schools were common, like the Butlers (mentioned above); R. L. and A. D. James; M. L. and H. B. Jacks. In a similar way C. J. and W. W. Vaughan were related, if a little more distantly.

Behind most of these headmasterly examples was a background that was eminent, not only in teaching but elsewhere in the whole range of public service and intellectualism. Samuel Butler of Shrewsbury is a case in point,[1] but a better example comes from the Wordsworth family, including not only William, the poet, and his sister Dorothy, but two heads of Oxford or Cambridge colleges and three bishops, one of whom, Christopher, was headmaster of Harrow, and another, Charles, second master of Winchester—all of them extremely closely linked (see Family Linkage 2). This case is also interesting for its sidelight on the relative worth of a public-school reputation. Charles Wordsworth must have been near the apex of quality for a public schoolmaster:

1. The grandson of Samuel Butler, Headmaster of Shrewsbury and Bishop of Lichfield, was Samuel Butler, the painter, who wrote *Erewhon* and *The Way of all Flesh*. This last book must be read by anyone who hopes to understand public school and social problems of the middle nineteenth century. It is usually assumed that it is semi-autobiographical.

Nephew of the poet, god-son of the Archbishop of Canterbury, a scholar of exquisite taste and instant facility in Greek and Latin verse, disciple and friend at Christ Church of Pusey, tutor and intimate friend of Gladstone and Manning, of a personal life judged saintly by contemporaries who applied rigorous tests, among the best cricketers, oarsmen, skaters, rackets and tennis players of his day, joint founder of the University Cricket Match and Boat Race, Wordsworth brought to an assistant mastership a 'background' and an assemblage of gifts surely unrivalled in public-school history.[1]

On paper Charles Wordsworth was certainly impressive, but there is far more to being a great man than this. Even con-

Family Linkage 2. *The Wordsworth family.*

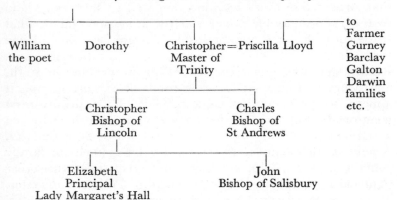

sidered within his own family, this particular Wordsworth was not at all outstanding and hardly in the same class as his uncle. It is a sad and sobering reflection on the so-called elevated level that we are considering.

A more involved case of family relationship was that of the headmasters of Wellington (Benson) and Clifton (Wilson). Linked directly to both these in the same generation, in an in-law kind of relationship, were Henry Sidgwick, Lord Rayleigh and Arthur Balfour, the prime minister, with automatic introductions to philosophical, scholastic, scientific, religious, political and indeed almost every important circle in the country. The two men—Benson and Wilson—were major figures in the headmasterly world, but here again, as with the Wordsworths and even allowing for the archbishopric, they

1. Firth, op. cit., p. 141.

11

were small fry in this company. Balfour was not the only prime minister with such connections; Gladstone's son-in-law, Wickham, was in the chair at Wellington, while the fourteenth Earl of Home married C. A. Alington's daughter.

The nineteenth century saw a growth of the professional ranks both in number and variety, helped in part by the growth of the public schools. Some of the professions were based on expert knowledge acquired by years of study and applied as a service to the community. Such were medicine, the Civil Service, the armed forces. For some of the other professions the dominant feature was that of perpetual quest, of opening the mind to new ideas and new aspects of truth. It is sometimes said that Arnold rose every morning prepared to start again and treat every issue of life from scratch with an open mind. That is the spirit, however impracticable it might be, which drives the radical, the teacher, the researcher, the university don. Restless questioning is at the root of this freedom of the spirit, and, whether this attitude is the result of nurture or not, it appears to go in families, some of which have already been mentioned. Occasionally a headmaster appears to have played a significant role or even to have started such a dynasty. Arnold is an example. Not only did his immediate family contain famous names, but there are direct links with other significant families—Huxley, Ward, Penrose, Forster, Trevelyan. Moreover, it is possible to extend these relationships, laterally as it were, into more families: Macaulay, Babington, Rose, Vaughan, Conybeare, Cartwright, as indicated in Family Linkage 3. Elsewhere it is shown that the Vaughans were also related to the Symonds, Green, Stanley, Hare, Maurice families (Family Linkage 5). From these the lines can be extended to Fisher, Strickland, Cornish, Warre, Bowdler, Booth—and so on, almost indefinitely. In this web are many headmasters, although the significant feature of this particular instance is the widespread nature of the fame over many fields, from politics to literature, from radicals to men of science.

Occasionally a family develops that seems to possess a special interest in education. The best example of this is the family that stemmed from George Butler, who became headmaster of Harrow in 1805. Four headmasters are to be found here, besides heads of Oxford or Cambridge colleges, dons, a diplomatist,

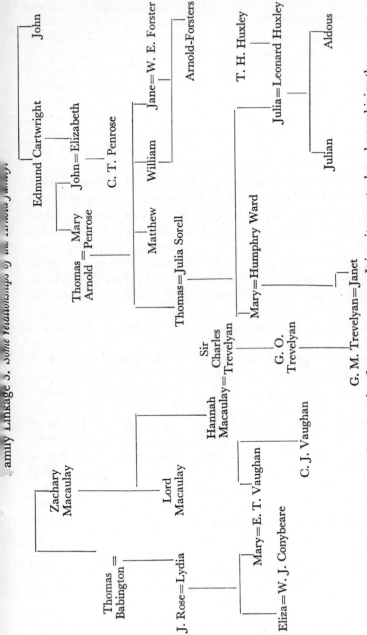

1. The linkages shown here are taken from many sources. It is quite easy to show, by combining the linkages shown in this book, that almost all the great intellectual names are inter-linked. This linkage is only a skeleton. Only the significant names are included. Thus only four of the very large family of Thomas Arnold are indicated. For other purposes it would be fairer to include all children, so that the effects of character, ability, marriage and influence could be assessed. This would lead us into the realm of statistics and its purpose would be different if relevant. It is our main purpose here to show that the great headmasters were part of a network, both in the background and in the creative sense. This clearly affected views, ambitions, character, appointments and many other matters.

major social reformers, besides another outstanding descendant, R. A. Butler (now Lord Butler). In addition, there are linkages with at least three other families also distinguished in scholasticism and research—the Darwins, Galtons and Edgeworths. Again, from these starting-points, it is possible to construct extremely elaborate links not only across the families of one era but also in historical depth. In this case we can trace the ancestry back in time to the Norman dukes and royal houses, including Charles Martel and Charlemagne. A simple indication of the more modern educational relationships of this elaborate example is given in Family Linkage 4.

George Butler and Thomas Arnold were not unique. Other heads have started intellectual dynasties, which have not only produced eminent men and women in a direct line, but have intermarried with other intellectual families. Such relationships are obvious to anyone interested in genealogy, and have been a matter of comment from time to time. One of the most complete investigations in depth was due to Francis Galton, and a glance at work of this nature indicates that a considerable proportion of the intellectual field of the nineteenth and twentieth centuries was locked within a select group. This is not really surprising, for the main opportunity for young people to meet came through the meeting of families. Any reading of nineteenth-century biographies will confirm how much visiting took place between friends. That so many from these families occupied commanding and influential positions is also not surprising, since those in the same circle possessed the power of appointment. This section of society formed a kind of intellectual aristocracy,[1] to use the phrase of Noel Annan, and new names suddenly appeared within it as men of great ability entered the lists and started growing-points of their own. Two outstanding examples appear to be George Butler and Thomas Arnold, and any headmaster of an influential school stands some chance of repeating the achievement.

Not every headmaster, even when he had a large family, formed a growing-point. In theory the combined brilliance of Benson and Mary Sidgwick was an even more promising source

1. The concept of the intellectual aristocracy has been stressed by Noel Annan; see N. G. Annan, 'The Intellectual Aristocracy', *Studies in Social History—A Tribute to G. M. Trevelyan*, edited by J. J. Plumb, 1955, Part 8.

Family Linkage 4. *Brief outline of the George Butler family tree.*[1]

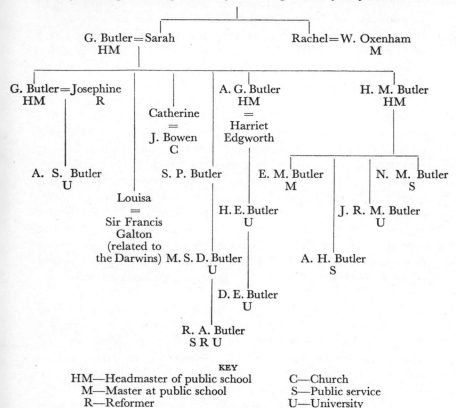

than any of the others we have considered. Unfortunately, however, this family, instead of expanding its talents, held a strange quality of self-extinction, and all the promise petered out since none of their eminent children married. The same long-term tragedy is seen to a lesser degree in the descendants of Thomas Jex-Blake, the father of T. W. Jex-Blake, the head of Cheltenham and Rugby. In this immediate family were three of the most outstanding women, all of them unmarried.[2]

1. Only a skeleton outline is shown to indicate the relationships.
2. The Jex-Blake women were: Sophia, Founder of London School of Medicine for Women, etc.; Henrietta, Principal, Lady Margaret Hall, Oxford; Katherine, Mistress of Girton College.

A different kind of situation existed in those families, commonly seen in the aristocracy, where many members held prominent official positions. Usually these were posts of responsibility where creative thinking was not essential, and certainly not so important as other factors, such as the need for reliability, discretion and solidarity to the point of secrecy. This can be guaranteed only by kinship, as in the bankers, or in the family business of Eton, or in politics, or in foreign service, as shown elsewhere (p. 238). Here again elaborate relationships can be spread over most, if not all, the titled families, as shown typically by Anthony Sampson.[1] However, the Galton, Butler, Arnold and the abortive Benson trees are somewhat different, for they do not depend merely on eminence derived from filling gaps in a hierarchy, even at top level, but rather on the self-achievement of their members. There is much to be said for the argument that the real contribution of Thomas Arnold to the country's welfare did not lie so much in his school work as in this particular quality of handing down his abilities, and certainly that is true for the original George Butler.

Headmasters of the great schools did not need to fear superannuation nor the rust of old age, for the post was only a stepping-stone to higher things. Promotion to deaneries and bishoprics were common enough, if there was any trace of ability. Sometimes one gets the impression that elevation came as a mere reward for faithful service, as perhaps with Pollock, and sometimes even as a means of removing an unsuccessful man, as in the case of Goulburn.[2] No less than four headmasters found themselves at Canterbury—Longley, Tait, Frederick Temple and Benson—and this tradition continues to the present day through William Temple and Geoffrey Fisher. It is really beyond dispute that the opportunities and the offers were there, even if they were not always accepted, as in the refusal of bishoprics by C. J. Vaughan and J. M. Wilson. The Victorian scene cannot usually be taken at face value, and the case of

1. See A. Sampson, *Anatomy of Britain*, 1962, charts between pp. 34–5.
2. It was assumed in the last century that men in power looked after the welfare of their old schools. The only way of removing an unsuccessful headmaster was by promotion. Certainly this was commonly reckoned to be the background to Goulburn's elevation. Details are, however, unknown.

Vaughan is a particularly good illustration. His early life at
Rugby under Arnold had been full of promise, and he went on
to great success at Cambridge. At twenty-six he tried unsuccess-
fully for Rugby, but was appointed to Harrow two years later.
This in itself would rule out modesty. From that moment the
fortunes of Harrow improved markedly and have already been
the subject of comment. However, he resigned in 1859 and
accepted a bishopric in 1863 only to decline it a week later. In
1879 he became Dean of Llandaff. This story of moderate
success has always seemed mysterious for such an ambitious
man. His resignation from Harrow and the manner of his
refusal of the see of Rochester were not entirely in character.
It has recently been revealed that Vaughan was forced to resign
by the father of J. A. Symonds because of his sexual relations
with at least one boy, and it was agreed to keep the matter
secret on condition that Vaughan did not accept any important
ecclesiastical post. When he defied the ban and accepted the
bishopric four years later, he was promptly threatened with
exposure and had no option but to withdraw.[1] A. P. Stanley
had been drawn into this affair from the beginning, and the
personal tragedy became a family matter, with the Symonds,
Stanley and Vaughan families intermarried in an extraordinary
way, as outlined briefly in Family Linkage 5. One can only
guess at the gossip and recriminations behind the scenes in a
situation which held every ingredient of Victorian melodrama.
It is clear that a magnificent family tree can be not only a
source of pride, promise and fulfilment, but also a potential
source of tragedy.

The church was a common and traditional outlet for headmasters, but by no means the only one. Some were attracted
back to the university, to the more leisurely and rewarding
mastership of an Oxford or Cambridge college, like H. M.
Butler, Cyril Norwood and John Percival, or even in recent
times to become vice-chancellors of red-brick universities, like
Sir Charles Morris, Sir John Wolfenden and Lord James, or
heads of major corporations or government departments, like
Sir Arthur fforde and Sir John Wolfenden again. The more
exotic possibilities, however, were limited largely to schools at
the top end of the hierarchy, to the original seven, to

1. For the story of Vaughan and Harrow, see Grosskurth, op. cit.

Family Linkage 5. *Brief outline of some of the Vaughan family relationships.*[1]

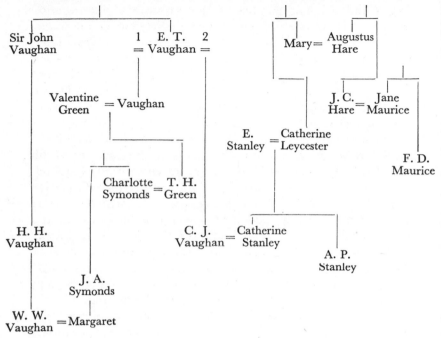

Wellington, Marlborough in the nineteenth century, and to a
very few additional ones since.

THE REPUTATION OF HEADMASTERS

Any headmaster's achievement is complex and differs fundamentally from that of the normal teacher since he is responsible
not only for teaching, but for buildings, the estate, the staff, the
boys and health, besides the reputation of the school in the
public eye. It is true that governing bodies exist, but, as we have
said, it is undeniable that the power lies in the headmaster's
study. Success can, therefore, be judged by many criteria.

Schools are institutions housed in open country and made of
stone, bricks and mortar. This solid aspect is, in fact, the only
part that visibly endures and the one that springs naturally to

1. The relationships are taken from many sources and no details of families
are given. This family linkage should be read in conjunction with the others
in the chapter.

mind. Is the man who extends the buildings or spreads the estate over acres of countryside of more account than the man who merely increases the number of pupils? On the basis of buildings, Wooll and Goulburn at Rugby, usually dismissed as unsuccessful, would rank far higher than Arnold and Temple, and similar examples could easily be quoted from the records of other schools.

The details behind any expansion are usually dull and lengthy, with architects, solicitors, headmasters and governors in a perpetual wrangle, but occasionally a head managed to cut through the delays with a grand gesture, as at Uppingham, where Thring defied his governors and financed his schemes himself. In the same way, at Winchester, Ridding's wealth was impressive. He could and did pour his own money into any project he liked. It made his position unchallengeable and brought with it immense power:

> He was thus enabled to devote his substantial private means to public purposes, in all his successive offices, from the Second Mastership to his Bishopric, never keeping for himself a penny of his salary. . . . In all he put into his reforms twenty thousand pounds of his own money, of which eventually he was repaid a little less than half . . . only so could the passive obstruction of the Warden and Fellows be brushed aside, and the new Governing Body be confronted with a *fait accompli*.[1]

In a similar way H. W. Moss's real achievement at Shrewsbury was the movement of the school from the central site, where Butler and Kennedy did their teaching, to Kingsland. Although logic would suggest that the permanency reflected in buildings would be the most important achievement of all, yet, in fact, a local fame appears to be the maximum lot of such a man if he is lucky.

A headmaster is often judged by the quality of his products. E. Graham discovered that 342 of the boys who served under H. M. Butler at Harrow became prominent in after-life, including ninety-six who excelled at sport, besides one archbishop, four viceroys, sixty-four generals and five headmasters of public schools.[2] If these figures are any guide, it would be hard to convict the generation of Harrovians trained under

1. Firth, op. cit., p. 149.
2. Graham, op. cit., p. 300.

Dr Butler of inefficiency or stagnation, in spite of the advantages they enjoyed.

J. M. Wilson noted that a small school is apt to produce more significant pupils than a large one, and this was certainly true of Goulburn's time at Rugby and confirmed by C. H. Pearson's subjective comparison with Rugby under Arnold.

His son Matthew and Clough and Arthur Stanley are three of his [Arnold's] pupils who really achieved eminence; Tom Hughes and Hodson, of Hodson's Horse, are known creditably by their work; and Henry Smith made himself the greatest of living English mathematicians by striking into a line for which Rugby was no preparation. Now this cannot be called a large list for fourteen years of scholastic activity, and Eton has repeatedly furnished more brilliant lists for a shorter period, while Rugby itself, under one of its very worst headmasters, turned out a whole muster-roll of distinguished men, such as Goschen, Lord Justice Bowen, and Professor Sidgwick.[1]

It is possible that this criticism might be true in spite of Arnold's reputation for producing prominent men, but it certainly cannot be accepted without caution. For one thing, the reign of Tait separated Goulburn from Arnold, so there were distinct differences of time and circumstance. The situation becomes even more complicated if we try to compare two headmasters in different schools (say Benson and Temple), since the raw material, facilities, opportunities, reputation and general background are so far apart. Moreover, 'eminence' is a difficult quality to assess without a strict definition. However, if we consider two successive heads in the same school to eliminate some of the differences owing to background and period, and take precise arbitrary values of success in adult life, then perhaps a more worth-while comparison can be made. For this purpose a so-called unsuccessful head, Wooll, has been compared with Arnold himself, using the following criteria of success: the rank of major or above in the army, of commander or above in the navy, of a professor or a fellow of a college, of a dean or above in the church, of an M.P. in politics, of a judge, Q.C. or high sheriff. This covers most assessable careers, and although one may quarrel about the lowest rank of each of these, at least it is constant for both headmasters and will include a wider selection than any thorny assessment of 'eminence'. The results are seen in Table 7.

1. C. H. Pearson, *Memorials*, edited by William Stebbing, 1900, pp. 18–19.

At once it can be said that there is little evidence here that Arnold so altered the complexion of the school that unlikely boys became successful in after-life. A very slight increase in percentage over the achievements of Wooll is all that can possibly be claimed, and certainly nothing that anyone is likely to make a point of argument. Arnold, then, had no secret. He no more placed the wreath of success on the brows of his boys than did Wooll before him. One feels that much the same conclusion would be reached in other instances, although an interesting case for this kind of analysis would be that of Shrewsbury with its three heads—Samuel Butler, Kennedy,

Table 7. *Successful men in the Victorian era produced from Rugby school entrants, 1818–34.*[1]

Date of entry	Total Number of entrants	Number of entrants becoming successful	Percentage	Headmaster
1818	77	10	13	
1819	71	9	13	Wooll
1820	63	7	11	only
1821	49	4	8	
1822	34	2	6	
1823	35	3	9	
1824	31	5	16	
1825	32	2	6	Wooll
1826	32	4	12	and
1827	31	3	10	Arnold
1828	67	6	9	
1829	96	9	9	
1830	113	12	11	
1831	106	13	12	
1832	80	13	16	Arnold
1833	89	8	9	only
1834	71	12	17	

NOTE: The definition of 'successful' is given in the text. Further years would include some coming under the influence of Tait, the next headmaster.

1. Material deduced from information in *Rugby School Register* (Rev. A. T. Michell). For a similar analysis for the different purpose of *élite* contributions, see Chapter 9, pp. 217-18.

Moss—spread over more than a century. It would combine the problems of extraordinary examination results with small and medium schools, the issue of staff longevity and change of site.

Allied to general success in adult life is another criterion often advanced in favour of some headmasters—namely, the number of boys or staff who came to direct public schools themselves later in their careers. We have seen that H. M. Butler was responsible for five of these. The ideas of Arnold are supposed to have been spread throughout the system by his pupils and colleagues. In a similar way Temple has the reputation of a maker of headmasters, and was certainly responsible for the advancement of nine colleagues.[1]

An analysis of school records reveals that almost twice as many men were promoted from the staff at Rugby than from any other public school, the nearest rival being Harrow. From a superficial view this could mean that Rugby was the best vehicle for advancement in the nineteenth century, but it must be explained that one school at least, Eton, was not in the race at all, for the good reason that service there was superior to a job of responsibility elsewhere, and the number seeking promotion was correspondingly small. Even at Rugby, promotion to a headship somewhere else often meant a drop in salary, so that, for financial reasons, a move was not usually made.[2] Apart from the over-all view, this problem was also complex in detail. It can be demonstrated quite easily that not only did the best headmasters create opportunities for their staffs, but that heads, often dismissed as unsuccessful, have also at times produced equal or even more striking results. As an example, members of Wickham's staff at Wellington went on to headships at Haileybury (and then to Eton), Cranleigh, Lancing (then on to Durham and Uppingham), Winchester, Sedbergh (and on to Tonbridge), Birkenhead (and then to Epsom), St Edward's, Highgate, Ipswich, Trent College. This is no mean record, equal to or better than the rest, but even this is not to be compared with the record of his father, Edward Wickham, who was not a public-school head at all, but ran a preparatory

1. The nine masters under Temple who became headmasters were Bradley, Benson, A. Butler, Jex-Blake, Percival, C. Evans, Kitchener, Phillpotts, Potts.
2. For comparison of the salaries at Rugby and the headmastership at Wellington, see Newsome, *Wellington College*, op. cit. (references to Benson).

school, known as Eagle House, at Hammersmith.[1] David Newsome reveals that six major headmasters were all boys together under him, namely Ridding of Winchester, Butler of Harrow, A. G. Butler of Haileybury, G. J. Blore of King's School, Canterbury, E. C. Wickham of Wellington and Edmond Warre of Eton. This school appears to have been exceptional, not only in its clientele but also in its scholastic approach:

Then there was Eagle House, Hammersmith, under Edward Wickham, father of the editor of Horace. Here was given what by the standards of earlier times was a complete grammar-school course. Henry Montagu Butler, when he left at the age of twelve, had read two Greek plays with choruses, a fair amount of the *Iliad*, of Xenophon's *Hellenica* and of the Greek Testament, Cicero's *De Amicitia*, much of Virgil, a book of Horace's Odes and a little Livy. In addition to this he had composed themes and, every week, sixteen lines of original hexameters. It is doubtful whether so high a standard of scholarship, in Greek at any rate, was reached at so early an age before the nineteenth century, and certain that it is not reached today. For those who went from a good private to a good public school, the nineteenth century was the golden age, if not of classical scholarship, at least of classical education.[2]

This particular case takes the problem of major influence one stage further back in time, into the preparatory school, and only goes to confuse the issue still more. On one interpretation it would make the subsequent public-school experience of each of these boys irrelevant, and the elder Wickham a greater moulder of future headmasters than any actual public-school man.

Allied to the criterion of producing worthy men is the question of teaching quality. On this theory headmasters must not only be good teachers but the best teachers. The need for inspiring the sixth seemed to be an obsession with them all, as though it were the most important part of their work. It is difficult to find a name that did not succumb to this vanity, and certainly when the school was as small as Shrewsbury under Butler and Kennedy, there may have been some justice in claiming it to be important. However, with a big school the idea that the head, with all his other commitments, can be as vital

1. References to the Wickhams, father and son, taken from Newsome, *Godliness and Good Learning*, op. cit., pp. 221 and 222.
2. Clarke, op. cit., p. 84.

a teacher as when teaching was his sole occupation at assistant-master level is ludicrous. Certainly teaching experience before appointment appears to be irrelevant. Two of the greatest names on any reckoning, Arnold[1] and Temple,[2] had none, and neither had Thring.[3] As outsiders they were able to bring in other ideas which may have been more important, and they were really picked for their other qualities. As an outsider himself Clement Dukes supported such appointments very strongly, on the grounds not only that such a person was more likely to be a man of the world and a magnet to the boys, but that he could then be chosen for the real qualities that a headmaster ought to possess: 'It is an indisputable fact that a head-master is not required as a teacher any more than a general is needed to fight in the ranks.' [4]

A large school requires qualities of administration, however these are defined, together with a certain ruthlessness. All headmasters of any stature had their goals firmly before them. It is perhaps a sign of this stature that these aims were not allowed to degenerate into obstinacy or into that rapid elimination of anyone critical which is essentially a sign of weakness. However, ruthlessness seems to be essential if the examples of Thring, Benson, Sanderson and Temple are any guide. Sometimes this ruthless quality becomes heartless and threatens the very foundations of any claim to headmasterly status. The most significant example of this is Arnold himself.[5] His deliberate act of sacrificing many young boys over a long period of time to achieve the object of eliminating them and their kind from his school makes very unpleasant reading indeed. He would no doubt have argued that the desired end was ample justification, but it remains as a flaw in his record which grows in significance with the years. This Arnold episode, like that of C. J. Vaughan,

1. Arnold had run a private school of his own for boys and young men wanting to enter Oxford and Cambridge. At one time it was run in partnership with his brother-in-law. It was at Laleham.
2. Temple had been connected with the central authority (Whitehall) and had been in charge of the effort to educate teachers for workhouses (Kneller Hall).
3. Thring had taught for a while in a National School in Gloucester (lower-class elementary school): '. . . he looked upon a clergyman's work in a parish as an excellent preparation for the duties of a schoolmaster.' (Parkin, op. cit., pp. 46–7).
4. Dukes, op. cit., p. 41.
5. For the ruthless side of Arnold, see Bamford, op. cit., Chapter 12.

has only recently come to light. In a similar way the many claims to reform in the field of discipline and curriculum must be treated with the greatest reserve.

Anyone's reputation must, in the last resort, rest on public opinion. To attain wide recognition a man must somehow acquire publicity.[1] Men must write about him and argue. It would appear from the examples of Temple, Arnold, Benson and, to a lesser extent, Thring, that it is immaterial whether the arguments are about school affairs or not—it is the publicity that counts. The man must be constantly in the newspapers and talked about. Boys and parents do the rest. If the man has any pretence to stature then he will acquire not only scholastic reputation, but also advancement in the world, for so many of his products will have strong connections. It is not without significance that the greatest names became dynamic personalities in the world at large. This quality can be the essence of good teaching too, but it also carries with it great dangers. Vivid personalities necessarily risk indoctrinating children by their influence. Denials by headmasters have not stood the test of time. One might well ask how a man whose name appears regularly in the papers and who deliberately sets out to shock society can possibly fail to influence his pupils. This is not an idle question but one vital to the whole public-school story, since the greatest headmasters have by common repute been violent radicals, both within and without the church, while, conversely, many with dim reputations were reactionaries, like Balston. Both the Rugby men in the first category were a nightmare to their governing bodies, so that Arnold was almost dismissed and Temple's resignation was received with such obvious relief that they appointed Hayman, a man totally opposite in every respect, with disastrous and sensational results. Such masters and headmasters were not passive administrative robots; their demand for passionate religion meant that both allegiance and repulsion were strong. We know that they

1. It is a significant fact that, of the great headmasters, Temple and Benson went on to eminence in later life and therefore acquired immense publicity. Arnold acquired fame and notoriety in his own lifetime on account of his ideas on the Church, politics and the social system—all of them unconnected with the school. Thring acquired great publicity because of the continual arguments about the school, and in particular in its migration to Borth (see Chapter 8, pp. 205–6).

argued with their sixth forms, and even when they did not they were still the men behind the words that the boys read in pamphlets and newspaper reports. The example of all these, including Benson, and even those who courted publicity without being successful, like Hayman, shows clearly how impossible it is to divorce a man's public life from his work in school. Such headmasters, by their very dominance, cannot be avoided, and to suggest otherwise betrays complete ignorance of the educative process, and suggests that it is a mere parrot-like recital and absorption of facts that would turn the very best teachers into an inefficient machine. It raises questions of whether or not pressure of an intense kind, for whatever purpose, is legitimate, though it is worth mentioning that those headmasters who lacked this controversial dynamic quality are not considered in the top rank. They may have inspired men after they left; they failed to do so with children. This applies to Longley and Tait.

A matter of some significance linked with the publicity surrounding radically-minded heads and founders of schools is their relationship to society and the 'true' purpose of education. Fundamentally Woodard was not so much trying to educate children as independent human beings as to create a force that would change the face of Britain—for the better, as he saw it. The same was true of some of the others. This raises the whole problem of whether a school should reflect society as it is and ease the adjustment of boys to it, or whether the school should anticipate change and actively try to mould society into a different shape. Many people would distinguish the first as education, and the second as propaganda or indoctrination. It is, of course, impossible for anyone to be exactly neutral in these matters, or even to realize what are the norms of society at any particular time. It is also true that social class-values and objectives are involved. Thus the background and education of the average teacher produced today automatically means that he will not necessarily be reflecting lower-class standards, even in a lower-class area. In spite of these difficulties there is still a gulf between the extremes, between a man who tries to educate without a definite political or religious goal and a man to whom education is a tool for the creation of a new and different society. Of the men we have been considering, Woodard, Arnold, Temple were of the 'propaganda' variety, and perhaps some

others, like Moberly, would have followed this line had they been built of stronger fibre. On the other hand, men like Samuel Butler, Kennedy, Cotton and Thring had no positive 'world-changing' ambitions. Sanderson might also come into this category, although some might consider his curricular revolutions as 'threats' to society. The point which has been elaborated here in a general form lies at the root of the outcry against Woodard, Arnold and Temple in their own lifetimes, and any assessment of their stature depends to some extent on the view taken of this question. It contains, however, philosophical considerations which are too deep and extensive for the scope of the present work. It is enough to say that, for many people, this question is so important that these headmasters would have to be eliminated from any accolade of greatness based on their educational achievements.

One outstanding difficulty which clouds our judgement of headmasters is that many of them became successful men of the world after they left. Theoretically, the latter part of such lives is irrelevant to us. They should be considered purely by their direct influence on the school itself during their period of office, anything that happened afterwards being ignored. In practice it is impossible to free the mind entirely of any subsequent climb to fame, although one should guard against the easy assumption that later glory meant a correspondingly outstanding headmastership. It has, in fact, been assumed that Arnold's stature as a national figure in religious controversy and social questions merely reflected his greatness within the school itself. This is far too involved a question to be pursued at the moment, and has indeed been considered elsewhere, but the same point can be made from the example of another man, E. W. Benson.

Benson as a person obviously possessed qualities which in the outside world were recognized in successive advancement leading to Canterbury, but these are not necessarily the qualities required of a headmaster. We can take for granted that he was an efficient administrator in that he saw a new and complicated project through from the bricks-and-mortar stage to recognition as a new public school. But a school is not so much architecture and reputation as an assembly of boys, and how can any headmaster be truly great who is so disliked, even

12

hated, by so many of his pupils? David Newsome, in his study of Wellington College, wrote:

> If Benson was sometimes severe with his staff, he was more so—and more frequently—with the boys. There is no doubt that many feared him, and that he allowed his temper on occasion to get out of hand.[1]

Among the remarks of old boys comes this gem from Sir Ian Hamilton: 'Whenever Benson was on view, I watched him exactly as a mouse does a cat, and for exactly the same reason.' [2]

Perhaps for a first headmaster a stern administrator with a goal and determination is what a school really needs. All the same, it seems a pity that there should exist such a blemish that would not perhaps matter in any other post but that of a man in charge of a school. It is sufficient to raise doubts on the question of whether Benson was at all a successful headmaster in the fundamental issue of his care of boys.

To any boy, the headmaster is a great man, for he wields immense power and is the ultimate authority of his little world. Outside the school, however, the situation is quite different. Mere possession of a high post, even an archbishopric, is no guarantee of immortality. Which of the headmasters are really significant? To some extent this is like the fruitless but fascinating pastime of comparing the relative worth of great musicians or great artists, but the significant fact is that they are not really on this creative level, and are so very few in number in any case, and could certainly be counted on the fingers of one hand. With substantial flaws and misgivings in Arnold, Temple, Benson and Moberly it is clearly unrealistic to expect a perfect specimen. Figures like Hawtrey, Cotton, Sanderson, Thring, Ridding, Kennedy, Malim may have been great headmasters in a narrower sense, but they hardly knock on the door of national fame, even if history supports their claims. It is a sobering thought that the stature of the most famous names of all—Arnold, Temple, Benson—rests far more on their achievements and thoughts in the adult rather than in the child's world. Perhaps, indeed, the strength of Thring and Sanderson lies in this very fact that their reputation rests entirely on their work in schools.

1. Newsome, *Wellington College*, op. cit., 156.
2. ibid.

The public-school head is, at one and the same time, the manager of a business, a public-relations officer, a teacher and a man with pastoral responsibility. One has a suspicion that the greatest of these duties—pastoral care—does not get the attention it deserves, and that the best headmasters are often laid to rest unsung.

CHAPTER SEVEN

The Growth of the System (II): National Policy and New-Type Public Schools

At the lower-class level education was minimal and geared to the three R.s. Such schools could not thrive on fees alone, and their existence was eked out by grants given by Whitehall on the recommendation of the school inspector. Except at this lower-class, elementary level the state held aloof. It gave no help whatever to the education of the upper and middle classes. Until the late 1860s it did not even give any encouragement, and the situation may be summed up in the words of J. P. Fearon: 'It might give test, stimulus, advice, dignity; it witholds them all. . . .'[1]

Three kinds of school catered for the middle and upper classes: the private, the proprietary and the endowed. Broadly speaking, private schools were owned and run by individuals, often in families, for their own private profit. They varied in quality from the worthless to preparatory schools owned and run by Oxford or Cambridge graduates and patronized by the well-to-do. Proprietary schools, as already illustrated for the cases of Marlborough and Cheltenham, began like a business, with shareholders. Only endowed schools relied on money or property donated as a charity for the purpose of education. This was public money, and the result was that they alone were directly vulnerable to state interference. The state indeed had a duty to see that the money was wisely spent.

The seven main public schools were among the oldest and most extensive charities in the country. The fact that magnificent buildings sheltered the Fellows and scholars and saw the rearing of the nation's leaders did not necessarily mean that the charities had been administered well and the money spent to

1. SIC, I, 1868, pp. 107–8.

the best advantage. A committee of the House of Commons under Henry Brougham looked at some of these charities in 1816 and 1818, and their investigations were summed up in these words:

> It unquestionably shows that considerable unauthorized deviations have been made, both at Eton and Winchester, from the original plans of the founders; that these deviations have been made more by a regard to the interests of the fellows than of the scholars . . . and that although in some respects they have proved beneficial upon the whole to the institutions, yet they have, by gradual encroachment, been carried too far.[1]

That investigation was only a preliminary, and a national survey began in 1818 with the appointment of charity commissioners. Unfortunately the situation was complicated and the number of charities so great that the work was spread over eighteen years; even so, many charities were missed. Moreover, some charities lay outside their powers of investigation, and these, as we have seen earlier, included the major schools. In spite of this, Brougham's committee had already shown that abuses did exist in the old schools, and it was naturally expected that Eton would put its own house in order, and perhaps bring its general attitude on discipline and curriculum more into line with modern thought. But as the years went on and decade followed decade, there was little sign of any fundamental change, apart from the abolition of Montem.[2] The stories of boys and old boys went to confirm that all the old privileges and oddities were still being preserved. These traditions were even hotly defended: 'We should be jealous of any reform . . . which would either diminish to any considerable extent the power of the College to maintain a liberal hospitality or trench materially on the comforts of the individual members.'[3]

For an age of reform, progress was dreadfully slow. Criticism was sporadic and only occasionally severe. However, the matter came to a head in 1860 when Matthew James Higgins produced three articles in the *Cornhill Magazine* and Sir John Coleridge

1. *Edinburgh Review*, April 1861.
2. In the early days Montem arose from the effort to provide funds to enable the head boy to go to the university. By the early nineteenth century this had developed into a glorious mixture of fête, bazaar, fun-fair, spectacle and triumphal procession which attracted crowds who went to Eton by excursion trains from London. It was finally abolished by Hawtrey.
3. *Quarterly Review*, LII, 1834, p. 144.

delivered strictures at Tiverton. These were followed by others, and notably by a violent onslaught in the *Edinburgh Review* of April 1861, which concentrated not so much on the outmoded education as the illegalities exposed by Brougham's Committee forty years before, which, presumably, still went on unchecked. They summed up the position as follows:

> That the statutes of such a foundation as Eton College should be carried out to the letter in the present day is, we admit, neither possible nor desirable; but it is both possible and desirable that the enormous revenues willed by an English king for the promotion of education amongst the upper and middle classes of this country, should not be illegally diverted from their original destination into the pockets of a small number of individuals who are not entitled to them. . . .[1]

The article finally called for a Royal Commission to probe these problems, together with similar ones at Westminster, Winchester, Harrow and Rugby.

This was a challenge which accused the teachers of Cabinet Ministers of embezzlement, and the issue could no longer be ignored. In three months a commission was set up 'to inquire into the Revenues and Management of certain Colleges and Schools and the studies pursued and instruction given therein . . .'.[2]

The seven major boarding schools forming the core of the public-school system were chosen for this investigation, together with the day schools of St Paul's and Merchant Taylors'. Ostensibly, therefore, nine schools were involved, but in many ways eight were included only for comparative purposes, the main target being Eton itself.

On the very first day of the investigation, 4 July 1862, the provost, bursar and registrar of Eton went through a gruelling time on the question of property owned by the college. It was quickly established that the fines on the renewal of leases had never been audited, and that over the years an enormous sum of money had found its way into the pockets of the Fellows in a furtive manner that was quite unethical and could hardly be dismissed as technically legal. Lord Clarendon, the chairman, put it quite bluntly to the Rev. G. J. Dupuis, the senior bursar:

1. *Edinburgh Review*, April 1861, p. 45.
2. The commission now known as the Public Schools Commission (PSC).

... it seems to me that the appropriation of these fines, and their division between members of the governing body ... is in direct contravention of the statutes, because each of these statutes over and over again bind the Provost and Fellows by the most solemn oaths to adhere strictly to the stipendiary salaries specified by the founder, and to apply the whole of whatever surplus may remain to the College for the common use and advantage of the foundation. ... I should like to know in what way they can reconcile the division of the fines with the observance of the statutes?

MR DUPUIS: The only answer that I feel I can make to what your Lordship has asked is that it has always been so; a bad reason, perhaps you will say, but I really do not know any other. We have been elected one after the other, with this system coming down to us, and we took it as we found it, and have been carrying it on.[1]

Later, on that same day, Lord Clarendon tried to summarize the position:

CLARENDON: And the fines on renewal of leases during the last 20 years amount to £127,700?

MR BATCHELOR (the Registrar of Eton): Yes.

CLARENDON: And that amount of fines has been divided during the last 20 years among the Provosts and Fellows?

REGISTRAR: Yes.

CLARENDON: The Provost taking two shares to each Fellow's one?

REGISTRAR: Yes, that has been so.

CLARENDON: And it has appeared to the Provost and Fellows that there is nothing contrary to the statutes in their so doing?

REGISTRAR: No.[2]

The provost and the others could give no satisfactory explanation of their conduct. The abuses and duplicity had been going on for centuries, and while it is easy to see how the continuity of the Fellows had brought about the system and made it difficult to alter, none the less the resort to history and tradition as an excuse was fundamentally weak and would not have saved men in humbler positions. They really had no defence, for Brougham had exposed enough over forty years before to make any honest and responsible man uneasy, to say the least.

The particular problem of fines, used here as an illustration, is only one small sample of the irregularities and privileges that were laid bare day after day, not only at Eton, but at other

1. PSC, III, p. 6, Q. 117.
2. ibid., p. 8, Qq. 171–4.

schools also, in lesser and different degree. Cupidity is clearly a stronger force than honesty, even for clergymen who were supposed to be guiding the morals of the young. No headmaster came out of the revelations of the Public Schools Commission with the honour of his school intact, and it is not surprising that most school historians have wished to ignore the episode entirely. Only in recent years, after almost a century, has it been possible to find suitably acid comments, like this one for Winchester:

> But the law of the land, on whose letter they [the Warden and Fellows] had relied for centuries to cheat the children and starve the ushers, now turned its bleak face against the exploiters themselves. They might whimper and snarl, like old dogs driven off a juicy and familiar bone; but their teeth were drawn.[1]

THE TAUNTON COMMISSION

One lesson of the Public Schools Commission was not so much the deplorable examples of morality it exposed as the wider fears and inferences. If this was the situation at schools which bred prime ministers and lord chancellors, then how could anyone blame irregularities in the thousands of other educational endowments to be found elsewhere in the country. Eton, Winchester, Harrow, Rugby and the rest of the seven were only the most prominent examples of a host of other endowed schools designed to give a 'grammar'-school education. The condition of these other schools was clearly a matter of public concern, and when the Public Schools (Clarendon) Commission had finished its work, a new Commission, under Lord Taunton, was appointed in 1864 to explore this wider field. If we can consider the Clarendon Commission as primarily concerned with the education of the upper classes, then, in broad terms, the Taunton Commission was confined to the education of the middle classes, in so far as the endowed schools were involved. Some of these schools were famous already and destined to join the exclusive higher ranks later on.

The first task of the new commission was to explore the situation, and to this end headmasters and trustees were asked to supply information about their schools. Experts were then sent out into the field to check and amplify on these claims—

1. Firth, op. cit., pp. 148–9.

a very wise precaution, as it turned out, since in thirty-eight schools which claimed to be providing a classical education in Yorkshire and Durham alone, there were in fact no scholars to take advantage of it. Such abuses had arisen largely as the result of legal problems which had by 1865 produced an educational stalemate on endowments. Most of the money concerned had been left hundreds of years before at a time when ideas on education were quite different from those in the nineteenth century. Everyone involved realized this, but was powerless to act since the exact interpretation of wills and the persistence of Greek and Latin as the bases of grammar-school education had been strengthened by Lord Eldon's judgement in 1805. It is true that a new scheme for any particular school could be arranged and sanctioned by the Court of Chancery or the Charity Commission, but only on condition that everyone concerned was in full agreement—i.e. the headmaster, usher (if any), trustees and any interested members of the public. However, this kind of co-operation was extremely rare, and the usual disputes meant that the whole machinery of the law came into play. This could be a long-drawn-out business, and very expensive indeed with the endowment swallowed up in costs and the trustees impoverished. One case at Ludlow had cost £20,000 and absorbed the whole of the estate. An effort to get rid of the master at Fremington had dragged on from 1844 to 1864, and was still unresolved in 1868. Masters could, therefore, and often did, defy their own trustees with the threat of legal action.[1]

This problem of endowments was one situation which the Taunton Commission had to face; another concerned fundamental questions of education and social class. How many social classes were there? How many children of each category? How many types of school should there be? What types of curriculum were suitable, and in what ways were the wishes of the parents to be met? After an exhaustive investigation the commissioners came to the following conclusion:

> The wishes of the parents can best be defined in the first instance by the length of time during which they are willing to keep their children under instruction. It is found that, viewed in this way, education, as distinct from the direct preparation for employment,

1. Information taken from SIC, i, Chapter 4.

can at present be classified as that which is to stop at about 14, that which is to stop at about 16, and that which is to continue till 18 or 19; and for convenience we shall call these the Third, the Second, and the First Grade of education respectively. The difference in the time assigned makes some difference in the very nature of the education itself; if a boy cannot remain at school beyond the age of 14 it is useless to begin teaching him such subjects as require a longer time for their proper study; if he can continue till 18 or 19, it may be expedient to postpone some studies that would otherwise be commenced early. Both the substance and the arrangement of the instruction will thus greatly depend on the length of time that can be devoted to it. It is obvious that these distinctions correspond roughly, but by no means exactly, to the graduations in society. Those who can afford to pay more for their children's education will also, as a general rule, continue that education for a longer time.[1]

In their opinion, parents of the first grade comprised the aristocracy, the gentry, both rich and poor, and professional men (such as clergymen, doctors, lawyers). All these people put their faith in the classics. In theory, they were in favour of any reasonable experiments, like that of the modern sides, i.e. with science and modern languages as part of the curriculum, provided such developments did not involve their own sons:

In fact, they are often timid; and while very desirous that experiments should be tried, not ready to let their own children be the subjects on which the trial should be made . . . it seems often to be difficult to prevent these modern departments from being a refuge for boys whose inferior ability or diligence has prevented their success in classical studies. . . .[2]

This first grade was evidently conservative by nature and willing to subordinate educational to social requirements. This was an attitude which was unlikely to alter greatly with time, and we find, fifty years later, another official committee making precisely the same comments. The study of the classics was closely linked with the upper class, and the poorer gentry in particular clung to it for reasons of status.

They [the great majority of professional men and poorer gentry] would, no doubt, in most instances be glad to secure something more than classics and mathematics. But they value these highly for their own sake, and perhaps even more for the value at present assigned to them in English society. They have nothing to look to

1. ibid., pp. 15–16.
2. ibid., pp. 16–17.

but education to keep their sons on a high social level. And they would not wish to have what might be more readily converted into money, if in any degree it tended to let their children sink in the social scale.[1]

The second and third grades of schools corresponded with further subdivisions of the middle class, but they are not strictly our concern here since they dealt with a shallower education coupled with a leaving age of sixteen or below, which was insufficient for that pre-university study which was one of the essential criteria of the public school. A summary of these divisions together with the lower-class situation in 1865 is given in Table 8.

The term 'middle class' was used in a multitude of ways. Most commentators referred to all three grades of education as middle class, including the strictly classical education of the topmost schools, including Eton. On the other hand, some, including Fearon, excluded some or all of the first grade (A) from any consideration of the middle class. Whether the others had mental reservations about including Eton and its fellow-schools with the rest is not very clear. Similarly, at the lower end, the inclusion of artisans among the third grade is a little surprising in terms of the social thinking and attitudes of the time, but not in terms of the fluid situation which education reflected and which has already been shown in the vision of Woodard.

On a practical note, we have seen that the headmasters of the major schools screened pupils and parents with ruthless efficiency. They were acutely aware of the amount of social mixing which parents would tolerate; their actions, words and entrance registers reflect this. A close reading of the twenty-one volumes of the Taunton Commission shows clearly that the same principles applied on the much wider field of endowed schools generally. As an example, we may consider the three grades of parents noted in Table 8 patronizing schools in five counties of southern England (Kent, Surrey, Sussex, Hampshire, Berkshire). There were seventeen schools of the first grade (A), with boarders and restricted to classical education, and in nine of them entry was restricted entirely, or almost entirely, to children of the first grade. Only in four cases did

1. ibid., pp. 17–18.

Table 8. The education of boys as seen in 1865.[1]

Type of School	Leaving age	Parents	Kind and purpose of education	Curriculum	Schools	Children 8-15 per 1,000 population*
1st grade (A)	18 or 19	Aristocracy, gentry, gentlemen of independent means	Cultural. Boarding. Leading to university. Some private-tutoring	Classical	The Seven. High fees. Graduate clerical staff	2-3
		Professionals, businessmen, Large manufacturers, etc	Cultural and professional. Leading to learned professions. Boarding and/or day	Modern sides, Latin, maths, modern languages, some science	Proprietary and endowed. Moderate fees. Graduate staff. Clerical, Headmaster	
2nd grade (B)	16	Tradesmen in considerable business, farmers, agents, managers, upper clerks, etc	Training for trade and agriculture	English, maths, modern languages, geography, science, some Latin	Day grammar schools. Commercial academies, day and boarding†	3-5
3rd grade (C)	14	Small tradesmen, shopmen, clerks, upper artisans, 'decayed tradesmen'	The essentials well done	3 R's plus some show of the above	Private schools. Low fees. Some overlap above and below	6-8
—	12, 13 or none	Artisans, labourers, etc	The rudiments	3 R's	National school type. Dame schools. Often no school at all	
Work-house	—	Paupers	The barest rudiments	—	Workhouse schools	

* This is an average of many calculations (Farr, Richmond, Acland and others) based on different criteria
† Special teachers for music, art, dancing, etc.

1. The information given in this table is based on many sources, partly on SIC itself. Although this table may give the impression of clear-cut categories, there were in fact many schools on the borderline. Similar remarks apply to parents and curricula. This table should be used as a guide only. The pattern began to change drastically in the 1880s, as a result of the working of the 1870 Act. This, therefore, only represents a transient picture.

parents of the second grade (B) exceed those of the first—
one of them being Hurstpierpoint, where an abnormal social
situation was deliberately contrived. Moreover, in all the
schools in these counties, of whatever grade, not one had
boarders spread over all three sections of the middle class, as
defined in this table. There is ample evidence, therefore, of
selection by social criteria.

Socially, this was a time of change. The old days when the
aristocracy reigned supreme had gone, and, in theory at any
rate, the topmost positions were open to men of ability, although
this was obviously more evident in Scotland than England.
The power which had rested in the land and the large landowners had passed to the industrial and business moguls. Men
of foresight and alarm had been aware of this change for half a
century before J. S. Mill expressed it in 1870: '. . . human
beings are no longer born to their place in life . . . but are free
to employ their faculties, and such favourable chances as offer,
to achieve the lot which may appear to them most desirable'.[1]

Although this may be true for the rising spheres of influence
in the country, and was manifest at the adult level, education
itself appeared to act in the reverse direction by actually
hardening class differences through the process of segregation,
as we have already seen. Headmasters were in the unique
position of realizing social change in action, and some had
made a serious study of the implications of the new industrialism
and democracy. Their statements and the continuing exclusiveness of the schools, not to mention the same phenomenon in the
schools investigated by the Taunton Commission, show that
distinct layers appeared to exist in their reckoning and in the
opinions of their clients. These were represented not only by
the three grades enumerated by the commission, as seen in
Table 8, but by further subdivisions. This exclusiveness,
brought about, perhaps, by the demands of parents, had
dangers for society and leadership. Matthew Arnold saw this
clearly. He wanted to see the barriers indicated in Table 8
broken down (1868):

> So we have amongst us the spectacle of a middle class cut in two
> in a way unexampled anywhere else; of a professional class brought
> up on the first plane with fine and governing qualities, but without

1. Houghton, op. cit., p. 4.

the idea of science; while that immense business class, which is becoming so important a power in all countries, on which the future so much depends, and which in the leading schools of other countries fills so large a place, is in England brought up on the second plane, cut off from the aristocracy and the professions, and without governing qualities.[1]

Any attempt to label all the types of education we have been considering as middle class is to concentrate unduly on the classroom. It ignores altogether the environment of the school itself and the style which went to create an expensive upbringing. Indeed, for the upper class, this was the essential core of education, and it has already been noted that, as the century progressed, so the major schools improved their surroundings and facilities, particularly in the last quarter, until they were unique in the educational world and resembled landed estates. Whether we should still persist in calling this middle-class education, as so many commentators appeared to do, is perhaps immaterial, but there is no doubt that it grew progressively more exclusive.

All this would appear to emphasize that a boarding school with a wide social intake was a difficult if not an impossible proposition. In practice it was also linked with money in terms of fees and standards of living, seen particularly well in the Woodard arrangement. Indeed, Woodard's concept of the triple-tier kind of education for the middle classes is almost identical with that of the Schools Inquiry (Taunton) Commission, even down to details of the different kinds of occupation in each grade. Where they differed was in the question of purpose. The commission was content to provide something that appeared to suit the parents and the situation as it was, while Woodard was using boarding education as a social weapon to mould the situation to his liking and provide Anglican growing-points at all levels. He was not, therefore, concerned with the leaving-age question at all.

The Taunton Commission revealed that out of a total of 3,000 endowed schools in England and Wales, 791 were entitled to give an education higher than the necessities reserved for the manual and lower classes. A summary of its findings, together

1. W. F. Connell, *The Educational Thought and Influence of Matthew Arnold* 1950, pp. 265–6.

with the nine schools of the Clarendon Commission, is given in Table 9. It will be seen at once that only 218 of these 791

Table 9. *Endowed schools in England and Wales, c. 1865.*[1]

Curriculum in existence	Number of endowed schools
Classical	218
Semi-classical	183
Schools in abeyance	50
Elementary	340
Total number of schools within the scope of the Taunton Commission	791
Endowed schools outside the scope of the Taunton Commission	2,218 approx.
Total number of endowed schools	3,000 approx.

schools gave an education that could be compared with Eton and Harrow in the narrow and strictly curricular sense, and of these almost half (actually 101) made no effort to fulfil the purpose of a public school by preparing boys for the university. This means that about 110 endowed grammar schools were taking classics seriously, although it should not be inferred from this that they were all geared solely, or even mainly, to the task of preparing boys for Oxford and Cambridge. On the average about seventy of these schools sent one boy to the university a year, and in less than fifty of them was the school successful enough to get 20 per cent or more of its scholars to Oxford or Cambridge.

This raises the whole question of the purpose of schools which prepared pupils for the university, and yet only succeeded with ones or twos. If these few represented star pupils, then the main body were failures, and the classics had been delivered in vain, apart from possible claims to culture or brain-development. On the other hand, if these few were privileged and received a

1. For information about endowed schools, see SIC, i. This Table is compiled from information given there.

kind of education different from the rest, then an undue proportion of the master's time was being spent on one or two pupils. In either case the school stood condemned, for it could be argued strongly that the school was sacrificing the many for the few. On this criterion only forty-two or so endowed schools, including the big nine and Marlborough, were in fact giving an effective education and not sacrificing the main mass of the scholars to the ego of the headmaster. From the strictly educational point of view, forty-two out of 791 represents the potential endowed grammar-school recruitment to the public schools in 1865. The other 749 had lost the race.

This is the most optimistic view of endowed schools that can be taken at this time. If, in addition to the successful teaching of the classics, we also add the normal criteria for a public school outlined in Chapter 2—expense, and a significant boarding element of, say, eighty boys at least—then the forty-two is reduced to twenty-one. Of all the endowed schools the number of potential public schools therefore varies from twenty-one to forty-two according to the criteria of boarding, cost or education. In addition, ten proprietary boarding schools were already successful enough to satisfy the above standards. It follows that thirty-one public boarding schools represent the maximum strength of the system in 1865. This does not mean that all thirty-one had arrived in the sense of being accepted by the others, but, as we shall see, it represents the potential pool. Perhaps this number errs on the generous side, and an objection might be made that the arbitrary figure of eighty boarders is too low. It is important, however, not to judge the situation by modern standards. Not only were the curriculum and facilities different from those of today, but most schools, even famous ones, were small. If all the classical schools of 1865, or thereabouts, whether endowed or proprietary, are arranged by size according to the number of boarders or day scholars, then the tenth largest boarding establishment had 270 boarders, the corresponding figure for a day school being 175 (Table 10). It should be noted, however, that this includes schools which did not cater for the 'upper' classes (like Christ's Hospital and Hurstpierpoint, at this stage), and were therefore not equivalent to the others. Three of the boarding schools were proprietary, and if only endowed schools are considered, then the tenth

Table 10. *Classical schools (endowed and proprietary)*, c. 1865,
arranged by order of size and type of pupil.[1]

Rank by size	Classical schools arranged by:	
	Number of boarders	Number of day scholars
1	Eton (804)	City of London (641)
2	Christ's Hospital (775)	§King's College School (412)
3	§Marlborough (518)	§North London Collegiate (380)
4	†Harrow (475)	§University College S. (347)
5	§†Cheltenham (473)	Merchant Taylors' (258)
6	†Rugby (450)	Manchester G.S. (252)
7	§Rossall (370)	Newcastle upon Tyne G.S. (230)
8	†Hurstpierpoint (324)	Bristol G.S. (225)
9	Haileybury (320)	*Birmingham K.E.S. (216)
10	Wellington (270)	*Leeds G.S. (175)

* In addition there were some boarders.
† In addition there were some day scholars.[2]
§ Proprietary schools.[3]

largest establishment was Repton with less than 200 boarders
(actually 170).

A small school may produce an intimate atmosphere, and
only in this situation may the headmaster imagine that he can
know every boy well, but there were, and still are, grave
disadvantages to outweigh any possible gain. Apart from the
economic tightrope, a small school involves a tiny staff. This
limits educational quality, particularly at a high level, while
the situation of three or four men isolated in a world of boys is
rarely a happy one. Co-operation can easily degenerate into a
mental agony of internal jealousy and pride. A classic example
comes from the inspection of Sedbergh by Joshua Fitch in
1867:

1. Material for this table is derived from various sections of SIC and
elsewhere. The following schools are omitted for lack of detail about the
curriculum or about numbers: Stonyhurst, Blackheath, Mill Hill.
2. In addition to its boarders, Cheltenham had 220 day scholars.
3. The difference between proprietary and endowed schools is fundamental
in theory, but in practice has little importance provided the seat of power,
the headmaster, is safeguarded. This is clear when it is realized that Cheltenham, Rossall and many others were officially proprietary in 1865.

13

. . . the Masterships are held by two Clergymen, who have not
been on speaking terms for fifteen years. Each of these gentlemen
took me privately aside to assure me that the other was not to be
trusted, and that it was impossible to work harmoniously with him.
The headmaster accounted for the ignorance of the Upper Forms
by complaining of the stupidity of the methods adopted in the
lower classes, methods over which he, the headmaster, had no sort
of control. The Usher, on the other hand, assigned as a reason for
the worthlessness of his own teaching, that it was no use to prepare
them for a course so absurd and useless as was pursued in the upper
classes.[1]

Or again:

As to Sedbergh, I despair of putting it into any class at all. In its
present state it simply cumbers the ground.[2]

Internal warfare was found not only in remote places, but
over the whole country. It has occurred in most schools at some
time in their history, and in particularly severe form under
Samuel Butler at Shrewsbury, and at Eton and Rugby too, not
to mention the Moberly–Charles Wordsworth clash at
Winchester.[3]

Educational quality was not the only feature that separated
one school from another. Some were very rich indeed,
some very poor, and some had virtually lost all trace of their
endowments. The Taunton Commission summed up this
situation:

The amount of endowment of these [grammar] schools ranges
from that of Christ's Hospital, which includes a net income of over
£42,000 a year, besides a very valuable site and large buildings, to
some which consist simply of a rent charge of £5 or £6 or less a
year. But these are extreme cases. The usual case is that the school
possesses a school house, a master's house, and an annual income.[4]

Fifteen schools (Christ's Hospital, Eton, Winchester, St
Paul's, Charterhouse, Merchant Taylors', Rugby, Dulwich,
St Olave's, Birmingham, Manchester, Tonbridge, Bedford,
Aldenham and Monmouth) had net incomes exceeding £2,000
a year, sixteen others more than £1,000, fifty-five with at least

1. H. L. Clarke and W. N. Weech, *History of Sedbergh School*, 1925, pp. 98–9.
2. ibid., p. 99.
3. See Firth, op. cit.
4. SIC, I, p. 110.

£500, 222 with £100 to £500, and all the rest under £100 a year.[1]

These endowments were scattered very unevenly over the country. Lancashire and the West Riding were well provided for, but it was not really the numbers that mattered but the state the schools were in. On paper, Cornwall possessed eleven endowed schools, but six had ceased to exist and the net income of them all was less than £400 a year. Out of forty schools in Westmorland, thirty had either closed or were purely elementary in character, and only three made any sort of showing at the classics.[2]

The national picture was, therefore, quite chaotic. As a summary we might say that, of the 791 schools which were endowed and which might possibly have developed in other circumstances into rivals of Eton, Harrow and the rest, less than fifty were tackling the job in any serious way, and only twenty-one had developed the barest minimum qualifications for a viable boarding school.

Yet in this chaos was great potential. If only the endowments of unsuccessful schools could be gathered together, and then redistributed as part of a national plan, the core of a great system of 'secondary' education would emerge. Many people were hypnotized by this dream in early and mid-Victorian times. Even if the total picture was not absolutely clear till 1868, it had been suspected long enough. The abuse and redirection of charities had become an obvious and acute probem ever since Brougham's Committee and the agitations in the post-Napoleonic period, reinforced by the steady outpouring of volumes by the Charity Commission from 1819 to 1837. Henry Brougham and Lytton Bulwer[3] had pressed for reform long before Victoria, and this was kept up later not only by laymen but by professional educationists and public-school headmasters like Frederick Temple,[4] E. R. Humphreys[5] and A. C. Tait.[6]

1. Information from ibid.
2. See ibid, pp. 110–11, and also detailed tables.
3. See Lytton Bulwer, op. cit. (fourth edition), i, p. 335 *et seq.*
4. See F. Temple, 'National Education', *Oxford Essays*, 1856.
5. Humphreys was headmaster of Cheltenham Grammar School; see *Transactions of the National Association for the Promotion of Social Science*, 1857, pp. 134–6.
6. See A. C. Tait, *Middle Class Education*, 1865.

They all wanted the dormant endowments confiscated where necessary, and put to use for the benefit of national education in some form or other.[1] Matthew Arnold also had a grandiose scheme reminiscent of Brereton:

> . . . amalgamation [of endowed schools] should be used, the most useful of these institutions strengthened, the most useless suppressed, the whole body of them be treated as one whole, destined harmoniously to co-operate towards one end. What should be had in view is to constitute, in every county, at least one great centre of secondary instruction, with low charges, with the security of inspection, and with a public character. These institutions should bear some such title as that of *Royal Schools*, and should derive their support, mainly, of course, from school-fees, but partly, also, from endowments— their own, or those appropriated to them—and partly from scholarships supplied by public grants. Wherever it is possible, wherever, that is, their scale of charges is not too high, or their situation not too unsuitable, existing schools of good repute should be adopted as the *Royal Schools*.[2]

He thought that a little competition of this kind would benefit the existing schools:

> Probably the very best medicine which could be devised for the defects of Eton, Harrow, and the other schools which the Royal Commissioners have been scrutinizing, would be the juxtaposition, and, to a certain extent, the competition, of establishments of this kind. No wise man will desire to see root-and-branch work made with schools like Eton or Harrow, or to see them diverted from the function which they at present discharge, and, on the whole, usefully. Great subversive changes would here be out of place; it is an addition of new that our secondary instruction wants, not a demolition of old, or, at least, not of this old.[3]

In view of the influence of Matthew Arnold, Temple, Tait and the other experts on education, it is not surprising that the same solution was, in effect, favoured by the Taunton Commission in its report of 1868, especially in view of the fact that Temple and W. E. Forster were members of it.[4]

The Commission wanted four boarding schools of the first grade (A) for every million inhabitants, with corresponding day

1. For other ideas, see F. V. Thornton, *The Education of the Middle Classes in England*, 1862; also various works by J. G. Sheppard, H. Hayman. etc.
2. M. Arnold, *A French Eton*, 1892 edition, pp. 70–1.
3. ibid., pp. 71–2.
4. Matthew Arnold, Temple, Tait and Forster knew each other very well indeed, and Forster and Arnold were brothers-in-law.

schools for built-up areas; one boarding school of the second grade (B) for every 100,000 persons, and a day school of the third grade (C) for every town. The country was to be divided into eleven divisions, as used by the Registrar-General for census purposes, and the whole question of the redistribution of schools, including closures, would be dealt with by provincial machinery working with the Charity Commission. At the centre, control was to be strengthened and the overall development subject to the approval of Parliament. Apart from the grand design, the Commission had thoughts on the curriculum and the place of science in it, and gave advice on a wide variety of other topics, including selection, examining bodies and administration.

THE AFTERMATH OF THE TAUNTON COMMISSION

Looking back at the year 1868, it is easy to see the Taunton Commission as something positive. The manifest industry behind the vast report certainly revealed the situation, gave an indication of the abuses and reforms necessary and pleased the radicals. But that is not really how the schools saw it at the time. Those vitally concerned were frightened. For Woodard and the supporters of a vigorous established church the proposals were tragic. Education was the traditional and rightful province of the church, and these new events threatened to bring the state in as a major arbiter in school affairs, virtually splitting English education into secular and religious camps. The church was left with responsibility for the lower orders, while the really influential 'middle' section was surrendered to the enemy. Moreover, for Woodard the new situation was a threat to his ambition to create a national network of Anglican middle-class schools. To anyone with a knowledge of the world, like Matthew Arnold, such a scheme had been hopeless from the very beginning, and indeed the tempo of Woodard's creations had slackened off by the late 1860s. Judged by other public-school standards, Woodard's efforts may have been phenomenal, but in terms of the national need, it was paltry. Nevertheless the dream had been so much part of his life that the threat to it was like a betrayal. He quarrelled with Gladstone and with those people who had once supported him and now supported the Taunton proposals. A particular case

was that of Lord Lyttelton, a member of the Taunton Commission and a future Chief Commissioner of Endowed Schools.[1]

Although Woodard's ambition for the church was destroyed
by Taunton, his own schools were not involved since they were
part of an empire that was independent and, therefore, beyond
state interference; the same could not be said for others. The
headmasters of endowed grammar schools had real and
immediate cause for concern. The unsuccessful would almost
certainly disappear, while even the successful had no guarantee
of survival and might easily emerge with a different identity.
That a great change was imminent was certain, while an
Endowed Schools Bill presented to Parliament threatened to
strike at the very roots of education in the classroom. It proposed
not only to revise endowments, but also contemplated a national
examination system and diplomas for teachers.

The headmasters of the endowed schools were angry. They
looked on this new development as an interference rather than
a reform. Even more galling was the fact that Eton, Harrow
and the other select few were to be exempt. Such privileged
treatment made the rest bitter, and the most vehement
objections came from Thring, Benson, Bradley, Harper and
Mitchinson. They were hard-working, independent men with a
fine sense of achievement. Uppingham, for instance, had grown
under Thring from a school of twenty-five to 330 or so; he
considered that he now had the best school in the country.
With his own upper-class background and success, he could
afford to be frank and pour scorn on the Taunton Commission
and its recommendations: 'How ridiculous it will seem in years
to come appointing a lot of squires and a stray lord or two to
gather promiscuous evidence on an intricate professional
question, and sum up, and pronounce infallible judgement
on it.' [2]

Benson, at Wellington, was even more incensed, if that were
possible. To him it was almost a personal insult that his solid
work could be jeopardized by mixing his own school with a lot
of others inferior in quality to become part of a nebulous system.
He wrote to Gladstone, Forster, the Archbishop of Canterbury

1. For the relations of Woodard, Gladstone, Lyttleton and others, see
Heeney, op. cit.
2. Parkin, op. cit., pp. 146–7.

and others. As head of an establishment that was virtually royal, his protest carried more weight, perhaps, than most—enough at least to make Forster hesitate and seek the advice of the most eminent headmaster of the day, Frederick Temple himself. Rugby had already been dealt with under the Public Schools Act of 1868, so that Temple stood outside the controversy. He took an extremely radical view. Not only was the Bill before Parliament sound, but, in his opinion, it was a great pity that the seven old schools—his own, Rugby, among them—were not also included in its provisions. As for the particular point at issue, Temple wrote to Benson telling him bluntly what he had written to Forster, adding the unpalatable truth that, in his opinion, 'Wellington had less claim [for exemption] than most other places'.[1]

It sobered a great friendship once and for all. Temple's attitude was perhaps rather tactless and cruel, and it is easy to dismiss it loftily as a reflection of his safe and superior position, but there was soundness, even statesmanship, in this view, and it really is the greatest pity that Forster's original plan for professional standards came to nothing.

More important in the long run than the jealousy of the smaller fry for the seven, or even Thring's contempt for them, was the reaction of Mitchinson of Canterbury. He realized that individual freedom for each school might be a precious asset, but its inevitable result was an appalling weakness in opposing parliamentary action. He called for a meeting of headmasters in London or Oxford. Eventually, twenty-five or twenty-six met at the Freemasons' Tavern on 2 March 1869, and the outcome was a deputation to Forster to present a joint view on the bill. Thring had been reluctant to join, and only turned up at the first meeting after refusing the invitation once. By the second occasion he had changed his attitude completely and was enthusiastic; it was he who suggested the logical outcome of a regular annual meeting. As a beginning he invited them all to Uppingham for the following Christmas. So it was that in October Thring sent out sixty or seventy invitations, only to find that a mere fourteen headmasters accepted. Why the occasion was unpopular is difficult to say. Uppingham is not the easiest place in the world to get to, and, apart from the

1. Newsome, *Wellington College*, p. 138.

arguments, there was very little else there to amuse the headmasters at Christmas time. It is possible that such mundane
considerations lay behind the refusals, but it is more probable
that the absent headmasters were over-cautious and wanted to
see the reactions of others first.[1]

The names of the schools represented on that first occasion
have some significance: Sherborne, Repton, Tonbridge, Liverpool, Bury St Edmunds, Richmond, Bromsgrove, Oakham,
Canterbury, Felsted, Highgate, Norwich, Dulwich. They were
a mixture of day and boarding schools, mostly ancient grammar
in type, with headmasters proud of their independence, jealous
of their freedom and hankering after undisputed recognition.[2]
The top schools in the new 'proprietary' class—Marlborough,
Cheltenham and the rest—were not there.

The only schools at that time with an undoubted national
reputation were the seven, and it was in the mind of some of
these men that the surest way to their aims and to a recognition
of their status was to bring the old schools into their discussions
at the very beginning. The suggestion was made that the
headmaster of Eton should be invited to attend the conference
as president, and Thring at once protested. He was an Old
Etonian himself, Captain of Montem and head of the school.
He therefore knew Eton thoroughly and spoke with the voice
of authority and experience. For him the buildings reflected a
certain grace through their architectural and historic merit, but
that was all. The rest of the education was worthless. But while
he might despise Eton as a school, he knew only too well that
the rest of the world regarded it with awe. It was this conflict
of opinion between those who knew and those who did not that
annoyed Thring. It spurred him to revolt and turned him into
a schoolmaster determined to prove that his own ideas on
education were right and the Etonian system wrong. On the
question of inviting the head of Eton to their conference, he

1. For background of the first meetings of headmasters, see G. R. Parkin
op. cit.
2. The nature of the schools represented at Uppingham has some interest:
    Boarding schools: Sherborne, Repton, Tonbridge, Bromsgrove, Felsted.
    Day schools: Liverpool, Highgate, Dulwich.
    Mixed boarding and day: Bury St Edmunds, Richmond, Oakham, Canter-
bury, Norwich.
    Those labelled boarding or day above contain some scholars of the other
category. There were, of course, considerable differences in size.

thought that overtures to the great schools at that particular time would be taken as a sign of inferiority; it would not strengthen their hand but weaken it. In his own words: 'I laid down plainly that I thought it was simple death to do so; we rested on our vitality and work, they on their prestige and false glory: if they would meet us on common ground, well and good; if not, not.' [1] The wisdom of Thring's delaying tactics was shown at the next meeting: 'The seven school delusion broken up. Winchester and Shrewsbury there; Eton has joined since. A committee formed to look after school interests.' [2] This was the turning-point. The Headmasters' Conference was now an established fact, and the lesser schools no longer felt isolated and alone.

After the first excitement the urgency slowly evaporated. There were times when business dwindled so much that annual meetings were unnecessary, and from 1882 to 1895 meetings were only held every two years. In the early days, while policy was still fluid, there were efforts to spread the representation on the conference and include assistant masters, but these had finally come to nothing by 1875.

All attempts to define an arbitrary basis for membership also failed. The idea that a school could automatically qualify was ruled out in preference for 'a sort of club of schoolmasters, who are at liberty to elect their own members'.[3] A school, no matter how important, had to curry favour with the existing club members to get in, and the Conference was soon completely dominated by the old schools. According to Baron, the 'nine' filled 104 out of the 261 Committee places available up to 1902, while G. W. S. Howson, speaking in 1914, complained that:

Eighty schools of the Conference have never been represented at all [on the Committee]; that three schools have each furnished a member of the Committee fifteen times in twenty-two years, and three other schools have furnished a member twelve to fourteen times. During eighteen years, no school of less than 400 boys has ever been represented. The headmasters of such schools as Oundle, Dulwich, Berkhamsted and Felsted have never served. Towns like Leeds, Liverpool, Bristol, Newcastle, Oxford and Cambridge have

1. Parkin, op. cit., pp. 175–6.
2. ibid, p. 177.
3. G. Baron, 'The Origins and Early History of the Headmasters' Conference, 1869–1914', *Educational Review*, VII, June 1955, pp. 223–4.

never had a voice on the Committee. Out of a Committee of nine, in the past there has always been a majority of six from the same ten schools.[1]

What a change this represents from the origins of the conference as indicated by the gathering at Uppingham! No commercial company was ever more completely dominated and taken over by rivals than this. All efforts to alter this situation by some form of rotation or regional representation failed.

On paper the list of headmasters and schools makes a most impressive sight, and it is true that until the First World War the conference did play a part in bringing some cohesion into the examination system and into the question of training, but this was really a secondary activity. Its main function was undoubtedly the provision of a platform for the airing of views and meeting others in the profession. For the first forty years at least it was ineffective as an instrument of reform. The common front could not disguise the fact that this was a collection of very individual minds with very individual problems. In 1913, no less an authority than A. F. Leach wrote:

> The Headmasters of the Public Schools have also organized a sort of association called the Headmasters' Conference, founded by Thring, but each of them is too much of an autocrat in his own sphere to be prepared for any large measure of co-operative activity, and they usually hold aloof from any form of State inspection or control. Indeed there is probably no position in English civic life where a single individual exercises such uncontrolled power over others as does the head of a successful Public School. . . .[2]

Meanwhile the worst fears of the headmasters and others were not realized, for the more offending passages of the Bill were not included in the final Endowed Schools Act of 1869. Neither did many of the Taunton recommendations like regional organization and the formation of a ministry materialize. This Act did, however, authorize the appointment of a Commission to draw up schemes of management for each of the endowed schools in turn. Five years later these powers were transferred to the Charity Commissioners, and, ultimately, to the Board of Education, when that body was created in 1899.

1. ibid., pp. 230–1.
2. *Cyclopedia of Education.*

These commissioners were very active. Between 1873 and 1886 almost 450 schemes were published, and an analysis of 189 schools reorganized under the Endowed Schools Commission showed that the number of pupils had more than doubled between 1868 and 1883. In this period many old-established schools were virtually re-created, some of them developing into the renowned public boarding schools of the present time.

A good example is that of Sedbergh.[1] In 1870 this school looked like disappearing altogether. A combination of internal squabbles and poor attendance had so weakened the tradition that it seemed kinder and best to end the agony once and for all, and either hand over the endowments to Giggleswick, so that at least one good school could be made out of two, or else to lower the sights a little and turn Sedbergh into a 'modern' school. At one time one of these two solutions appeared to be the most likely outcome, but obstinacy and local agitation refused to accept defeat. A scheme was eventually formed in 1874, and a new set of governors took over with a new set of rules and a new headmaster. At once all the old sense of failure vanished, and the intake graph rose steadily for thirty years almost without a break.

In the same kind of way a large number of schools were able to reorganize themselves and obtain a new freedom and a chance to expand, including Aldenham, Sherborne, St Peter's, Stamford. But for some, alas, the new powers came too late.

Looking back at the years 1868 and 1869 it is clear that the combination of the Taunton Report, and the Endowed Schools Act which followed, brought about directly and indirectly a solid increase in numbers in the upper part of the independent school sector, and also, as an indirect result, the first signs of cohesion. In its role of watchdog, the Headmasters' Conference was a natural development, but it was an artificial body also. No amount of common threat or scholastic unity within the classroom could disguise the fact that Eton and any day grammar school, however exalted, were miles apart. For parents and old boys the old-established public school was an educational engine designed to produce a common approach to life for the *élite* of society; boarding was essential and so were high fees and an exclusive clientele and curriculum. Nothing,

1. See Clarke and Weech, op. cit.

as we shall see, could bridge the gap from this conception to that of the day school open to all and sundry.

PROBLEMS OF RECOGNITION

A constant feature of the public-school system has been its exclusiveness. At one time the club was more or less limited to the seven schools, and from time to time others were added to the fold. Exactly when a particular school reached the stature necessary for it to be associated with the others without question is difficult to determine. Looking back, it is easy to fall into the trap of assuming that famous schools were accepted by the others long before they in fact were simply because they are so well known to us now. It is even easier to ignore the many promising schools which succeeded for a time and then fell out of the race. Criteria have altered too. Early opinion concentrated on the social-boarding aspect, and it is safe to say that, by 1889, there were about thirty schools forming a select group of similar character. In that year the *Public Schools' Year Book* was published for the first time, with the following statement in the Preface:

> In order that the book may be published at a low price it has been thought best to fix the number of schools to be included at thirty. Within this limit, the principle of selection has been to admit such schools as the Editors—representatives respectively of Eton, Harrow and Winchester—regard as belonging to the same genus as their own.

What significance, if any, should be attached to the statement that the limit of thirty was arbitrary, owing to considerations of space, is a matter of opinion, but presumably the number chosen was a minimum. These schools included the two historic day schools of the Clarendon Commission (St Paul's and Merchant Taylors') as well as three in Scotland, so that in our consideration of boarding schools in England and Wales the number is reduced to twenty-five.

It is of some interest to compare these twenty-five schools of 1889 with the total of thirty-one deduced from other considerations as potential public boarding schools in 1865 (see p. 176 above). The details given in Table 11 show that twenty of the schools were common, and that real discrepancies were few and based on the different nature of the criteria used. Sectarian

schools, for instance, were still not accepted by the *Year Book* editors of 1889, while two of the new schools included in the later list were not functioning in time for the 1865 assessment. It is clear that boarding size and the style of education, as reported by the Taunton Commission, were reasonable signs of potential, and that, from the names omitted in 1889, the compilers of the first *Year Book* were conservative in their selection.

Table 11. *Lists of English public boarding schools, 1865 and 1889.*

---

20 schools common to both lists:
> The seven: Eton, Harrow, Winchester, Rugby, West-minster, Shrewsbury, Charterhouse
> Other old grammar schools: Repton, Sherborne, Tonbridge, Uppingham
> New schools: Bradfield, Brighton, Cheltenham, Clifton, Haileybury, Lancing, Marlborough, Rossall, Wellington

---

11 schools on the 1865 list[1] only:
> Old grammar schools: Bromsgrove, Durham, Felsted, Oundle, St Peter's (York)
> New schools: Epsom
> Sectarian schools: Moravian (Leeds), Wesleyan (Sheffield), Wesleyan (Taunton), Mount St Mary's, Oscott St Mary's

---

5 schools on the 1889 list[2] only:
> Old grammar schools: Bedford, Dulwich
> New schools: Dover, Malvern,* Radley*
> * These schools were not open till 1865 or later, and therefore could not have appeared on the earlier list.

Few outsiders would have disagreed with the names in the first *Year Book*, and they still form the hard-core of the genuine public-school system at the present time. The common elements, if we omit St Paul's and Merchant Taylors' as being day schools, arise from the significance of boarding education, a unified

1. 1865 Source: Based on the number of boarders and style of education (see pages 174–7).
2. 1889 Source: *Public Schools Year Book.* The 1889 List also included two day schools (St Paul's and Merchant Taylors') and three in Scotland (Fettes, Glenalmond, Loretto).

Anglican outlook within each school and an exclusiveness derived from a prohibitive cost and a positive restriction of the intake to the higher classes. The great day grammar schools at Manchester, Birmingham and elsewhere were still obviously beyond the fringe.

The city grammar schools did not, and still do not, conform to the general plan set by the leading boarding schools in at least four ways: in being local, in their religious aspect, in their boarding requirements and in their social intake. This is seen even at the hey-day of public-school development in the 1850s. We have particularly detailed knowledge of three main schools for this period—Manchester, Birmingham and Liverpool.[1] All show the same trend. They catered for boys who could walk to school and for boys from widely different religious backgrounds —in spite of the fact that the headmasters were Anglican clergymen. Analyses show that dissenters, Anglicans, Roman Catholics, Unitarians, Irvingites, atheists and Jews all rubbed shoulders together in the classrooms. As for the background of the boys, they came mainly from professional, industrial, commercial and lower-class circles. At Birmingham in 1857, in the classical school, there were two sons of naval officers and twenty-six of clergymen of varying denominations; forty-seven had a professional background and another forty-seven came from commerce and industry. Fifty-one were the sons of tradesmen; thirty-one had clerks for parents. Policemen were responsible for three children, teachers for one, while various lower-class groups, including widows whose status cannot be determined, accounted for another forty-one. Liverpool and Manchester were much the same. Such an intake would have been unthinkable at Eton or Harrow, or indeed at any private school, and incompatible with the Victorian upper-class horror of trading and shopkeeping.

On the other hand, in spite of the gulf that separated them, there were close links, particularly on the teaching side, between

1. For details of these three main schools, see A. A. Mumford, *The Manchester Grammar School, 1515 to 1915*, 1919; J. S. Howson, 'Statistics of the Liverpool Collegiate Institution', *Transactions of the National Association for the Promotion of Social Science*, 1858, pp. 241–9; D. Wainwright, *Liverpool Gentlemen*, 1960 (see p. 308 for a comparison of 1858 and 1958); E. H. Giffard, 'Statistics of King Edward's Grammar School, Birmingham', *Transactions of the National Association for the Promotion of Social Science*, 1857, pp. 130–4.

the genuine public boarding school and the city day grammar school. They were both concerned with preparing boys for the old universities, and in this respect there was no difference between Harrow and Manchester. The closest ties, however, lay in the common educational origin and social element in the staffs. It was shown in an earlier chapter (pp. 121–3) that more masters at Eton, Rugby, Harrow and Shrewsbury, taken collectively, were educated at day grammar schools than at boarding schools other than the original seven. In the production of these masters, King Edward's School, Birmingham, and Manchester Grammar were outstanding, and the traffic was not entirely one way, for it was a recognized promotion for masters at the seven, apart from Eton, to become headmasters at day grammar schools. Four men at Birmingham and three at Manchester arrived by this route. It is a statement of fact, therefore, that headmasters at major grammar schools and the staff at major public schools were of the same genus. By itself, however, this is not enough, since, in public esteem, the boys are of more consequence than the staff. Unlike departments at the universities, it is the non-scholastic attitude of the parents that makes the school, not the academic brilliance of the masters.

There has been a slow evolution in the social side of school life. It is commonly assumed that with general changes of attitude and the decline in families living on inherited income, the number of middle-class children has increased at all the main public schools. Nowadays trade is almost respectable (although a great deal obviously depends on the nature of the word 'trade'), so it could be argued that boarding and day schools have grown together a little in this respect at least. Generalizations of this kind, however, should not blind us to the fact that the details and significance of the change still elude us and remain to be explored.

Reactions on the Local Scene[1]

Any school is a source of local wealth. In the nineteenth century the masters of the big schools and their families occupied large houses, employed servants and paid high rates. Boys had to be housed and fed, their clothes washed, their shoes repaired. The school itself had to be built, extended, altered, maintained, swept and scrubbed, the gardens tended, the playing-fields cut.

With everything taken into account, it has been estimated that, in 1851, Rugby School's value to the town was about £70,000 in trade and 'the life-blood of 1,400 inhabitants'.[2] Taking Rugby as a typical example, it being one of the most successful schools of that time, in the country as a whole no less than 8,000 people were probably directly dependent on upper-class boarding education. We have little knowledge of the corresponding situation in connection with other forms of education.

The year 1851 may not have represented the ebb, but it was close to it, for the major schools were not only about to expand, but, as we have seen, a large number of new schools were being founded and were becoming successful competitors. With this expansion the benefits to their localities, both in cash and employment, grew rapidly. At the same time the growth of the railways, and with it the mechanics of retail trade, meant a change in the relationship of school and town. From the 1870s, at least, the schools began to rely less on local tradesmen and more on the cut-price stores in the big cities. As a counter-measure, local councils began to look beyond their own

1. For this chapter generally, see T. W. Bamford, 'Public School Town in the Nineteenth Century', *B.J.Ed.S.*, November 1957, pp. 25–36.
2. ibid, p. 33.

boundaries for more stable sources of rate and trade income in the encouragement of new industries.

Until this stage was reached local employment and prosperity in any public-school town depended largely on the prosperity of the school itself, and in some cases, like Oundle and Uppingham, the situation is practically the same today. School depressions were town depressions—times of unrelieved gloom with unemployment, empty houses and lounges deserted in the hotels. Strangely enough, sojourners only aggravated the situation, since, for reasons quite unexplained except in terms of publicity, they tended to stay away in lean periods, when the common sense of the situation would have suggested a flood to take advantage of the obvious vacancies at such times. In every case except for those schools in a large city, as with Westminster or Charterhouse, it is clear that the welfare of both town and school were linked indissolubly, and yet the prevalent nineteenth century view was that school affairs were a private matter and the concern of itself alone.

The see-saws of prosperity, which were such a feature of public-school life in the Victorian era, were a constant source of hope and fear, not only for the school itself and the old boys, but for all dependants of the school. The most unpopular of men was the headmaster of a dwindling establishment. Parents, traders, old boys, staff, the world at large blamed him for hanging on and not resigning, or for not following one or other of a hundred panaceas. Meanwhile the locality looked on, vociferous at times, but quite helpless. In the celebrated case of Goulburn at Rugby, community concern was reflected in editorials and articles in the local press. In 1855:

Four years ago there was much difficulty in procuring a house suitable for a family in Rugby. We wish it was the case now, but the ticketed windows on the once favoured Hillmorton Road tell a different tale. . . .[1]

It was calculated at the time that a bare £15,000 was involved as cash, apart from employment and other intangibles. For a small town this was serious, since the situation appeared to be progressive, and it is no wonder that they openly expressed the hope that the headmaster might be called to higher office in the church as soon as possible, and leave the school in more

1. *Rugby Advertiser*, 27 January 1855.

14

capable hands. When their prayers were answered and Goulburn was translated to Norwich as dean, the locals were still in agony lest the trustees fail them again by appointing an inferior man: 'All good men interested in Rugby School, will join us in the prayer that the Trustees may be Divinely inspired in their choice.'[1]

The traders were the most vitally concerned of all local groups, and were naturally sensitive, as at Eton, to anything that threatened their welfare and profits. A shop out of bounds, the alterations in the boarding-house tradition, the establishment of an internal tuck-shop, bulk buying—all these were resisted by aggrieved individuals but never by joint action, for that smacked too much of trade-unionism, and those who were still dependent on school trade, or hopeful of it, feared reprisal and ruin. The same fear kept the traders quiet, not only over wholesale and retail matters, but over the wider issues of health and education, which will be discussed later. Indeed, the silence of the traders at times of crisis made up a neutral block in town affairs concerning the school, which effectively split the most worthy causes.

A feature of the Victorian era was the slow and progressive divorce of school from town which continued throughout the nineteenth century and was almost complete by the end of it.

At one time boys fed and slept in the town. Boarding-houses were small and kept by the wives, daughters and relatives of professional men such as doctors and solicitors, and even, in some places, by close relatives of masters and headmasters, as at Eton. These 'dames' houses were often very popular, largely, no doubt, on account of the presence of the motherly, middle-aged women in charge, but they suffered from at least two fatal defects from the school's point of view. For one thing, a boy lodged within a private house was outside the power of the masters for a considerable period of the day. Another, and more important point, was that the profit which went into the pockets of private people attracted the cupidity of the staff. Headmasters came to realize that these plums could be used to increase the rewards of schoolmastering and to enhance their own power in the bestowal of houses on individual members of staff, rather like a potentate bestowing estates on a favourite or

1. *Rugby Advertiser*, 27 June 1857.

a member of the aristocracy installing a friend in a church living. A whole set of unwritten rules and ritual grew up around this practice. Such customs were jealously guarded, and the situation was liable to explode if the rules were violated, as we have seen in the case of Henry Hayman (p. 142).

By the advent of Victoria the change-over in the domestic care of boys from private houses to the houses of schoolmasters was already far advanced, and was more or less complete by the 1850s, although the old system still partly persists in some places. It was the key element of a tidying-up process that was transforming the easy, intimate relationships of town and school in the eighteenth and early nineteenth centuries. Masters became more deeply immersed in school work, till it occupied their thoughts and activities day and night. No longer did they have time to hold local curacies and be responsible for the welfare of a community, although some headmasters in the middle and late years of the century, like C. J. Vaughan, Moberly, A. C. Tait and Temple, interested themselves in politics, education and health. Farmers and landowners still allowed the boys to wander where they liked, and only occasionally was this freedom abused to the extent of local warfare, as at Harrow and Rugby. At the boys' level skirmishing between town and school occurred throughout the century everywhere and was not cured until they were virtually cut off from one another and time-tabling had reduced the amount of leisure spent out of school. Casual meetings between the two sets of youths in out-of-the-way places started with insults and peltings as the parties approached, liable to break out into open fighting if numbers were anything like even. In the main it was just youthful high spirits—a kind of game which both groups rather enjoyed. It was open and had none of the psychological agony endured by town boys who happened to be members of the school. Only rarely was an adult involved, as in the case of T. W. Tipler.[1]

Until the early years of the twentieth century at least, a local boy in this kind of school environment led a miserable existence,

1. Fighting between school boys and town boys is a feature of most schoolboy tales, from *Tom Brown* onwards. That these stories were reflections of actual events is occasionally shown by local papers, e.g. *Rugby Advertiser*. Sometimes the animosity appears to have crystallized about a particular adult person, as in the case of Mr Tipler.

and indeed had to be a tough character to survive for any length of time—he could hardly expect happiness. In spite of statements to the contrary, most schools distinguished sharply between foundationers and the rest. The boys who lived out were ostracized at the best of schools and subjected to subtle jibes. Mostly it was a boy battle, and only rarely do we find a headmaster involved—as at Bromsgrove, where the man openly sneered at the shabby clothing of local day boys and called them by insulting nicknames publicly: ' "Bacon" was the grocer's son and "Carthorse" the farmer's.' [1]

It is easy to imagine the treatment handed out by the rest of the staff when the head gave such a lead as this. It smacks of the technique of a bad headmaster using the easiest, most effective and beastliest form of domination. At the boys' level there was never any pretence about the hostility which existed:

> Friendship cannot exist except as between equals, and absurd as the statement may appear to one who has not been a public-school boy, a boarder in the school does not regard a home-boarder [local boy] as his equal. It is not just to the boy himself to send him to a school where he will be looked down upon as an inferior. . . . In our opinion a Home Boarder misses half the good of a public-school education . . . a home boarder's education is at best but a hot-house education with the east wind left out of it. [2]

This was written in 1901, by a man who knew the schools inside out, and it is confirmed in detail for the whole century and beyond by such men as T. Hughes, H. V. Weisse[3] and J. M. Wilson. Even so stern and just a disciplinarian as Temple confessed that the local boy in his school was not very happy unless he happened to be clever, in which case there were compensations. Arnold in the early period, and Percival fifty years later, may well have felt that the day boy at the public school got the better education, but the psychological effects were often withering.

This special situation of the local boy in the big school was a relatively rare but long-term one. It naturally coloured local relations whenever there was any dispute between school and

1. Lamb, op. cit., p. 144.
2. Minchin, op. cit., pp. 384–5.
3. H. V. Weisse had a varied career as master and headmaster in the twentieth century.

town. At such times letters of complaint would appear in the press and details be blurted out in public meetings. However, if one ignores this running sore, then it is fair to say that there was plenty of goodwill between the locals and the schools on matters of mutual interest, although occasionally problems became so deeply embedded in local pride, class-consciousness and money that compromise became impossible. Two such problems concerned local education and health.

THE CONFLICT OVER LOCAL EDUCATION

Most public schools in the middle and late nineteenth century were merely successful and specialized examples of endowed grammar schools. There were almost eight hundred foundations, each one with a founder and an intricate legal history extending, in many cases, over several centuries. Statements of policy, where they existed at all, were usually contained in wills mixed up with personal eccentricities and donations to the family and servants. A school of the least ambitious type could easily accumulate a frightening pile of documents. Considering the whole national picture, the mass lay scattered, uncatalogued and vast, representing, as it still does, one of the most tangled problems in educational history, aggravated by the fact that the documents are often difficult to read and that the very meaning of words like 'free', 'children', 'poverty' and 'grammar' has changed with time and made the wishes of the founders correspondingly difficult to interpret.[1]

By the nineteenth century the word 'free', as in 'free grammar school', meant legally that no charge should be made to the children attending, and very occasionally this certainly was the exact meaning of the word, as at Manchester and Stamford. On the other hand, B. H. Kennedy pointed out that 'free' often meant something quite different. For one thing, it could infer freedom from control or coercion, as in 'free man' or 'free city'.

1. Change in the meanings of words, and their relationship to the schools, can be traced, in part, in SIC in various volumes, but is summarized in I, pp. 126–7, together with summaries of definitions of the following: 'Religious instruction', p. 140; 'Diverse nature of the schools, etc.', pp. 112–116; Social rank of scholars and sex, pp. 111–12, 121–2; Geographical problems, pp. 125–6; Curriculum, pp. 119–20 *et seq.* For Dr Kennedy's important viewpoint on the meaning of 'free', see particularly pp. 122–3 and Note 3.

If this applied to schools, as Kennedy insisted that it should, then the headmaster should be free from the control and interference of a superior body or person like a college, chapter or provost of the kind already existing at Eton, Winchester, Westminster, or created in more modern times at Bradfield, Lancing and elsewhere. Moreover, it was illogical and against the spirit of past ages to supply education free to everyone, to the sons of the rich and the poor indiscriminately. In some places fees were specifically graded, as in the quaint and picturesque language of the school at Llanrwst:

> Entrance: every knight sonne, 2/6
> every doctor or esq. sonne, 2/-
> every gentleman or minister sonne, . . . 1/-
> every yeomane sonne . . . 9d
> poor and meaner men's sonne . . . 6d
> but poore indeed gratis.[1]

There was no intention of establishing this school for any particular section of society at least, and the same was true for most grammar schools. In this sense education should be 'free' from hindrance on financial or social grounds, to be open to the sons of rich and poor alike. The question of sex is more difficult, for the original provisions were usually vague or only the word 'children' used. What, precisely, founders had in mind in each case is a matter of opinion, but the result was the development of grammar education almost exclusively into a male monopoly.

The geographical problem is, perhaps, a little easier. A few schools, like St Paul's,[2] were certainly not conceived in local terms at all, while Winchester and Charterhouse were designed for special sections of the populace in one way or another. But such cases were exceptional. The fact that schools were usually founded in small towns by a local boy who had made good infers that he had his own hearth in mind. Indeed, in many cases, the actual villages to be served were specifically mentioned by the founders. It is difficult to see how Elizabethan merchants, for instance, living in their relatively stable world, could have foreseen the problems of growth and invention

1. SIC, I, p. 125.
2. St Paul's was founded by John Colet, in or about 1511, 'for 153 boys of all nations and countries . . .'; see PSC, II, p. 239.

which would alter the whole concept of the word 'inhabitant'. How many of Harrow's present population of 200,000, for example, would qualify as inhabitants in the eyes of the founder, John Lyon? Perhaps this is an extreme case, but the same situation is seen at Rugby. Lawrence Sheriff, the founder of the school there, saw the town as a place of 350 where everyone knew everyone else. How precisely would he view the situation when the population had grown to 50,000, under a different form of government and with different codes of manners? Is the child who has resided there for only one night a citizen, and if not, then what precise residential qualifications are necessary for free education in a local school? This argumentative and apparently trivial question became of vital importance when sojourners descended on the towns of Harrow, Bedford and elsewhere and took advantage of the situation.[1] Their migrant children were accepted with reluctance, and the only alternative would have been to challenge the rights of these parents in the courts. As we have already seen, this could be a very expensive business, which might have dragged on and impoverished the charity without producing any firm or desirable decision.

Local people with a stronger residential claim to free education on the foundation were permanent residents like shopkeepers, the manual classes and some professional men. Professional men, however, were often sojourners themselves and the heads were in any case virtually obliged to take their sons. Doctors attended the headmaster when he was sick, let alone the families of the staff and the boys; their co-operation was obviously desirable in preventing any uneasy relationships which might reflect on health. Solicitors, on the other hand, could be and were often militant. They knew their rights, could size up the legal chances where the free clauses of local schools were applicable, and were educated men. They could not be browbeaten or convinced by the specious arguments which

1. One of the working sojourners was a well-known educationist, H. B. Bingham, who kept a school for deaf children of the upper classes, and moved after his son had finished his education at Rugby. Bingham's school is extraordinary in many ways, particularly in its self-contained element, had its own farm, bakery, etc., and its unique subjects of interest, like the small zoo that he kept in the grounds and the visual aids that were displayed on ceilings and walls.

heads delivered to parents of tradesmen and other low ranks. Their sons were usually accepted without demur.

The net result was that, until the 1880s, there was a constant local battle between any endowed school which wanted to grow more and more exclusive by admitting only boarders, and the locals who saw the foundation as existing for the town's benefit and the school as the town's property. This conflict broke surface whenever any incident occurred which appeared to threaten severance of school from town. At such times the local middle classes and professional men, some of them magistrates, would form an uneasy alliance, as at Shrewsbury, Rugby, Harrow and no doubt in many other places as well. Often there was one man as a dominant personality representing each point of view—professional, trader, manual worker—and in the case of Rugby names can be given for these champions at successive periods.

Even before Victoria a solicitor of Rugby, William Ferdinand Wratislaw,[1] had fought the trustees successfully. Again, when Arnold, by a series of tricks incredible in their ruthlessness, managed to prevent local and other boys from attending at an early age, he fought this action successfully in the courts in 1839. The Victorian era, therefore, began with this particular town triumphant, and every prospect of a break-through for the local child. Unfortunately this prospect faded rapidly, although the sons of local professional men and sojourners continued to attend. No attempt was made to replace the lower forms of the school, so that new boys were necessarily older in years and had to obtain their preparatory schooling elsewhere. The sons of traders were now not only unwelcome as children, but did not usually possess the necessary grounding in Latin. Their fathers condemned this situation in public meetings as unjust and illegal, and as evidence of privilege; to them the founder, Lawrence Sheriff, who had been a trader himself, had the traders particularly in mind when he created the school in the first place, and they were encouraged in this belief in the 1860s by the national agitation for a comprehensive system of grammar schools. One of these writers was Frederick Temple,

1. See Bamford, *Arnold*, op. cit., particularly Chapter 12. This family was radically minded, and had a great deal to do with agitation about the school and local matters until the end of the century.

whose long essay on 'National Education' appeared to favour the claims of local people:

They [the grammar schools] were intended for the education of the whole community, but especially for that of the middle classes ... yet the schools were assuredly not intended for the gentry alone, but rather looked to poverty as a special qualification for admission. The middle classes were thus marked out as the chief objects of the goodwill of the founders.[1]

When this man was appointed headmaster of Rugby in 1858, it is no wonder that the news was received with acclamation by the town, and that twenty-four middle-class (trader) parents sent their sons in the next four years—a unique feature. But that was the end. Temple's words did not survive the practical test; he had no more liking for local boys than the headmasters before or after. The same general story is seen at Harrow and Shrewsbury, though with considerable variation in detail. At all these places, however, there were antagonisms between school and town which only began to subside with the Acts of 1868 and 1869.

From the whole century it is difficult to find a headmaster of a major school who was really sympathetic to the claims of the locality, and perhaps this is not surprising as they were paid to put the interests of the school first. The nearest, perhaps, was C. J. Vaughan, who, to a large extent, defied his governors at Harrow and set up a special form for local boys in May 1853, with Latin taught free and a charge of £15 per annum for the rest of the curriculum. Even though these boys were kept apart from the rest of the school, it was at least a gesture that saw permanence in the building of the Lower School; and a similar school was set up for the middle classes in Rugby in 1878. Other men worked hard at helping the town, but this was often akin to religious pastoralism, not because they had true sympathy. Indeed, some of the headmasters—Temple among them—revealed an attitude almost of contempt in their private conversations.

It is difficult to live in a town for twenty or thirty years, as many of the masters did, and pay no attention whatever to local society. Wives were generally more active than husbands at this level, and the nineteenth-century ethic entailed at least a

1. F. Temple, 'National Education', *Oxford Essays*, 1856.

show of good works and charity. The headmaster, with his social position, had every opportunity to carve out a prominent career for himself in local affairs, as Vaughan did at Harrow and as many have done in recent years. In the same way it is not surprising to find Mrs Vaughan starting and directing an industrial home for girls. In a rural situation this was simple enough, for the headmaster and his wife were automatic leaders, but in large towns the position was more difficult, and extremely so at Eton, where the staff may have been important educationally but were really quite insignificant socially. Even so, the most singular case of education involving school and locality was undoubtedly that of Stephen Hawtrey.[1] He used the Etonian style of education in a school for working-class children that he ran at Windsor. Latin was taught and Hawtrey's assistants at Eton helped to inject a good deal of mathematics. In their turn, the older boys, who paid 9*d.* a week for their own lessons, went to Eton to teach the young aristocracy and face the bribery of small gifts in return for sums done 'on the sly'.

Elsewhere many masters laboured at the local Mechanics' Institutes, as at Rugby, only to be rewarded by falling numbers and general apathy. Some of the special public lectures and series by J. M. Wilson[2] and T. N. Hutchinson[3] displayed an astonishing virtuosity, but these successes were not repeated in the more routine work. The Mechanics' Institute at Rugby was itself saved time and again by the money and devotion of masters at the school, but their efforts were only rewarded by miserable attendances, while identical classes held elsewhere in the town at inconvenient centres, and at far greater cost to the students, thrived. Superficially, it was an absurd and illogical situation. It may be that the explanation lay in the undertones of charity so beloved of the gentry and so hated by the lower classes. Rugby was a town that grew rapidly, and to judge by the census details a multitude of accents would have been present in any audience; it is more than possible that the speech

1. See PSC, III, evidence of S. T. Hawtrey; also Brinsley-Richards, op. cit., p. 21 *et seq.*
2. Wilson gave lectures, apart from series, on such topics as meteors, the sun, the aurora, the comets. These were reported at length in the local press.
3. Hutchinson gave series of lectures on electricity.

of the masters only stressed social gulfs. Whatever the explanation, this phenomenon of the absent audiences remained one of the most enigmatic and apparently unkind features of local life. For thirty years the public schoolmasters struggled against every kind of disappointment, until, by 1870, they gave up at last, and their names largely disappeared from the teaching-lists except in the special case of art. Meanwhile, this adult education work was carried on by their wives as a venture for promoting the education of women. All this would appear to be as much a sociological as an educational problem, though how far this example was typical is impossible to say at present.

One matter beyond dispute is the active role of the schools as local promoters of culture. They employed musicians who were active within the town, often in search of clients, but also as performers, as organizers of recitals and the encouragement of music at all levels and for all ages. This is a long tradition that is still present, most notably at Rugby.

THE CONFLICT OVER LOCAL HEALTH

Early Victorian towns are sometimes thought of as romantic places, with their stage-coaches, solid houses, warm inns, great roaring fires and elegant fashions, but in fact they were neither pleasant nor healthy. Piped water, clean streets, a pure atmosphere and water sanitation did not exist. People were huddled together in warrens as close as the builders could manage. T. H. Simms describes the life of one of our major public-school towns in the early Victorian period (1842–8):

> Each fetid court of beaten earth in the centre of the town contained a pump for drinking water, a drain which often took the overflow from a cesspool, and a small enclosure, surrounded by a low brick wall to hold more solid filth . . . the value of the eight wider roads that radiated from the town in providing constant through winds was lessened by the ditches which ran alongside them. In these ditches the sewage from the town was collected and spread as manure upon the undrained fields 'little better than a morass'. From ditches and cesspools the sewage of the town seeped into the drift gravels. . . . Held in this gravel subsoil, 'the receptacle for the chief fluid filth of the town', the water was drawn up from wells about twelve feet deep. This the inhabitants drank.[1]

1. T. H. Simms, *The Rise of a Midland Town, Rugby, 1800–1900*, 1949, pp. 6–7.

Piggeries, kennels and stables were part of the every-day scene. At fair-times the refuse left by stalls, cattle and horses was indescribable and 'the accumulated filth in the streets took over a week to remove'.[1]

Such conditions were a vital concern of the schools. Elegant buildings and surroundings were ludicrous alongside tenements and alleys that were an offence to the eye and nostril. It was no idle chance that headmasters, almost without exception, took an active interest in sanitary reform, whether it was water supply or sewage. As for the more positive nuisances of cesspools, piggeries and cattle markets, they were intent on getting them removed as far from the school and the gentry areas as possible.

Whenever they could, the headmasters placed the blame for any decline in prosperity, either short or long term, on to typhus, cholera or any other convenient infection raging at the time. Epidemics at Winchester in 1846, 1848 and 1861 provided Moberly with a wonderful excuse for attacking the local authorities over faulty drainage. The approach of his own school to educational matters may have been one of the most conservative in the land, but he was exceedingly quick to point out conservative tendencies in others, and in the local council in particular. It was not only that the schemes for the clearance of refuse and smell, either here or elsewhere, were novel and expensive, but that they also meant a new way of life with the rejection of the old standards and a corresponding revolution in thought, attitude and practice. It was not easy for any man used to the well and the village pump and the traditional earthy life to see it all thrown on to the scrap-heap as outmoded and indecent. This is not a matter of intelligence and appreciation, but rather one of habit and loyalty; it was really too much for the older leaders of any community. The new ideas were only introduced in the face of bitter opposition, and usually adopted in apathy. Headmasters, like all men who have reform thrust upon them, ignored the problem as long as they could. Even in the late nineteenth century we get a comment from one of the experts:

I have *seen* cesspools at one of the most popular and expensive schools in the kingdom in such a state of repletion that it would be impossible for the boys to use them without defiling themselves

1. ibid., p. 5.

with the decomposing ordure. I may add that I saw this condition, on the occasion I refer to, on the last day of the vacation, and the state of things had existed probably since the end of the previous term.[1]

Even at Rugby, one of the first two towns in the country to take up powers under the Public Health Act of 1848, progress was painfully slow.[2] Successive schemes for water and sewage were tried and abandoned for thirty long years until a satisfactory solution came in 1876. Every headmaster was interested and took a hand in the arguments, particularly Arnold's successor, A. C. Tait. Indeed, it is ironic that Tait's passionate work for the cure of infectious disease should have been rewarded in 1856, years after leaving Rugby, with such tragic personal loss as the deaths from scarlet fever of five of his own children within the space of five weeks.

Disease is frightening at any time. Headmasters, renowned for rebuking archbishops and Cabinet Ministers, were brought to their knees at the first sign of infection. It was not uncommon for schools outside London to cut their terms short or send the boys home at a moment's notice. Sometimes the malady lingered so long that emergency measures had to be taken. On one occasion, in 1841, most of the school at Rugby dispersed, various groups going to Churchover, Leamington and the Lake District. As an evacuation, it was a Sunday-afternoon picnic compared with the moonlight treks of the old dissenting academies, or even with Thring's epic flight from Uppingham to Borth.[3]

The Uppingham suggestion first came from a group of masters, and finally, after repeated outbreaks of fever directly connected with the health of the town, Thring set out on Monday, 13 March 1876, in deep snow to find a suitable place of refuge. Forty-eight hours later, on the day of a hurricane, he

1. Dukes, op. cit., p. 63.
2. For health progress in a public-school town, see Simms, op. cit., p. 9.
3. General note on evacuations: the temporary movement of schools has taken many forms. Undoubtedly the most romantic, from our point of view, were the sudden movements of dissenting academies, often with only the briefest warning. Perhaps the most extreme instances of evacuation were the movements of Catholic schools from various countries owing to religious persecution, as mentioned earlier (Introduction). Parallel instances in our own day concerned the movement of schools on evacuation of civilian populations during the Second World War.

entered the Cambrian Hotel at Borth on the Welsh coast, six miles north of Aberystwyth. This was to be his home and that of 290 boys for over a year. With the mountains and the sea-shore, and the occasional illness, they found plenty of excitement in improvization, in fumigation, in new forms of games and scientific rambling, all of it handled with superb publicity in the columns of *The Times*.

Meanwhile the traders back home had been having a lean time. They had missed the school's food and clothing account, the spending of the families, the pocket money, the rent and rates of the houses. But for all their entreaties Thring was adamant; he would not go back until the town's sanitation had been put in order. In the end he was triumphant and returned to take an invited interest in local affairs and to be elected president of the Mutual Improvement Society.

The operation had attracted great attention. It had gone so smoothly that there had been rumours that the school would never return. When ultimately they did come back, it was only after they had shown that the buildings in Rutland were not so essential after all. Numbers had actually increased in exile, and a third of the school was new and were strangers to the town. Popularity was a new experience for Thring. His relationships with the town, with his staff and indeed with his own trustees had hardly been models of coexistence. Undoubtedly he was impulsive and dictatorial, and he also had the annoying habit of backing his own judgement with his own money. Typically, he had sunk £3,000 into the Borth migration. Other members of staff were also greatly out of pocket, but the trustees grew stubborn and the staff were only repaid for the Borth adventure after an appeal to the Charity Commissioners.[1]

Public health was not really understood until the funda-mental causes of infectious diseases were appreciated and the work of Pasteur widely known. This, however, did not affect the role and importance of the public-school doctor, but only his efficiency. He was the expert, and almost always the outcome of medical opinion was some expensive reconstruction of the buildings and drainage, or some equally expensive change

1. For this episode as a whole, see Parkin, op. cit., and J. H. Skrine, *Uppingham by the Sea*, 1878.

in the sleeping or living arrangements of the boys. Whatever the advice, it could not be dismissed lightly, and the headmasters knew it and often resented it. The fundamental issue was that both these men had responsibilities which could not easily admit of a superior judgement, and they both necessarily looked at the same problem through different eyes. Both were professional men, jealous of their rights, insisting that due recognition should be given to their expert knowledge. In times of epidemic the doctor was supreme, but from the long-term viewpoint of planning, his advice on the need for new and expensive facilities after such an emergency could nullify other projects which the headmaster had in mind, and could, if pressed, amount to interference with policy.

The growing influence of the doctor and the spread of his empire beyond the strict confines of sickness could easily be considered as a status question and as a bid for greater power and recognition. Superficially, this view can be supported by a glance at a standard textbook of the late Victorian age, like *Health at School* by Clement Dukes, which went through several editions. Here are not only discussions of clothes and sanitation, sickness and meals, but also such matters as discipline, the time-table, curriculum, rewards and punishments, examinations, and even comments on the appointments of masters and headmasters. All these matters are, in part at any rate, the rightful sphere of medicine, though not so by tradition. It is only in recent times that the complexities of the roles of nature and nurture upon the individual have begun to be understood. We now realize that much of the teacher's effort in the past was at least a waste and often positively injurious.

The clash between doctors and headmasters was a question of rights and recognition. When the medical man was full-time, his subordinate position was clear, but when he was only part-time and only semi-dependent on the school, he was free from authority, and in several cases acted as an independent individual carrying his side of any dispute into the local and national press.[1] Of the many examples, the best is probably that of Dr Barford at Wellington. In the early days he had

1. A good example of the power of a medical expert in early Victorian times is connected with the alterations at Rugby carried out on the recommendations of Sir James Clarke.

complained about the drains and was still complaining twenty years later, when the health of the college had become a serious matter, with the deaths of boys in two successive years, followed by a serious throat epidemic. A drastic overhaul of the drainage system was the only way out and Barford mentioned an expense of £20,000. In his long fight he may certainly have grown 'officious, overbearing and independent', but he had protested too often and too long for the governing body, who sacked him. But removing the main objector did not remove the embarrassment or the illnesses any more than covering the spots removes a rash. Repairs were made, but still Barford carried on an independent campaign against the school's health in the papers and the *Lancet*. Boys continued to fall ill, the climax coming in 1891 with a diphtheria epidemic. The entire site was abandoned and, in the wake of the Thring tradition, the school settled down again in the Imperial Hotel at Malvern while the buildings were disinfected and the drains put right.[1]

1. For Wellington, Dr Barford and the evacuation to Malvern, see Newsome, *Wellington College*, op.cit.

CHAPTER NINE

Contributions of the Public Schools to the Victorian Era

A school may be regarded as an essential, if minute, part of the national educational framework. Within these limits the public schools appeared to satisfy a particular stratum of Victorian society. A school may also be judged by its success in producing men of ability and position on the assumption that the influence of the school permeates the whole life and career of its scholars and thereby brings about success or failure. On this basis, the reputation of a public school has rested on its assumed ability to create men specially suited for leadership and government. In trying to assess claims of this kind it will be necessary to consider each of the three general categories of public school existing in the nineteenth century—(1) the original seven, (2) the new foundations and (3) the revived grammar schools —starting with (1).

Many schools have produced a printed register of boys containing summaries of subsequent careers.[1] Such a book can yield a wealth of information, although there are difficulties in presenting the material in a simple form. What, for instance, is an occupation? Does a J.P. qualify for inclusion? What precisely is to be done about a person with multiple occupations, as in the actual case of a barrister who was also a journalist, an assistant editor and an M.P.? This is not an isolated example; no less than thirty-five boys who entered Rugby in the year 1875 had more than one career. On the other hand, it is tidier to allot one occupation to each boy so that totals can be squared

---

1. An interesting contrast to the main public boarding schools is Christ's Hospital. The subsequent careers of the old boys of this school would provide a comparison of boarding education which might reduce family influence to a minimum.

Table 12. *The future occupations of boys who entered Harrow and Rugby at five-yearly intervals from 1830 to 1880.*[1]

Year	Armed forces	Church	Law	Administration and politics	Scholastics	Business	Overseas	Medicine	Science and Engineering	Other Occupation	Died young	No information
RUGBY												
1830	9	28	13	12	3	3	3	1	0	0	1	40
1835	11	19	9	8	0	0	0	1	0	0	4	21
1840	21	22	9	11	4	5	3	0	1	0	4	39
1845	35	19	12	23	2	4	7	5	0	1	3	32
1850	38	15	15	16	5	5	9	2	0	4	10	28
1855	20	9	16	9	4	5	6	1	0	0	2	18
1860	26	16	27	7	5	9	14	2	3	3	3	28
1865	19	13	26	13	10	18	17	4	3	2	2	34
1870	18	11	19	8	2	34	11	3	4	5	5	21
1875	15	7	24	8	5	30	23	5	5	12	2	18
1880	8	5	22	5	6	26	11	7	6	2	3	13
HARROW												
1830	14	8	11	8	0	4	0	0	0	1	3	26
1835	7	6	3	10	0	2	1	0	0	0	0	8
1840	4	3	2	3	2	2	3	0	0	1	0	11
1845	14	9	10	16	2	6	2	0	1	2	4	9
1850	36	12	14	22	1	8	1	2	0	3	7	16
1855	42	13	25	23	1	9	3	0	1	0	0	22
1860	39	9	19	26	1	8	9	2	4	2	10	33
1865	26	9	13	19	1	24	16	1	2	4	5	38
1870	37	5	21	22	5	24	12	1	2	7	6	27
1875	32	9	22	21	2	23	13	3	1	9	1	23
1880	33	4	18	5	8	21	11	2	3	3	4	53
RUGBY AND HARROW COMBINED												
1830	23	36	24	20	3	7	3	1	0	1	4	66
1835	18	25	12	19	0	2	1	1	0	0	4	29
1840	25	25	11	15	6	7	6	0	1	1	4	50
1845	49	28	22	43	4	11	9	5	1	3	7	41
1850	74	27	29	39	6	13	10	4	0	7	17	44
1855	62	22	41	32	5	14	9	1	1	0	2	40
1860	65	25	46	33	6	17	23	4	7	5	13	61
1865	45	22	39	33	11	42	33	5	5	6	7	72
1870	55	16	40	30	7	58	23	4	6	12	11	48
1875	47	16	46	29	7	53	36	8	6	21	3	41
1880	41	9	40	10	14	47	22	9	9	5	7	66

1. Details compiled from Dauglish and Stephenson, op. cit. (Harrow), and Michell, op. cit. (Rugby). The obvious subjective element for classification by categories, and the arbitrary rules for priorities are discussed in the text. 'Died Young' refers to those dying either at school or soon afterwards who had no time to adopt a career. Several varieties of some categories were itemized, including different hierarchical levels reached. It is difficult to justify fine subdivisions without elaborate research into each individual case. Thus it was clear that in the six subdivisions that were made of 'business' a great deal depended on the quality and understanding of the person making the original entries.

and a mere transient acquaintance with an occupation be ignored. A simple analysis of the future occupations of boys entering Harrow and Rugby at five-yearly intervals from 1830 to 1880 is given in Table 12. The construction of such a table involves some degree of personal judgement to decide on the 'major' occupation for each entrant. In those cases where it was difficult to pick out the dominant feature of a man's career, the procedure adopted was to choose the first occupation on leaving school or university, since this was, presumably, most nearly related to the influence of the school itself. Inevitably, this means that important facts have sometimes been excluded, as in the case of a barrister who was an M.P. for only a short period in middle age. The nature and extent of the residual 'minor' occupations are of some interest, if only to remove doubts about the nature of the personal element involved in selection. An analysis of this point for Harrow for the year 1875 is shown in Table 13. The effect of minor occupations on the figures for the professions, including science, is small, and the only items for comment concern the relatively large numbers affecting 'administration' and 'other occupations'. The administration figure for minor occupations includes four M.P.s and seventeen local magistrates and dignitaries. 'Other occupations' include all those who are not easily classified. A few boys chose middle- or even lower-class occupations instead of the usual professions. Such were the sons of local tradesmen, forced into the schools on the foundation. Mostly they became farmers, shopkeepers or skilled workers, but their numbers were small and their stay at the school usually brief. In addition there were 'gentleman farmers', and the seven instances of minor 'other' occupations recorded in Table 13 include an author, a journalist, an artist, the inventor of an airship and a trainer of racehorses.

Another difficulty concerns the lack of information about the large number of boys recorded in the last column of Table 12. In some cases this is the result of losing touch, but equally there were many who inherited wealth and estates and therefore followed no occupation in the usual meaning of the term. In the case of Harrow, twenty-one of these came from aristocratic families, and it is likely, therefore, that many members of the gentry are also hidden in the figures under

'No Information'; indeed, for Rugby, this is known to be so from personal knowledge.

The armed forces were undoubtedly the most popular outlet for the two old schools, and the same was true for Winchester. Of the 504 instances recorded here only one was not an officer, while sixty-five reached the rank of at least full colonel or its naval equivalent of captain. Not only was this occupation acceptable to the aristocracy, but it held glamour and royal

Table 13. *Major and minor occupations of the Harrow entrants, 1875.*[1]

Occupation	Armed forces	Church	Law	Administration and politics	Scholastics	Business	Overseas	Medicine	Science and Engineering	Other Occupations	Died young	No Information
Major	32	9	22	21	2	23	13	3	1	9	1	23
Minor	2	2	1	22	1	4	3	0	0	7	0	0
Total	34 62*	11	23	43	3	27	16	3	1	16	1	23

* This is the figure if volunteers are included.

approval. Any school with pretensions had old boys among a few selected regiments, and the prestige of this profession continued throughout the century and is still high today. It will be noted that, for both schools, there was an increase in numbers after 1845. Since these numbers refer to boys entering the school at about twelve or thirteen, it follows that the effect on the armed forces was some five or more years later. This would appear to reflect the situation introduced by the Crimean War and the Indian Mutiny, although there are differences between the schools in that Rugby's contribution faded with the years while the strength of the Harrow contingent remained fairly steady. On the other hand there was a decline at Winchester from 1840 to 1859, with a steady increase thereafter. J. G. C. Minchin claimed that, 'Above all Harrow is a soldier's school.'[2] The figures here would support this view to a limited

1. Major and minor lists were made of all years concerned, but 1875 may be taken as typical of the difficulties.
2. Minchin, op. cit., p. 151.

extent, but the law, gentry pursuits and business in later years were also important, while other schools, like Cheltenham, appear to have been dominated by the military theme.

In addition to their contribution to the regular armed forces, many old boys joined the militia, and from the 1875 entrants alone, twenty-eight from Harrow (seven with no other recorded occupation) and at least four from Rugby served in this way.

If the armed forces represented the most popular occupation, then, conversely, the least favoured outlets were science, engineering and medicine, where the attitude of the schools amounted to a virtual boycott until the 1860s; even then the increase was largely confined to Rugby. This is clearly indicated by the figures in Table 12, and has also been demonstrated for Victorian Winchester in a study over ten decades by T. J. H. Bishop (1820–1919).[1] But even a few scientists may be important. It could be argued, for instance, that, compared with the size of the army as a whole, the numbers recruited from Harrow and Rugby were negligible, but this is to ignore the significance of their role as officers, in particular as high-ranking officers. This brings in the question of *élites*. In the same way it could be argued that quality in science is important too, and this is a point to which we shall return later.

Of the professions, the law attracted about 10 per cent of the boys until 1850, and became even more popular thereafter. Of those recorded here, eleven were promoted to the bench.

Apart from the extremes of the armed forces and science, the century saw the one or two other interesting and significant changes brought out in the figures of Table 12.

'Business' is a wide term, but if defined as including directors, bankers, stockbrokers, merchants, manufacturers, shipowners and similar occupations, then it becomes an acceptable and indeed popular pursuit. Business in this sense always involved a superior 'desk-job' without anything vigorous or hand-soiling. In the earlier period it was almost invariably a by-product of some other occupation. Many lawyers and politicians became directors of railways incidentally to their main work, and it was not until the later years of the century that leavers were entering business for its own sake. This change occurred rather suddenly and affected boys entering the two schools concerned

1. Bishop, op. cit.

after 1860 and before 1870 (Figure 3). This appears to coincide with the corresponding phenomenon at Durham and Sedbergh, as representatives of the revived grammar schools, although detailed figures for Winchester would indicate a somewhat earlier date, in the late 1840s and 1850s.[1] In spite of a general agreement it would be rash to assume that business was growing steadily more respectable. There are other possibilities to be

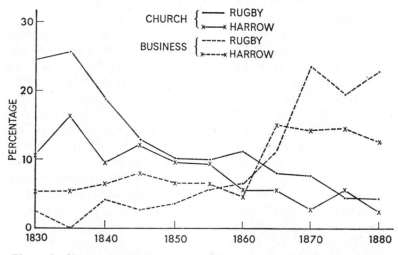

Figure 3. *Harrow and Rugby entrants, at five-yearly intervals from 1830 to 1880, with church and business careers*

considered. The schools may have been taking more children with a business background, or, alternatively, this may have been one of the growing occupations for which the public-school background, whether in education, influence or kinship, was especially suited. Certainly there was a need for new outlets to absorb younger sons, although why this particular one was chosen rather than others is uncertain, and may be related to the influence of family connections and the lack of necessary expertise. In the political field, Aydelotte's analysis of the Parliament of 1841–7 shows that 14 per cent of the 478 M.P.s who were gentry on a broad definition of that term were also businessmen.[2] This is clear evidence that the gentry were

1. Bishop, op.cit.
2. See W. O. Aydelotte in G. Kitson Clark, *The Making of Victorian England,* 1962, pp. 290–305.

becoming involved in business early in the reign, although it is perhaps true that these M.P.s were more likely to be interested in business than were other gentry, and some support for this hypothesis is to be seen in Figure 3. In the years before 1860 Harrow had a consistently higher percentage of boys who went into business, and, of the two schools, Harrow was more closely associated with the House of Commons. Altogether, these results confirm that the landed nature of this class was being diluted.

As an opposing trend in the old public schools, there was a marked and steady decline of boys entering the church, confirmed in detail by Winchester figures for over a century (Figure 3). This is a very surprising result indeed in view of the emphasis placed on religion and the pulpit orations of the headmasters, and with so many of the staff being in orders. With so much emphasis on the moral aspects of life, one would have assumed that there would have been a corresponding reflection in church figures. However, it is clear that the publicized great age of the schools in terms of the moral revolution of the 1840s and 1850s had no real effect on the boys of that generation, if their ultimate choice of careers is any guide, and neither did the aftermath of experience at the universities with the Oxford Movement drama. Figure 3 indicates that the slide began for Rugby soon after 1835, in the middle of Arnold's headship and twenty years before there was any significant introduction of lay staff to replace those in orders. The reduction noted here cannot be explained by a possible decline in the number of parents who were clergymen, since Rugby was particularly favoured by them and the percentage of clergy among the parents sending children was consistently higher (except for 1835) than the percentage of children entering the church. The 1830s might well have been a time of religious regeneration for some adults, and certainly the Oxford Movement was a burning topic of conversation; but it had no positive lasting effect on the boys of Harrow and Rugby,[1] in spite of a few notable exceptions. It would indicate that the seeds of a growing secularism are to be found in the schools

1. For Rugby, the following represents the figures for the percentages of parents in the church and sons going into the church, at five-yearly intervals from 1830 to 1875.

Parents:	25	8	22	18	15	14	17	9	10	13
Sons :	25	26	18	13	10	10	11	8	8	5

very early on. One element appears to have been the head-masters' complete misunderstanding of the effect of words on children, for it is an axiom of teaching that moral exhortation is worthless in the long run and this could well have accelerated the process. Perhaps it was a contributory cause to other changes, such as supply and demand, the gradual diminution in the value of church livings with their loss of financial bait, and the growing sense of doubt and agnosticism in a scientific environment. Some of the facts are plain even if the reasons behind them are not. In terms of recruitment religion was already losing its grip before the Victorian era began.

The century also saw an increase in the number of public-school men going overseas. This feature was connected with the growth and glamour of empire, and was only to be expected for careerist schools catering for younger sons. On the other hand, overseas service was unpopular in the highest circles, both in the army and the administration. It is doubtful if a similar tendency could ever be shown at Eton, and it is perhaps significant that this feature is less marked in Harrow than in Rugby.

The column in Table 12 headed 'Administration and Politics' covers the Civil Service and Diplomatic Corps (both at home and overseas), politicians and those holding positions of responsibility and status in local and regional affairs. In the last instance responsibility usually came in the middle or late years of life, and in all the cases recorded here this was the only 'occupation' recorded for these boys. Fifty-four boys from Rugby and ninety-four from Harrow were involved in these local posts in the years mentioned—they were presumably combining this service with a wealthy influential background. As one might expect from the general aspects of the two schools discussed in Chapter One, Harrow outpaced Rugby in the fields of politics and the diplomatic service, with forty-five entrants as against twenty-one. There was an element of privilege and influence in these appointments, and the same aspect was seen in boys going into the Civil Services overseas (including the Indian Civil Service) where the combined figures for the two schools are[1]:

1830	1835	1840	1845	1850	1855	1860	1865	1870	1875	1880
1	6	6	8	13	8	3	3	1	2	3

1. The figures for 1830–80 are only indicative. The problems involved in

The first absolutely open competition for these overseas posts occurred in 1854. Previously the appointment of civil servants lay wholly in the hands of patrons, and the explanation of the sudden drop in the figures after the 1850–5 period might lie in the assumption that the amount of privilege would grow less with exalted schools once competition had been adopted as the method of entry.[1] We have seen that other schools, formed from 1842 onwards, specialized in overseas work and would, in theory at least, draw off some of the posts from those schools who would have held them on privilege in pre-competition days.

Any organization comprises many people working towards a common end. The nature of the end and the means of achieving it are determined by a very few people within the organization who have the power to make key decisions. Such a key group may be looked upon as an *élite* and their power is usually reflected in the status of individuals involved, as indicated by the rank of 'general', 'secretary of state', 'dean', 'cardinal', etc. One method of evaluating schools is by their contribution to *élites* in a similar way to that in which the relative claims of successful and unsuccessful headmasters were determined earlier (pp. 154–5). The percentages quoted there for 'successful' products of Rugby among the entrants of 1818 to 1834 varied between eight and sixteen. Although this procedure was useful for comparing headmasters, in the question of *élites* rather different definitions should perhaps be made. If we take the rank of colonel (or its equivalent) in the armed forces, an archdeacon or above in the church, a Q.C. or judge in law, and service in the government for M.P.s, then an analysis of the Harrow and Rugby years shown in Table 12 is given in Table 14. Percentages of boys entering the *élites*, as here defined, varied between 4 and 15 per cent, and were generally higher for Harrow than for Rugby. Using similar criteria for the period 1820–1922, and covering the whole range of livelihood, Bishop obtained for Winchester a figure of

combining the figures of schools is particularly difficult with public schools, where each institution has clientele and staff both with individualistic approaches and a headmaster with an overall guiding influence.
1. Dates concerned with Civil Service examinations are complicated, since different dates can refer to the same phenomenon in different sections of the service, while it was common for both old and new methods to continue side by side.

almost 25 per cent. At first sight the difference between
Winchester and the other two schools would appear to
be striking, but there are difficulties whenever different time
sequences or social catchment are involved. Thus at some
periods opportunities for public-school men in some professions
are greater, as in the armed forces in time of war, and the
significance of the rank of colonel also changes with the size of
the organization. Similarly, entry into the Guards, for example,

Table 14. *Percentage of boys of Harrow and Rugby who
achieved élite status in selected professions, based on entrants
at five-yearly intervals from 1830 to 1880.*[1]

	Percentage of boys entering professions who achieved 'élite' status			
	Armed forces	*Church*	*Law*	*Parliament*
Rugby	10	7	6	4
Harrow	15	15	6	13

(For the arbitrary definition of *élite*, see text.)

is not always based on an army career centred on ambition.
Again, the clientele of both Harrow and Rugby was based on
the gentry, and the attitudes of this class to work and ambition
are not the same as those lower down the hierarchy. Eldest
sons, in any case, have an assured future without *élite* ambition.
All these points have to be borne in mind before schools can
be reasonably compared.

This summary represents some of the significant points in the
broad destiny of boys from Harrow and Rugby. How far they
can be considered as typical of the seven is a matter of opinion.
The significant differences between Harrow and Rugby have
been demonstrated, yet, of all the schools, these two are closest

1. The four occupations given perhaps show the public schools in their
best light. Estimates of *élites* in other fields, e.g. science, are more difficult to
achieve because of the nature of the ill-defined hierarchy in the last century.
How far the 'success' of boys varied with time is a matter for later development. Altogether this table lends support to the importance of 'influence' in
achieving success in life. This theme receives some attention later on.

to one another. Winchester is different, as the work of Bishop shows, and in many ways that difference has grown with the years. On general grounds one would expect Shrewsbury, Westminster and Charterhouse to show even greater differences, with Eton remaining unique.

Of the newer variety of public school, Cheltenham and Clifton may perhaps be taken as examples. An analysis of Cheltenham's register over seventy years, from 1841 to 1910, produces overall figures for the occupations of boys on leaving (Table 15).

Table 15. *Occupations of boys leaving Cheltenham College, 1841–1910.*[1]

Old boys entering	Numbers
Armed forces—home	2,301
Armed forces—India	595
Clergy	449
The Law	444
Medicine (including Forces)	178
Civil engineers (including overseas)	161
Civil Service $\begin{cases} 24 \text{ to East India College*} \\ 81 \text{ to I.C.S. (1855–99)} \\ 18 \text{ to India, Home and Colonial C.S.} \end{cases}$	99

* The figure for entry to the East India College has been omitted from the total because the failure rate is said to have been high.[2]

There is no question but that the armed forces were the major outlet, and the same was true of Clifton. Other occupations almost pale into insignificance. Cheltenham was the first new major school of the Victorian era, and the first to be set up in answer to professional demand. Even so, the figures clearly indicate that it did not produce the major influx into science and engineering, outside the army and posts overseas, that one might reasonably have expected, and the same is true of Clifton.[3]

1. Figures calculated from information given in A. H. Hunter, *Cheltenham College Register, 1841–1910*, 1911, pp. 798–835. Among the 178 boys entering medicine, thirty-eight were in the armed forces, fifteen in the army, fifteen in the Indian army, eight in the navy.
2. S. P. Woodruff, *The Men Who Ruled India: The Founders*, 1953, p. 283.
3. For some Clifton figures, see notes under p. 221 below.

For Cheltenham the number of clergy was small, and at Clifton, too, the drop from 1863 to 1905 in boys entering the church was quite pronounced. It would be most interesting to know if the same trend could be confirmed for Marlborough, a school designed for the sons of clergymen, and for those schools catering for dissenters. For Cheltenham 3 per cent of those entering the church reached the rank of archdeacon at least, and for the law 9 per cent reached the rank of Q.C.

If Cheltenham and Clifton are any guide, then the new public schools followed the same pattern as the old, and the change in curriculum, so marked at school level, was not reflected in similar changes in the nature of the occupations. In the case of the army, the attraction seems to have been the social status involved; the non-classical sides were successful because the magnet of the army and similar targets were achieved more easily that way. The armed forces benefited at a technical level —we have enough evidence of that in the overspill from the forces into the inspectorates—but the benefit was not passed on generally to civilian society and industry. The country's needs, which Playfair and others were so concerned about, had obviously met with no response, and a career in science as such was not acceptable.

In the third category of public school in the nineteenth century, changes were taking place also. Here again, at the old grammar-school level, is the marked decline in products for the church and an increase in old boys going overseas. In an analysis of selected years from 1830 to 1885, both Sedbergh and Durham showed these features.[1] In addition, there was a dramatic increase in the number of boys who, between 1860 and 1880, chose business as a career, and this reflects the changes already seen at Harrow and Rugby. On the other hand, in contrast to the other public schools, they also showed a marked upward swing in the number of boys attracted to science and engineering late in the century. It is possible that this was connected with the reorganization under new schemes —the pressure of parents drawn from a different social class and the proximity of red-brick universities—but actual evidence

1. Selected details of the future occupations of boys entering Clifton, Durham and Sedbergh, in selected years are as shown at the foot of opposite page.

for this as an underlying cause is thin. A similar situation was to be seen at Manchester Grammar School, as we shall indicate later, and probably in other grammar schools.

General conclusions must be tentative. Public schools are notoriously individualistic, and the trends noted here are based on the few schools which have been investigated—none of them adequately from our point of view. It is possible to say, however, that in all three main varieties of public school—the seven, the new creations and the old grammar schools fighting for recognition—a common pattern emerges with individual variations. Church provision was everywhere on the decline. Science and engineering were almost ignored, except towards the end of the century (after 1870), and then limited to the reconstituted grammar schools, apart from the special case of the supply of technical officers to the armed forces. There was a marked increase in boys going overseas, and business gained rapidly in prestige in all schools, even those in the top bracket. Rather strangely, this last development occurred rather quickly with boys who entered during the 1860s, but again with inter-school variations. Of the other professions, the armed forces and the law continued to be popular, while the position of medicine varied considerably.

It is important to realize that there are subtle depths to these figures which can easily upset obvious conclusions. A decline in over-all contribution, for instance, does not necessarily mean

School	Year or years	Church	Business	Overseas	Science and Engineering
Clifton	1863	9	12	11	1
	1880	5	12	15	4
	1905	1	11	15	1
Durham	1840–4	28	4	3	0
	1855–9	12	5	10	2
	1880–4	11	30	17	19
Sedbergh	1830–5	22	4	6	0
	1855–9	11	16	4	1
	1880–5	5	61	26	14

(Compiled from the published registers of Sedbergh School, Durham School and Clifton College. The other categories shown in Table 12 have been omitted.)

that public-school influence declined as well. The church is a case in point. The evidence shows that the social pattern and recruitment within the church was changing rapidly, even if posts at top level were still largely restricted to public-school products. Indeed, this restriction persisted at least into the twentieth century. Out of eighty deans and bishops in 1927 who would have had their schooldays in Victorian times, only eight had been educated outside the public-school ranks, and no less than thirty-eight were educated at the 'fourteen principal schools'.[1] The public-school recruitment may have dwindled in mid-Victorian times, but it clearly remained important and dominant. This situation, though gratifying for the schools, was not healthy for the profession, and neither was the habit of translating headmasters directly to deaneries or the bench. This was already obvious in the last century, and commented upon by Clement Dukes:

> At the present time [1894] the highest rewards of the *clerical* profession . . . are usually bestowed upon those who have held the chief positions in the *scholastic* profession. It can scarcely be urged that this is either wise or just. It casts an undeserved slur upon the members of the clerical profession by the implicit assumption that it does not contain men with sufficient ability to occupy the highest posts . . . it tends to prevent able men entering the Church . . . and induces men to enter the teaching profession as a stepping stone to Church preferment. . . .[2]

Whether the elevation of headmasters and the decline in the contribution of the schools to the church are related is a matter that cannot be pursued here.

PROBLEMS OF QUANTITY AND QUALITY

It is clear from the example of the church alone that the value of public-school contributions to Victorian society depends on the relative accent placed on both quantity and quality. Quality exists at various subjective levels from the failure to the genius, and perhaps it would be simpler to consider the situation in science as a test-case.

Even though we can dismiss the contribution of public schools to Victorian science as a whole, it is still a fact that, among the

1. See R. H. Tawney, *Equality*, 1952, pp. 278–9.
2. Dukes, op. cit., p. 47.

few scientists the schools produced, there are one or two formidable names. Charles Darwin is a case in point.

Darwin was a product of pre-Victorian Shrewsbury, when Samuel Butler fed his boys on the classics and very little else, and certainly not on science. Yet Darwin's work came to shake the Victorian era in every aspect from religion to science, morals and social thinking. His work, in fact, was so significant, comparable in many ways to that of Galileo and Newton in previous eras, that Shrewsbury could well claim on the evidence of this one old boy alone that they made up in quality whatever may be lacking in quantity. The point at issue is therefore, how far could Samuel Butler, as headmaster of Shrewsbury, have claimed to have influenced Darwin so that his fame was a direct outcome of public-school education? Or alternatively, would Darwin have been the same figure had he not gone to Shrewsbury at all?

Samuel Butler would have been in no doubt about this. Although he died twenty years before the publication of *The Origin of Species* in 1859, Butler would have greeted the rise of Darwin into the ranks of immortality with some surprise, no doubt, but as confirmation of the fact that the classics were the best 'brain-sharpener' known. This view was widely held and must be taken seriously if only for the reason that Butler was certainly the most successful schoolmaster in terms of the quality of his examination successes that this country has ever known.[1] The secret behind this epic of teaching lay perhaps in the fact that Butler was not only a remarkable conveyor of enthusiasm and classical insight to some boys at least, but that he studied the market with infinite care. Whatever the reason, the curriculum was narrow and the results were outstanding in a narrow classical groove, and we now know from countless experiments that such an education does not necessarily indicate future quality. There is, in fact, no evidence whatever that the classics, or indeed any other single subject, is the long-sought-after

1. The examination successes of Shrewsbury under Butler and Kennedy can be judged from *The Honours Boards of Shrewsbury School*, 1806–1882. These results should, of course, be compared with the corresponding achievements of other schools, as given in their registers. The school which was supposed to rival Shrewsbury at one time—Rugby—did have excellent results, though centred on a different university, but they do not appear to have the unique quality of the other school, and neither, as far as is known, does any other establishment.

philosopher's stone of education. In any case, this argument would be irrelevant here, for Darwin was a late developer. His potential was not revealed at school at all. Either the classics had a very delayed action or the roots of his excellence lay elsewhere. Certainly he himself had no faith in the public-school panacea:

> Nothing could have been worse for the development of my mind than Doctor Butler's school. . . . When I left the school I was for my age neither high nor low in it; and I believe that I was considered by all my masters and by my Father as a very ordinary boy, rather below the common standard in intellect.[1]

There is little point in stretching the influence of the school in an attempt to explain Darwin's success, for he came from a scientifically eminent family with a grandfather, Erasmus, who had been a famous medical man with a poetical insight into the evolution of nature.[2] The same is largely true of other public-school men of science who achieved fame in the nineteenth century. The numbers of these are extremely few, as indicated in Chapter 5, and the difficulty in coming to any conclusion about them is in the impossibility of finding an unbiased list. For this reason it is, perhaps, as well to take a list of major English scientists from 1800 to 1866 (made for another purpose by George Haines)[3] in which public-school education was not even considered. This at least forms a convenient 'non-prejudiced' list to work on. Of all those reaching eminence in Victorian times, and born between 1828 and 1838, thirty-three names are given, and of these only four came from public boarding schools. Of the four, John Lubbock obtained his inspiration from Darwin himself, whom he happened to know when he was a child, while T. G. Bonney's enthusiasm came through his parents, and V. Harcourt was a product of a scientifically minded family. This only leaves one person unresolved—W. Dawkins—a product of Rossall. There is nothing here to show that scientific achievement owed anything to the public schools either as a whole or from the very few

1. C. Darwin, *Autobiography*, 1958, pp. 27–8.
2. The scientific spirit of Erasmus Darwin can be gathered from Anna Seward, *Memoirs of the Life of Dr Darwin*, etc., 1804; R. L. and Maria Edgeworth, *Memoirs of Richard Lovell Edgeworth, Esq.*, 2 vols., 1820; H. Pearson, *Dr Darwin*, 1943.
3. G. Haines, *German Influence upon English Education and Science, 1800–1866*, 1957.

individuals concerned. Darwin, indeed, may have been an outstanding old boy, but in owing little to his school in terms of his success in life he is not exceptional.

Similar instances can be seen elsewhere, and particularly in the field of literature. Did eminent Victorian authors owe anything to their education? Certainly an upbringing that involved a study of language was unimportant, for the major ones who have survived owed little to their schools and the classics. The women writers and Dickens are evidence of that. Even literary old boys of the seven present difficult problems. How can anyone argue, for instance, that Anthony Trollope owed anything to his stay at Harrow: 'The indignities I endured are not to be described. . . . I was allowed to join in no play. Nor did I learn anything—for I was taught nothing.' [1] Did this experience, or the equally obnoxious one of Lewis Carroll at Rugby,[2] go to form part of the character that made them successful men of letters? This is a vital question that covers the whole range of human endeavour, and is too important an issue to be dismissed by a few quotations. What is really needed is a full exploration of the education of men of genius from the public-school point of view before we can include their names as part of the schools' contribution to the nineteenth century.

A similar problem concerns those boys who acted in ways diametrically opposed to the policy and influence of their own public schools. It is no part of any school's job to produce rubber stamps, yet there are clearly limits to the amount of divergence that a school would acknowledge as the legitimate outcome of its teaching. What can be said, for instance, of the position of those who rejected the very religion that nurtured them? Sometimes there was a family conflict, too, as between Matthew Arnold and his father and the sons of two archbishop-headmasters who became Roman Catholics. Another instance comes from the Oxford Movement. How far could it be said that Hurrell Froude and Pusey were Etonian in outlook when their campaign was against the spirit of the school, and when

1. E. C. Mack, *Public Schools and British Opinion, 1760–1860*, 1938, p. 134, n. 3.
2. S. D. Collingwood, *The Life and Letters of Lewis Carroll*, 1898, p. 30. Similar quotations for other men could be multiplied almost indefinitely.

16

they were influenced so profoundly by Newman and Keble, who had never been to a public school at all? In any case, such men are exceptional. As special cases it is dangerous and difficult to draw conclusions from them. As F. H. Spencer put it:

> Neither Gladstone nor Wellington was great because he was an Etonian but because he was Gladstone or Wellington. Even the factor that enabled them to get an early start and to use opportunities was not a school advantage, but family wealth sufficient to enable them to emerge. . . . They, like Peel [of Harrow] and Salisbury [Eton] . . . glorified their schools, not vice versa.[1]

No one can seriously doubt this, and it is with lesser clay that we have to deal to present any profit-and-loss account, although why we should assume that the weaker brethren are more subject to school influence is another matter. What evidence is there, in fact, that a boy going to a Victorian public school obtained such an advantage by his education that he was able to defeat others in the struggle for recognition? Dr Hans attempted to answer this fundamental question by analysing the *Authors' Who's Who*, 1948 edition. The advantage of doing this lay in the fact that the selection of names had already been made by external agency and was to that extent less liable to prejudice, while the number of Victorian cases taken—975— ensured a very wide selection, including those well outside the first rank of genius besides the very few within it. It is of course a questionable assumption that a man who writes enough books to get his name included in this volume is fairly advanced in his profession, but at first sight this would appear reasonable. The results for those born before 1885 are classified by profession and are given in Table 16.

To take one example is probably the simplest way of realizing the significance of these results. We can show, for instance, that eighteen out of 102 medical men (as authors) were educated at the top nine schools. If this kind of talent were evenly distributed, it follows that these particular schools should have been producing between them about a fifth to a sixth of all the doctors in the country, whereas in fact, as we have seen, their contribution to the national medical pool was meagre. The same kind of remarks apply to the figures for science and

1. F. H. Spencer, *The Public School Question*, 1944, p. 20.

engineering. It follows that the small numbers actually produced contained a disproportionately high percentage of men writing books on their particular field. If we combine the main and the newer public schools together, then the contribution of them all is very striking indeed. Dr Hans sums it up in the following manner:

Table 16. *Education of authors born before 1885, and having a Victorian education.*[1]

Profession of author	9 Public schools	51 Independent schools	Other English schools	Schools elsewhere, private, etc.	Total
Clergy	30	61	58	27	176
Academic	57	106	108	90	361
Legal	17	15	8	8	48
Medical	18	41	20	23	102
Technical	34	49	28	18	129
Literary	45	36	20	13	114
Political	18	9	6	12	45
Total	219	317	248	191	975
Percentage	22·4	32·6	25·3	19·7	100

About 66 per cent of the leading members of all the liberal professions discussed in this article are alumni of sixty public schools represented at the Headmasters' Conference. . . . This position has remained stationary since the eighteenth century.[2]

There are three possible explanations for this dominance. The first assumes a superior natural ability in public schoolboys, the second a better training and the third involves social privilege. Dr Hans had no difficulty in dismissing the first two and coming to a definite conclusion that '. . . the main cause of the dominance of public school boys must be the socially and financially privileged position of their parents'.[3]

1. The material in this table comes from N. Hans, 'Independent Schools and the Liberal Professions', *Year Book of Education*, 1950, p. 224. See also N. Hans, *Educational Trends in the Eighteenth Century*, 1951.
2. Hans, 'Independent Schools', art. cit., p. 236.
3. ibid., p. 238.

F. H. Spencer came to much the same conclusion from different premises. A study of church development and church dignitaries discussed earlier also lends powerful support to this thesis, and we shall see further evidence on the same lines in the special cases of Parliament, the Empire and affairs at home.

The quality of the successful man is one of the great themes of life, and it cannot be pretended that our particular aspect of the problem is closed. Whereas public-school men do not seem to be represented in large numbers at the very top in science and its ancillaries, judging by their reputation as great scientists,[1] yet they are prominent in the wider field of 'science writing'.[2] The explanation may lie in criteria, or in the bias of a literary education, or perhaps in the possibility that public-school men tend to gravitate in unusual numbers to positions at the 'sub-top' level. The whole problem is complicated by the fact that any assumptions of common properties concerning the nature of the 'top' in any occupation are probably false. The top scientist or artist is a creative person in a specialized field and not essentially a writer or administrator, while the properties of a top man in the church, as identified in bishops and archbishops, are different again. The creative person is likely to be a rarer phenomenon than the man of success reckoned as a holder of office. Thus, there must be a new archbishop whenever one dies; there need not be a scientist or artist or musician of equivalent creative ability to replace another. Such a person does not necessarily wield power in the positive sense of a politician or a trade-union leader. He does not form part of an *élite* in the usual sense of that word, and may often stand alone or even be unknown. In the similar case of poetry, how should the schools be judged—by poets who found fame in their lifetime, and oblivion thereafter (in many cases), or by those like Gerard Manley Hopkins, who found fame only after death?

Altogether, it seems fair to conclude that the contribution of public schools to Victorian professional life was, in a few cases like engineering and science, both negligible and significant— negligible in overall numbers, but significant in men towards

1. Haines, op. cit.
2. Hans, op. cit.

the top. Moreover, where the study of a subject like science was not exactly encouraged in any school, it seems obvious that schooling had little to do with this phenomenon. The particular case of science was a most serious matter since England relied on its industry and trade, both of which rested ultimately on scientific 'know-how'. English backwardness in academic science was notorious. In the early years of the century we appear to have relied on Scottish talent, while in the Victorian period the gap created by new developments, particularly in chemistry, were made up by some of our men going overseas for their education, especially to Germany, and by the employment of August Hofmann in the Royal College of Chemistry in England. Neither the public schools nor Oxford or Cambridge encouraged these studies, and yet these were major institutions, which could have given a lead and lent an air of respectability to such new developments. From many aspects this neglect bore the stamp of irresponsibility.

PUBLIC SCHOOLS AND PARLIAMENT

For at least a hundred years before the advent of Victoria a large number of the men who formed policy at the highest level had been old boys of the seven. About one Member of Parliament in five at the general election of 1734 came from this source, and this proportion had increased to almost half the House at the general election of 1830. Of all the 5,034 M.P.s in the century from 1734 to the Reform Bill of 1832: '. . . 1,714, or about a third had gone to one or more of the seven English public schools of the old régime: Charterhouse, Eton, Harrow, Rugby, Shrewsbury, Westminster and Winchester'.[1]

The high proportion of public-school men in the House to be found at the accession of Queen Victoria was constant throughout her reign and into the twentieth century, although the exclusiveness of the seven diminished with the advent of new schools. Even in the period 1918–35, 43 per cent of M.P.s had attended a public school, though by 1945 this had fallen to under 30 per cent.[2]

1. G. P. Judd, *Members of Parliament, 1734–1832*, 1955, p. 37.
2. For other information about M.P.s, etc., see ibid, p. 37, n. 6, and pp. 37–8.

Eton had been the dominant school. In the long view, Old Etonians comprised over a quarter of the Cabinet from 1801 to 1924, and even today they are still prominent, with a tenth of the members elected in both 1945 and 1950. The last three Conservative prime ministers have been Old Etonians, and the products of this school have dominated the topmost position of all, in spite of a gap of fifty years from Campbell Bannerman to Attlee.

The English Cabinet system ensures that power is held in a few hands, and some would argue that real political power at any one time is limited to a mere handful of people. Until the 1860s Cabinets were essentially aristocratic, with the House of Lords well represented and sometimes in a majority, as under Peel and Russell. After the second Reform Bill of 1868 the landowning section began to lose its ascendency, and some Cabinet posts went to professional people and others, particularly in the Liberal party. By the end of the century this new type of politician had come to positions of power within that party at the expense of the landowners, including such names as Herbert Asquith, Lloyd George, R. B. Haldane, Augustine Birrell, while aristocrats still maintained their hold over the Conservatives (see Table 17).[1]

In the aristocratic form of political leadership there has always been a tendency to convert part of the influential group into a family group, a tendency which Peel resisted, but which is shown particularly well in the Cabinets of Lord Grey and Lord Salisbury in the last century, and in our own day in the cases of Churchill and Macmillan.

The advent of the Labour party and the eclipse of the Liberals in the present century has brought more men from the lower classes into Parliament, and has eliminated, on that side at least, any undue influence of family and aristocracy. In spite of this fact 'upper-class education' within the Labour party is significant and has grown rapidly, particularly at the top.[2] A famous case was the Wykehamist quintet of Sir Stafford Cripps, Hugh Gaitskell, Richard Crossman, Kenneth Younger

1. For the general background to politics and public schools, see W. L. Guttsman, *The British Political Élite*, 1963.
2. For an analysis of a recent House of Commons, see H. B. Berrington and S. E. Finer, 'The British House of Commons', *International Social Science Journal*, xiii, 1961, pp. 600–19.

and Douglas Jay,[1] while: 'Of those who sat in MacDonald's Cabinet, only four were public-school products. Among Mr Attlee's 34 colleagues, 11 passed through these institutions.'[2]

Taking a broad view, public-school education from 1918 to 1955 has been persistently dominant in the Conservative party and significant in the Labour party, as is shown in Figure 4.

Around the hub of Parliament and the ministries are a constellation of select bodies whose duty it is to advise and

Table 17. *Class structure of cabinets, 1868–1955, according to party.*[3]

	1868–86 Con. Lib.		1886–1916 Con. Lib.		1916–35 Con. Lab.		1935–55 Con. Lab.		1868–1955 Con. Lib. Lab.		
Aristocracy	13	15	26	23	19	3	20	1	60	32	4
Middle class	8	14	21	28	33	12	40	14	86	54	25
Working class	–	–	–	2	1	19	2	19	3	3	36
Total	21	29	47	53	53	34	62	34	149	89	65

(This breakdown concentrates on the two major governmental parties. It leaves out one Labour Cabinet Minister for the period 1886–1916 and all Liberal Ministers since 1916. Owing to the fact that nine Ministers sat in Cabinets of two different parties the total for the three parties adds up to 303, not 294.)

conduct the affairs of various governmental agencies. Guttsman investigated three such groups: the governors of cultural organizations; members of scientific and industrial councils; membership of Royal Commissions and chairmen of committees.

Among the 339 persons in the three groups of the influential here analysed, 151, or 45 per cent, had received their pre-university education in public boarding schools—two thirds of them in the

1. There are Wykehamist parallels to the quintet in politics, as in the contribution to educational administration at an earlier period of Robert Morant, H. A. L. Fisher and Selby Bigge.
2. Guttsman, op. cit., p. 96.
3. From Guttsman, op. cit., p. 79.

232 *Rise of the Public Schools*

twenty major public schools specially investigated. Almost the same number (154) were educated at Oxford and Cambridge.[1]

Here again we see a reflection of Hans's studies for influential men in earlier times—the over-representation of people with a particular kind of schooling, and the corresponding dangerous generalization that the way to the top lies through a particular kind of school, the more exclusive the better:

There exists today in Britain [1963] a 'ruling class', if we mean by it a group which provides the majority of those who occupy positions of power, and who, in their turn, can materially assist *their* sons to reach similar positions.[2]

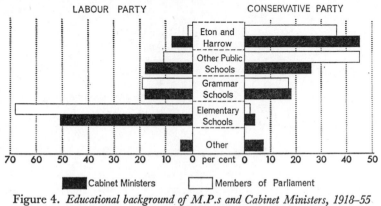

Figure 4. *Educational background of M.P.s and Cabinet Ministers, 1918–55 (after Guttsman)*[3]

The fact that the independent boarding schools produce 30 to 40 per cent of the ruling class, in Guttsman's definition, can hardly be doubted. Such an *élite* is not necessarily undesirable, and the mechanics of government and business, coupled with human psychology, appear to make an *élite* system inevitable. What is really doubtful is whether *élites* of our kind have worked in the true interests of democracy, as we know it, and whether special roads of entry to such *élites*—whether public schools, Oxford and Cambridge, family influence—are not denials of justice, and therefore not to be tolerated. These are key questions which partly lie outside our scope. As for the attitudes of public-school products, it should be remembered that they were not and are not men of one mind, and do not in fact form

1. ibid., p. 354.
2. ibid., p. 356.
3. ibid., p. 76.

a solid phalanx against the rest of the world, protecting their own class exclusively. What in fact had the first Victorian prime minister, Lord Melbourne, got in common with the second, Sir Robert Peel, the one a product of Eton and the other of Harrow? Or either of them with Gladstone (Eton)? Certainly there was a common background, and common views on some forms of education, but that was all. This common ground may have been slim, and they may have held divergent views on welfare and reform, if not on progress, but over the fundamental place of the public schools they were united.

The field of education remains a vital sector of administration at Ministry level since it can affect not only the upbringing and chances of the ordinary man, but the very existence of the public schools as well. Some acquaintance with the central power in education is, therefore, of interest to us here apart from the impressions that a closer look at one specific ministry might add to our understanding. We shall also have to stray a little outside the Victorian era for the sake of continuity.

Apart from the Cabinet as a whole, the responsibility for state education and reform rested, and still rests, with prime ministers, the political heads of the education office and the permanent secretaries. The state first entered the educational field in a major and direct way in 1870 with the Elementary Education Act of that year, and the educational background of these men at the educational summit since that date is of some interest. The general picture is shown in Table 18.

Only five prime ministers have been educated outside the public schools—Disraeli, Campbell-Bannerman, Lloyd George, Bonar Law, Ramsay MacDonald—and four of these were brought up outside England where the public-school tradition hardly exists. Old Etonians have dominated the beginning and the end of the series, separated by a fallow period of fifty years from Campbell-Bannerman to Attlee. Rather surprisingly, five of the six Etonians were Oxford men, and this in itself suggests the importance of influence rather than education.

Of the forty-three politicians at the head of the educational service, only seven had attended a state school and therefore had any contact with the state system in their formative years— W. Runciman, Sir John Gorst, Sir D. Maclean, A. J. Mundella, A. Henderson, Ellen Wilkinson and George Tomlinson—

Table 18. *The education of the seventy leading figures in the administration of education, 1870–1963.*[1]

	School education				
	Eton	Other major public schools	Minor public schools	English state schools	Wales and Scotland. Private schools
Prime ministers	6	4	1	0	5
Political heads of education	8	17	5	7	6
Permanent secretaries	2	5	2	0	2
Totals	16	26	8	7	13

	Post-school education				
	Oxford	Cambridge	Other universities	Professional	None
Prime ministers	7	3	1	3	2
Political heads of education	18	12	2	3	8
Permanent secretaries	11	0	0	0	0
Totals	36	15	3	6	10

and only in the last four cases was their experience below the grammar-school level. Only Mundella, Henderson and Tomlinson had their experience solely in lower-class schools, without the ameliorating influence of the grammar school or

1. Information from many sources. Political heads=Lord Presidents of the Council, Vice-Presidents, Presidents of the Board of Education, Ministers. Other major public schools: Harrow, Westminster, Winchester, Rugby, Shrewsbury, Haileybury, Marlborough, Uppingham, Wellington. (Omitted: Lord E. Percy.)

university. If this situation appears to be anomalous on the political side, it is even more significant at the level of permanent secretary. Apart from the very first two permanent secretaries in our series, who were Scots, the rest have been products of public schools and Oxford. It is clear that those who have directed the national system of education, both in Parliament and outside, have been drawn overwhelmingly from a public-school background.

It could be argued that these educational facts are irrelevant, that it is the job of the administrator to administer, and that it makes little difference whether the 'material' to be administered is defence, or coal or a colony. Education is, however, different to the extent that we are all cradled by our own experiences and loyalties. These experiences form a framework of personal reference which becomes important in a situation where particularly trenchant reform would certainly involve the welfare of one's own old school. Moreover, the independent schools (as represented by the public schools) were outside the system of state help, and to that extent in competition with it, while the men who ran the national system were not only aloof in terms of their own experience, but were not even involved at second hand since they did not even send their sons to the schools they administered. This is a contradictory situation which provides a constantly recurring theme for study.

The figures already given suggest that successive governments have insisted on public-school men being in charge of the education of the common, non-public-school man. Since the only real threat to public-school existence is administrative and political, the only conclusion that seems reasonable is that the whole background of men at top level was, and still is, favourable to public-school existence and ideals. As a corollary, it is not surprising that they looked at their responsibility for lower- and middle-class education through public-school eyes. On some questions this perhaps did not matter, and might even have been an asset on the criteria of excellence, but there arose at the end of the nineteenth century a problem which affected the whole future of state education in its elementary and secondary phases, and about which decisions had to be made.[1]

1. The magnitude and nature of these fateful decisions will be considered in the specific context of education on pp. 259–61.

Another striking fact more difficult to interpret concerns the subsequent careers of top men linked with education. In 1894 Lord Rosebery combined the posts of prime minister and lord president of the council, and this is the only instance of any politician directly responsible for education who also occupied the position of head of government at any time in his career. Even that case is exceptional, for it could be argued that the lord president was less concerned with education than the vice-president. There have been near-misses, as in the cases of the Duke of Devonshire and R. A. Butler, but that is all. If the post of First Lord of the Treasury represents the political goal of any ambitious man, then all forty-four holders of high educational office since 1870 have failed to reach it. It is a remarkable record, and it seems a fair inference that the way to political heights has not up to now lain through education—indeed, experience of it might be a hindrance. Certainly the reputations of many promising men like Birrell, or Runciman or even Arthur Balfour were tarnished by their educational experience.

PUBLIC SCHOOLS AND THE EMPIRE

One aspect of a top *élite* concerns their luxurious and particular style of living, for therein lie the doubts of many of their ability to appreciate other standards of culture both within and outside our society, or to understand the underlying needs of squalor and poverty. It is often assumed that this aloofness and style are inevitable consequences of life at the top and are indeed a necessary part of it. In a similar way, there is a traditional argument that men holding supreme power, or representing directly supreme power overseas, should have some of the trappings of this power, and should, at least, possess the style of men of the highest class if they are to inspire confidence. Lord Strang has made out a strong case for the aristocratic Diplomatic Service of the past on these very grounds.

So long as the conduct of foreign affairs in most countries remained the preserve of social oligarchies with an acute sense of class—and this was so till the early years of the twentieth century—there were compelling reasons for choosing candidates for the diplomatic career from the most intelligent members of a restricted social

stratum, however regrettable the class system itself might be. When, however, class prejudice ceased to dominate the pattern of international life, the methods of selection for the British Diplomatic Service could be, and were, gradually changed to the extent allowed by the continuing need for academic qualifications. By the end of the first world war what used to be known as 'birth' had ceased to be a criterion for the selection of entrants; and so had wealth in itself. . . . It was no longer required of a candidate that he should possess private means . . . but the field was still restricted by the fact that [university] scholarships were confined for the most part to private endowment. As state aid for education developed, the entrance doors . . . could be opened still wider, and were. But the process was necessarily gradual and has not yet [1955] been completed.[1]

For the period of high empire it is difficult to refute this argument. A Victorian viceroy, for instance, was in competition with some of the richest men in the world, many of them well acquainted with western standards and way of life. This explains perhaps why so many chosen for this task of government formed a close community with kinship in rich, influential and aristocratic groups.[2] A celebrated case is that of the Elgin–Grey– Halifax–Baring–Sydenham families, which contained no less than eight men of viceroy rank, besides a host of lesser men holding important posts overseas and others in Cabinets at home with special responsibility for colonial affairs. With space, the kinship relationships shown in Family Linkage 6 could easily have been continued into most families of note, and including other men of high standing. The strength of an aristocratic appointment lay in the fact that the viceroy represented in India a projection of a family web which comprised a power group in its own right, with relations in every *élite* group in England that mattered—politics, the armed forces, wealth, commerce—as Family Linkage 6 amply shows. Their power came indeed not so much from their own ability as from their intimate contacts. They were on personal, Christian-name terms with the centre of power, and there was no lack of support at home to look after their interests.

1. Lord Strang, *The Foreign Office*, 1955, p. 72.
2. For appointment in some posts overseas money was quite as important as the status of wife and relations. Lack of it was certainly a handicap. It is well known that men for the Diplomatic Service before the First World War had to possess a private income; £400 is said to have been the minimum in 1918. See R. Wilkinson, *The Prefects*, 1964, pp. 23–4.

As in the Cabinet problems discussed earlier there appears to be a strong link at times with the public schools. This applied particularly to the Elgins, Halifaxes and Greys. Such links are absent, however, or at least are not apparent, in the Baring–Sydenham examples, where the background of banking had not the same landowning values. Even the key figure of the second

Family Linkage 6. *Family Relationships of Some Overseas Governors.*[1]

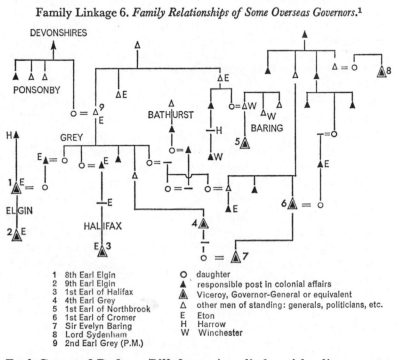

1	8th Earl Elgin	O	daughter
2	9th Earl Elgin	▲	responsible post in colonial affairs
3	1st Earl of Halifax	⬟	Viceroy, Governor-General or equivalent
4	4th Earl Grey	△	other men of standing: generals, politicians, etc.
5	1st Earl of Northbrook	E	Eton
6	1st Earl of Cromer	H	Harrow
7	Sir Evelyn Baring	W	Winchester
8	Lord Sydenham		
9	2nd Earl Grey (P.M.)		

Earl Grey, of Reform Bill fame, is a little misleading as presented here and in similar pedigrees. He married a Ponsonby and had thirteen children, eight of them sons without obvious allegiance to public schools. It is, indeed, through three of his daughters that the real cohesion of this extraordinary 'colonial' family tree depends. The same mixture of public-school and non-public-school background, seen in Family Linkage 6, is also to be seen in a summary of men at the apex of the Indian situation:

1. Some of the possibilities of extending this linkage may be seen from the relationships shown in the charts between pp. 34–5 of Sampson, *Anatomy of Britain,* op. cit.

One hundred years divided the Marquis Wellesley as Governor General from Lord Curzon as Viceroy 1798–1898. Omitting the 'officiating' Governors, there have been in that period of time twenty-two Governors General and Viceroys. Of these, nine have been Etonians—Lords Wellesley, Cornwallis, Ellenborough, Canning, Elgin (father and son), Dufferin, Lansdowne and Curzon. Of these Cornwallis alone filled the posts of Viceroy of Ireland and Governor General, while Lords Dufferin and Lansdowne have filled those of Viceroy of India and Governor General of Canada. Another Old Etonian, Sir Charles Metcalfe, acted as 'officiating' Governor General of India and was subsequently appointed Governor General of Canada. . . . Of the remaining thirteen Satraps of India, three were Old Harrovians, two (Lord Amherst and Lord William Bentinck) were Old Westminsters, one (Lawrence) came from the East India College of Haileybury, and eight from private schools or tutors.[1]

Looking at the men at top level overseas, there is, therefore, some reason for suggesting that here public-school influence is illusory. Of all the important factors—ability, school, university, wealth, family—we should be inclined to ascribe appointment at the highest level in government circles to those suggested by Lord Strang—ability, wealth and family—making experience of an aristocratic style of living important and essential within the context of the nineteenth century. Opportunities for governing at this level have diminished with the dissolution of the Empire, but it is possible that education—particularly university education—would have become more important as a factor in elevation with the change in *élite* social structure both at home and abroad.

A somewhat similar case to the rulers of empire abroad is found in the rulers of commercial empires at home, and it is no coincidence that these two were interlinked, as the Baring family relationships and the East India Company activities would indicate. Here again, T. Lupton and C. S. Wilson have shown that the decision-makers (the directors) in banking and big business still rely on the informal relationships that spring from a shared social background.[2] In practice, this means a way of life associated with the rich, with public schools, with the old universities, and especially with prominent kinship. There is no

1. Minchin, op. cit., pp. 107–8.
2. For banking and big business, see T. Lupton and C. S. Wilson, 'The Social Background and Connections of "Top Decision Makers" ', *Manchester School of Economics and Social Studies*, xxviii, 1959, pp. 30–51.

reason to suppose that this was not the situation in the last century. There is no doubt that both the quality of education and the quality of the kinship are important.

Viceroys and governors were men filling a hierarchical niche, becoming almost equivalent in stature to Gladstone, Peel and similar figures. If not world famous in their own right, they were at least on the fringe of fame, though it should be remembered that even this is largely a question of relative viewpoint. Modern histories of India, for instance, written from the Indian standpoint, are apt to be divided into chapters headed 'Cornwallis', 'Bentinck', 'Metcalfe', 'Dalhousie' . . .,[1] and through Indian eyes these men are far more significant than Peel and the others at home. In any event, these men were exceptional, and it is with lesser men of empire that we must deal to discover the real influence which the public schools had.

The expansion and consolidation of the Empire created a need to staff it with soldiers, administrators and professional men of all kinds. The cream was the Indian Civil Service. Until 1919 these men wielded immense power, and it can be said quite simply that they were both the government of the country and its administrative Civil Service.[2] For this work the public schools have taken the credit, and headmasters have frequently boasted about it. They regarded their success as beyond dispute and attributed it to their method of stressing intellectual ability (in classical terms) as a criterion for entering the sixth and to the opportunities given to the prefects for handling boys. This sense of achievement was felt not only in the main boarding schools, but also with lesser brethren of the day variety, as in this statement by the headmaster of University College School: 'The public schools pride themselves on fostering these qualities (of enterprise and the spirit of adventure) and claim that it is they who, if they did not make the Empire (for most of them

1. These histories of India are those published in India for Indian readers and for Indian education. The visitor to both India and Pakistan is faced on every hand with the legacy of Englishmen as major figures whose memory is dimmed in this country by names more notable in British history. This presents a readjustment of thinking which is an outstanding educational experience. It has ramifications into the importance of opportunity and the size of the national pool of ability.
2. See J. Coatman, in *The British Civil Servant*, edited by W. A. Robson, p. 209, *et. seq.*

were hardly in existence when the Empire was made), at least maintain and administer it through their members.' [1]

The situation, however, was far from simple. For the Victorian era it is hardly too much to say that the real preparation for entry into the Overseas Service began after schooldays had finished, and that success in the examination depended on the polish acquired elsewhere: 'As evidence of the inappropriateness of our public school education for contact with the world, I would ask, How many of our first-grade schools are capable of passing boys into Woolwich, Sandhurst, Cooper's Hill, or the English and Indian Civil Services, without their intermediate passage through the hands of a "crammer"?' [2]

It would be novel, to say the least, to place the credit for the good selection of overseas administrators, and the whole business and glory of empire, directly on to the crammers. Although their contribution has not yet been recognized and really warrants more than a passing reference, there are other difficulties in accepting the claims of the public schools without reservation.

The Empire was at no time the homogeneous mass of countries that a glance at the red areas in Victorian and Edwardian atlases might lead us to believe. The similarities, for instance, of Uganda, India, Jamaica and Australia were, and still are, far less than their differences. It would be strange, indeed, if public-school influence had been uniform over such a disparate assembly, and the very qualities which may have helped to achieve temporary stability in some areas were anathema in others. In the new 'white' regions the public-school man was unwanted, ridiculed, even rejected. This was common knowledge, and was emphasized by H. B. Gray,[3] a man of immense experience both at home and abroad: '. . . the English boy, as he emerges from the crucible of the public-school laboratory, is generally a more conspicuous failure—especially at first—in

1. G. Kendall, *A Headmaster Reflects*, 1937, p. 218. A further extract, which perhaps, stresses the school aspect more precisely, is to be found in A. A. David, *Life and the Public Schools*, 1932, p. 145.
2. Dukes, op. cit.
3. He went to Winchester and Oxford and was on the staff at Westminster. He was headmaster of Louth Grammar School, chairman of the Council, warden and headmaster of Bradfield College from 1880 to 1910. He was a member of Commissions to the U.S.A. and in Canada. He was also intimately involved with the British Association.

17

those new and partially discovered Continents [Australia and Canada], than he has proved himself to be a conspicuous success in dealing with lower or more submissive races in the wilds of Africa or in the plains of India.' [1]

There were, then, two sides of empire at least. The more stable and successful (white) part developed without public-school help; the other side varied from the simple and primitive life of isolated tribes to the mountains and forests of India with a time-depth of civilization making Europeans appear brash and newly rich. The penetration and understanding of this new culture fascinated many an eighteenth-century Englishman, and since that period there has been the continual exploration, preservation and recording of antiquities and natural resources which is one of the main contributions of Britain to the modern Indian sub-continent. How far public-school products were directly responsible for this is unknown, but there is no good reason to suppose that it is great, or indeed that they contributed in any significant way to the industrialization which took place throughout the nineteenth and twentieth centuries.

The Indian scene is complicated by changes in attitude and environment over the last two hundred years, brought about by changes in science, industry and commerce in Europe. The Englishman before the Mutiny had to settle down in India and consider it a life-time job, but afterwards the developments of faster travel, telegraphy and the cutting of the Suez Canal made it possible for him to keep one eye on home. The new western developments had profound effects. In the words of Amaury de Riencourt:

> This technological development had two important consequences: the growth of administrative and political centralization and the development of a growing barrier between colonizers and colonized . . . the former independence of the colonial proconsuls, on whose political acumen, judgement and strength of character the safety of the imperial possession depended was progressively curtailed. Viceroys and governors became messenger boys. . . . The gulf between white and coloured races was great enough in the old days, but it was more the perennial gulf between conqueror and conquered than that between two entirely different species increasingly separated by the growth of industrial technological knowledge and facilities. Modernization made it easier for the Europeans to import

1. H. B. Gray, *The Public Schools and the Empire*, 1913, p. 30.

their own style of life to Asia than to adapt themselves to local customs as their predecessors had in the old days.[1]

In other words, public-school products in high office in London were limiting the power of their brethren in the field. This was virtually a clash of responsibility, and the same problem was seen in the coolness, even enmity, that developed between the administrator on the spot and the local army men responsible for peace and frontier (if not for conquest). The same clash was to be seen in the officers of the English and Indian Armies in the Crimea. The public-school bond was only relative, and it would appear that in some cases the social rank and responsibility given by one's own individual consignment of power was superior to school loyalty.

There was a significant difference in the social content of the English and Indian Army officer, though both showed an influx of landed gentry at the end of the eighteenth and the beginning of the nineteenth centuries which remained at approximately a third of the intake for the home army until the First World War. There is no doubt that many in the officer ranks of both armies came from the public schools, with different records for each school, as we have already seen, and for some at least, service in India was unpopular.[2] There has also been a change with time, as shown by the fact that the catchment area for the home force has widened in recent years: '. . . in 1891, 55 well-known public schools and universities supplied the total of 373 cadets [at Sandhurst], whereas by 1961 roughly twice as many cadets came from nearly six times as many schools [308] . . .'. [3]

The number going into the Indian Army from Cheltenham (Table 15) indicates that the public-school contribution was large for this kind of school, and relatively greater than the contribution from other types of school, like Rugby, Harrow and Durham. It was supposed that the public-school character was something special, and that it gave to the Indian Civil Service and army overseas a trustworthy and unifying core that worked for the benefit of self, Britain and the Empire. Such a suggestion had its seeds in the games and rough-and-tumble of

1. A. de Riencourt, *The Soul of India*, 1961, pp. 218–19.
2. For information about the army, see P. E. Razzell, 'Social Origins of Officers in the Indian and British Home Army', *British Journal of Sociology*, xiv, no. 3, 1963, pp. 248–60.
3. ibid., p. 259.

Tom Brown, was developed in the *Boys' Own Paper* and then stylized by G. A. Henty among many others: 'The young reader was enabled to identify himself with a hero who might accompany *Moore to Corunna, Wolfe to Canada*, might go *With Roberts to Pretoria*, or *With Kitchener to the Soudan*, and win his imperial spurs with them all.' [1]

This was not entirely romantic fiction: 'A view of the record of additions to the Empire in the last 20 years of the nineteenth century shows that the subaltern had ample occasion for the exercise of his skills.' [2]

There was, however, a distinct difference in viewpoint between the military man of action and the civilian ruler-administrator, in spite of their common education. Perhaps it is a little naïve to suggest that this conflict was a reflection of the tensions within each school between the classical and modern sides that were such a notable feature of the late nineteenth and early twentieth-century scene. At the same time the entry regulations for the Civil Service and army do suggest that different kinds of career did develop from the different sides, were indeed designed for that purpose, and that they did correspond to different ideals within the schools.

A complicating factor for both the overseas civil servant and army officer was the changing attitude to empire at home. The acquisition and retention of this vast collection of countries was in many ways brought about reluctantly and in the teeth of much criticism. Many people, like Cobden, had great reservations on the desirability of the whole operation.[3] However, with the Mutiny and the 1860s the complaints virtually disappeared, since disengagement had ceased to be a practical proposition. No one could contemplate withdrawal with the consequences of civil war, if not barbarism, which might ensue. Moreover, many on the left disliked the very idea of the parochial nationalism of small nations.[4] British rule appeared to be the only immediate guarantee of good rule, and the future hand-over of India and the colonies could only be achieved after

1. A. P. Thornton, *The Imperial Idea and its Enemies*, 1959, pp. 92–3.
2. ibid., p. 95.
3. Other anti-imperialists included Goldwin Smith. For a brief survey, see G. D. H. Cole and R. Postgate, *The Common People, 1746–1946*, fourth edition, p. 366.
4. E. Halévy, *Imperialism and the Rise of Labour*, 1951, p. 105.

sustained tutelage under British occupation. In this light, Britain was the conveyor of the benefits of European civilization, and our residents in India and elsewhere were agents towards this end. This was the period of high empire which coincided with the great period of public-school growth, and the two events are not entirely unconnected. The problem is really whether the two agents—the public-school civil servant and the army staffed by so many public-school products—were satisfactory for the purposes of handover.

The overwhelming impression from contemporary memoirs is of the British Raj, polo and the like, with civil servants a kind of well-paid set of secular missionaries combining 'a competent and industrious official career with a modicum of pleasure in the way of pig-sticking, shooting and fishing'. [1] Their life was magnificent and ideally suited to the gentry-administrative grade of civil servant, and yet slow reform of the kind needed in this situation was alien both to his duty and to his background, and indeed alien to the whole spirit of British administration. [2]

Until 1854 vacancies were filled by nomination and replaced thereafter by competition in which the crammer played a significant part. Writing in 1937, Sir Edward Blunt commented:

> It is often argued that though appointment by competition may provide India with more brilliant servants, yet appointment by nomination secured for her more devoted servants, because the nominees mostly came from families with old traditions of Indian service. But there are, in fact, still many civil servants in India who come from such families. [3]

Against the long Victorian background the results achieved by these men appeared to be solid and everlasting, but the inevitability of it all was rudely shaken by the Boer War, and the impressiveness slowly wilted under growing criticism at home and rising nationalism abroad. The basis of these complaints amounted to the fact that Britain, through her administrators, gave the non-white parts of the Empire peace, law, health and stability—everything except responsibility, social equality and social evolution, not to say revolution. Whether

1. Wainwright, op. cit., p. 184.
2. See C. H. Sisson, *The Spirit of British Administration and Some European Comparisons*, 1959. This is discussed in detail later.
3. Sir Edward Blunt, *The I.C.S.*, 1937, p. 46.

such a revision of policy was possible within the spirit of permanency that existed is not our direct concern, but it does appear, in hindsight, that there was much truth in these criticisms. The public schools, however, were only one factor in the situation, and how much of the blame can be placed on them, how much on family standards and universities, how much on politics, on the accidental development of science, on local patriotism, and how much on plain inertia is a matter of opinion. The point here is that the public schools can hardly claim the credit for running the Empire without accepting some of the blame for the acute problems attending its dissolution.

Some men diagnosed the disease as the erroneous view taken of administrative responsibility, and that it was the duty of the men on the spot to reflect new developments and trends. Writing in 1929, Michael Sadler put it like this: 'The upper middle class, or middle class, Englishmen of whom the Treasury official and the magnates of the Indian Civil Service are typical have shown during the last thirty years a mulish inability to transmit the life of the educational and social tradition which bred them.' [1] Sadler regarded this as the end of a social order leading those who followed it blindly to extinction. Such conservatism may have been magnificent in its day, but these people suffered from great limitations which stood out gauntly 'against the subtle Indian scene and in rooms at the Treasury where the rising champions of social change make financial demands'.[2] Perhaps the reasons in India and England for what was in appearance the same malaise were different, but fundamentally they concerned the same group of people.

In India one loses touch with a good deal of what is going on in England, especially if it is reported in newspapers or in reviews. And left wing books and novels and poetry are not the favourite reading of European officials in their Indian clubs. But why have the middle class and upper middle class who stayed in England been only half awake to the signs of the times? Partly because they have been comfortable. Comfortable, and meritoriously busy.[3]

1. M. Sadler, 'The Philosophy Underlying the System of Education in England (I)', *Educational Year Book of the International Institute of Teachers' College*, Columbia University, 1929, pp. 25–7.
2. ibid.
3. ibid.

That is how one of the great minds of education saw this problem, and that is undoubtedly somewhere near the truth for the non-white parts of the Empire. The administrative officers overseas were not suited to a rapidly changing situation that was already apparent at home and to which their education was not attuned. Their upbringing almost denied the value of science, engineering and industry, on which the strength of the West really rested. Whether any other selection of men—from research perhaps, or maybe Hofmann's pupils in the last century—would have done better is doubtful, except that these were presumably involved with the doctrine of change rather than with the myth of permanency. Leaving aside the interesting but fruitless game of 'might have been', the open-competition system ensured that administrative branches overseas were recruited widely from private students or Durham as well as from Harrow or Eton. For interpretation we have to be certain that the public-school ideal, whatever that might be, was constant and ensured that school influence not only persisted into adult life, but also influenced colleagues educated outside.

There is both profit and loss to be counted into the final reckoning, and it is significant that other continental countries without public schools have had equivalent problems of empire and even less success in solving them, judging by the aftermath. Altogether, the Victorian achievement overseas, as carried out by high-ranking administrators, was magnificent viewed superficially and in the podesta sense, but it was also self-satisfied and self-centred, and thereby nurtured all the seeds of disaster.

Apart from its governmental aspects, the Empire also became the arena for free enterprise in the development of plantations and the creation of business interests. The public schools were certainly involved in this phase of overseas development, but its nature and extent is not so narrowly defined as the Civil Service and an adequate consideration cannot be given at this stage.

There is one final word to be said. The overseas visitor cannot fail to be struck by the faith in the English public-school system that exists today at top level in the Indian sub-continent. The boarding schools deliberately set up by the British Raj long ago were not scrapped at independence and partition. Rather they were strengthened both in numbers and influence. An Indian.

Headmasters' Conference flourishes. These boarding schools are now being used by their respective governments in the hope of raising an *élite* for their rapidly developing society, based on a democratically selected intake into the schools. To judge by English experience these schemes have a fair chance of success, though whether the cohesive spirit produced by boarding is better achieved at the school level or at the university or polytechnic later is another matter. In spite of this, it could indeed be claimed, independently of the past, that the public schools themselves have succeeded in at least convincing two new nations of their worth. It is one of the more striking and lasting influences of Britain on India.

PUBLIC SCHOOLS, REFORM AND WELFARE[1]

A feature of Victorian Britain was the fight of the lower classes for the recognition of their rights, brought about mainly by agitation and joint action in trade unions. Both methods were universally condemned by headmasters. Arnold was the only one to be vitally concerned with wide social issues and willing to sacrifice himself as a champion of lower-class rights; he had plans for a guided social revolution, but he died before he could come to grips with a massive attempt to solve the problem. Arnold was unique; both Temple and Percival, who emulated his example to some extent, were pale shadows beside him, and as far as we know, with the exception perhaps of G. Butler, other scholastics ignored his example altogether and kept their gaze within their own environment. Social evils, agitation and unrest forced a good deal of reform on to various governments, and these measures were unpopular with large sections of the community, and especially with the gentry and aristocracy providing the core of the major schools' clientele.

Outside Parliament, where policy was carried into effect, the Ministers of the Crown had to work with men whom they could trust and understand. It has already been shown that the Cabinet was drawn largely from public-school men, and it is not surprising that those in power chose many fellow old boys for the top jobs of the Civil Service, or that posts in the old departments went more by patronage and political favour than

1. For the background of social reform, see D. Roberts, *Victorian Origins of the British Welfare State*, 1960.

by merit.[1] Whereas this remained a possibility for administrative posts where personal relations were regarded as all-important—provided they were coupled with an alert mind and character as measured by personal recommendation or a university degree—the same general qualities were not enough for posts requiring technical knowledge.

The Victorian era saw the rapid growth of government concern over the people enmeshed in the new industrial society, and this was expressed in the appointment of men as inspectors of factories, health, prisons, education, railways and mines, in addition to those acting as lunacy commissioners, poor-law assistant-commissioners and the like. In some ways these were the first signs of the Welfare State and the driving-force behind them came from Benthamites like Edwin Chadwick and Kay Shuttleworth, neither of whom were public-school products. The new inspectors were destined to be influential entrepreneurs between the central offices and the outback, and were often chosen from a wide field, as in the case of the twelve poor-law commissioners chosen from 2,000 applicants.[2] In the words of David Roberts:

> Whether they were lawyers or journalists, engineers or clergymen . . . the inspectors were usually men of more than common attainments. The patricians of the governing class generally selected able men, sincere in the wish to alleviate social evils. They did not employ those mediocre political favourites who dominated the revenue departments, and who became the objects of Anthony Trollope's satires.[3]

Men to look after sanitation, the mines, health, railways, factories and the like had to be chosen from among competent doctors and engineers, both private and military, and they came mainly from middle-class and professional backgrounds. They were men of distinction, and the fact that eleven of them were elected to the Royal Society indicates their quality. Although well educated they were not public-school products, for the school curriculum there did not exactly encourage a serious study of engineering and other technologies. Only in the case of education do we find a dominance of men with a public school–Oxford/Cambridge background.

1. ibid., p. 123.
2. ibid., p. 164.
3. ibid., pp. 157–8.

Inspectors of education, familiarly known as H.M.I.s, were mature men on appointment with schooldays well in the past, and they were already prominent in some scholastic niche or in some professional field, like the church, which might vaguely be regarded as educational. Indeed, the vested interests of the church in education through its possession of the majority of schools in the Victorian era meant that the early inspectors had to be acceptable to the church itself. The schools they inspected were lower class and educational experience was not demanded —indeed, less than a third of these men had had any kind of educational experience, and none at all had that real acquaintance with the elementary school floor and rostrum that was essential for an appreciation of these particular lower-class problems.

The first two school inspectors—John Allen and Hugh S. Tremenheere—were typically old boys of the seven, and yet represented entirely opposite views on education:

> Where Allen believed with Coleridge that all social evils arose from sin, Tremenheere believed that they arose from ignorance. He put his faith in political economy, industrial training and the development of all the faculties of man.[1]

Usually the two viewpoints were incompatible, and only the most vivid characters, like Arnold, were able to fuse them together in one person. Such viewpoints, however, were not the result of school influence and were found typically in rebellious Victorian youth everywhere, although both Jacobinic and churchly thought may, of course, be moulded in the school environment with a suitable circle of friends and influence. Arnold had both trends in his make-up before ever he went to Winchester.

Like the public schools which nurtured them, school inspectors grew and expanded with the Victorian era. The middle and late years of the reign saw them at the summit of their power, when the simple result of a visit to a lower-class school could be a matter of poverty or affluence for the ordinary teacher. It is no wonder that their pre-arranged visits produced an early-warning system, subservience and red-carpet treatment. In the words of Kekewich:

1. ibid., p. 188.

Imagine the feelings of the unfortunate teacher when he looked over the Inspector's shoulder [at the annual examination of the children] and saw the failures [of the pupils] being recorded wholesale, and knew that his annual salary was being reduced by two and eight pence for each failure.[1]

They were lordly men separated by a vast social, educational and cultural gulf from those whose welfare was their concern. There was no question of professional co-operation here, for the power in the inspector's hand prevented it. The relationship was really one of master and servant, and the contempt of H.M.I. for lower-class teachers was actually expressed a little later, as we shall see. It could be argued that this antagonism reflected the education of the two sets of individuals—the expensive public boarding school for the one and the cheap day elementary for the other. However, if this gulf was a social one, rooted partly in the public-school background of the top men, at least that same background helped to encourage their individualistic and fearless attitude which was so much a feature of these inspectors until the 1880s or 1890s at least. They wrote reports which were models of candour. When they disapproved, they said so bluntly—masters, schools, children, managers, anything within their view could be and was castigated—even to the point of publicly criticizing official policy.[2] This is the spirit of individuality and response to duty that was so typical of Thomas Arnold and the mid-Victorian headmasters. They would have applauded this standpoint as being in line with their teaching, and it is not without significance that the major figure of the inspectorate, and the most outspoken, was no less a figure than the famous son of Thomas, Matthew Arnold himself. The early inspectors fought to maintain this freedom and the vice-president of the Council, Robert Lowe, was censured in 1864 and forced to resign for mutilating their reports. As the central authority became more organized towards the end of the century, this freedom appears to have been less evident. One is tempted to attribute the conflict entirely to public-school change in the nineteenth century—to the stress on individualism in the great

1. E. L. Edmonds, *The School Inspector*, 1962, p. 81.
2. The reports of H.M.I.s were printed and can be seen in the *Minutes of the Committee of Council on Education*.

headmaster period, and to the stress on regimentation and team spirit in the last quarter of the century and beyond.

The H.M.I.s were only one of at least eight equivalent services created for supervisory purposes, and the only one recruited extensively from the old boys of public schools. Yet all these services were successful, and it is clear that the specialisms of medicine and engineering, with their non-public-school background, could produce men of character equally imbued with the spirit of service as easily as the amateuristic approach of the public schools themselves. This indicates that the so-called character of public-school boys, in so far as it was desirable for this kind of work, was not the product of schooling at all.

In clinging to their traditions, there can be no doubt that the public schools let a great opportunity slip. Had they taken to science wholeheartedly it is highly probable that they would have filled most of the technical inspectorates as well as the educational, and thereby have held a virtual monopoly. As it was, they merely contributed to a small but important part of general social development. This gap in their contribution to state welfare, and the realization that others were quite able and willing to fill it, was disturbing to those in authority who wanted the major schools to play a leading role on a wide front.

Education inspectors were only one section of the educational *élite*, and certainly not the most influential. Although they played an important part in the development of elementary education and social change, and at one period formed an effective kind of pressure-group, it was at the administrative and political level that key decisions were made.

PUBLIC SCHOOLS AND EDUCATION

Public-school influence was felt in education in different ways at different levels of society. If admiration and imitation are any guide to the success of an institution, then the seven had a direct major effect on the education of the upper and upper middle classes, and those schools which professed at one time to be rooted in other ideas, like Uppingham, ended finally in the same mould. The same was true of Woodard's efforts to spread public-school ideas lower down the social pyramid to the middle and lower classes (see pp. 30–3). The end result of

public-school reverence was to limit it in type and to confine it to a small section of society. On the middle classes generally (traders, manufacturers, professional men) upper-class education had little effect until the end of the century, except perhaps for the token inclusion of classics in many academies to lend an air of culture. It could well be argued that any real influence between the two systems was in a reverse direction, with the middle-class insistence on a wide educational range, including some of the practical arts and sciences, being forced slowly on the upper-class schools. But it is in their influence on the rather remote lower-class education that we see both their strength and their limitations.[1]

Public-school clientele and staff were socially too distant from the lower classes for there to have been any direct general contact and influence. Those towns which housed public schools felt their presence strongly since the headmasters were often involved with lower-class education at the 'managerial' level. Their visits to the schools were akin to the presence of the inspector, and there are known instances which bordered upon interference. These towns also tended to accumulate a large core of gentry and the gentry-minded—as at Harrow, Eton, Rugby—who interested themselves in charity with help for local church schools as one of their main objectives. All this was a local matter; it cannot be put forward as a national influence. It was of less significance than the situation existing in a large number of rural areas which by 1850 already possessed ample educational provision for the lower classes, often owing to the patronage of lords of the manor and their wives, seen typically in Lady Sykes and Lady Wenlock in the East Riding of Yorkshire.[2]

Public-school influence on lower-class education as a whole was felt most strongly in a direct supervisory way at top level, and indirectly from pressure-groups. It was strong over a wide

1. The headmasters at Rugby, for instance, were locally very influential in the nineteenth century. We not only find them intimately involved with local projects, e.g. Rugby Education Society, the Institute, but they interfered in the schools to some extent. A typical example from the log book of Trinity Parochial School, for 19 June 1865, reads as follows: 'Dr Temple wished H. Linnell (a pupil teacher) to go to the Big School to sing for part of the day: he went.'
2. See T. W. Bamford, *The Evolution of Rural Education*, 1965.

field, but particularly so in the higher-grade problem, that major lower-class development after the 1870 Act. Public-school opinion may be considered as involving both the school, as represented by headmasters, and the opinions of old boys who became influential in later years.

As with all matters of importance, there were varying ideas expressed by headmasters on the problem of lower-class education, but Thring and Temple probably represented the extremes.

Thring was an example of ultra-conservative reaction. He was not convinced of the need for elementary-school expansion. He thought of education as a kind of reward, whether from man or God, already provided in ample quantity for those who wanted it and strove for it. He had no time for a schooling that was distributed for nothing, and he was therefore against the spirit of the 1870 Act, which contemplated, if it did not provide, an education for everyone. He expressed his point of view very forcibly indeed:

> You cannot break the laws of nature which have made the work and powers of men vary in value. This is what I mean when I ask why should I maintain my neighbour's illegitimate child. I mean by illegitimate, every child brought into the world who demands more than his parents can give him, or to whom the Government makes a present of money. The School Boards are promising to be an excellent example of public robbery.[1]

This is a hard view, but typical of the middle and late nineteenth century, and typical too of one extreme of religious opinion founded on divine will and original sin, which sought a kind of social *status quo* by preaching contentment with one's lot. Thring's view was typical of most headmasters. Perhaps their own position in fee-paying schools had something to do with this, together with their isolation in rural areas, where the problems were not so vivid or acute. Whatever the reason, most headmasters were frightened of lower-class power.

In Temple's view, education for the masses was a necessary reform.[2] He wanted the creation of character to go hand in

1. Parkin, op. cit., p. 313.
2. For Temple's views on lower-class education, see Sandford, op. cit. Also his speeches in Parliament and at meetings. See particularly his views expressed in arguments about the curriculum, etc., to be followed at the Lower School of Lawrence Sheriff.

hand with the 3 R.s, and for this religion was essential. He therefore wanted an expansion of education with the position of religion strengthened. At the same time, he was a realist and wanted to keep lower-class education separate on the grounds of the different attitudes, habits and morals in the children. Mixing would have degraded the middle classes, let alone the upper. Whether he regarded the separation as permanent, or merely as a temporary measure to accommodate the time-lag for adjustment, is another matter. If one side of headmasterly opinion objected to state provision, and wanted a restricted competitive free system, the other favoured expansion with social reservations, and contemplated educational apartheid, if not educational neglect. This makes our problem complex and presents another example of Sadler's two sides to social revolution. At the actual public-school level, the bridges between the two—the conservative and the active reformer —were very few indeed. Frederick Temple qualifies on some counts, and so did Arnold before him, but the rest had no real appreciation or insight into what was happening or bound to happen. Perhaps at the headmaster level such insight and drive was not desirable, for both these men were highly unpopular and attacked for trying to face wide problems squarely and honestly.

In both extremes there are typical public-school attitudes: the advocacy of independence and competition, the accent on character development and the spirit of social isolation. But whereas Thring interpreted these in a very restrictive way, Temple did not. The importance of these attitudes can be seen when Tait, Benson and Temple became archbishops. As former headmasters of public schools they found themselves in virtual control of the national school network which covered the land and provided education for the vast majority of the lower classes. In the successive crises over the attempt to reorganize education in the 1890s, two archbishops were therefore at the heart of the problems, trying to maintain independence, to avoid rates (Benson) and to hold on to religion against the secular trend. It is sometimes said that the new look had to wait for Benson's death and the coming of Temple and a new century, but even Temple's effort to see this reform (the 1902 Education Act) through the Lords virtually killed

him, for he collapsed during his speech and died a few days later.[1]

The headmasters may have represented the schools in many ways, but they were, in fact, only one aspect of public-school influence, some of it difficult to evaluate. The fact that men like Gladstone or Palmerston were responsible for certain reforms does not mean that this related to their background. It could only be so interpreted if this influence, either from headmasterly pressure or the influence of their own schooldays, could be shown to be a motivation in the reform. This is often difficult, if not impossible, to demonstrate, as is the case with the 1870 Elementary Education Act itself.

The man usually held responsible for this Act was W. E. Forster, the vice-president of the Committee of Council on Education, holding office in Gladstone's last Cabinet. He was educated at a Quaker school in Tottenham, so that he was outside the influence of the public schools in his early years. However, his marriage with Jane, Arnold's eldest daughter, brought him immediately within a circle of people prominent in public-school life, including Temple. This was not the kind of marriage where the in-laws were meant only for social occasions. Forster found himself immersed in the Arnolds—he adopted Arnold children and Matthew became a confidant. Matthew had to be careful not to press their relationship too far, and yet he was keen to make his brother-in-law aware of educational needs, as in this example connected with the Taunton Commission: 'I must talk to William before the Commission meets, because I think someone should go to America also.' [2]

It is not surprising that the 1870 Act had some of the Arnold influences behind it. It could be argued, on the other hand, that a great deal of top-level influence in those days had to be public school in any case, and also that the Arnold–Temple type of advice was on the radical brink and therefore not generally typical of public schools. Moreover, the 1870 Act can only be assessed within the context of other unsuccessful Bills

1. For some of the relationships between church and state (the 'dual system'), see M. A. Cruickshank, *A History of the Origin and Development of the Dual System in England and Wales with Special Reference to the Period 1870–1944.* (Ph.D. thesis for Leeds University) 2 vols., 1955.
2. Matthew Arnold, *Schools and Universities on the Continent*, edited by R. H. Super, 1964, p. 346.

introduced earlier, many of them with similar provisions. It may be that a full analysis would show that public-school influence would be so radical as to be atypical, though the remoteness of this lower-class problem meant that there was no clash of interests at this particular time. With the advance of the century, however, lower-class education began to reach beyond the 3 R.s to threaten middle-class academies and even grammar schools. It is in this situation that the influence of the public schools becomes clearer.

The schooling of the lower classes after 1870 was, in fact, elementary in character and organized in standards.[1] Seven such standards were allowed after 1882, and the regulations governing this education were enshrined in a document called the Code, which was amended year by year. For reasons that do not vitally concern us here, this elementary education (mainly the 3 R.s) was expanded in some areas until it became almost secondary in the manner of a grammar school. The development of this education was directed by the Education Department in Whitehall, although another branch of the central authority—the Department of Science and Art in South Kensington—was intimately involved. This second body was created from the results of the 1851 Exhibition, and was directly linked with the educational needs of schools, colleges, industry, design and craftsmanship. As the name implies, it was primarily interested in art, design, science and technology as educational cogs towards a new industrial society, and the more

1. The period from 1870 to 1902 is of immense complexity outside the public schools. It is fair to say that the School Board case has never been adequately represented and that the participation of individuals has been romanticized. This is, perhaps, inevitable in any situation where one organization succeeds another. The denigration proceeds in both subtle and obvious ways, and this was clearly the case here. Some idea of the problems involved can be gathered from E. Eaglesham, *From School Board to Local Authority*, 1956. The romantic story presented by B. M. Allen in his two biographies and by G. A. N. Lowndes must be considered against the two biographies of Sadler, the memoirs of Kekewich and FitzRoy, the personalities and actions of Balfour, Joseph Chamberlain, the Webbs and other radicals, not to mention churchmen, scientists, headmasters and pressure-groups on behalf of local authorities, etc. The following provide an initial study: B. M. Allen, *William Garnett*, 1933 and *Sir Robert Morant*, 1934; Cruickshank, op. cit.; G. A. N. Lowndes, *The Silent Social Revolution*, 1937; M. Sadleir, *Michael Ernest Sadler*, 1949; L. Grier, *Achievement in Education*, 1952; G. W. Kekewich, *The Education Department and After*, 1920; A. Fitzroy, *Memoirs*, 2 vols., 1925.

18

active it became the nearer it drew to the dream of so many Victorian intellectuals from Huxley to Ruskin, not to mention the original driving-force of the Prince Consort himself. South Kensington gave grants to help science teaching and secondary education in general, including the new developments in lower-class education. This meant that the curriculum of these newly formed 'elementary' schools, pursuing a higher form of education, placed a greater emphasis on science than did the traditional grammar schools.

This process was known as higher-grade development on account of the higher level of work being done, and Huxley voiced the hopes of many who wanted to see it develop into a bridge between the elementary schools and the universities. There was nothing fundamentally new in this idea, for some people, like C. S. Parker,[1] had even before 1870 wanted to see the village or community school catering both for the elementals and for advanced work leading directly to the university in the Scottish manner. But from this point of view the efforts of the Education Department in Whitehall had been disastrous, since their regulations only allowed for grants for elementary work and prevented the development of 'liberal' education. Higher-grade schools were, to this extent, a step in the right direction. On the other hand, many people in authority saw these schools as serious competitors to the old-established grammar schools and the traditional (academy) type of middle-class education. Questions concerning the legality of these higher-grade schools arose, and their whole future was jeopardized by a decision in the courts. Ultimately, a new Act of Parliament in 1902 resolved the situation by reinforcing the distinction between elementary and secondary education, thereby eliminating the broad ladder from the elementary schools, for the time being at least. Later, by new regulations in 1904 and 1907, the new secondary schools were reduced to a common pattern with Latin as part of the curriculum. In this, secondary schools were guided along public-school lines with the classics as an integral part of their liberal education.

Higher-grade schools, with their scientific and practical bias, had represented the peak of elementary-school progress and had

1. C. S. Parker, 'On the History of Classical Education', *Essays on a Liberal Education*, edited by F. W. Farrar, 1868, p. 77.

been identified by many with lower-class hopes. There can be little doubt that between 1896 and 1904 one potential kind of higher education based on lower-class elementary schools and tradition was blotted out, and another created around the old grammar schools fashioned in the public-school mould. No matter what views are taken of the relative merits of the operation, this period was one of the most crucial in English educational history, and it is here that public-school influence, directly and indirectly, was at its more significant.

The background details of the story are complex, for many people were involved, and there were several related interweaving themes, some of them heavily charged with public-school attitudes. The emphasis on science teaching as a condition for grants by the Department of Science and Art at South Kensington was clearly against public-school culture and tradition and the upbringing of most men in power in Whitehall. Many thought them non-educational in the 'liberal' sense and the rivalry of the two departments and the relationships of South Kensington to the education of the lower classes lay at the kernel of educational problems in the late nineteenth century.

The changes were brought about by men at the top, and it is perhaps easier to consider the elimination of the higher aspirations of the elementary schools in two phases.

The first phase brought about the downfall of the school boards (which administered many elementary schools) by demonstrating that their more ambitious efforts to educate lower-class children and adults were illegal. This involved many people whose names are known to us—Sir John Gorst, William Garnett, Francis Black, William Hales, Barclay Cockerton among others—but the driving-force behind their actions, whether of ambition, religious conviction, educational belief or sheer mischievousness, is largely unknown. Certainly this part of the affair has a most disreputable side.

The second phase is a different matter. It concerned the planning, passing and interpretation of the 1902 Education Act. The two men credited with the achievement are Arthur Balfour, the prime minister, and Robert Morant, later permanent secretary at the Board of Education. Balfour was Eton and Cambridge; Morant, Winchester and Oxford. Morant was

certainly influenced by his public-school connections, while Balfour, apart from his own background, had two public-school heads within his own family.

The details of this human and exciting but long story do not concern us, but the final result was an intimacy between Morant and Balfour, and the eclipse of Gorst, Kekewich (the permanent secretary) and Michael Sadler in a series of bitter feuds which left Sadler and Morant estranged for life and Kekewich deposed to make way for 'a younger man'. The net result was the elevation of Morant, the obliteration of higher-grade development, the preservation of the identity of the grammar schools, and the reinforcement of a public-school pattern by new regulations in 1904 and 1907. It was a constant accusation thereafter that Morant, in particular, had converted English secondary schools into imitations of Winchester. Typical of the critics was Chuter Ede, who exclaimed in Parliament on 4 February 1943:

. . . when the Act of 1902 was passed its administration was left to one of the greatest autocrats who ever dwelt in the Civil Service, the late Sir Robert Morant, of whom it was said, 'He was not unprincipled, but he was unscrupulous.' He believed that the best form of education was that which had been given to him at Winchester. . . .

Recent research has shown that Morant's part in these developments has been greatly exaggerated, but his influence remains formidable enough. The main interest from our point of view is not so much the drama or the personalities, but the public-school implications.

As in politics, or in the antagonism between administration and the army, we find a clash of ideas which overrides even an outward show of agreement. It has been stressed by leaders in business that they rely on the mutual confidence that springs from a shared social background and, in many cases, kinship. The instance we are discussing here also indicates that there can be opposite views of public-school ethics and even of Civil Service procedure. Certainly there was an interference in state policy by the Civil Service that must be almost unique, and some would also argue against the spirit of the public-school background—indeed, it was this fact of forgetting the basic principles of character that so shocked Sadler and sent him into

the wilderness for so many years. Further, in the period 1896–1902 a choice of three future patterns of secondary education presented itself. The first was to encourage the upward development of lower-class elementary education through higher-grade schools. The second was to develop along middle-class grammar-school lines with the traditional literary and public-school influences. The third was to compromise between the two. Undoubtedly Kekewich was in favour of compromise, and to this end he did in fact manage to bring about an agreement between the rival associations of headmasters. Balfour, Morant, Headlam and the church were in favour of the second choice. So were the public schools:

> Throughout the years of debate preceding the 1902 Act the [Headmasters'] Conference and the [Headmasters'] Association pursued the same end. They aimed at preserving the dominance of the headmaster in all matters relating to the organization of his school and hence at limiting the powers of the proposed Local Education Authorities as narrowly as possible. It was constantly stressed that, when a Central Authority was set up, there should be a sharp distinction between the secondary and the elementary systems. . . .' [1]

The adoption of the second solution exclusively meant that a wide interpretation of education was lost and lower-class (elementary-school) aspirations were delayed for a generation and more. With those aspirations went any hope of a massive development of technical and scientific education that the scientists and industrialists had been urging for half a century. The result was a triumph for traditional thought and the adoption of a public-school cloak for the higher parts of the educational system as a whole. Whether this was the best solution is a matter of opinion, but the outcome may well represent the greatest single contribution of the Victorian public school to the immediate post-Victorian era, and one which has affected every single inhabitant in this country directly in one way or another.

One effect of this scholastic revolution was to widen the gulf between lower-class and middle-class education, and even though the class connotations faded, the gulf persisted strongly till the Second World War and can even be felt today. This

1. Baron, op. cit., pp. 228–9.

distinction applied not only to children, buildings and facilities, but also to teachers themselves. Government inspectors treated elementary-school teachers as inferiors, and dismissed their education with contempt. They made no secret of the fact and even committed these opinions to paper for the Chief Inspector of Elementary Schools to summarize in a document dated as late as 6 January 1910.[1] They spoke of lower-class education and lower-class teachers as inferior and beyond redemption, and insisted that anyone with such a background was quite unfitted for authority:

> The difference in respect to efficiency between ex-elementary teacher Inspectors and those who have a more liberal education is very great. Very few of our Inspectors (H.M.I.s) have a good word to say for local Inspectors of the former type. . . . It is interesting to note that the two local Inspectors about whom *our* Inspectors are really enthusiastic hail, one from Winchester and Trinity, Cambridge, the other from Charterhouse and Corpus Christi College, Oxford. . . . Apart from the fact that the elementary teachers are, as a rule, uncultured and imperfectly educated, and that many, if not most, of them are creatures of tradition and routine, there are special reasons why the bulk of the local Inspectors in this country should be unequal to the discharge of their responsible duties. . . . The local authorities have inherited . . . not merely a vicious system of local inspection, but also a large number of vicious local Inspectors. . . . Having regard to all these facts, we cannot wonder that local inspection as at present conducted in the large towns is on the whole a hindrance rather than an aid to educational progress, and we can only hope that the local Chief Inspectors, who are the fountain heads of a vicious officialdom, will be gradually pensioned off. . . .

However palatable these opinions may have been to their old public-school masters, there is no doubt that their products had no appreciation of local class values, difficulties, culture or objectives. It is no wonder too that with such men advising on educational affairs the events of 1895–1902 should have turned out in the way they did.

It is perhaps unfair to blame the public schools directly for problems outside their range, but none the less their old boys,

1. This document is usually referred to as the Holmes Circular, after the chief-inspector involved. Though it was meant to be confidential some of the contents leaked out, but the whole document has never been published. It created an outcry that succeeded in eliminating Robert Morant from th e educational scene. For some details, see F. H. Hayward, *Educational A d ministration and Criticism*, 1912, pp. 574–5.

in basing their ideas firmly and openly on public-school methods and practice, created the situations which occurred. In this, therefore, the schools contributed indirectly to the national educational dilemma and to scientific backwardness. Some people have also seen in the tripartite system of Hadow–Norwood[1] the hand of the public schools in desiring the production of an *élite*. However, it was not anticipated, even by the Labour party, that the 'secondary education for all' scheme that had its origins in the Hadow Report of 1926 (even though that report did not mention it as such) would result in the segregation of children by social class. It was confidently expected that the result of the 1944 Act, as expressed by eleven plus, would break down social barriers.

It has already been noted that the makers of the Education Acts of 1870 and 1902 had intimate public-school connections, including family relationships, through W. E. Forster and Arthur Balfour. The same is true of the remaining two major Acts—those of 1918 and 1944. In the former case the mothers of H. A. L. Fisher and W. W. Vaughan[2] were sisters, while R. A. Butler of the 1944 Act is a member of the scholastic family which was started when the first George Butler became headmaster of Harrow in 1805.[3] The fact that every major step in the building of the state system of education had such an intimate public-school aura is quite remarkable. These, however, are complicated issues which lie far beyond our scope and outside the Victorian era.

One may summarize the complex influence of public schools on state education in the following way. First of all, their products managed to create a system of secondary schools in the public-school image, and secondly, this development created and to some extent perpetuated a schism in the national framework. That this schism was real and deep and unjust, if expedient, cannot be doubted by anyone with experience, or who has read extensively the educational literature before and between the wars. Furthermore, the result was a virtual obliteration of the promising expansion in science and applied science that had been building up in some lower-class schools.

1. For the Hadow and Norwood Reports, see pp. 288–9, n. 2, and p. 293, n. 2, below.
2. See Family Linkage 5, p. 152.
3. See Family Linkage 4, p. 149.

If public-school influence on state education was indirect, yet important and extremely controversial to say the least, its influence on universities was no less important and direct. The further education of boys leaving Winchester and Harrow for the decade 1878–87 is indicated in Table 19, with corresponding

Table 19. *Further (non-military) education of pupils entering Winchester and Harrow from 1878 to 1887 compared with figures for the same decade for Manchester Grammar School.*[1]

| | Boys proceeding to: | | | | | |
	Oxford	Cambridge	London	Red-brick	Technical, medical, agriculture	Scotland, Ireland, overseas
Winchester	348	139	10	4	19	6
Harrow	258	356	6	2	3	12
Total	606	495	16	6	22	18
Manchester Grammar School	93	44	?	199	?	?

figures for Manchester Grammar School. Several points are immediately apparent. Winchester and Harrow sent their sons to Oxford and Cambridge, and only very exceptional boys went elsewhere. Those proceeding to London and the red-brick universities went to take advantage of science, engineering and similar specialized studies not offered at the old universities. They fall into the same category as those who became medical students or who went to the agricultural colleges at Cirencester or Downton, or travelled abroad to the polytechnics of Zürich or Dresden, or to Heidelberg for chemistry. Manchester Grammar School, on the other hand, supported the older universities, presumably wherever possible, but the main-stream of its contribution to higher learning went to the local institution.

1. The Harrow and Winchester figures are taken from the relevant school registers. The Manchester figures are taken from Mumford, op. cit., p. 457.

The boys represented here would be passing on to the universities from the mid 1880s to the mid 1890s, and this picture is therefore a reflection of the situation in the late Victorian age. Details for Winchester, worked out by T. J. H. Bishop over a much longer period (1820–1922),[1] show that this pattern persisted well into the twentieth century at least, although, as a rather surprising matter of detail, Winchester has now reversed its patronage within the two older universities and its sons have come to favour Cambridge rather than Oxford.

All this lends powerful support to the often quoted statement that public schoolboys would rather forego a university education altogether than proceed to red-brick. The solidarity presented in the figures quoted here is extraordinary, since in terms of the boy–boy and boy–teacher relationships one would have expected more rebels as the outcome of boy and master pressure. Clearly there were subtle pressures of an overwhelming nature which had the effect of denigrating any possible appeal the newer universities might have had. This Oxford/Cambridge tradition still persists, and red-brick deans of faculties at the present day complain of the very few recruits from leading schools. Red-brick universities have, therefore, had to build themselves up with a different kind of clientele, on the products of local schools like Manchester Grammar at best, and with the main intake from the secondary schools in the state system.

The situation within the universities is linked with the problems of science and industry. Victorian industry was self-sufficient in many ways, producing its results without an intake of well-trained university men. The technical 'know-how' was passed on from expert to apprentice or in the mechanics' and technical institutes. Such a system, however, was limited and not necessarily progressive or expansionist. A surer base for the whole country's industry would have been to create technical university-like institutions with the stress on science, applied science and research. This is what Prince Albert tried to do with some of his schemes. But even though pure science gained recognition at red-brick establishments and even at Oxford and Cambridge by the end of the century, the same recognition was not given to technology, and undoubtedly the

1. Bishop, op. cit.

strong links between Oxford and Cambridge and the public schools aided this short-sightedness in the older universities.[1]

Altogether it may be said that the present glory of England's post-school education—the growth of science, technology and red-brick—had very little encouragement indeed from the public schools, and owes virtually nothing to them historically, except in the provision of some teachers and vice-chancellors. Even so, the Oxford/Cambridge spirit of boarding education, which is akin to that of the public schools, is still thought of nostalgically by many at red-brick, especially those products of the older universities who have migrated there, while some almost apologize for their paucity of halls of residence.

1. The following quotation summarizes the position: 'One thing at any rate was beyond dispute—the high esteem in which the study of the natural sciences was held in England at the close of the nineteenth century. The position had changed, vastly, since those early days of the century when the pioneers of modern chemistry and physics were self-educated men outside the official centres of learning. Today all the leaders of science were university professors . . . Lord Rayleigh and Ramsay in London, J. J. Thomson and James Dewar at Cambridge, Ray Lankester at Oxford, Oliver Lodge at Liverpool, Lord Kelvin at Glasgow, P. G. Tait at Edinburgh, what country in Europe could boast of more famous names than these?'—from E. Halevy, *Imperialism and the Rise of Labour*, 1951, pp. 147–8.

CHAPTER TEN

Twentieth-Century Developments

Public schools have in the twentieth century been dominated by a slow change in the nature and extent of the system, by a persistence of the conservative approach apparent in the Victorian age and by problems connected with their relationships to the state.

The definition of a public school has been difficult ever since the earliest days of Victoria when the seven held the field, and Samuel Butler had already outlined their distinguishing features as prosperity, national recruitment (and thereby boarding), ample endowment, ancient lineage and sound scholarship. Substantial fees also assured that they dealt with the education of the sons of the rich. Each one of these schools was unique in its own way, and it followed that every school thereafter founded on the same principles complicated the issue, diluting criteria so that the absence of antiquity was quickly forgiven, and so too were some of the more unsavoury details of foundation. Using the arbitrary distinction of size, thirty-one schools of public-school type in England and Wales were recognized in 1865, while in 1889 the compilers of the first *Public Schools' Year Book* agreed on twenty-five, relying on personal judgement. The discrepancy in these figures was accounted for by borderline cases and the inclusion or exclusion of non-Anglican schools. One difficulty in following the growth of this system from 1837 is that values changed with time, as in the opinion of what comprised a small or large school, or the paramount virtues of religion or the classics, while new developments like the Headmasters' Conference only complicated the issue still further. The ultimate result of these fluctuating criteria is today's position, and in many ways it is simpler to survey this

evolution by considering the system as it stands now before tracing back its growth.

THE EXTENT OF THE SYSTEM IN 1962[1]

Whatever may be said about other schools, there is no doubt that the original seven are still very much at the heart of the system. We cannot, therefore, go far wrong in starting a consideration of the modern public school with these seven, exactly as we would if we were considering the same question at the accession of Queen Victoria, or, for that matter, at the end of the eighteenth century.

Westminster, by virtue of its eminent but restricted position, is easily the smallest, but the rest are very large schools indeed, varying in size from 500 boarders to 1,190. Apart from Westminster, only Rugby and Shrewsbury have any appreciable number of day scholars, and even there they do not exceed 9 per cent. All these schools take boys between thirteen and eighteen. The large size and particular age-range is important, for it enables advanced work to take place in large sixth forms and hence tailors work to fit university standards, particularly those of Oxford and Cambridge. They are also very expensive, with fees ranging from £441 to £508 per annum, and these have since been increased substantially. With the exception of one or two special cases, to be mentioned later, they are the most expensive schools in the country, in spite of their endowments, and are consequently very exclusive from a purely financial viewpoint. With this exclusiveness go many other less tangible features traditionally associated with a leisured and wealthy class which will be the subject of comment later.

If we are to find genuine modern companions of this group, they must be sought among those independent schools which have a large number of boarders, which concentrate on high quality work and which are exclusive by virtue of their fees, whatever the reason for that might be.

1. Particulars and details of modern public schools, taken from a wide variety of sources, including individual information, is given in the Appendix. It has been stressed that statistics of this kind are liable to vary rapidly and are subject to sudden 'jumps'. This becomes clear when it is realized that any change in total numbers takes place with rebuilding, etc.

There are more than 4,000 independent schools of various types in this country today,[1] but if we adopt as our criterion, for the reasons stated above, a bare minimum of 200 boarders in the thirteen to eighteen age-range to allow the significance of boarding to be felt, then we can reduce this number drastically. The picture which emerges for the year 1962 is given in detail in the Appendix. There are eighty-four schools, perhaps eighty-five, satisfying these precise requirements. If we relaxed the independent clause and included direct-grant boarding schools as well, then another ten or twelve would have to be added. In a similar way, if we relaxed the number of boarders slightly, say to 170, then another eight independent and another two direct-grant schools would be involved. The figure of 106 boarding schools, therefore, represents a maximum, and, if we eliminated the direct grant—a most important category to be considered in detail later—the maximum is ninety-two.

If we look at the eighty-five schools given in the Appendix a little more closely, we find that all but nine have fees of £360 per annum or more, and that two of these nine are virtually free or close to it, one being the special case of Christ's Hospital. Again, nine of the eighty-five were not represented on the Headmasters' Conference, and while this does not mean that they were not doing useful work, at least one of the normal qualities for acceptance was therefore not in evidence. It is, perhaps, not without significance that six of these nine are grouped towards the bottom of the list when the eighty-five are arranged in fees order. Similarly, with one exception, they are all near the minimum size. In this way it is possible to pare our list down to about seventy schools for England and Wales.

This method is, of course, arbitrary, but it is necessary to know in general terms the extent of the system with which we are dealing. At the same time it is necessary to scrutinize other possible boarding schools, whether independent, direct-grant or maintained, so that any omissions can be accounted for. Such schools not on the independent list will be considered later. If we restrict our attention to the schools in the Appendix, the exclusion of only half a dozen well-known names is a matter of some surprise to the non-committed student, and three of

1. For the number of independent schools at any particular time, see *Statistics of Education*, H.M.S.O., published annually.

these are borderline. We may take it, therefore, that approximately seventy schools in England and Wales represent almost the entire public-school group, defined as producing significant boarding, expensive, independent education with strong links to Oxford or Cambridge. Other schools of a direct-grant or experimental nature will be considered in another context.

THE GROWTH OF THE SYSTEM

The obvious method of considering this growth is by utilizing the dates of foundation for individual schools. A convenient

Table 20. *The foundation, by decades since 1830, of public schools according to three definitions.*[1]

Decade	Number of New Foundations by Definition		
	A	B	C
1830–9	0	3	8
1840–9	9	15	1
1850–9	5	6	3
1860–9	10	14	2
1870–9	4	7	–
1880–9	5	10	–
1890–9	3	6	–
1900–9	1	3	–
1910–19	0	0	–
1920–9	3	3	–
1930–9	1	1	1
1940–9	0	0	–
1950–9	0	0	–

A = Members of H.M.C. (1962), 200 or more boarders, independent (see text).
B = Members of H.M.C. (1962) all schools.
C = Other equivalent boarding schools, mostly now extinct.

starting-point would be the seventy schools already mentioned, working backwards in time. On this basis we find that twenty-two, apart from the seven, were founded before the accession of Victoria, many of them old grammar schools.

1. Material obtained from the references given in the Appendix. Material in column 'C' from many sources.

The newer additions were not spread evenly over the years but limited largely to the last century, as shown in Table 20, column A. This, however, ignores the fact that many schools still surviving have changed their nature over the years and have few boarders or none at all today, and yet have historical significance. Accordingly, column B embraces all schools in the Headmasters' Conference. There is still a further complication since the public-school system is a dynamic one—many schools are still either not recognized by their fellows or have passed out of view; some of them are now extinct, having once been prosperous. Estimates of these are given in column C. In this way it is very unlikely that many successful and 'recognized' schools have been omitted.

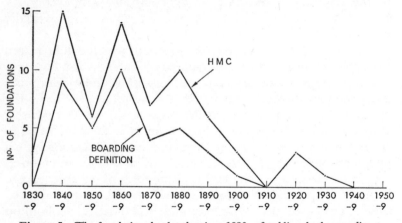

Figure 5. *The foundation, by decades since 1830, of public schools according to two definitions*

Two of these relationships (A and B) are shown in graph form in Figure 5. It is clear from this that, whichever definition is used, the same general picture emerges.

The high-water mark for new foundations was in the thirty-year period 1840 to 1870, followed by a moderately active period till 1900. Since then new foundations have been remarkably few. Thus the sixty years since 1900 have yielded only five new schools compared with thirty-five in the sixty years before that date. This contrast would be even more marked if we included those schools which were eligible at one time to be included but which have since slipped into obscurity.

The differences in the figures given in Table 1 (p. 18) and those in Table 20 are entirely due to problems of changing status.

An illustration of the change in standards and public school potential over a century occurs in a comparison of the 1865 and 1962 lists. All thirty-one of the 1865 schools are included in the later list with the exception of five, three of which were sectarian. Of these exceptions, two have now faded from sight, one is border-line in numbers, one continues as a very prominent state school, and the other appears to have changed its policy over boarding. The whole of development over the hundred years, therefore, is not just a simple accretion, but a continual profit-and-loss account as reckoned at different times. Many schools have risen and then fallen according to the arbitrary criteria we have taken, and whatever yardstick is adopted a similar phenomenon would automatically develop.

It is important to consider the objections which can be raised to the picture of growth as represented by Table 20 and Figure 5. It may be argued, for instance, that our stress on boarding and independence is outmoded, but that does not appear to be the opinion of the 'top' schools at the present day, as we shall see. It is also true that there are many other schools, mentioned in the Appendix, which have not been included here for analytical purposes since they do not come within the rather modest requirements we have made, but some form of selection has to be made for practical purposes, while it should not be forgotten that an even greater number of similar (excluded) schools could have been itemized for earlier decades in the nineteenth century. Pleas may also be made that this or that particular school ought to have been included, and it has been admitted that one or two omissions are surprising, but this procedure would have meant adopting prejudiced for arbitrary criteria, and the numbers involved would probably have been few in any case. A much more serious objection would be that the number of schools is unimportant and may even present a false picture; that growth should be reckoned in terms of pupils. This, however, would present a much more complicated and formidable task. In any case, this objection could not affect the facts already given for the number of schools involved.

Altogether there is no mistaking the conclusion of Figure 5

that a most significant change in development occurred about the year 1900.

The glory of the public-school system in the nineteenth century lay in the creation from scratch of new schools—the Marlboroughs, Wellingtons and Lancings—and this century has nothing really comparable to offer. There is no denying that a change in tempo occurred quite sharply at the turn of the century, and this lends support to the common assumption that the public schools were largely a Victorian development. The impetus underlying this growth seemed to vanish suddenly with the death of the Queen.

A milestone of this importance calls for some explanation, and there are several tempting possibilities.

The market may have become saturated after the work of the Charity Commission, whose intensified efforts over the previous thirty years had created so many new schools out of old ones. This work was helped by a new form of state aid to many independent schools through local authorities and their responsibilities under the 1889 Act. All this was helped in turn by the so-called 'whisky money' [1] which eased the finances of many schools now on the Headmasters' Conference. The net result may have been that the number and variety of independent boarding schools in existence by 1900 was already more than sufficient to absorb all the clientele able and willing to pay substantial fees. This theory, however, ignores the fact that founding a school is an act of faith rather than an accounting procedure, and many schools, as we have seen, began in the nineteenth century at unpropitious times. In this sense 1900 must also have corresponded with a change in the educational missionary spirit.

Rising population, increasing wealth and changing values among the social classes are matters to be weighed here as well as changing standards of education. Whether these would account adequately for the sudden change in public-school growth is very doubtful, and we need to know more about such effects.

The change in public-school vitality also happened to coincide roughly with the Education Act of 1902, which dealt

1. The 'whisky money' resulted from the sale of spirits and was devoted to helping the work of local authorities (as set up under the 1888 Act) in operating their duties under the 1889 Act.

19

exclusively with state education and placed secondary (grammar) education on the rates and under the control of local authorities. This coincidence has been developed by many into an explanation of the sudden failure to continue the creation of new public schools.

The Act of 1902 was interpreted by politicians and civil servants in such a way that a common kind of secondary school emerged providing a grammar type of education on a broad basis for the middle classes, and, after 1907, to a growing number of lower-class children as well.[1] This brought into existence a strong parallel system of education of high quality, with a curriculum comparable to the boarding schools and preparing scholars for the university. These new schools were built solidly, and developed into frank imitations of Eton, Harrow and the rest as far as funds and the provision of day scholars would allow, with first-class equipment and staffed by graduates, even if they were usually only derivatives of red-brick. Each area soon had its own grammar school with boys able to graduate from the slums to Oxford or Cambridge, and in this way a national grammar-school system was built up and paid for by rates and taxes. Whether the success of the 1902 Act, however, prevented a further expansion of public boarding schools in the twentieth century is very doubtful. For one thing, the existing schools were not full and had to struggle for clients. Secondly, there is no evidence that the municipal grammar schools accepted pupils who would otherwise have gone to boarding schools. What evidence there is, and it is by no means conclusive, indicates that the day grammar school filled up with local middle-class children whose parents could not possibly have afforded the fees of a major boarding school.

It is also possible that the 1902 Act had a psychological as distinct from an economic and practical effect. The fact that the state had now entered the secondary field might have reduced missionary ardour, since the needs of the middle classes

1. The Education Act, 1902 did not specifically mention secondary education. It was concerned, on paper, with both elementary and higher education. A great deal was left to the interpretation of Presidents of the Board of Education and other policy-makers. Thus the present-day supporters of Morant claim that the grammar-school system is his monument and that this represents the most significant educational achievement of the century. See Frank Roscoe, *Year Book of Education*, 1932, p. 277.

became the concern of officialdom. It is true that the clientele was not typical of the public schools we have in mind, but it is precisely in the same way that Woodard and many others founded schools which later raised their ambitions.

Altogether the reason behind the sudden change in the rate of public-school formation is not likely to be simple; it may well be as elusive as the corresponding problem of school popularity in the 1830s and 1840s, which was discussed in Chapter 1.

As the years went by and the free-place system began to work and elementary boys on scholarships flooded the local grammar schools and began to squeeze out a growing proportion of the fee payers, the situation seemed ripe for change. It was confidently expected that the wealthier middle classes who patronized the local day schools would begin to resent the infiltration of the lower-class element, and would begin to look elsewhere for the education of their children. The obvious result should have been an increased pressure on boarding schools. In 1928 Norwood, in a typical comment, expressed the opinion that this would give rise to a new surge in the independent sector:

At the present moment all the public schools are full to the point of inconvenience, and new boarding schools have made their appearance only to be filled at once. Stowe, the Wrekin School, Canford, and others, are in my opinion only the vanguard of a new wave of foundations, which will have various subjects and varying curricula, but all will be built on the basis of the public school tradition.[1]

Even if we accept these statements and the doubtful inclusion of Wrekin, the examples quoted are deceptive, for how many more can anyone add to Stowe and Canford?[2] It was the threat of a flood that never came, although several other schools which were founded at this period do not appear to have received their due recognition. New schools were not the only answer—a

1. C. Norwood, 'The Boys' Boarding School', *The Schools of England*, edited by J. Dover Wilson, 1928, p. 119.
2. According to *The Public and Preparatory Schools Year Book*, 'Wrekin College was founded in 1880 by Sir John Bayley. On the retirement of the Founder in 1920 the College passed into the control of a constituted Board of Governors.' Other examples to be added are: Bryanston, All Hallows and Gordonstoun (Scotland). There are others. Perhaps the most significant omission is Millfield, while co-educational schools like Bedales should not be forgotten.

general increase in size would have achieved the same result. None the less there is something of a mystery in the situation.

Another aspect of growth concerns the Headmasters' Conference.[1]

In 1902 the Conference was thirty-three years old. Out of 103 schools which were represented in that year, no less than twenty-one were day schools serving large cities, and twenty more had only the merest token of a boarding house. In those days schools as widely different as this were closer together than are their descendants now. Apart from the scholasticism which presented common problems, they were all independent. In that same year, however, the Balfour Act began to alter the significance of independence since 'higher education' became a responsibility of the local education authorities, and this resulted in the production of an extensive network of state secondary schools all over the country, many of them old grammar schools. This change in ownership, together with some direct state relationships, has had an unknown but undoubtedly considerable effect on the membership of the Conference, since the freedom of the headmaster has always been a major criterion.

In spite of competition from the state system the Conference has grown from 103 to 200 over the last sixty years. This doubling of numbers has not affected the pattern of recruitment —there is still a hard core of independent boarding schools and an exclusive set of day grammar schools, with others lying in between, and, indeed, a few state schools as well. Whatever else they may mean, the figures quoted for the Headmasters' Conference do not represent any growth in the public-school system, except perhaps in recognition. Any appreciation of the subtleties here entails an understanding of the terms 'direct grant', 'voluntary' and 'maintained', together with the sub-divisions of 'voluntary', and these will be considered in the context of status and independence later.

THE PUBLIC SCHOOLS AND EDUCATION

In the light of their Victorian development, the growth of the public schools in this century has been a disappointment, and so has been their attitude to the curriculum. Victorian pressures

1. A fuller discussion of the Conference today is given in Chapter 11. The origins of the Conference are discussed in Chapter 7

certainly produced laboratories, but they aroused no general conviction among the heads that science was a necessary part of education. Schoolmasters at this level had not learnt the lesson that culture was possible without the classics, and not every school had a Professor Armstrong on its governing body to press the claims of science with vigour. They were still fighting a rearguard action sixty and seventy years after the Public Schools Commission, and were still producing the same arguments that were applicable in a Victorian world of empire where science and industry were left to lesser folk. In times of peace it had been pleasant, perhaps, to pass the time in arguments with the successors of Huxley, but the new type of total war brought by 1914 showed that the question was no longer merely one of academic preference. Science had become a necessity for national survival, and in particular for many posts of leadership at the topmost levels. The scarcity was frightening and in August 1916 Asquith himself set up an inquiry into science teaching with the following results:

. . . while the great majority of these schools [independent schools of the Headmasters' Conference] offer adequate opportunities for the study of science to those boys whose parents desire it, there has in the public schools as a whole been no general recognition of the principle that science should form an essential part of secondary education. . . . Further, the establishment of modern sides had the unforeseen result of providing an excuse for the neglect of science on the classical side. In our view it is a very real defect in public school organization that boys should in many schools have to make their choice between a classical side in which science is almost wholly neglected and a modern side in which the general educational conditions are in many ways unfavourable.[1]

This conclusion was not a matter of opinion, but based on an exhaustive analysis. In spite of the Clarendon Commission it was clear that the schools had managed to evade the spirit of reform. Undoubtedly this was due to the circular effect, with classicists being fed back into the schools and leading positions in society. In this conservatism the schools forgot the consequences of their example—as leaders in education other schools followed them and the nation suffered a crisis. Important though it may have been, Asquith's Committee produced little

1. *Report of the Committee Appointed by the Prime Minister to Enquire into The Position of Natural Science in the Educational System of Great Britain*, 1919, pp. 11–12.

effect and the bright boys were still encouraged to take up classics and the arts. Wherever one puts the blame, the same rearguard action was maintained throughout the 1920s and 1930s, and continued right on to the present day through the Second World War, which again almost led to disaster. Only within the last few years, with the reforms at Oxford and Cambridge, has the classical grip been shaken a little.

All this is generalization and within it there must have been the same variations from school to school that we found in science teaching in the last century and which had significance for the development of the public-school system. Until the most recent years, which will receive attention later, we have little positive knowledge of the corresponding internal patterns in this century until the late 1950s at least. This is owing to the fact that adequate statistical material is not readily available, and that working on the individual differences of seventy different schools presents obvious difficulties for the research worker.

It is important to realize that criticism of the scientific contribution of our schools arose from radicals who were concerned with national prosperity; it found little response in the clientele and the lack of science created no difficulties for the school leaver. There is no doubt that the education given, however outmoded it may have been, was suited to the schools' traditional role of feeding the ancient universities. Although the neglect of science for the abler pupils appears to be established, one cannot complain that these schools neglected higher education generally. About a third of Etonians passed on to Oxford or Cambridge in a steady stream—a proportion that is rather low, as one might expect, by the more competitive standards of Rugby and Winchester. There the percentage passing on to these universities has varied from 40 to almost 60 per cent from 1864 to 1955, and the corresponding figures have been high in all schools aiming at genuine public-school status. Although Oxford and Cambridge were the main target, some schools have specialized in links with the professions as well, from the army to medicine, and these links are still seen strongly at Wellington, Clifton, Haileybury and Epsom. Sir John Smyth's figures for the educational background of cadets at Sandhurst in 1891 and 1961 illustrate this point well.[1]

1. Sir John Smyth, *Sandhurst*, 1961, pp. 261, 263–9.

Information for the early part of the last century indicates that an old boy sending his own son to the same school was a very rare phenomenon outside Eton but that the proportion climbed to 10 per cent or so at Rugby until the second half of the century at least. A recent analysis of the same phenomenon at Winchester confirms the picture until 1880, when the percentage rose to over 30 per cent between then and 1920. This means that about a third of the boys had fathers at the same school before them, a feature that is not unusual and is said to be the case at Oundle and elsewhere. Very rarely the continuity may be greater still, as at Harrow, where it is said that: 'At present there are about 40 per cent second generation, about 15 per cent third generation, 3 per cent fourth generation and about 2 per cent fifth or more generation boys studying in the school.' [1]

All this is important evidence to show that the schools have been attractive enough to the boys—either as educational institutions or for their influence in later life—for them to send their own sons after them in a kind of family loyalty.

Important as the relationships with the universities and the old boys may be, there is no doubt that the real success of any school lies in the life and happiness of the boys, and yet of all matters concerning boarding establishments this is the greatest enigma. Fundamentally boys do not seem to have changed in a hundred years, in spite of a new world, expanded curricula and modern techniques. There still remains that code of loyalty between boy and boy that cuts him off from the adult world of master and parent and prevents the truth from emerging. Years afterwards a little may filter through in a faded or exaggerated way that the unwary and the rash will assume represents a total picture of the school. In fact the vital experiences of sex and brutality are secret, hole-in-the-corner affairs, known only to a small clique, perhaps half a dozen or so at most. It is therefore possible to obtain completely true but completely opposite views of the same school at the same time. In this situation masters often confuse the issue. They write in memoirs of the reform of evils rampant in their youth, and as teachers they are sensitive when anyone reveals that

1. Y. P. Johri, *Punjab Public School Chronicle*, September 1964, p. 6.

vice, sexual or otherwise, still exists, as though they were in some way responsible for it and stand condemned. The existence of abuse has already been demonstrated beyond all doubt for the last century, and Norwood as headmaster of Harrow in the 1920s called this kind of accusation 'a beastly libel',[1] and certainly it was so if it inferred any reflection on the staff. After all, vice is not unknown in day schools where the opportunities are few, while any parent can confirm the shock of bringing up children. This is part of the eternal dilemma—if you give too much freedom then a few will respect it and a few will abuse it and the great mass are willing to be drawn in either direction (with a bias towards abuse since it contains the fascination of forbidden fruit); while if you give no freedom at all, then all true education ceases and so does the whole point of being a public school. That sexual relationships between boys are very difficult to prevent is shown by the continuous series of revelations from the late Edwardian era, as given in Robert Graves's autobiography,[2] to the most recent times, as at Gordonstoun, or by open-eyed schoolmasters like Heckstall-Smith. Perhaps the most famous exposure of all was the novel *The Loom of Youth*, written by Alec Waugh in six and a half weeks. This book has all the zest to be expected from a boy caught up in the gap between the comparative peace of his schooldays and war in 1917, recording the events while they were still fresh in the mind.

> I was in a nostalgic mood, but I was also in a rebellious mood. Intensely though I had enjoyed my four years at Sherborne, I had been in constant conflict with authority. That conflict, so it seemed to me, had been in the main caused and determined by authority's inability or refusal to recognize the true nature of school life.[3]

The book was very popular although heavily criticized, and Alec Waugh's own preface to a later edition, long after the uproar had died, has some significance for us now:

> Two points are to be remembered. First, that before World War I Britain's imperial destiny was never questioned, and the public-school system as a bulwark of Empire was held sacrosanct. Second that no book before *The Loom of Youth* had accepted as part of the

1. Norwood, 'The Boys' Boarding School', art cit., p. 133.
2. R. Graves, *Goodbye to all That*, 1929, rev. ed., 1957. See also H. Heckstall-Smith, *Doubtful Schoolmaster*, 1962.
3. Alec Waugh, *The Loom of Youth*, Preface to the 1954 edition.

fabric of school life the inevitable emotional consequences of monastic herding together for eight months of the year of thirteen-year-old children and eighteen-year-old adolescents. On that issue such a complete conspiracy of silence had been maintained that when fathers were asked by their wives, and schoolmasters by parents who had not themselves been at public schools whether 'such things really could take place', the only defence was a grudging admission 'Perhaps in a bad house, in a bad school, in a bad time.' [1]

This is as neat a summary of the internal public-school dilemma as exists. It was written by a man really sympathetic to their cause, and anxious, when he wrote the book, for them to put things right, as distinct from those authors who were destructive and wanted to see the schools abolished as undemocratic relics in a new society.[2]

If the last 150 years are any guide, the changes have been ones of degree only. The enormities of the early and middle nineteenth century have perhaps gone, but the more subtle psychological terrors and sexual desires remain, as they must in a society of boys whose passions mature five or six years before they can find any kind of legitimate outlet. The situation is, if anything, deteriorating owing to the earlier onset of puberty—a phenomenon that has been engaging the wits of psychologists in recent years and can hardly have made the task of the housemaster any easier. Any headmaster who claims to have solved the grosser problems of sex—and some almost do— is either blind or conducting an institution nearer to a penitentiary than a school.

Over the years the schools have tried various devices to keep the attentions of the boys on the more manly and 'clean' pursuits and away from the natural position of their hands, and away also from the urges of their own inbuilt endocrine system. Incentives in sport and work were part of the answer.

From the 1870s to the 1920s, rugger and cricket graduated from pastimes and boyish enthusiasms to the status of major educational engines. There was safety in numbers, especially with a referee or umpire, while the idea of 'team spirit' that

1. ibid.
2. For a detailed account of the influence of novels and opinion in the period before and after the First World War, see A. C. Mack, *Public Schools and British Opinion Since 1860*, 1941, especially Chapters 9 and 10, though earlier chapters should be read for earlier literary work concerning public schools.

games were supposed to foster became a major factor in the stability of the community, the nation and the Empire. Even boys without spirit and without the slightest interest had to conform. At one time each school had different rules, but once agreements were reached, and the development of railways allowed the teams to travel, the cult grew quickly, and some idea of its grip can be seen in the first *Public School Year Book* (1889). There 215 pages are devot ed to the details of the schools, including some preparatory schools, entrance scholarships, examination papers and the regulations for Woolwich and Sandhurst. After this, 122 pages are devoted to nothing but sport, including the names of the players and the results of the matches.

In some schools the cult of games was taken to absurd lengths, and the games pitch replaced the classroom as a work unit, bringing with it all the same problems of misfitting and unhappiness that had marked the classics era.[1] This was the situation that H. B. Gray had complained about and that we are very close to in *The Loom of Youth*. Schools were slow to learn that boys do not fall easily into a single mould, no matter what its character and shape. After a dominance of fifty years or so, this particular concept of team sport was beginning to fade by the early 1920s.

As for the classroom, the secret of hard work and application was sought in one incentive after another, as though all children would respond if only a correct diagnosis of pedagogy was made, and the art of teaching was reduced to a search for the right incentive. In its early days the School Certificate was hailed as a solution for all the problems of classroom and discipline: '. . . they [problem boys] have ceased to exist as a class completely, just because there is now open to their efforts an examination which is within their compass, and has given direction and a sense of achievement, however humble, to their work'.[2]

This is typical of the exaggerated claims made in education. This examination and its successors have certainly helped in supplying an overall goal, but it is not the complete answer, for children cannot keep goals before them twenty-four hours

1. For criticism before the First World War, see Gray, op. cit., ch. 11 *et seq.*
2. Norwood, in Wilson, op. cit., p. 121.

a day. Spectacular results for new methods are not uncommon in the short run. What most enthusiasts have failed to see is that the psychological background of any experiment is often more important than the new idea being tested, and that children have great powers of adaptability. Moreover, the infinite variations in our genetic make-up, apart from the infinite variations in our environment, make it very unlikely that simple solutions are possible to a complex learning process. This is not to say that examinations have not played their part, but misfits still have an annoying habit of turning up under the most reasonable circumstances. And this can be a sociological phenomenon within the school itself rather than a lapse in teaching or understanding.

The real advances of this century have come not so much from panaceas as from a greater tolerance towards the interests of children and the way they spend their time. The boy has become a person in his own right, with his own special desires and interests. It is considered desirable that he should even like what he is doing. In some ways we are back to the pre and early Victorian idea of spare-time individualism, but this time with a watchful eye and without the licence of the former period.

One of the main arguments against the old methods was that they failed with an appalling number of boys. Crichton-Miller put this wastage at 25 per cent, and this is a conservative estimate:

> But about the time of the First World War the older public schools began to eliminate the wastage which had been a reproach for years—perhaps since their inception. By 'wastage' I mean not only the boys who left the school in cabs which arrived for them mysteriously at odd times in the term, and many others who stayed the course but hated every moment of it both at the time and retrospectively, but also that much greater number who gained little from their time at school and for whom those priceless years were shockingly wasted. . . . This wastage appears to have been mainly —but not entirely—among those who were intellectually or physically below average. But great enlightenment took place between the wars, and my own estimate is that at the good public schools these losses fell from perhaps 25 per cent to something below 10 per cent—and I doubt whether we will ever get this much lower. . . .[1]

1. D. Crichton-Miller, 'The Public Schools and the Welfare State', *B.J.Ed.S.*, November 1956, p. 7.

Whether one agrees with these precise figures or not, there is
no doubt of the change. It has arrived slowly but certainly, as
a kind of last resort after all the much-heralded solutions—
classics, religion, sport, examinations—had failed. It can, however, be traced back in time through the men who have
encouraged the spare-time occupations of boys at all periods,
and often in a non-academic and non-athletic way. It is really
the spirit of Thring without his preaching or classical short-
sightedness. It is the respect for boys as boys, and not merely
that proportion of them with a superior I.Q. This is really the
difference between good headmasters past and present. There
is no lack of evidence from the last century of the indulgence of
headmasters in the antics and whims of brilliant youth—what
is new is the present-day tolerance of similar eccentricity
at a much lower level of achievement, in terms of unusual
work and desires in the less able, even of dull and stupid
individuals.

All this is only one aspect of a new approach seen everywhere,
even in the treatment of rebels. In the early days arguments of
an immoral, treasonable or irreligious nature were common,
even physical rebellion was not unknown, but they produced
only one result. This iron hand has now largely gone, and the
one-time spirit of Eton that a school had some responsibility for
its own misfits prevails, and has done so since the 1920s. This
does not mean that expulsions do not occur; they still do in
fair numbers, but it is said that the whole business is handled
more reasonably. Judgement, however, must be withheld, since
factual details of expulsions and superannuation are not available. Undoubtedly there would be great differences between
schools in this respect. The moral basis of expulsion has also
changed; it should be remembered that removal below the age
of fifteen (soon to be sixteen) could easily be interpreted as a
mark of cowardice, since, in view of the compulsory school-
leaving age, the school is merely passing on its own problems
for some state headmaster to deal with. A good example of the
modern attitude occurred at Wellington, of all places, in the
1930s, where the Romilly brothers developed pacific and
communistic tendencies with a great flare for publicity and yet
managed to survive.[1]

1. Newsome, *Wellington College*, op. cit., p. 340 *et seq.*

The new spirit of tolerance and humanity in the schools was a slow creation, and it is difficult to know what exactly nurtured it. It is easy to say that this was the next approach after other methods had failed, but in fact the time-scale of educational change in the public schools is too extended for there to be any personal continuity with previously discarded ventures. As we have seen, the roots of tolerance can be traced well into the past, and even such a severe character as Arnold had large streaks of it in his make-up. However this may be, there is no doubt that the modern impetus came from a reaction to all things Victorian, seen so well in Lytton Strachey,[1] and helped by the shattering experience of the First World War. A single school, Clifton, sent over 3,100 boys to war and 578 lost their lives.[2] This is typical of many schools. No wonder the survivors were shaken, uncertain and cynical. The Edwardian confidence seemed part of another world, and the reaction brought a crop of novels. We have still not recovered, and, if anything, the Second World War only intensified the attitude.

In the nature of things, judgements on the schools, as far as they concern the lives of boys, can only be tentative. Any reflection on adult life must wait for the proper records to be made available in the form of completed registers, letters and memoirs. But this inevitably means a time-lag of thirty or forty years.

PUBLIC SCHOOLS AND THE STATE

The state system of secondary schools, organized after 1902 under the local education authorities, was not only competitive with the public schools, but also competitive within itself. This is seen in the way different salaries were paid for men with the same qualifications and experience in secondary schools in different parts of the country. This was a situation that suited the independent schools; they more than held their own and maintained their dominance in prestige and influence with ease. It was not until the First World War had been going for two or three years that this dominance was challenged and it became

1. L. Strachey, *Eminent Victorians*. From our point of view his study of Dr Arnold is especially interesting.
2. *Clifton College Annals and Register, 1862–1925*, 1925, edited by F. Borwick, ch. xviii, especially p. cxxv.

apparent for the very first time that there might be certain
spheres of education in which ordinary state grammar schools
might well give a lead. This occurred as an indirect result of
H. A. L. Fisher's determination to bring some unity to the
profession of teaching by a national system of pay. Secondary
(grammar) school salaries were made uniform, and superannuation was introduced. From the comments made earlier when
discussing the lot of the assistant master, it will be clear that the
new situation did not affect the major schools. It was, however,
a serious matter for schools lower down the scale who paid
miserable salaries to assistants while handsomely rewarding the
headmasters. If these independent schools were not to lose their
staffs, then the governing bodies had now to watch national
salary scales jealously, and provide pension schemes of their
own.[1] This has remained a perpetual problem for the smaller
school, and in the early years the situation was acute. It was
even argued that this new situation was quite unfair to the
independent schools, and this was clearly in the minds of the
May Committee in 1931—a 'Businessmen's Committee'—when
they recommended a cut in salary for teachers of the state
system. Every increase in the Burnham scale has meant a
corresponding spiral of fees at independent schools to meet the
extra expense.[2] The ironic outcome of this situation was that
the old curse of the public schools—the poverty of the assistant
staff that Norwood and others had complained about so bitterly
in the Victorian and Edwardian eras—was cured, not by their
own efforts, but by competition from the despised day schools.

In a similar way, just as assistant masters of boarding schools
were attracted to day grammar-school headships in the nineteenth century, so now many were attracted to the new
secondary schools. This ensured a spread of influence both ways
and brought about a common *esprit de corps* in the state system
analogous to and derived directly from the public schools. It
was a development that justified all the labours of men like

1. F. B. Malim, in *Year Book of Education*, 1932, p. 221.
2. The Burnham scale of salaries in the state system is that fixed by the
Burnham Committee. At various times there have been several different
scales referring to elementary-school teachers, secondary-school teachers,
technical teachers. After the 1944 Act one scale for school teachers was
introduced with suitable differentials. This Committee was a statutory
body. Lord Burnham was the first Chairman.

Morant who had toiled to create the state system in this mould in spite of bitter opposition.

In these ways, as in their influence on building and other standards to be discussed later, the pressure of the state has been indirect, but it has also had direct effects, both fulfilled and unfulfilled.

The state has threatened to interfere with public schools at various times, notably in individual cases whenever endowments were involved, and again at the period of the formation of the Headmasters' Conference, and later still at the time of the Bryce Commission. In this century it opened the door a little with the offer of official inspection, and again when independent schools were investigated for the first time under the terms of the 1918 Act.[1] These, however, were timid affairs.

With their selected clientele, the schools had always been a natural target for radicals, and the growing political force of the Labour party after the First World War made renewed attacks certain and even abolition possible. Perhaps the most interesting criticisms of all came from a succession of eminent men like H. B. Gray, Sadler, Norwood and Alec Waugh, whose real aim was to strengthen the schools by revealing the folly of their ways in their lack of realism and evolution. Added to all this uncertainty, many of the schools at the end of the First World War found themselves in difficulties over two related matters, the scarcity of clients and the problem of finance, rendered more difficult by the Teachers' Superannuation Act, already mentioned.[2] They could not see their way out of the financial and social problems without state help. In this difficulty the independent schools of the Headmasters' Conference decided to act together in bridging the gap between themselves and the schools of the state system. How far they were concerned about the growing success of the secondary (grammar) schools and how far concerned about their social isolation is a matter

1. The 1918 Act did not call for annual or periodic returns, and thus no continuous link with the central authority was forged. The 1944 Act made provision for a registration procedure.
2. The situation in the public schools at the end of the First World War and in the 1920s is somewhat obscure. Whereas many complained of difficulties, some appeared to consider the situation satisfactory. Research on the prosperity of the schools in the crucial period between 1910 and 1950 is badly needed, and without it all conclusions must be tentative.

of debate. One of the main arguments against them has always been the social one—namely that they were upper-class schools and one of the main organs or avenues of privilege, and that they selected their children accordingly. The headmasters have usually denied that there was any deliberate attempt on their part to create a social barrier, as distinct from their Victorian counterparts. When this change of attitude occurred we do not know. Modern headmasters have usually regretted, in print at any rate, that they could only afford to take in the richest section of the community—they had nothing against the other social classes as such. In their view the only difficulties in accepting poor boys were practical and financial, and both of these could easily be resolved if the Board of Education were willing enough to co-operate. The new situation was that they were now willing to accept a certain percentage of ex-elementary (poor) schoolboys as evidence of good faith.

On 3 April 1919, after discussions with the headmasters of state schools in 1918, the headmasters of Charterhouse, Eton and Marlborough made this offer officially to H. A. L. Fisher, the president of the Board of Education. He welcomed the overture but declined it with thanks, and made an interesting suggestion as a counter-proposal:

> It is full of encouragement for the future of education. It represents a sincere desire to make the public system of education as comprehensive, as accessible, and as effective as possible, and a readiness to co-operate with the Board of Education which I am bound to acknowledge with gratitude. I think that possibly the schools might render the best service by educating promising pupils from other schools at a relatively late age—say fifteen or over. . . .[1]

Nothing came of Fisher's suggestion, and the problems of finance remained to haunt those on the lower fringe.

The period between the wars was marked by a review of the whole state system of education, and a series of reports were issued based on the continuous work of the Consultative Committee. Four of these concern us here, three of them associated with the chairmanship of W. H. Hadow and one with Sir Will Spens;[2] in all they covered nursery, infant, junior,

1. J. Graves, *Policy and Progress in Secondary Education*, 1943, p. 189.
2. Details of the Reports made by the Consultative Committee of the Board of Education are as follows:

elementary and secondary schools of every type, with suitable suggestions about their future. By the time of the Second World War the only remaining part of normal education to be considered was the independent sector. Here the public schools were quite unimportant in terms of numbers but by far the most significant in terms of stability and principle.

The war brought in a coalition government, and with it the possibility of successful reform of the state system. A determination to solve the social evils of gross inequality arose not only from the revelations of pre-war unemployment and left-wing writers, but from the bitter experience of evacuation. Education was regarded by everyone, from the church to the government, as the key to the new world. In this the public schools were an essential element, since any major form of educational reconstruction without them was unrealistic, yet there had been no official review of them for seventy years.[1]

War brought another significant development in organization. Responsibility for public schools was shared between headmasters and governing bodies. A parallel development to the Conference was obviously possible for the governors, and a preliminary meeting was held in 1940. A draft scheme for an association was introduced and the Governing Bodies Association formed in 1942. A committee of this association had already considered the wider relationships:

Hadow I: *The Education of the Adolescent*, 1926. This deals essentially with senior pupils in elementary schools, although it presented a general plan as well, including a separation by age about eleven.
Hadow II: *Primary Schools*, 1931.
Hadow III: *Infant and Nursery Schools*, 1933.
Spens: *Grammar and Technical High Schools*, 1938.
These four Reports cover the whole range of state education apart from special categories (e.g. handicapped pupils) and post-school youth and adult education.
1. The situation had changed considerably, and so had some of the key definitions. Before 1902, secondary education was essentially independent in nature, and therefore any investigation of secondary schools could include public schools since they were also, in most cases, endowed schools. The 1902 Act brought a fundamental change. The secondary phase became part of the state system and could be compared to elementary education, which was suited to a different kind of clientele. After 1902 independent schools (including the public schools) lay outside the state system, so that any investigation of secondary schools after 1902 would not necessarily include public schools unless the terms of reference specifically included them.

20

At its first Annual General Meeting in February, 1942, the G.B.A. endorsed a memorandum submitted by its committee, which proposed that the Board of Education be asked to set up a special committee to work out, in consultation with the G.B.A., a system for the selection and allocation of state-aided scholars to the public schools, and to offer advice to the board in regard to the continuance and development of the direct grant system.[1]

This reflects the composition of the first association, with 138 members, including eighty independent schools, fifty-three direct grant and five others.

The appeal of the Governing Bodies Association produced results, although it came at a time when reconstruction was in the air, and these schools became the object of one of those wartime explorations of the educational scene that preceded the 1944 Education Act. In July 1942, R. A. Butler, as president of the Board of Education, appointed twenty people under Lord Fleming:

To consider means whereby the association between the Public Schools (by which term is meant schools which are in membership of the Governing Bodies Association or Headmasters' Conference) and the general education system of the country could be developed and extended; also to consider how far any measures recommended in the case of boys' Public Schools could be applied to comparable schools for girls.[2]

It was an astonishing recognition of the Association after so short an existence, and a most disappointing start for the investigation. The terms of reference completely ignored the fundamental problems; the whole position of these schools in our society, their role and their desirability, was taken for granted. It is hardly surprising that there was no bite to the report when it appeared two years later, since any sifting of the roots was outside the terms of reference.

The committee produced two schemes, one for day schools and another for boarding. The day variety had been receiving grants directly from the government for over eighty years, and from local authorities for over fifty. Of the schools in the Headmasters' Conference of 1944, seventeen had been receiving grants from local authorities since 1893, while the system of

1. G. Fisher, 'Origins and Scope of the Governing Bodies Association', *The Times*, December 1963.
2. Terms of reference of the Fleming Report.

some schools receiving their support exclusively from the central authority—the so-called direct-grant schools—dated from 1919.[1] There was no lack of historical precedent to judge the case for day schools; there were indeed no fundamental problems that had not already been explored and settled long before.

The real difficulties lay with the major boarding schools— those that spring naturally to mind at the mention of the term 'public school'. It was the integration of these into the state system that was the whole purpose of the exercise, and the committee came out in favour of diluting the sons of the rich, who could afford the education, with ordinary boys from ordinary homes. An elaborate procedure was devised for selecting these children. They were to be 'capable of profiting thereby', to be chosen without regard to parental means and to have spent at least two years at a state primary school.

In the first instance parents were to apply to their local authority, and in due course the application would be sent on to the Board of Education (Ministry) together with:

(a) the candidates' Primary School or Secondary School records . . .
(b) reports from the Head Masters or Head Mistresses . . .
(c) the observations of the Local Education Authorities . . .[2]

The application would then be sent to a Regional Interviewing Board 'who would arrange to see the candidates selected by them for further consideration accompanied, wherever possible, by their parents or guardians . . .'.[3]

Any boy who survived that hurdle would be interviewed again, this time by the head of his selected school, and, if accepted, would be granted a bursary by the central authority, his parents paying any difference according to their income.

This elaborate procedure meant that no less than three bureaucratic bodies would be involved, each one adding to the pile of documents in the boy's dossier. Since written examinations were not favoured as a technique in selection, it followed that decisions would have to be made on the basis of reports from men in totally different parts of the country and with different backgrounds and experience. The net result would

1. Fleming Report, op. cit., p. 31.
2. ibid., pp. 73–4.
3. ibid.

have been a reliance on personal opinion on the results of interviews, notoriously ineffective for adults and palpably absurd for such a period of change as boyhood. Compared with the simple sizing up of a possible new boy by the headmaster, it was an incredible procedure. Headmasters, like all human beings, are fallible and liable to bias, but their judgement was replaced by an even more hazardous chain of selective steps which could easily have degenerated into a sieve based on social attitude and experience.

Under this scheme—B, as it was called—a new social element amounting to a third of the total was designed to find its way to Eton, Harrow, Marlborough and the rest, and represent a ladder from the slum to the most exclusive boarding houses in the country.

Such a procedure required an elaborate organization with a clearing-house mechanism, and for this purpose a special Central Advisory Committee was to be set up at the summit. In trying to be fair to everybody, the Fleming Committee had produced a scheme that was cumbersome and top-heavy—one cannot evade the conclusion that their terms of reference had prevented them from investigating the matters which would have helped them most—the relative successfulness of these schools, the amount of privilege that was involved, the use of endowments and their possible redistribution, the limits of reasonable school expenditure, and matters of this kind.

The report was not well received. There were too many strings for many headmasters, although the independent schools as a whole 'were ready to accept the report in principle, and a committee under Sir Maurice Holmes was set up and issued a report in which the practical details were worked out'.[1] Many outside critics dismissed it as superficial, since the concept of the place of the public school in modern society was not challenged. From the wider view of education it was a most disappointing document, redeemed by one or two minor discussions of an academic interest. Opinion in influential circles had hardly advanced from the position of 1919, or from Norwood's suggestions fifteen years before in 1928:

. . . the boarding schools should offer free tuition and the state should pay the boarding fees together with a bursary where necessary

1. G. Fisher, op. cit.

. . . the boys . . . selected by interview on the basis of school record: and that the qualifications for election should not be intellectual pre-eminence in an examination. Such a scheme can have no chance unless it emanates from the Board of Education, and has the government behind it.[1]

It is ironic to think that at the very time the Fleming Committee was sitting and trying to bring some cohesion into our social system, Norwood himself was engaged with his own committee,[2] which had the opposite effect of consolidating the tripartite system in state secondary schools and splitting children into types.

The death-blow came quickly. The government decided against the bursary scheme and suggested that any money needed to send boys from state schools to boarding public schools should be provided by the local authorities. This evaded the issue and put an end to any successful outcome, as Norwood had predicted, for it raised at once all the emotional tensions of rates and local politics. The Minister, Ellen Wilkinson, in her Foreword to *The New Secondary Education*, put the matter very plainly indeed:

Until education in the state secondary schools is as good as the best that money can buy outside the state system, so long will inequalities remain. For that matter even when that end has been achieved, if people prefer to pay high fees for education less good or no better than that which the state provides free of charge to its tax payers, there is certainly no reason, in a free country, why they should not spend their money that way. Variety in education is a needed spice. But no state money will go to a school which does not provide places for children from the state primary schools either free or for fees paid by the local authority.[3]

There has been no change of heart since.

The relationships of the public schools to the state is defined in the 1944 Education Act, although public schools are not

1. Norwood, in Wilson, op. cit., p. 136.
2. The Norwood Committee referred to investigated changes in the curriculum and examinations in secondary schools. It was a committee of the Secondary School Examinations Council appointed by Mr Butler in October 1941. This committee tried to relate the curriculum to the character, aptitudes and abilities of children. Their statements on the three broad types of child did much to encourage the development of the tripartite system, although the seeds of this can be found in the Hadow and Spens reports mentioned above, if not in the 1902 and 1918 Acts.
3. E. Wilkinson, *The New Secondary Education*, 1947, Foreword.

mentioned specifically. They come under the heading of independent schools, and the provisions of this Act which are
relevant were designed to ensure a minimum level of efficiency
through a system of registration and inspection.

Altogether there are more than 4,000 independent schools in
this country, and public schools of the type which we have been
dealing with here are swamped by a host of day and boarding
schools of a bewildering variety. Educationally there is nothing
cohesive about this group at all, and usually they only share
common problems of finance and administration. The introduction of compulsory registration and inspection was very
necessary with the large number of small private schools of
doubtful viability since the state must see that its youth is not
exploited, but the new procedures do not really affect the public
schools proper since they possess standards at least as high as
state schools, and some are incomparably higher, as we shall
see.

A more promising clause of the Act for state–boarding-
school co-operation comes in Section 8, which at first sight
appears to encourage an open approach:

> . . . a local education authority shall, in particular, have regard to
> the expediency of securing the provision of boarding accommodation,
> either in boarding schools or otherwise, for pupils for whom educa-
> tion as boarders is considered by their parents and by the authority
> to be desirable.

There are children for whom boarding education is the only
possible solution. The victims of multiple handicaps, or of
broken homes, or those with parents overseas are cases in point,
but the expense is great and numbers are few and tend to be
exceptional. Sending boys or girls away in large numbers at
£400 or more each at the expense of the ratepayers would be a
very bold move indeed on the part of any council, especially as
fees go up year by year. It is equally doubtful if large-scale
bursaries will be contemplated by the national government, in
spite of the very large number of M.P.s educated at and
favourably inclined towards public schools.[1] Certainly the
Governing Bodies Association has few hopes in this direction.[2]
At the very least bursaries would demand some limits on

1. See p. 321.
2. Fisher, op. cit.

expenditure, as Ellen Wilkinson suggested, and this would automatically cut off the best and most important schools with their costly facilities. It would in fact evade the most vital part of the problem, which is that concerned with the schools at the very top.

There are practical problems too about filling a quarter, a half or even three-quarters of the places from state schools. From which particular category of the pupils at thirteen are the lucky ones to be chosen if the vague, unrealistic and bureaucratic approach of Fleming is not to be considered? From the ablest grammar pupils, or a cross-section of school society, including the secondary modern? Would recruitment be local or national? If past solutions of similar problems are any guide, it would probably end in creaming off the ablest grammar-school boys two years after entry, with disastrous results to the depleted schools, just as further creaming at twelve and thirteen robbed the secondary moderns of their best pupils and affected school morale. In effect the state system would become second best, officially stamped as such. For their part the public schools may well benefit from such a creaming process by continuing to educate a potentially privileged class, an *élite*. Moreover, by this method one could possibly justify the high expenses of the major schools on the plea that exceptional people require exceptional education. Robert Birley, who was a member of the Fleming Committee, put it this way:

The principle of 'creaming' would then be fully established in the English Educational system. The only alternative would be to insist on these schools foregoing their privileges; staff salaries would be fixed at Burnham rates, staff ratios would be raised to the general average, and, I suppose, the outer parts of the playing fields would be given over for Council housing estates.[1]

Many local authorities have their own boarding schools for sick and handicapped children, but only a few have gone to the length of starting their own boarding schools on the public-school pattern. At one time it seemed likely that the precedent set by Surrey and other authorities would be widely followed, but it is doubtful now if these pioneer efforts will be repeated to any significant degree, for there has been a general shift in

1. R. Birley, *The Public Schools*, Occasional Publications No. 3, University of Sheffield Institute of Education, 1957.

emphasis. The old accent on the development of secondary education has changed, and although this is still a pregnant part of the system, the major effort will soon be directed to further education in its various forms, in the expansion of technical education, in the growth of universities and in the freer distribution of scholarships. The whole picture points inevitably in this direction. The school has to some extent ceased to be an end in itself, and has become an intermediate part of a wider process—a sandwich, in effect, between the primary school and eighteen plus.

CHAPTER ELEVEN

The Modern Situation[1]

It has already been demonstrated that, by using the seven as a yardstick, we can arrive at certain arbitrary criteria for a public school, namely independence, boarding, size, exclusiveness and links with the traditional universities of Oxford and Cambridge. This approach, developed in Chapter 10 for the purposes of considering development and growth, produced a list of some seventy schools—a very large number if public schools are to claim any unique properties. In the opinion of many the range of facilities offered by such a large number of independent schools would automatically destroy any cohesive elements there might be. On the other hand, the words 'public school' have for many acquired such an aura of desirability as a sign of status, if not of education, that there is a constant tendency to extend the term so that schools without one or more of these criteria may claim companionship with the more exclusive.

Perhaps the most common effort to widen the field is to regard membership of the Headmasters' Conference or Governing Bodies Association as the main criterion. This has had a

1. General note on terms used in this chapter:
Aided: This is a voluntary school (i.e. one that is owned privately, usually by one of the churches). The church has two-thirds of the seats on the Board of Governors, and the schools can appoint and dismiss (through the Governors) their own teachers. They have control over the teaching of religion with safeguards for individual children under the normal conscience clauses. The cost of new fittings, and a quarter of the cost of external repairs, together with any improvements and enlargements, is borne by the owners. Internal repairs, maintenance, salaries, etc., are provided by the local authority. Apart from direct-grant schools, this is the maximum latitude allowed by the state to any organization running a school.
Controlled: This is a voluntary school, owned privately, usually by a church. A third of the seats on the Governing Body are occupied by the church, and denominational teaching can only take place on two periods a week. Teachers are appointed and dismissed by the local authority, with the provision that some (a fifth in some cases) must be reserved for teaching

paper claim to recognition since the Board of Education took this view in defining the scope of the Fleming Committee (1942), and there is no doubt that it has a simplifying convenience. However, administrative tidiness is not really a deciding factor, and since this wider approach would increase the numbers to 200 at least it becomes necessary to look more closely at the members of the conference.

There is a list of the conference schools in the official publication, *The Public and Preparatory Schools' Year Book*, and superficially the title of this volume provides in itself a case for considering any entry here as a public school. If, however, we are to infer from this that these schools, taken together, form a unified group, each one a little Eton bestowing some mystical benefit on its products, then we meet formidable objections.

For one thing, the conference has been growing in numbers since its inception, and its composition has varied slightly from year to year with a considerable cumulative effect. Of the fifteen schools represented at the birth of the conference at Uppingham at Christmas 1869, two are no longer members. Of those present in 1902, nine have disappeared. The birth- and death-rate of those on the borderline is therefore high, and the problem arises whether one should be ruthless and strictly up to date, only admitting those appearing in the latest *Year*

---

the religion of the foundation where this is an essential feature of the school. Finance is really the responsibility of the local authority. It will be seen that the foundation has much reduced powers compared to a school of the aided variety. This is the most freedom allowed by the state to a denominational school that wishes to maintain its independence without having any financial burden under normal circumstances.

County: This is the normal state school, owned by and maintained by the local authority.

There is a third variety of voluntary school, known as *special agreement*. It is derived from the 1936 Act and in terms of independence it is close to the aided variety. It does not concern us here since examples are relatively rare and no particular instances have been relevant in our discussions of the Headmasters' Conference.

The essential difference between aided and direct-grant schools (if we limit our consideration of the aided variety to grammar schools only) is not so much one of finance, or of facilities, but rather one of status. The direct-grant school works directly through the central authority, and the aided through the local council.

The number of direct-grant schools varies from time to time. The eighty-two given here rose to eighty-five in the next year, the latter figure being derived from a list kindly supplied by the Ministry of Education.

Book, or whether even a transitory membership justifies the accolade of public school. If we are going to include the latter, then the number approaches 400 rather than 200.

Another difficulty arises from the complex nature of the composition. In 1962 it not only included 108 schools that were independent, but also fifty-four direct-grant, six aided, three controlled and three county schools. In addition there were twenty-one other schools not in England at all—three in Wales, thirteen in Scotland, four in Ireland and one in Jersey.

The terms 'direct grant', 'aided', 'controlled' and 'county' are technical. They refer to schools which come under the umbrella of the state. In the case of direct-grant schools the relationship with the central authority is direct, in the other cases it lies through local education authorities. A county school is a normal state school. The aided and controlled varieties are maintained by the local authorities, who nominate a third of the governors in the case of aided and two thirds in the case of controlled schools. These proportions reflect the power and freedom of these schools in the appointment of staff or in teaching religious instruction. In the normal way, however, they are an integral part of the state system and their standards are, or should be, virtually identical. As for the direct-grant schools, these also lie within the state system and cannot really be distinguished from the others in any fundamental way apart from the technicalities of administration. However, since direct-grant schools include some examples of historical significance, like Manchester Grammar, it is necessary to dwell a little on this particular category to realize the essential differences between them and the independent schools.[1]

In 1962 there were eighty-two grammar schools for boys receiving grants directly from the Ministry of Education under Section 100 of the 1944 Act. Fifty-four of these were members of the Headmasters' Conference and were therefore connected in some respect with the main independent schools while

---

1. Although this is true, nevertheless there are outstanding similarities between schools. This has arisen through parental and public pressure concerning examinations as a basis for entry into suitable professions or universities. Much the same applies to the state system. In theory the headmaster of a state secondary school has complete control over his own curriculum, but in fact time-tables in schools as far apart as Cornwall and Northumberland bear an astonishing resemblance.

twenty-eight were not. Which particular set of properties excluded the headmasters of the twenty-eight from sitting at the conference table with their more fortunate fifty-four brothers, only detailed investigation or the conference itself could disclose. Details vary from year to year, but, in 1962, a day grammar school of this type received a grant of £39 a head, together with £66 for each boy in the sixth, as well as balances to cover experiments and losses due to any reduction of fees allowable on parental income. The local authority of a district has a considerable say in the choice of boys. A quarter must have spent at least two years in a 'state' primary school, and another quarter must be placed at the disposal of the authority if it so desires; while the rest, although fee payers, are drawn from the same locality since these are predominantly day schools. In addition, the rest of the regulations, from meals and milk to teachers and collective worship, bears an astonishing resemblance to the work of the normal grammar school in the state system. As for the key question of administration, either a third of the seats on the governing body must be given to the local authority directly, or else a majority of the governors must be 'representative' in the following manner: 'A Member of Parliament, a Mayor, a chairman or vice-chairman or member of a local authority . . . or a chairman or vice-chairman of an education committee of an authority, or of a parish meeting; or . . .' [1]

Again we see a considerable resemblance to the governing bodies of voluntary schools in the state system. With so many local people involved, from boys to governors, these are local schools in every sense. This is not surprising, since the major influences—Whitehall and the locality—have the state schools as their main responsibilities. Indeed, in staffing, buildings, playing-fields and the like, there is little to choose between the best of direct-grant and the best of state schools.

The position of the independent schools is quite different. They can do what they like. They recruit from the whole nation. They are not essentially linked with large centres of population and are therefore neither concerned with nor affected by local feeling. They can construct their own scale of fees and pay

1. *Direct Grant Schools Regulations*, issued by the government in the form of a statutory instrument. Amendments are issued from time to time.

salaries accordingly. They can alter policy, acquire property and expand or not as they wish, irrespective of the state of the nation. They can accept what boys they like. The headmasters are omnipotent.

These two kinds of school, independent and direct grant, are altogether different in kind, and the other varieties represented

Table 21. *Categories of schools in England and Wales represented on the Headmasters' Conference (1962).*[1]

Boys schools only	Number of schools	Percentage in H.M.C. (approx.)
Independent schools:		
All types	1,062	10%
Grammar type only	212	51%
Grammar with boarders	197	53%
Grammar with>200 boarders	85	89%
Direct-grant schools:		
All types	116	46%
Grammar type only	82	66%
Grammar with boarders	42	60%
Grammar with>200 boarders	10†	60%
County and voluntary schools:		
Grammar only	417*	3%

† Arbitrary allowances made for the lower starting age.
* Modern variants, e.g. comprehensive, omitted.

on the conference—the aided, the controlled and the county— are even more remote from the independent set.

Apart from the different problems of different types of school, the proportions elected to the conference from each group show that in no category is membership automatically guaranteed (Table 21). This table shows that there are important factors contributing to membership, most of which we have already assumed, namely, a grammar type of education, independence, boarding size and a direct grant for those schools which are not

1. Boys schools only are considered; mixed schools are omitted. For sources, see Appendix. Also Ministry of Education Statistics, Part I, 1962; list of direct-grant grammar schools in England and Wales.

independent. Although the common factors are interesting, it is the proportion omitted from each group which is most puzzling. What, for instance, is lacking in the excluded 34 per cent of direct-grant grammar schools that they too are not included? Why are experimental schools frowned upon? It is perhaps pointless to pursue these matters too deeply, for it would give to the conference undue significance. There is no doubt that it supplies a need and is useful to its members, but such a service does not necessarily imply status any more than belonging to a trade union or a bank. Again we are back with the problems of hierarchy, with definitions and the misuse of words. If we have to give a name to this miscellaneous collection of schools, then 'Conference Schools' would be a better umbrella word, if one were needed, leaving the old phrase 'public school', absurd though it may be to foreigners, for its original purpose before the conference was ever thought of. Perhaps the last word on this issue may be left to Robert Birley, headmaster of Eton, who put the matter in the clearest possible terms:

> . . . no one can define a Public School. The only definition I have ever come across is that which was employed by the Board of Education in setting up the Fleming Committee, 'a school which is represented on the Governing Bodies Association or the Headmasters' Conference', and one can hardly imagine anything less helpful than that.[1]

MODERN PROBLEMS

Essentially the problems of independent boarding schools concern finance, their clientele and their relationship to the state.

In line with the argument of the last chapter, it is easiest and most sensible to confine our considerations largely to those independent schools with 200 boarders or more, aged thirteen or over. In this way we can be sure of considering reasonably sized schools where the boarding element is significant.

FINANCE

The relationship of fees to the size of the schools in 1962 is listed in the Appendix and shown graphically in Figure 6. With the exception of Millfield, six of the original seven are the most expensive in the country, but what is really surprising is the

1. Birley, op. cit., p. 1.

general relationship which emerges. The larger the school, the higher the fees. By an analogy with industry one would have expected the opposite, namely, that the larger the plant the

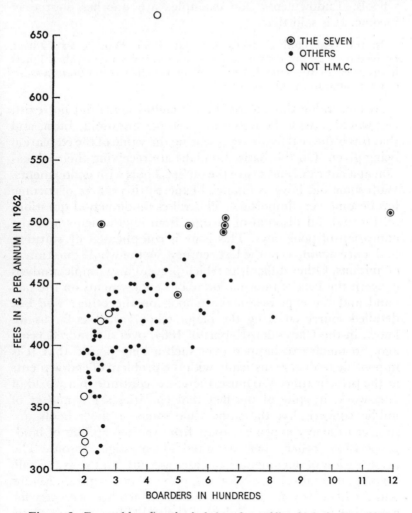

Figure 6. *Fees and boarding size in independent public schools for boys, 1962*

cheaper the cost of creating the product. This situation emphasizes that there are factors at work here which are unlikely to be defined neatly in economic terms.

In 1962 the basic fees at the better schools were about £500

per annum, and it would appear that £320 or so represented
the lowest reasonable limit. There are several matters, however,
which prevent us using these fees as simple comparisons between
schools. Endowments, for example, are another source of
income. It is said that:

> In the year ending December 31st, 1955, Winchester College
> derived over 20 per cent of its income from investments, the highest
> figure ever for this school. Eton College is believed to obtain a third
> of its income from this source.[1]

At face value this means that, if endowments did not exist,
fees would have to be raised to £750 per annum at Eton, and
that this is the real figure representing the value of the education
being given. On this basis, Etonians are receiving their education at a cut rate, and so are the other schools with endowments.
With some old boys as financial experts, this source of income
has become very important. This raises fundamental questions
on the rightful disposal of income from endowments and the
education of poor boys. This issue is complicated by statutes,
and, once again, as in the last century, by the whole question of
definitions. Other difficulties which prevent any simple analysis
concern the lack of information about endowments on the one
hand and the expenses of the schools on the other. The last
detailed source covering the major schools was, as far as we
know, in the Clarendon Report of 1864, over a hundred years
ago. So much can happen over such a long period that it is
impossible to deal realistically with the problem of endowments
at the present time. We must, therefore, continue in a world of
guesswork, in spite of the fact that charities are a matter of
public concern. At the same time some of the schools are
subject to heavy expenses, apart from the stockpiling of land,
property or other assets acquired for prestige reasons. The
preservation of documents is a case in point, and so is the safe
keeping, if not display, of pictures, plate, manuscripts, museums
and the like. How far these are matters which are necessary for
education or the responsibility of the individual schools alone
is a matter of opinion and will certainly vary greatly in each case.

Some of the fees are high, but whether they are too high
depends on the value placed on the returns which are given.

1. R. Williams, *Whose Public Schools?* Bow Group Publication, No. 11,
1957, p. 26.

Not all schools are expensive. In two schools at least there are either no fees at all or only token charges (Christ's Hospital and Royal Masonic).

The systematic study of fees is also made difficult by the way in which they change. In practice they increase in sharp jumps rather than gradually over time, each school presenting a different pattern. This means that any conclusions drawn from an analysis of a particular month or year must be treated with reserve. This applies equally to the figures given in the Appendix, and in view of the manner in which the schools are grouped in that list, it is clear that a great deal depends on whether or not a particular school had just raised its fees. The same remarks apply to a simple comparison of two occasions a few years apart. Nevertheless the change in twenty-three years, from the pre-war position of 1939 to 1962, using the same reference sources,[1] does indicate certain trends. If we examine the size of the fees, then the actual increase over this period varies from £223 to £318 for various independent boarding schools, and is distributed fairly evenly over both 'expensive' and 'cheap' schools. Thus Eton increased its fees from £245 to £508, a rise of £263, while, towards the lower end of the scale, Dover College has increased fees from £120 to £411, a rise of £291. Although problems of growing prestige should be taken into account, these two schools may perhaps be taken as typical, and it follows that there has been a levelling off over these twenty-three years and that, correspondingly, the largest increased percentages are to be found in those schools at the lower end of the table in 1939. Over this period Eton has increased its fees by 107 per cent, the increase for Dover College is 243 per cent and for Brecon 292 per cent. Were it not for the complexities of endowments and other matters we should be inclined to argue from these facts that standards have been altering so that the lower members are being lifted gradually into the same bracket as the major schools. This, however, would be a rash conclusion, as we shall see.

At a top school fees already stand over the £500 mark (1962), with the prospect of further increases to come,[2] and

1. *Public Schools' Year Book.*
2. Four years later (1966) fees at Eton had risen to £595 per annum, and altogether twenty-eight schools on our list were charging more than £500 per annum.

21

to these amounts must be added the usual quota for extra
subjects, private coaching, sports gear, clothing, holidays,
travel and the like. Altogether, if a boy stays at school for five
years, a parent must be prepared to spend between £2,500
and £3,000. This, however, only provides for the years
from thirteen to eighteen, and merely represents the second
stage of schooling and the second stage of expense, for
it is usual for a boy to pass through a preparatory school
first, entailing another five years or so of boarding between
the ages of seven or eight and thirteen. At a good preparatory
school this would add £1,600 or more. That does not end the
matter, for the public school leads naturally to the university
(old style), and three years there might well cost little
less per annum than at the public school itself, say a total
of £1,200 to £1,500. Altogether, without extravagance and
without the luck of scholarships, a child's education from the
age of eight to an honours degree could easily cost between
£5,000 and £6,000. If the parent has more than one son, then
this amount must be multiplied accordingly. Three sons will
cost him little short of £18,000. There are ways of reducing the
burden without dropping sights and choosing a less expensive
school further down the list, or even of abandoning boarding
education altogether. There are insurance schemes to spread
the load from birth or on a kind of delayed payment not
completed till some years after the schooldays have finished. In
some cases a deed of covenant or payment in advance can save
considerable sums of money, or even estate duty for grandparents. The following was one practical possibility existing
in 1965:

> As an example, if £400 per annum for five years will be required
> towards fees, and the payment is made thirteen years before the
> child's entry to the school (i.e. at his birth), the capital sum required
> will be about £1,290.[1]

Grandparents are often involved in this kind of financial
arrangement, and the efforts to maintain their income can lead
to complicated insurance schemes. Some occupations have
special boarding-school provisions. Opportunities overseas often
include very generous help with fees as well as holiday air travel

1. *The Times*, 8 February 1965.

for children as part of the contract. The same kind of social aid for staff is also creeping into British industry. Somewhat rarer is the case of a boy who wins a scholarship or obtains a grant from a local authority. There is no doubt, however, that for many parents the cost appears to be prodigious.

Although we know that the problem of fees can be alleviated in one or other of the various ways mentioned above, and no doubt in others too, we are ignorant of their impact—the number of boys involved in particular schools, the sums of money concerned. These, like the problems of endowments and expenses, are complicated and comprise a vast area for research. Without this vital internal information all talk of public-school aid or reform must be based on guesswork and hence be of limited value.

It is essential to be realistic about costs. There is no compulsion about any expenditure; the parent is a free agent. He could use the same amount of money on his children in a thousand ways other than education, since every penny of capital expenditure could be saved by sending his child to a series of state schools. Moreover, if his son were able and lucky enough, the end result could easily be the same. Oxford or Cambridge could still be the goal, even perhaps the same college. This is neither impossible nor unusual. Why, then, does any parent sacrifice this vast sum, and what precisely does he obtain in exchange for it?

BENEFITS OF PUBLIC-SCHOOL LIFE

Many of the benefits usually cited for public-school life are intangible, at best matters of prejudice or opinion. Norwood, in line with many others, once wrote a book about this,[1] and gave the assets of the English tradition as the Christian spirit, self-restraint, English culture, the true spirit of athletics and the spirit of service. One could well add the themes of scholarship wedded to the classics, and an increasing standard of excellence. These features by Norwood and others may well be the important ones, although they are by no means the exclusive prerogative of public schools, and an equally convincing case could be made out for education at home or at day schools. Unfortunately, Norwood's criteria suffer from the

1. C. Norwood, *The English Tradition of Education*, 1929.

defect of being difficult to measure, and are therefore the source
of a continual argument which, by its very nature, is endless.
A headmaster may well think that these are the important
issues by which a school should be judged, even if they are
intensely subjective, but the average parent, or child for that
matter, is more down to earth, and some of the educational
by-products which they would consider important *are* measurable and subject to analysis.

These measurable items concern examinations, the degree of
attention paid to individual boys, living-conditions at the school
itself and the success of old boys in later life.

All schools giving this particular kind of academic education
are concerned with some form of external examination. A recent
survey by the Ministry of Education has indicated that the
highest rate of success in the General Certificate of Education
at both ordinary and advanced levels among school-leavers in
1960–1 was achieved by the direct-grant grammar schools. In
view of their clientele, highly selective in terms of intellectual
ability, this is hardly surprising. Moreover, independent schools
comprise such a wide variety that combining all the results
from this category is meaningless.

Even within one school there are often sharp divisions in
ability. At Winchester, for instance, seventy scholars are
admitted as a result of a stiff competitive examination, while
the pressure to get in at all ensures that commoners are selected
from a very large number of applicants. A detailed investigation
of the ability of these boys was published in 1953 by Kenneth
Hutton: '. . . it seems fairly certain that not more than 1 per
cent of boys at Winchester College are below the median of the
population, and that exceedingly few scholars are not in the
top 1 per cent of the population'.[1]

Although the scholars represent a core of boys of high ability,
there are sufficiently able numbers in the commoners to ensure
that 40 per cent of the school as a whole are in fact in the top
1 per cent of the population, and it is not surprising, therefore,
that Winchester is, as we shall see, perhaps the most successful

1. K. Hutton, 'Intelligence Quotients and Differential Fertility—Some
Observations From Winchester College', *Eugenics Review*, xliv, January
1953, pp. 205–15.

boarding school, judged by its examination results. This situation is not new; it has remained constant for forty or fifty years.

It is difficult to find a yardstick to distinguish individual schools, although they themselves stress their connections with Oxford and Cambridge. For this reason there is a long tradition

Table 22. *Scholarships and exhibitions to Oxford and Cambridge, 1957–61.*[1]

Type of school		Scholarships and exhibitions
Direct-grant day	Manchester Grammar School	140
Independent*	Dulwich	128
Independent boarding	Winchester	102
Independent*	St. Paul's	79
Direct-grant day	Bradford Grammar School	73
Independent boarding	Rugby	72
Direct-grant day	Bristol Grammar School	72
Independent†	King's Canterbury	72
Independent boarding	Marlborough	65
Independent boarding	Downside (R.C.)	62
Independent boarding	Christ's Hospital	58
Independent boarding	Eton	56
Direct-grant day	King Edward's Birmingham	55
Independent*	King's Coll. S., Wimbledon	54
County (L.E.A.) day	King Edward VII, Sheffield	53
Independent boarding	Shrewsbury	51
Independent boarding	Ampleforth (R.C.)	49
Direct-grant day	Latymer Upper	48
Independent‡	Clifton	46
Independent day	City of London	44

* Mainly day
† Mainly boarding.
‡ Boarding and day.

of comparison which relies on that crown of achievement, an open scholarship to one of the older universities. Here the magnet of Oxford and Cambridge is sufficient to draw in the brighter boys from a wide range of schools—state and independent—and the results of the top twenty in order of success, over five years from 1957 to 1961, is given in Table 22. As we

1. Figures taken from Sampson, *Anatomy of Britain*, op. cit. p. 191.

should expect, Winchester is near the top, and presumably other schools close to it have the same kind of 'intelligence' quality in their intake. All but one of these schools are members of the Headmasters' Conference. Nine are essentially boarding, ten are day and one is a mixture of the two, although some of the boarding schools have a few day scholars and vice versa. On this showing there is virtually nothing to choose between boarding and day schools. The boarding schools represented here are of several kinds, old established and relatively new, Anglican and Roman Catholic, and similarly the day schools are not homogeneous either, five of them being direct grant, four independent and one a state grammar school with a long and diverse tradition.

A merit list based simply on the number of scholarships gained makes no allowance for school size. A school of 500 boys that produces fifty scholarships in five years has a certain claim to superiority over another school with the same record but with 1,000 boys on roll. If we allow for size, then Winchester quite easily becomes the leading school, followed by King's Canterbury, Manchester Grammar, and a group consisting of Dulwich, St Paul's, Bradford Grammar, Downside, Christ's Hospital and King Edward's, Birmingham. Eton would move to the bottom of such a list. However, if we are to consider school size as important in itself, then a small school with results too modest to be included in Table 22 may well come higher than those mentioned.

Comparisons of this kind cannot be pressed too far, since open scholarships are not the goal of every headmaster, and many a brilliant scholar in a small school, or a school without this tradition, escapes the hothouse. The ethos of the school is important too. It is difficult to believe that the boys of Eton and Winchester are to the same degree really interested in the same goals and the same academic competitive achievements. Moreover, methods of entry and the quality of child, staff and surroundings vary enormously. What different types of education, boarding and day, public and non-public, would achieve with identical boys, identical masters and identical facilities is another matter.

It will be noted from Table 22 that only one state school was involved, and this may lead to the conclusion that state schools

are inferior. On this question the Robbins Committee on Higher Education also noted that, for men, 54 per cent of entrants to Oxford and Cambridge came from independent schools compared with 30 per cent from state schools, and that this represented a persistent state of affairs. They commented as follows:

We do not doubt that, in the past, prejudices weighted the scales against the applicants from maintained schools; and we think that such influences have not altogether ceased to operate. Moreover, the able boy from a small grammar school and a home with no tradition of higher education may not find it easy to make his quality apparent at interview to those responsible for selection. But in general we believe that nowadays the candidate from a maintained school who actually presents himself for entrance receives due consideration of his claims. A significant cause of the disproportionate representation of the independent schools seems to be that relatively fewer boys from maintained schools apply. The reasons for this are various. Many maintained schools, with staffing difficulties and shortages of specialist accommodation, cannot afford to organize for a few pupils the specialized instruction necessary to ensure success. Moreover, it is sometimes difficult for pupils in maintained schools, who are normally older when they gain passes at the Ordinary level than their fellows in independent schools, to spend three years in the sixth form. But we suspect that the main explanation is that they feel convinced that their chances are small. This in turn is probably connected with the relative lack of contact between the colleges of Oxford and Cambridge and maintained schools.[1]

Although independent schools may contribute so greatly to Oxford and Cambridge, and the fact of getting there at all may be a considerable achievement in itself, the quality of the university work is also important. Wastage in terms of men not obtaining a degree is high for boarding schools in relation to the others (6 per cent),[2] and the percentage obtaining first- and second-class degrees is low (50 per cent) compared with those from maintained schools (67 per cent).[3] Similar results have been obtained in other surveys where Oxford and Cambridge were taken separately.[4] These are very general and disappointing

1. Robbins Report, 1963, pp. 80–1. The official name for this Report was *Higher Education*. It was produced by the Committee on Higher Education. appointed by the prime minister under the chairmanship of Lord Robbins,
2. ibid, Appendix 2 (A), p. 134.
3. ibid.
4. ibid., pp. 317–19.

figures for the public schools, but what precise differences
they hide between different levels of the hierarchy are unknown.
Certainly such categories as 'boarding schools' and 'independent
schools' are far too broad. Individual and intensive details from
half a dozen diverse schools over the whole academic field are
needed before we can begin to appreciate the real situation.
As it is, we know that the university results for Winchester have,
on the whole, been unsatisfactory, with their Oxford contingents
of boys born between 1900 and 1919 having a record of 50 per
cent or more of fourths, passes or failures (Bishop).

On a less ambitious note there is evidence of successes at
O-level with less able boys. One study of all known boys in
public schools (1,172) who had failed eleven plus and were
therefore considered by the state (at that time) as being unfit
for grammar-school education, produced the following conclusions: 'About 70 per cent got 5 or more passes at "O" level
before leaving their public schools, the average number per boy
being between 5·5 and 6 showing signs of increasing. . . .' [1]

This is creditable, but it could be argued that similar results
have been obtained in some pockets of the state system, as in
part of the East Riding of Yorkshire. It all lends colour to the
belief that the national pool of ability is much greater than the
traditional grammar-school mind would admit, and, with
advancing medical science, it may well be limitless.

When all the present evidence is considered—and most of it
is very unsatisfactory—the parent of a boy at a public boarding
school can at least be assured that he will receive an education
which bears comparison with the best in terms of open competition, and that if his son possesses talent he will probably receive
his due reward.

The second kind of fact about education that is measurable
is the degree of personal tuition, the yardstick being size of class.
The Clarendon schools have moved a long way from the
position in the last century, when the more expensive the school
the larger the class. By and large the reverse is now the rule.

Dividing the number of boys by the number of teachers gives
a rough and ready indication of class size, although there are
difficulties. For one thing, the number of extra and part-time

1. *The Times Educational Supplement*, 17 May 1963, p. 1061.

teachers must be considered, while the lengths of terms and the number of hours taught per week by the average teacher varies from school to school. Again, some members of staff whose names appear on the lists have other duties. None the less the pupil–teacher ratio does give some indication of the amount of personal attention given to each boy. The statistics issued by the Ministry of Education, covering the whole country, boys and girls alike, are the only real source of information for a comparison. Four distinct categories of school are shown in Table 23.

Table 23. *Pupils per teacher in four types of school dealing with secondary pupils (1962).*[1]

Type of secondary school	Pupils per teacher	Notes
Independent schools recognized as efficient	11·5	284 schools involved, including the main public schools (boarding).
Direct - grant grammar schools	17·5	Includes 179 schools, of which 54 are in the H.M.C.
L.E.A. grammar schools (maintained)	18·0	This figure is based on 1,287 schools, mainly day, with a curriculum corresponding to the direct grant.
Secondary modern schools	20·8	For the less able pupils. 3,899 schools. Academic work often limited.

It is clear from this evidence that there are almost twice as many teachers per boy in the independent secondary (efficient) schools, which includes the public schools, than in the secondary modern. This is particularly important to the parent, because, until 1966 at any rate, the alternative scholastic route lies through the state system, and the sieve of eleven plus[2] does not

1. Figures taken from Ministry of Education, *Statistics of Education*, Part I, 1962 (1963). The figures include girls' schools. Allowances have been made for part-time teachers.
2. The 1944 Act states that all children in the state system, unless they suffer from disabilities, must pass from the primary to the secondary

give him a personal guarantee of a choice between the local
grammar and the modern schools, and the certainty that his
son may enjoy the somewhat preferable ratio and graduate
staffing of the grammar school. Again, if a grammar type of
approach is considered essential by the parent, by virtue
of his own particular educational reasoning, then the only
alternative may be, finances allowing, to withdraw the
boy from the state system altogether. The choice between
the figures 11·5 and 20·8 can be largely a question of
money. The obvious inference from these figures is that
a boy in an independent secondary school can get much
closer personal tuition and care than in any other kind of
school. The figure of 11·5 covers 284 schools, and takes care of
all the extremes to be found within them. The more exclusive
the school the fewer pupils to a teacher, and vice versa. In
the original seven, for instance, the ratio is nearer 10:1, and
it is lower still in some denominational schools, while in one
special case at least (Millfield) the proportion is almost half this
figure.

In view of what has already been said of the equivalence of
scholarship results between some direct-grant and boarding
schools (shown in Table 22), these pupil–teacher ratios have
most interesting educational implications.[1] There is no doubt

school—i.e. that there must be a break in surroundings. It also says that
children must be educated according to the three A's—age, ability and
aptitude—with a sufficient variety of school to suit the differing qualities of
children. This has meant (until the realization of universal comprehensive
education, foreshadowed in Circular 10/65) that some kind of selection of
children must be made so that they can go to appropriate secondary schools
at eleven-plus. Efforts have been made in some areas to eliminate the whole
problem of separation either by providing comprehensive schools or by
allowing parental wishes to be fulfilled, by having further breaks in education either earlier or later on, or in other ways. None the less it is still
generally true to say that before a child can be admitted to a grammar school
(or the 'grammar stream' of a comprehensive school) he must have attained
a certain minimum level of achievement, to be tested by examination, or at
least have certain measurable innate abilities. To this extent parental
desires and ambitions are limited. The only real alternative to the 'gamble'
of eleven-plus or its equivalent is to abandon the state system altogether and
patronize the independent schools, of which the public schools are the most
celebrated examples.
1. Pupil–teacher ratios can hide a multitude of significant differences in
teaching, besides the differences to be expected between individual schools.
A detailed analysis somewhat on the lines of the Clarendon Report of 1864
would be essential for any real understanding.

that many direct-grant day schools, and even some state schools, in spite of the greater number of pupils to a teacher, produce results which are equally good, and it is possible to argue, for instance, that class size may not be a matter of great importance for the outstanding pupil. Like all educational issues, this is a complex problem for the figures in Table 23 are general; there is no guarantee that such ratios apply in any particular school. Even in a situation where the figure is reduced to eleven or less, there are certainly large classes as well, while in state grammar schools many classes are small, especially in the sixth form. This is a most important matter about which we have very little information and none that is without prejudice. A modern review is needed, if only to indicate how far the interests of particular parents are being served. As a very general statement, however, it would seem likely that, for some public schools at any rate, boys of normal or less than normal ability have a chance of enjoying personal tuition in small classes which is denied to those in the state system. It is a mere matter of observation that in the top schools rooms are small and only hold half or two-thirds the number for which the state-school classroom is designed.

Whether a small pupil–teacher ratio is important only accurate long-term research could tell, but there is a strong feeling in the profession that it is so, and the situation existing at Millfield and elsewhere may well bear it out.

Another feature of school life, extremely difficult to measure, but nevertheless important, is the material background—the acres of land, the bricks and mortar. The difficulty of arriving at common criteria here is that each school is unique, and there is nothing in the independent system as a whole to correspond with the similarity between one state grammar school and the next. The facilities to be provided in the state system are laid down in one of the statutory instruments, amended and brought up to date at intervals and commonly called the building regulations. Here are to be found the ministerial limits of generosity. As an example we may quote from the provision for a day school of 600 pupils. An average school of this type should have a site of $3\frac{3}{4}$ acres, with a paved area of 34,200 square feet and 12 acres of playing-field (approximately thirty-six boys to

the acre).[1] The teaching area is also defined within limits, together with the number of sanitary fittings, wash basins, size of dining-hall and the rest. A national system with thousands of schools and thousands of headmasters to cope with, is dependent on architects and planners who are sensitive to public opinion and accusations of waste and favouritism. The result is a deadening effort to be fair to all areas, with inevitable ceilings on expenditure, standardization and a collaboration between many local authorities to cut costs. Whether this is a necessary part of a national system is a matter of opinion, but certainly the urge to economize is ever present, one typical outcome being that schools get far less than the one acre for thirty boys that R. F. Cholmeley thought a minimum as far back as 1928.[2] All this is common knowledge which the average person, expert or not, acquires instinctively as he attends school and observes the various buildings in the area. Direct-grant schools are usually old foundations, often older in appearance, but are essentially alike in design, purpose and general standard.

Public schools are quite different. Governing bodies consist of men picked for their eminence rather than local influence; they are certainly not concerned that the costs of their particular school should bear any relationship to the costs of another. With their national recruitment parents are strangers too, and the schools have developed according to their own policies without reference to the locality in which they happen to be. It is true that almost all the important and ancient schools were local in origin, but their rise to public-school status entailed a complete divorce from local influence in any meaningful way. It is usual for these schools to form communities of their own. The development of an impressive setting and façade is a distinctive feature. The landed gentry might be an outmoded class to which the schools were at one time wedded, but it is by no means a coincidence that the essential material background to that class—the estate atmosphere, the park, the seclusion, the acres, the architecture, the rows of trees—are

1. These figures are based on *The Standards for School Premises Regulations*, 1959, S.I. 1959, No. 890. It should be mentioned that there should be some increase for sixth forms. These same regulations give details for such matters as sanitary fittings, wash basins, meals, dormitories, heating, lighting, etc.
2. Wilson (ed.), op. cit., p. 12.

essential elements of this kind of education. The top schools
have no need to shout their wares or their statistics from the
housetops. Their place in history is common knowledge, and so
are their standards. They do not have to struggle for clients,
although excellence is expected of them none the less, but those
lower in the hierarchy make a point of mentioning their assets.
In state schools, as we have seen, it is a question of the number
of boys per acre, but in the independent variety there is often
more than one acre per boy, in some cases two or three, and in
one instance more than four (Lord Wandsworth College). This
superior style is deliberate. As one school expresses it, 'The
influence of this environment [1,200 acres] is held to be of
significance in the education of a boy whatever may be his
future career.' [1]

Some of the schools have acquired great wealth over the
years. Three of them—Eton, Winchester and Christ's Hospital
—have notable collections of plate.[2] Ancient manuscripts and
books are to be found at Stonyhurst, and in profusion at Eton.
Again, the archives at Eton are vast by any standards. The
older parts of some schools are scheduled as ancient monu-
ments; notable museums are common, and some have more
than one. This background, which is undeniably impressive, is
seen especially in those schools with a multiple foundation,
where the fabric is really the responsibility of a separate
institution, and where the in-coming head cannot sweep away
all the ancient stuff from pique or because he does not like or
understand it. This kind of historical disaster has happened
frequently in schools with ancient foundations where the
headmaster has been virtually the sole authority.

It is not only in their ancient relics that the old schools are
outstanding. It is their attitude to scholarship which is so
refreshing. It was seen in Arnold, but especially in Samuel
Butler and Kennedy, and among assistant staff members, like
J. M. Wilson.[3] Inevitably such attitudes are rare, for research

1. *Public and Preparatory Schools Year Book*, 1961, p. 310.
2. For the collection of plate at Winchester, see *The Connoisseur*, January
1962, pp. 24–33.
3. This is the true spirit of intellectualism, and is seen in the sharp contrast
between the average teacher and the university don. It is essentially the
difference between the workman and the professional. The real difficulty
lies in trying to explain the significance of research and of reading in depth

is the hardest taskmaster of all. Nevertheless, the view that good teaching at any level infers standing on the threshold of new knowledge is not understood in the state system, while here, in the independent sector, it is not unknown for the staff not only to do research, but to be expected and encouraged to do it. But whereas this certainly applies to the top schools, standards fall off markedly lower down the scale so that most of the eighty-five boarding schools mentioned in Chapter 10 on p. 269 have facilities no better than the state recognizes and supplies to its own schools. The need for the replacement of outdated buildings and the need to introduce new facilities, like laboratories for science, is a continual drain on resources, and the difficulties of the 'lesser' schools can be illustrated by the efforts of the Industrial Fund for the Advancement of Scientific Education in distributing money for buildings and apparatus for sixth forms in non-state schools. Major schools like Eton, Marlborough, Rugby and Winchester can always guarantee to raise funds from their wealthy old-boy connections, and all these have in fact done so in recent years. While a quarter or half a million pounds can be raised in this way, help of this magnitude is quite beyond the resources of lesser establishments. All these factors tend to make the rich schools richer and the poorer ones nearer to the level of viability and the state minimum.

The standards set by the major schools in space, buildings, equipment and sheer fullness of living are a perpetual challenge, and in this lies much of their educational justification. They are, indeed, a living example of what the environment of education can be. Whether all this produces better men and women in the long run is another matter, but there is no denying that it is expensive and thereby exclusive. It comprises a subtle elegance that the parent expects and that in fact he pays for.

Examinations, personal tuition and the outward signs of elegance may be important, but, strangely enough, for many of the boys and parents the most solid return for the money spent has nothing to do with the school in any educational sense.

to a teacher audience which has no appreciation of it. Such phrases as 'relevance to the classroom', 'child-centred education', 'ivory towers', 'feet on the ground' only help to obscure the real issues.

It refers to the greater chances in life enjoyed by public-school boys over boys of equal ability educated elsewhere, and is linked with the strength of school solidarity and its hold over scholars past and present. School loyalty usually begins in the school and continues in the Old Boys' Society, although for the 30 per cent or so of scholars in the old schools with old boys for fathers, the process had already begun in the cradle. From the age of thirteen, if not before, everything traps the boy in a web of awe and loyalty. The school atmosphere plays its part, and so does the stress on manliness, chapel, confirmation and common ways of speech and codes of behaviour. In time the boy's name will appear in the published register alongside his fellows, together with an appendage of notes, whose length will indicate his success in life. The school's importance is also inflated by frequent notices in *The Times*, in obituaries, in lists of scholarships, prize-winners, degrees and feats of sportsmanship at university. Behind it all is an implied success-story both for the school and the individual. Even those who do not make the print have an implied assurance from the richness and success of parents who can afford the fees. The linkage with important people is also seen in the parade at Speech Day, and at Lord's, and in the return of old boys in triumph, as with Churchill to Harrow, or even in the solemn burial of the dead, as in the case of Wavell at Winchester. Any important and influential links are thereby manifest, and, by inference, it is assumed that a step into Eton or Winchester or one of the other major schools is the first step to success. The justification for this assumption, if any, is our purpose here, bearing in mind the contribution of the schools to the Victorian era. It can be demonstrated either in particular schools dealt with intensively, or from a wide survey of successful posts in government, industry and elsewhere.

The school which has been analysed most intensively from the modern point of view is Winchester, and T. J. H. Bishop was able to trace the careers of boys over a long period from 1820 to 1922, working in decades.[1] This is as reasonably up to date as is possible, since most old boys of periods later than 1922 have not really had time to make their mark in the world. Almost all Wykehamists, where details are known, became professional people. As for the quality of professional men, these

1. Bishop, op. cit.

were divided into three levels with an *élite* at the top consisting
of the so-called leaders liable to receive honours. The rankings
adopted were similar to those used when we were discussing
the question of members of *élites* from Harrow and Rugby in
the Victorian age (see pp. 217–8). On this basis a quarter of
Wykehamists became members of the *élite*. It has been pointed
out already that Winchester is exceptional in its intellectual
intake, so that the mere fact that so many reach the higher
ranks of the armed forces, the law and other professions is not
surprising at first sight. However, when this problem is probed,
the intellectual background appears to matter less and less. Of
the high flyers who obtained firsts at the university, less than
half reached the *élite* state, while 38 per cent of those who
reached the same *élite* obtained no degree at all! The fact that
classics degrees were prominent among these successful men also
indicates that it was the spirit of amateurism—i.e. without the
indispensable and specialized knowledge necessary for technical
posts—that mattered, rather than the sphere of interest. All
this lends colour to the assumption that public schools capture
the heights through nurturing the spirit of amateurism and
social influence. This conclusion is strengthened by the fact
that these same researches stress the importance of having a
father within the *élite* ranks already. Winchester is virtually
two schools—a majority of able boys and a highly intelligent
core, as the work of Hutton indicates—and this has some
bearing on the particular *élite* into which a boy goes. The
products of Winchester do well in life—that is amply
demonstrated—but some of these results indicate that this is
not due to the efforts of the school itself so much as to the
particular selection of boys and to their social and influential
environment. This is a subtle but most important point, and
it is not surprising that the simpler view prevails of assuming
that Winchester itself conveys success.

Winchester is a very exceptional school, and one would
expect the social and family influences to be even more pronounced at Eton and Harrow, and perhaps at one or two others.
The generalizations we have made are in line with other recent
studies and with the Victorian and modern conclusions discussed in an earlier chapter. In an investigation of *Who's Who*,
made in 1961, 36 per cent of the names were found to belong

to conference schools, with Eton accounting for one in six of these entries.[1] The Etonian representation is not unexpected considering the automatic inclusion of many titled people, but such a bias will hardly be effective for more than two or three schools. If we make allowance for size of school, then Eton still heads the list, followed by Winchester, Wellington, Rugby, Harrow, Westminster, Haileybury, Bradfield, Marlborough, Repton, Tonbridge, Charterhouse, Clifton, Cheltenham, St Paul's, Shrewsbury, Uppingham, etc. It reads like a list of eminent schools of the last century, and is strangely different from the list based on open scholarship results seen in Table 22. Where, in fact, have all those day schools gone which, in terms of examinations, were on equal or better terms than the schools from *Who's Who*. The obvious initial argument would be that social influence is an overwhelming factor in obtaining top jobs.

Another way of viewing the success of public schools arises from the situation in politics, the City, industry and the Civil Service.

The importance of the public schools in politics and government has already been indicated in some detail (Chapter 9). The influence at top level, in the Cabinet, is well known, but it is the contribution to the lesser ranks—the back-benchers—which is perhaps more significant at the present day. An analysis of the 1955–9 Parliament shows that about 20 per cent of Labour and 74 per cent of Conservative back-benchers graduated from the public schools, while one school, Eton, supplied no less than a fifth of the Conservative places.[2] In a similar way only 10 per cent of Conservative back-benchers came up through the state system, and we are assured that similar figures applied to the Parliament of 1959–64. There is also a second-generation effect, for while 78 per cent of Labour M.P.s (1965) sent their children to state schools (including direct grant) only 17 per cent of Conservative M.P.s did so.[3] There are obvious important social and political implications here, apart from the relevance of the education itself, but from the particular aspect we are considering they are all unimportant beside the fact obvious to parents that public-school

1. *The Times Educational Supplement*, 20 October 1961, p. 526.
2. Berrington and Finer, op. cit.
3. *The Times Educational Supplement*, 26 March 1965, p. 938.

products are to be found in large numbers in high and
influential places. This does not mean that the rich, fond parent
is deluded enough to see his son as a potential prime minister
and decides on his education accordingly, but there is no
denying that a boy at a top school will be in class and living
with many boys who will grow into influential men later on,
and who are indeed already members of influential families.
At one time church livings were often given to family friends,
and acquaintance in youth was usually regarded as a convenient stepping-stone. If this situation has altered nowadays,
the principle remains the same—the technique of mixing and
getting to know the right people is still supposed to be one of
the assets that is the natural outcome of public-school life.
In some occupations, like those in the City, this is said to be
more important than ability. Anthony Sampson expresses it
like this:

'It doesn't matter *what* you know, but *who* you know', they say in
the City: personal contacts, and the personal background which
provides them, are still decisive. This helps to account, perhaps, for
the fact that the City remains the unchallenged bastion of the
minor public school, and within the square mile you hear more talk
about men's schools, background, and above all their families, than
anywhere else except perhaps in the Guards. The waves of the
meritocracy, of examination wallahs and the managerial revolution
which have swept through the Civil Service and industrial corporations, have hardly rippled the City. The 'Old Boy Net', which
has become a sheepish or satirical phrase in other areas, remains a
venerable concept.[1]

If the City is the refuge of the ignorant but reliable amateur,
the same is true for industry. Public-school men are to be found
in managerial posts everywhere, variously estimated at a third
or a half, depending on the level concerned. They enter as
'trainees' half-way up the ladder, and again it is the so-called
public-school character that is sought after rather than any
particular knowledge. In England the kind of wide-eyed superficial view that is considered so essential has not found favour
in countries abroad. This is brought out strongly in David
Granick's up-to-date study of the European executive:

The British system of management selection is marked by two
strands which sharply contrast with those of the French and Belgian

1. Sampson, op. cit., p. 347.

patterns. One of these is the emphasis on amateurism, so pronounced that half the directors in charge of production have not bothered to earn even a minimal paper-qualification certifying to their competence. The second strand is the absence of any intellectual pre-selection of candidates for management. With or without higher education, with or without professional qualifications, all are eligible for top management. Since management is considered to be neither a profession nor a field in which intellectual attainments are particularly important, pre-selection of managerial candidates on scholarly grounds is ruled out as irrelevant. This leaves the intangible of 'character' as the deciding factor in determining managerial potential. But how can character be recognized? The first rough-and-ready criterion is graduation from one of those institutions which devote themselves to building character. The Public Schools play this role. . . .[1]

Whether just or not, this system favours the public-school boy, makes academic ability seem unimportant and eleven plus part of another world. This trend of employing public-school men is increasing, particularly among those who rise to high positions early in life. It confirms the impression from Winchester and elsewhere.

It has been suggested that the present interest of the public schools in the sphere of management is due to the new social status acquired by industry after the dearth of suitable outlets following on the death of the Empire and the decline of the Colonial Service. However, it has been shown earlier that business was already among the leading occupations for boys among the entrants to the public schools in the 1870s and 1880s. These boys would correspond with leavers from 1875 onwards, and the actual situation therefore shows that business and the Empire were parallel outlets for a long period.[2] The superficial replacement of one outlet for another is false, and the background is clearly complex. However that might be, there is no doubt of the apparent favour given to independent-school products compared with those from the state system, and there is also evidence that even within the favoured group one can distinguish between major and minor schools both in their degree of success and their attitude to the job in hand.[3]

1. D. Granick, *The European Executive*, 1962, pp. 298–9.
2. For details, see the corresponding sections in Chapter 9 and elsewhere. For an opposite opinion, see Granick, op. cit., p. 101.
3. For the distinctive differences between schools, and the relationships of these to success and attitudes, see ibid., pp. 132–6.

Another well-publicized field in which the public-school product is favoured is the Civil Service. Although there may be no deliberate attempt to prefer one type of education to another, the facts reflect a higher proportion of success for public-school products at all levels than seems reasonable on a proportional basis. This is seen particularly well in Professor Kelsall's analysis of senior civil servants.[1] For instance, if one takes 1,045 men of the rank of assistant secretary and above in 1950, one finds that 113 (10·8 per cent) came from the nine Clarendon schools (the seven, plus St Paul's and Merchant Taylors'). In earlier years, 1929 and 1939, the corresponding figures were sixty-seven (22·6 per cent) and seventy-eight (16·5 per cent). Thus the numbers are going up even if the percentage is declining with the overall increase of posts. About a quarter (23·2 per cent) of those who in 1950 achieved the rank of assistant secretary and above came from one of the independent boarding schools.

The position in the Civil Service, the City and industry is in many ways the same, and in other ways quite different. All are based on the same spirit of amateurism, though to different degrees and at different intellectual levels. The Civil Service has a sieve for selecting character and brain power based on the apparent theory that it is immaterial on what particular pabulum the brain has been nurtured so long as the young man showed brilliance in it at an early age. Background knowledge, which many might consider relevant to the post of a top government executive, is not required, and indeed is not required at any level, even on entry. In contrast to the situation found in many other countries, the British Civil Service relies on the so-called 'open mind'—brilliant, no doubt, but without expertise.[2] Again we have the same fundamental reliance on amateurism which was seen elsewhere, while the new stop-gap training being introduced hardly alters the position.

One is tempted to ascribe the faith in amateurism and belief in character to public schools and family influence with an argument along the following lines. Men in top positions in this country are public-school products themselves, with sons who are also at public schools. It is in their interests to promote the

1. R. K. Kelsall, *Higher Civil Servants in Britain*, 1955.
2. For the working of the Civil Service, and its general attitude to expertise, etc., see Sisson, op. cit.

myth of the character-developing powers of these schools. On this basis, character combined with intellectual prowess counts for more than true insight of modern problems or knowledge of anything useful. Certainly this covers many of the facts, but whether it is an adequate explanation only research into the minds, interests and backgrounds of the men who devised and persisted with the selection procedures, could determine.

With the examples of the City, industry and the Civil Service enough has been said to indicate the usefulness of a public-school background. It is still true that many public-school products, particularly from the top schools, do not enter the competitive race for jobs, while, on the intellectual level, the implications of the open scholarship results already given (p. 309) show that many are well capable of carving their own way in the professional field, even if the results at Oxford and Cambridge are disappointing. All this adds up to the fact that the parent is sinking money into a long-term investment which stands at least a chance of paying off.

Apart from the intangible philosophies of education which headmasters love to extol, and which are piously given out from the platform at every speech day, the hard-headed parent knows that the real advantages for him and his son lie in scholastic achievement, in personal attention in class, in the 'gentry' standards of life, in acquiring friends and in the increased chances for the future over his 'equals' in the state system.

This may well be the situation now, and some students can find no reason for anticipating change for at least another twenty-five years, yet faith in public-school predominance rests on certain assumptions. How long, for instance, will the spirit of amateurism prevail? In spite of the fact that the Civil Service still appoints historians and classicists to the exclusion of more relevant subjects like economics and science, there are indications that it is on the wane, and once it has died, a great deal of preference must collapse with it. On the other hand, if history is any guide at all, one should not expect this to happen too suddenly, for there were indications a century ago that science might be coming in, but in fact it has taken a century to mature and there are still odd corners unconquered. There are signs too that secondary education to eighteen, whether public school or not, is ceasing to be regarded as an end in itself and an

adequate preparation for a lifetime. With the expansion of universities and technical institutions of all kinds,[1] a degree, or at least an adult education in depth, may well become a standard piece of equipment for the first rung of any serious career, and that will make schooling correspondingly less important.

Not every public boarding school is an Eton. Whereas most of what has been said applies to a select few, the farther one goes down the list so do advantages, in the sense of privilege, slowly disappear. The exact range of privilege from top to bottom is an open question, and it would be ludicrous in the extreme to suggest that the least popular schools convey the same advantages as those at the top. At the same time, some properties of the great rub off on the small, in general estimation at least. To some extent this means that many parents are living in vain hope rather than fact, and this makes the need for a comprehensive and recognized analysis even more urgent.

PROBLEMS OF RELATIONSHIPS TO THE STATE

It is no part of our purpose to look into a crystal ball, but there are threats to the existence of the public schools which must at least be mentioned.

The economic dangers have been greatly exaggerated, for the schools are full and the number of people able to afford the fees shows no signs of slackening. Nowadays the major schools are booked for twelve years ahead, and this virtually means that boys must be registered within a year or so of birth. This is excellent for the schools, since it guarantees their prosperity even if the educational implications from such an advanced pre-selection are not so laudable.

The income of the seventy or so reasonably sized and large independent boarding schools amounts to about £14,000,000 per annum at the present time (1963) from fees alone.[2] To this must be added income from investments and endowments, while their capital value in buildings, land, assets is clearly very great indeed and quite beyond private or research computation other than that inspired by an official source at the topmost

1. For an analysis of the need for expansion of universities and associated matters, see Robbins Report, op. cit.
2. Figures calculated from details of schools given in the Appendix.

level. This solid investment is sometimes thought to provide a margin of safety on the grounds that the state could not afford to deal piecemeal with a system of this magnitude, and could not, in the event of closure, readily provide a form of alternative education for the boys who would no longer be educated privately. This is a naïve view, not only in terms of national income and historical experience, but also in terms of education. The national recruitment of the present schools may have educational and social advantages, but it results in the grave weakness of the boys being very widely and thinly spread geographically. Correspondingly, the absorption of these children into the state system would not strain any particular local resources unduly, and would certainly not present problems of the same magnitude which arise whenever there is a rapid shift in population. The argument, therefore, that the public-school system is saving the state a vast sum of money is grossly exaggerated, to say the least. If the whole of this facility closed down tomorrow, the resultant cost to the state of educating the extra children would be comparatively small and a mere fraction of the cost to the independent system itself.

Equally dubious is the claim of the schools to represent a bulwark of educational freedom.[1] Educationally, they are sometimes said to justify themselves on their ability to experiment and develop along their own lines. In fact their history shows them to be ultra-conservative, only minor variations having ever occurred. A great deal has been made of some recent initiative in revising the content and approach to mathematics as well as in one or two other ways, but set against past attitudes and a multitude of similar developments in the state system there is nothing extraordinary here. The completely revolutionary approach, of which Summerhill is an outstanding

1. I have not tried to establish here any claim to originality in the public schools. This would have needed an analysis of precisely what is meant by originality, in particular through an examination of schools more on the fringe of the system than inside it. It would appear, however, that originality is related more to the personality of the man in charge than anything else. This is far easier with an institution started from scratch than from one that is well established. The uphill fight of Sanderson at Oundle is evidence of this, and other examples could be given of minor changes introduced elsewhere. Apart from Summerhill there have been several interesting experiments of a co-educational character which, strictly, lie outside our scope. The same remark applies to those schools which have concentrated on a 'tough' environment for older boys.

example, lies elsewhere in the independent system, and is, unfortunately, outside our field.

The real threat to the schools comes from a wider concept of freedom, from the social and political thinking involved in the whole idea of the Welfare State. This in turn concerns the role of the independent school—and in particular the independent boarding school—in modern society.

We have changed rapidly in political and sociological outlook, and the modern position bears little relationship to that of the nineteenth century. Completely free enterprise is no longer a tenable proposition, and nowadays the matter may be put like this: 'Is it or is it not permissible for parents in a Welfare State to do something more for their children than the state can afford?' [1]

That is how Crichton Miller saw the dilemma, and that is really the crux of the matter. The principle of freedom from state interference is only permissible in our own day where exploitation is impossible, and it no longer applies to those activities which bear directly upon the welfare of the individual, especially where that individual is a child. All institutions are subject to control in some degree, from the operation of factories to the provision of entertainment. Perhaps the issue is seen at its clearest in arguments about the Health Service, since many would place education in a similar category. If the best medical service and treatment irrespective of cost should be at the disposal of any member of the community according to need, merely because he is a member of that community, should not the same principle hold for education? Certainly the existence of the independent schools denies it, and people are correspondingly uneasy. It is important to realize that independent schools are not necessarily objected to as such, any more than independent doctors are objected to alongside the state system, but results from the two should be equivalent. It would, for instance, be intolerable for a patient under the National Health Service to be denied treatment because of lack of wealth, and similarly the ordinary child should have the education best suited to him and not the one dictated by some irrelevant factor connected with his parents. The arguments revolve around two different viewpoints—whether the individual concerned puts

1. Crichton Miller, op. cit.

the accent on the freedom of choice of a parent in a free society, or whether the viewpoint concerns the rights of the child himself. On the second issue it is immaterial whether the parents are rich or not. This clash of opinion is an ancient one and is seen particularly well in the provisions of the 1944 Education Act itself.[1]

The threat of the state may well become a reality soon, although legislation will be necessary first, since the major schools are too independent and too historically based to listen to pleas which are not to their advantage. At the same time so little is known of the essentials that legislation would be ludicrous before a thorough investigation was made of the problems of wealth, endowments, fees, facilities, curricula, day and boarding, distribution, examinations, careers, status of parents and pupils, staffing, recruitment, efficiency and similar matters. It is vital to have a complete and accurate investigation, and there is at least a possibility that such a radical approach may be used in the government's latest move.

On 22 December 1965 it was announced that Sir John Newsom was to be the chairman of a new Public Schools Commission with the task of advising on the integration of public schools with the state system of education. For this purpose public schools were defined as 'those independent schools now in membership of the Headmasters' Conference, Governing Bodies Association, or the Association of Governing Bodies of Girls' Schools'. Direct-grant schools are excluded. This definition at least narrows the field in some ways, although the Commission will be concerned with both day and boarding schools at all levels of complexity and richness from Eton downwards. How far this will involve an investigation in depth remains to be seen, but a report can hardly be expected before 1968.

As for possible solutions, everything depends on a concept of standards. The reversion of schools to direct-grant status assumes that they are equivalent to the corresponding schools of the state system. The recent growth of this particular

1. The conflict of provisions in the 1944 Education Act concern the rights of the child, the rights of the parent, the duties of the parent, the duties of the local authority, the overriding supervision of the central authority in matters of dispute and equality between the different areas of the country.

category, including several boarding schools, is perhaps a sign for the future, although there are dangers in the new comprehensive school reorganization. Even co-operation between public schools and the local authorities, in the manner of Rendcomb, also assumes some common approach. Where standards are little better than those in state schools—as is the case in the majority of the public schools—then either of these solutions is possible provided the problems of finance and the selection of children can be resolved. The major difficulty lies at the top level where the provision is lavish, since both parental choice and a different, if questionable, kind of educational value are involved. It is difficult indeed to see how the great public schools could be adapted or absorbed into any state system without a drastic relaxation and slashing of standards, for any other course would entail a reversal of the policy of equivalence between schools. It would be an admission that an *élite* required isolated and superior surroundings for their education, and would reintroduce all the past troubles of eleven plus in an even more intense form. At the same time any solution which takes no account of the seven would only be a half-measure.

Standards are relative. In a few years the good standards of today become the commonplace of tomorrow, and if somehow one could resolve the tendency to keep ahead of the field for prestige reasons, then most problems of standards could be resolved in a decade or two. Again the top schools are only extraordinary by normal school criteria; in other fields they would not be so exceptional and a future for them there could be very bright, no matter what happens. The real difficulty is the glutinous nature of tradition and the refusal of people to contemplate change.

Appendix : Independent Boys' Schools in England and Wales in 1962, with Boarding Education to Eighteen

(A) WITH 200 OR MORE BOARDERS, IN ORDER OF FEES CHARGED

* Not member of H.M.C.
† Not member of H.M.C. or G.B.A.
D Some day pupils also.
Prep Has a 'prep' school for younger boys.

School	Refers to age 13–18			Remarks
	Total fees (boarding)	Total pupils	Boarders	
The Seven:	£ p.a.			
Eton	508	1,190	1,190	
Rugby	504	715	657	D
Harrow	498	653	653	
Winchester	498	537	537	
Westminster	498	444	257	D
Charterhouse	492	650	650	
Shrewsbury	441	540	498	D
Millfield†	666–756 etc.	491	435	Mixed D
Radley	489	470	470	
Oundle	480	680	680	
Cheltenham	474	468	368	Prep D
Downside	470(?)	525	520(?)	R.C.
Gresham's	465	300	250	Prep D
Bryanston	462	460	460	
Malvern	456	580	550	D
Bradfield	456	420	420	
Uppingham	456	589	589	
Epsom	455	430	300	Prep D
Wellington	453–74	681	674	D
King's, Canterbury	450	–	–	Prep D
Eastbourne	450	424	355	D

School	Refers to age 13–18			Remarks
	Total fees (boarding)	*Total pupils*	*Boarders*	
	£ *p.a.*			
Clifton	450	650	400	Prep D
Repton	450	485	485	Prep
Leys	450	357	357	Methodist
St Edwards	450	500	466	D
Sedbergh	447	428	410	D
Ardingly	444	300	300	Prep Woodard
Cranleigh	444	424	390	Prep D
Lancing	441	430	430	Woodard
Seaford	441	280	280	
Aldenham	435	312	296	D
Stowe	435	600	600	
Mill Hill	435	435	365	D
Canford	432	442	380	D
Hurstpierpoint	429	340	300	Prep D Woodward
St Johns	429	350	292	D
Haileybury	429	578	577	
Sherborne	426	593	588	
Nautical*	426	280	280	
Marlborough	423	810	810	
Leighton Park	423	245	214	Friends D
Bloxham	420	261	261	Woodard
Rossall	420	515	460	Prep D
Dean Close	420	349	240	D
Felsted	420	438	430	Prep
Milton Abbey*	420	250	250	
Worksop	420	420	390	Woodard Prep D
St Lawrence's	420	352	317	D
Kingswood	416	325	309	Prep D Methodist
Tonbridge	414	535	418	D
Dover	411	301	233	D
Allhallows	408	240	238	
Bromsgrove	408	332	240	Prep D
Trent	405	230	230	Prep
Denstone	400	380	378	Prep Woodard
King's (Taunton)	399	330	300	Prep D Woodard

School	Total fees (boarding)	Total pupils	Boarders	Remarks
	£ p.a.			
Stonyhurst	399	350	350	R.C.
Ampleforth	399	570	555	R.C. D
Wrekin	396	390	390	
Rydal	396	284	284	
Monkton Combe	396	300	210	Prep D
Blundells	396	401	335	D
St Peter's	395	400	200	Prep D
Sutton Valence	393	295	225	D
Bedford	390	600	245(?)	Prep D
Wycliffe	390	270	230	Prep D
St Bees	385	261	257	
Beaumont	381	250	247	R.C.
Lord Wandsworth's	381	281	279	Prep
Kelly	378	258	216	
Clayesmore	375	218	218	
Ellesmere	370	236	220	Prep
				Woodard
King William's	363	285	220(?)	Prep I.O.M.
Douai	360	235	235	R.C.
Oratory*	360	240	200(?)	Prep R.C. D
Ratcliffe	360	250	250(?)	R.C.
King's (Bruton)	336	300	260	Prep D
Scarborough†	330	263	200	
Bembridge†	324	210	205	
Mount St Mary's	321	282	253	R.C. D
Reeds*	315	200	200(?)	Prep
Taunton	315	334	240	Prep D
Royal Wanstead†	258	200	200(?)	
Christ's Hospital	up to 200	530	530(?)	Prep?
Royal Masonic	Free	400	400	
Number of boarders near 200:				
Highgate	327	665	190	Prep D
Colston's*	330	300	170(?)	Prep D
Llandovery	312	185	175(?)	
Brighton	414	380	180	Prep D
Carmel†	400	200	190(?)	Prep Jewish
Giggleswick	405	250	191(?)	Prep D
Ushaw†	225	200	200(?)	Prep R.C.

For some others near the limit, see appropriate schools in (B).

The number of boarders, aged thirteen to eighteen, is often difficult to ascertain. There are yearly fluctuations and any starting age, between seven and twelve needs some estimation. Figures are only approximate.

All the above schools, in England, are recognized as efficient by the Department of Education and Science.

There are many other independent schools which have all the given criteria with the exception of size—see (B) below.

(B) OTHER INDEPENDENT SCHOOLS WITH AN EDUCATION TO EIGHTEEN, BUT WITH THE NUMBER OF BOARDERS LESS THAN 200

(i) Members of H.M.C.:

Berkhamsted, Bishops Stortford, Bootham, Chigwell, Dulwich, Durham, Eastbourne, Forest, Ipswich, King's College School, King's (Macclesfield), King's (Rochester), Liverpool College, St Edmunds, St Paul's, Sebright, Sevenoaks, Silcoates, Solihull, Warwick, Wellingborough, Worcester, Christ's (Brecon), Merchant Taylors' (Middlesex).

(ii) Others:

Abbotsholme, Ackworth, Friends (Saffron Walden), Bedales, Prior Park, Queen's (Taunton), Rendcomb, Rishworth, Ryde, St George's (Harpenden), St George's (Weybridge), Truro, Wells, King's (Gloucester), Presentation College, Reading Bluecoat, Franciscan College, Licensed Victuallers, Salesian Missionary, Tabley House, Austin Friars, Friends' (Wigton), Dartington Hall, Monkton Wylde, Endsleigh, King's (Sherborne), Wynstones, Embley Park, Hurn Court, St John's (Southsea), St Mary's (Southampton), St Peter's (Bournemouth), Salesian (Farnborough), Stanbridge, Belmont Abbey, Lucton, St Christopher, King's (Ely), St. Edmund's (Ware), St Michael (Hitchin), Sherrardswood, Stanborough, Bethany, St George's (Tunbridge), Thomas de la Rue, Chetham Hospital, Friends' (Lancaster), Langley, Blackfriars (Corby), St Hugh's (Tollerton), Kingham Hill, Salesian (Cowley), Sibford Ferris, Bedstone, Shottan Hall, Sidcot (Friends), Cotton, Royal (Wolverhampton), Tettenhall, Everton (Ipswich), Badingham, City of London (Freeman), Frensham Heights, John Fisher, King Edward's (Witley), Pierrepoint, Russell, St Joseph's (Croydon), Michael Hall, Whittingehame, School for Deaf (Malvern), Friends' (Great Ayton), Scorton, Bentham, Fulneck, Wennington, H.M.S. Conway, Lindisfarne, Ruthin, St Mary's (Colwyn Bay), Emmanuel (Swansea), Monkton House (Cardiff).

Many of these schools are co-educational, and are therefore outside our sphere of study.

It is possible that there may be other boys' boarding schools with an education to eighteen which have escaped detection or the normal reference lists, but if so the numbers are few.

*

This appendix has been compiled from: *The Public and Preparatory Schools' Year Book*, 1961, 1962; *Schools*, 1962; *List of Independent Schools in England and Wales* (H.M.S.O.); *Whitaker's Almanack*, 1962, 1963. There is an inevitable time-lag in the recording of fees and pupils, and these references were occasionally at variance.

Index